CW00957012

Consumer Experience and Decision-Making in the Metaverse

Theodore Tarnanidis
Independent Researcher, Greece

A volume in the Advances in
Marketing, Customer Relationship
Management, and E-Services
(AMCRMES) Book Series

Published in the United States of America by
    IGI Global
    Business Science Reference (an imprint of IGI Global)
    701 E. Chocolate Avenue
    Hershey PA, USA 17033
    Tel: 717-533-8845
    Fax: 717-533-8661
    E-mail: cust@igi-global.com
    Web site: http://www.igi-global.com

Library of Congress Cataloging-in-Publication Data

CIP DATA PROCESSING

2024 Business Science Reference
ISBN(hc) 9798369341674 | ISBN(sc) 9798369349069 | eISBN 9798369341681

This book is published in the IGI Global book series Advances in Marketing, Customer Relationship Management, and E-Services (AMCRMES) (ISSN: 2327-5502; eISSN: 2327-5529)

British Cataloguing in Publication Data
A Cataloguing in Publication record for this book is available from the British Library.

All work contributed to this book is new, previously-unpublished material.
The views expressed in this book are those of the authors, but not necessarily of the publisher.

For electronic access to this publication, please contact: eresources@igi-global.com.

Advances in Marketing, Customer Relationship Management, and E-Services (AMCRMES) Book Series

ISSN:2327-5502
EISSN:2327-5529

Editor-in-Chief: Eldon Y. Li, National Chengchi University, Taiwan & California Polytechnic State University, USA

MISSION

Business processes, services, and communications are important factors in the management of good customer relationship, which is the foundation of any well organized business. Technology continues to play a vital role in the organization and automation of business processes for marketing, sales, and customer service. These features aid in the attraction of new clients and maintaining existing relationships.

The Advances in Marketing, Customer Relationship Management, and E-Services (AMCRMES) Book Series

addresses success factors for customer relationship management, marketing, and electronic services and its performance outcomes. This collection of reference source covers aspects of consumer behavior and marketing business strategies aiming towards researchers, scholars, and practitioners in the fields of marketing management.

COVERAGE

- Data mining and marketing
- Customer Relationship Management
- Legal Considerations in E-Marketing
- Ethical Considerations in E-Marketing
- E-Service Innovation
- Text Mining and Marketing
- Relationship Marketing
- Cases on Electronic Services
- B2B Marketing
- Customer Retention

IGI Global is currently accepting manuscripts for publication within this series. To submit a proposal for a volume in this series, please contact our Acquisition Editors at Acquisitions@igi-global.com or visit: http://www.igi-global.com/publish/.

Titles in this Series

701 East Chocolate Avenue, Hershey, PA 17033, USA
Tel: 717-533-8845 x100 • Fax: 717-533-8661
E-Mail: cust@igi-global.com • www.igi-global.com

Editorial Advisory Board

Table of Contents

Detailed Table of Contents

Chapter 1

Manali Agrawal, NSB Academy, India
Rohit Paroji, Kaseya, India

Client satisfaction is a term used to describe how satisfied a customer is with a good or service. It is an essential indicator of how successfully a company meets the requirements and expectations of its clients. Wonderla is the largest chain of amusement parks in India. This study aims to determine how satisfied customers are with the level of safety and comfort provided by Wonderla Holidays Ltd. It also focuses on identifying customer revisiting intentions, and to know whether customers will recommend Wonderla for others. It is analyzed that it is very important to formulate effective strategies to connect customers and make them feel special include personalizing the experience, offering outstanding customer service, and establishing a loyalty programed. Maintaining a neat and welcoming workplace, asking for and acting on client input, and providing convenience and comfort all help to increase customer satisfaction.

Chapter 2

Riza Ergün Arsal, Istanbul Bilgi University, Turkey
Asli Elif Aydin, Istanbul Bilgi University, Turkey

The purpose of this chapter is to explore the evolving landscape of marketing in the metaverse era. Metaverse applications of marketing activities from various industries are examined with cases from an emerging country. Beginning with an evaluation of marketing practices leading up to the metaverse, the chapter examines the transition from traditional methods to digital, social media, and mobile marketing strategies. It then delves into the myriad uses of the metaverse for marketing practices, highlighting immersive experiences, gamification, virtual commerce, and personalized engagement. Recent examples showcase how brands are leveraging virtual environments to connect with consumers in innovative ways. Last, expected challenges for companies are discussed. Concluding remarks offer recommendations for marketing practitioners, particularly in emerging countries, emphasizing the importance of embracing emerging technologies and adapting strategies to leverage the opportunities presented by the metaverse for effective brand engagement and consumer interaction.

Praneet Poddar, School of Business and Management, Christ University, Bangalore, India
Karan Anand, School of Business and Management, Christ University, Bangalore, India
Babita, School of Business and Management, Christ University, Bangalore, India

This research delves into how OTT platforms are transforming media consumption patterns and explores the role of consumer ethnocentrism in shaping buying behaviors within this context. Through a literature review and quantitative research methodology using a Likert-scale questionnaire, the study investigates the relationship between consumer ethnocentrism, buying intentions, and various influencing factors on OTT platforms. Contrary to expectations, the findings show that consumer ethnocentrism has minimal impact on buying behavior. Instead, factors such as price, content variety, personalized recommendations, cultural alignment, ease of platform usage, familiarity with foreign content, and language preferences are crucial in determining viewers' buying intentions. The chapter concludes by recommending that OTT platforms integrate cultural sensitivities into their strategies to better cater to diverse viewer preferences, thereby enhancing market competitiveness and audience engagement.

Mani Tyagi, Manav Rachna International Institute of Research and Studies, India
Shenki Tyagi, Kiet Group of Institutions, India

Traditional advertising channels are being reimagined and transformed in this virtual space, offering marketers unprecedented opportunities to connect with consumers on a deeper level. In this context, this chapter focuses specifically on uncovering the latest trends and strategies shaping advertising practices in the metaverse.

From immersive brand experiences in virtual environments to targeted advertising campaigns using augmented reality overlays, the possibilities are vast and exciting. We will examine how brands are harnessing the power of virtual reality, augmented reality, and other emerging technologies to captivate audiences and drive meaningful engagement. Ultimately, this chapter serves as a roadmap for marketers navigating the complexities of advertising in the metaverse. By understanding the latest trends, technologies, and best practices, businesses can position themselves for success in this rapidly evolving landscape. Join us as we embark on this journey into the future of advertising in the metaverse.

Chapter 5

Consumer behaviour is a topic most sought after when it comes to creating successful marketing practices that affect consumers' psychology, acting as a stimulus and inducing them to make purchases. Evidence explains that the psychological pricing strategy communicates with the subconscious mind of consumers, creating a perceptual illusion. This makes the deal seem more appealing to them. This chapter entails a practical study examining the impact of psychological pricing strategies on consumers' buying behaviour. This study has used authentic primary data that has been collected directly from consumers in India based on their buying experiences when encountering psychological pricing. The findings of this research show how socio-demographic factors like age, income, education, gender and family size influence consumers' buying behaviour when encountered with psychological pricing and if psychological patterns such as the anchoring heuristics, recency bias, scarcity effect and halo effect can overpower the influence of psychological pricing strategies in consumer buying behaviour.

Chapter 6

Retail is changing as a result of the convergence of blockchain, virtual reality, and augmented reality technology. Since this is a dynamic setting, it is essential to address any ethical issues that come up. This study aims to provide practical guidance for the responsible adoption of VR, AR, and blockchain technologies in retail by synthesising case studies and existing ethical frameworks. It will also thoroughly examine the ethical challenges arising from the integration of these technologies, with a focus on consumer privacy and data security. The study employed a multifaceted approach, including a thorough review of the literature, a critical analysis of the state-of-the-art ethical frameworks, and an examination of real case studies. There are certain ethical issues with virtual and augmented reality that are discussed, along with some possible answers. The results highlight the importance of user education, strict data protection protocols, and international regulatory cooperation as crucial elements for tackling ethical dilemmas in the context of augmented retail reality.

Chapter 7

Sonia Mukherjee, MIT World Peace University, India

Businesses are gradually shifting from the traditional models to newer business models with the adoption of metaverse. Consumers are expected to benefit immensely as a result of higher usage of metaverse technology in the different sectors such as healthcare, IT, travel and tourism, real estate, fashion brands and education, etc. India has a high potential of adopting the metaverse technology in the online gaming sector. However, numerous challenges such as dearth of investments, lack of infrastructure, dearth of rules and regulations, online fraud and harassment are part of the daily lives in today's world. Against this backdrop, the study examines the potential benefits and disadvantages of adopting the metaverse technology by business and brands and its interaction with consumers. Lastly, the study discusses the future of metaverse technology with emphasis on the gaming sector, its notable challenges associated with metaverse and the remedial measures and solutions which can be used for better integration of metaverse technology for business efficiency and consumer usage.

Chapter 8

Anuradha Yadav, Dayananda Sagar College of Engineering, India
Vijaya Kittu Manda, PBMEIT, India
Mallikharjuna Rao Jitta, GITAM University, India

The metaverse is an emerging virtual frontier that is becoming a new marketing channel for brands to showcase their products and services. Brands can now use the services of influencers (both human and virtual) to influence consumer decisions. The metaverse and other new-generation Web 3.0 technologies are used in marketing campaigns to take advantage of immersive and augmented reality environments. Influencers use strategies different from traditional e-commerce, B2B, and social media marketing. Virtual showrooms, events, and product launches engage with consumers to co-create products and give a memorable consumer experience. The metaverse provides opportunities for community building and user-generated content that is more social proof. As technologies improve, influencers get more engaged in the metaverse. Measuring and evaluating influencer campaigns, ethical considerations, legal and regulatory frameworks, and long-term implications of influencer campaigns are some areas of future study.

Chapter 9

Theodore Tarnanidis, International Hellenic University, Greece
Lampros Gkiouzepas, Hellenic Open University, Greece

Metaverse technologies have become ground-breaking tools, changing the way businesses interact with consumers and analyze their behavior. This research examines innovative Metaverse marketing strategies that focus on enhancing customer experiences and comprehending consumer behavior through cutting-edge technologies, platforms, and models. Businesses can create interactive and realistic experiences for their clients in a vibrant and immersive setting provided by the Metaverse. Companies can create virtual storefronts by utilizing VR and AR technologies, allowing customers to explore products and services in visually compelling ways. The chapter provides a summary of the origins of the metaverse in marketing, with further explanations about the immersive technologies employed in the creation of marketing strategies. The main trends and their implications are presented, along with a discussion of the current state of the art research in marketing, which was originally developed by the 'father of modern marketing,' Philip Kotler.

Chapter 10

Pratap Chandra Mandal, Indian Institute of Management, Shillong, India

It is imperative for companies to develop and manage customer relationships effectively. The objective of the study is to analyze the effective management of customer relationships by companies. The methodology adopted is a conceptual analysis of the various strategies and initiatives adopted by companies for managing customer relationships. Companies customize and personalize their offerings with the help of permission marketing and engagement marketing. They empower their customers, manage customer word of mouth, and deal with customer complaints effectively. Academicians may analyze the existing strategies and initiatives and suggest effective strategies and initiatives for management of customer relationships. Practicing managers may evaluate the existing strategies and initiatives and implement effective strategies and initiatives in future. All these will enable companies to develop strong bondage with their customers, to manage customer relationships effectively, and to achieve business excellence in the long run.

The chapter explores how VR and AR technologies influence consumer behavior in the metaverse, emphasizing the need for businesses to understand these dynamics. It delves into cognitive processes, emotional responses, and socio-cultural influences shaping purchasing decisions in virtual environments. The research analyzes user interactions, interface design, sensory immersion, and social interactions to uncover factors driving consumer engagement and decision-making. It highlights the importance of user-centered design, personalized marketing, and immersive storytelling for creating compelling virtual experiences. The study also identifies challenges and opportunities for businesses leveraging VR and AR technologies to enhance consumer engagement and drive sales in the metaverse, offering practical recommendations for success in the digital marketplace of the future.

Similar to a rising global trend, Gen-Z consumers in Delhi-NCR are spending more time on social media sites such as YouTube and Instagram. Understanding how advertising on these sites affects their purchasing decisions is critical. This study investigates the influence of YouTube and Instagram advertising in recruiting Generation Z customers. Based on a recent study that highlighted entertainment, informativeness, customization, and irritation as important elements impacting advertising value on YouTube, this chapter analyzes how these features influence brand awareness and purchase intention among Gen-Z consumers in Delhi-NCR. The study predicts that, like YouTube, Instagram commercials that are entertaining, informative, and personalized will be more effective in attracting Gen-Z customers. In contrast, irritating advertisements will have a negative influence. By evaluating these aspects, the study provides useful insights for marketers looking to use YouTube and Instagram advertising to effectively attract Gen-Z consumers in Delhi-NCR.

Metaverse is a huge virtual world in which humans and digital twins (avatars) will interact in real-time, a world created by humans that exists beyond the analog world we live in, where individuals are lonely but also social, with humanoid appearances, traditions, and taboos, but also without rules and boundaries. It is a completely different, relatively free, relatively unregulated virtual world. The interaction of consumers in virtual spaces and the companies investing in this field have not only made some research in this field mandatory but also caused questions to arise in people's minds. The focus of the study is the excitement and anxiety of consumers. In general, the aim is to define the metaverse concept that will affect consumers and the positive and negative effects of the metaverse concept on consumers. On this basis, the concept of the metaverse will be approached from a SWOT perspective and predictions will be made regarding the situations that may be encountered in the metaverse field soon.

This research emerges as a starting point in analyzing the requirements that brand managers should consider leveraging the presence of brands in the metaverse, considering the consumers' degree of knowledge, expectations, and desired experiences, thus contributing with theoretical and practical implications to brand management. Through a qualitative methodology – employing the focus group technique – it was possible to understand the interests of consumers and their metaverse-related associations. The interactivity component is of utmost importance and must be developed, implemented, and complemented with the user's own creativity. This research has also shed light on important dimensions related to virtual content.

Preface

This publication seeks to motivate diverse academics, professionals, and researchers to conduct research on the metaverse in consumer decision-making and marketing strategy. The metaverse is a digital realm where people interact, socialize, and make decisions with the aid of virtual or augmented reality environments. This up-and-coming trend has significant implications for how businesses understand and approach their target audience, design marketing strategies and campaigns. In a nutshell, the metaverse has the ability to transform consumer decision-making and marketing strategies by offering immersive experiences, personalized interactions, and new avenues for brand engagement. In order to maximize its full potential, businesses must stay informed and creative as this space develops. The focus of this book is on how technology advances have expanded the service economy and improved customer relationships. Through a collection of research, the book presents insights into immersive consumer experiences, virtual brand presence, data-driven personalization, and other topics. It equips readers with the knowledge and strategies to adapt to this new digital landscape and engage with consumers in innovative ways.

The book is made up of 14 chapters that aim to showcase the main research areas on the subject and thus provide valuable findings to practitioners and readers.

In Chapter 1, customers are questioned about their satisfaction with the level of safety and comfort provided by Wonderla Holidays Ltd. The focus is on determining if customers will recommend Wonderland to others and identifying customer revisiting intentions. The analysis indicates that it is vital to formulate effective strategies that connect with customers and make them feel special, such as personalizing the experience, providing outstanding customer service, and establishing a loyalty program.

Chapter 2 explores how traditional methods can be replaced by digital, social media, and mobile marketing strategies. The article explores the numerous uses of the metaverse in marketing practices, emphasizing immersive experiences, gamification, virtual commerce, and personalized engagement.

The subject of Chapter 3 is the transformation of media consumption patterns by OTT platforms and the influence of consumer ethnocentrism on buying behaviors in this setting. Using a likert-scale questionnaire and a literature review, the study examines the connection between consumer ethnocentrism, purchasing intentions, and various influencing factors on OTT platforms.

Chapter 4 provides an overview of how traditional advertising channels are being reimagined and transformed in this virtual space, offering marketers unprecedented opportunities to connect with consumers on a deeper level. This chapter is specifically focused on uncovering the latest trends and strategies that are shaping advertising practices in the metaverse. The possibilities range from immersive brand experiences in virtual environments to targeted advertising campaigns using augmented reality overlays and are both wide-ranging and exciting.

Chapter 5 is a practical study that examines the effects of psychological pricing strategies on consumers' buying behavior. The study is based on authentic primary data collected directly from consumers in India regarding their purchasing experiences when facing psychological pricing. The findings of this research show how socio-demographic factors like age, income, education, gender and family size influence consumers' buying behavior when encountered with psychological pricing and if psychological patterns such as the anchoring heuristics, recency bias, scarcity effect and halo effect can overpower the influence of psychological pricing strategies in consumer buying behavior.

Chapter 6 intends to provide practical guidance on how to responsibly use VR, AR, and blockchain technologies in retail by combining case studies and existing ethical frameworks. Furthermore, it thoroughly examines the ethical challenges that arise when these technologies are combined, with an emphasis on consumer privacy and data security.

Chapter 7 explains how businesses are gradually shifting from traditional models to newer business models with the adoption of Metaverse. The increased usage of Metaverse technology in various sectors, such as Healthcare, IT, Travel and Tourism, Real estate, Fashion brands, and Education, is expected to bring great benefits to consumers. India has a significant chance of adopting Metaverse technology in the online gaming industry.

Chapter 8 provides explanations about the metaverse, a virtual frontier that is becoming a new marketing channel for brands to showcase their products and services. Marketing campaigns utilize Metaverse and other new-generation Web 3.0 technologies to capitalize on immersive and augmented reality environments.

In Chapter 9, there is a summary of the origins of the metaverse in marketing, along with additional explanations on the immersive technologies used to create marketing strategies. The current state of the art research in marketing, originally developed by Professor Philip Kotler, is discussed in addition to the main trends and their implications.

In Chapter 10, companies are examined for their effective management of customer relationships. The method employed involves a conceptual analysis of the various strategies and initiatives taken by companies to manage customer relationships.

Chapter 11 examines how VR and AR technologies affect consumer behavior in the metaverse, emphasizing the importance of businesses comprehending these dynamics. It explores cognitive processes, emotional responses, and socio-cultural influences that impact purchasing decisions in virtual environments.

The topic of Chapter 12 is the impact of YouTube and Instagram advertising on recruiting customers from Generation Z. Based on a recent study that highlighted entertainment, informativeness, customization, and irritation as important elements impacting advertising value on YouTube, this paper analyzes how these features influence brand awareness and purchase intention among Gen-Z consumers in Delhi-NCR.

In Chapter 13, the interaction between consumers in virtual spaces and the companies investing in this field is explored. The study is aimed at defining the Metaverse concept and analyzing its positive and negative effects on consumers.

Chapter 14 analyze the requirements that brand managers should consider leveraging the presence of brands in the Metaverse, considering the consumers' degree of knowledge, expectations and desired experiences, thus contributing with theoretical and practical implications to brand management.

This publication serves as a valuable reference for academics, researchers, undergraduate students, postgraduate students, consultants, technology developers, and policymakers who want to study how marketing is utilized in the Metaverse. We are confident that readers will find this book to be essential for improving their current work and education. We should express our final gratitude to the contributors of the accepted chapters.

Theodore Tarnanidis
International Hellenic University, Greece

Chapter 1
A Study on Customer Satisfaction and Revisiting Intention of Wonderla Holidays Limited

Manali Agrawal
ⓘ https://orcid.org/0009-0003-7283-3079
NSB Academy, India

Rohit Paroji
Kaseya, India

ABSTRACT

Client satisfaction is a term used to describe how satisfied a customer is with a good or service. It is an essential indicator of how successfully a company meets the requirements and expectations of its clients. Wonderla is the largest chain of amusement parks in India. This study aims to determine how satisfied customers are with the level of safety and comfort provided by Wonderla Holidays Ltd. It also focuses on identifying customer revisiting intentions, and to know whether customers will recommend Wonderla for others. It is analyzed that it is very important to formulate effective strategies to connect customers and make them feel special include personalizing the experience, offering outstanding customer service, and establishing a loyalty programed. Maintaining a neat and welcoming workplace, asking for and acting on client input, and providing convenience and comfort all help to increase customer satisfaction.

DOI: 10.4018/979-8-3693-4167-4.ch001

INTRODUCTION

High levels of customer satisfaction are usually linked to good word-of-mouth advertising and increased client loyalty. There are several factors that can contribute to customer satisfaction, such as: Timeliness of delivery or service

- Competence and friendliness of the staff
- Responsiveness to customer needs and concerns
- Price and value for money
- Convenience and ease of use

Using tools like surveys, feedback forms, and online reviews, businesses can gauge customer satisfaction. Businesses can define areas for improvement and alter their products or services to better serve their customers by analyzing customer feedback.

Advantages of Customer Satisfaction

- Customers that are impressed with a product or service are likely to do business with the company in the future, which can increase customer loyalty.
- Positive word-of-mouth recommendations: Content customers are inclined to promote the product or service to their friends and family, which can help draw in new customers.
- Higher sales: Customers who were satisfied are likely to make more purchases and repeat previous ones, which can increase sales and revenue for the company.
- Competitive advantage: By consistently delivering high-level of customer satisfaction, a business can differentiate itself from rivals and gain a competitive edge in market.
- A company can develop a good reputation and strengthen its brand by continually providing high levels of customer satisfaction.

Customer Satisfaction Was Measured for Following Parameters

- **Food caliber.**
- **High-quality services.**
- **Quality of the physical environment.**
- **Cost and worth.**

The hospitality industry is a broad category encompassing businesses that provide services and accommodations to guests. It revolves around the concept of making guests feel welcome, comfortable, and satisfied. Key sectors within the hospitality industry include:

1. Hotels and Accommodations: Ranging from budget motels to luxury resorts, hotels provide temporary lodging for travelers. They offer a variety of amenities and services to enhance the guest experience.
2. Restaurants and Food Services: Restaurants, cafes, bars, and catering services fall under this category. Hospitality in dining includes not only the quality of food but also the ambiance, service, and overall dining experience.
3. Travel and Tourism: Travel agencies, tour operators, and other travel-related businesses facilitate the movement of people for leisure or business purposes. This sector plays a vital role in providing travel-related services.
4. Event Planning and Management: Businesses in this sector organize and manage events, conferences, weddings, and other gatherings. They focus on creating memorable experiences for attendees.
5. Cruise Lines: Cruise companies provide hospitality services on ships, offering a unique travel experience with accommodations, dining, entertainment, and various onboard activities.
6. Entertainment and Recreation: Theme parks, casinos, and entertainment venues contribute to the hospitality industry by providing recreational services and attractions.
7. Spas and Wellness Centers: Facilities that offer spa treatments, fitness services, and wellness programs are part of the hospitality industry, focusing on relaxation and well-being.

Key Characteristics of the Hospitality Industry: Customer-Centric: Hospitality businesses prioritize customer satisfaction and aim to exceed guest expectations. Service-Oriented: The industry is heavily focused on providing services, encompassing everything from housekeeping to dining to event planning.

Dynamic and Competitive: The hospitality landscape is ever-evolving, with businesses constantly innovating to meet changing customer preferences and stay competitive.

Global Reach: Hospitality is a global industry, with businesses catering to diverse cultures and international travelers.

People-Driven: The success of the hospitality industry depends on the skills, hospitality, and professionalism of its personnel.

The hospitality industry plays a crucial role in the global economy, providing employment opportunities and contributing to tourism and travel. It thrives on creating positive and memorable experiences for guests across various sectors.

WONDERLA

Wonderla is the largest chain of amusement parks in India. It is owned and operated by Wonderla Holidays Limited which is headquartered near Bidadi, 28 kilometres (17 mi) from Bangalore, Karnataka. It operates 3 amusement parks in Kochi, Bangalore, and Hyderabad.

Wonderla is promoted by Kochouseph Chittilappilly and his son Arun Chittilappilly. The first amusement park project Wonderla Kochi was set up in 2000, followed by the second in Bangalore in 2005, and finally the third in Hyderabad was commissioned in April 2016. Wonderla is currently planning to open its 4th amusement park in Chennai. Wonderla amusement parks offer a variety of dry rides such as roller coasters, ferris wheels, drop towers and water rides for its customers.

About Company

CEO: Kochouseph Thomas Chittilappilly
Vice president: Ajikrishnan A G
Bangalore branch head: Rudresh
Employees: 501 to 1,000 employees in India
Total net worth: 105 crore INR (bangalore)
Based on: Entertainment place

Vision

Get on one of the many exhilarating rides, or simply laze by the pool. But whatever you do, here, everybody gets a little closer. And that is why we are India's only Amazement Park

Mission

The loudest, craziest, and the most amazing part of town. This simply is not just an amusement park, but a world of breath-taking charm. It's a place to celebrate the smaller moments and share big wonders.

LITERATURE REVIEW

- **An examination of the relationship between service quality, customer satisfaction, and store loyalty,** using a national random telephone survey of 542 shoppers, examines the relationship between service quality, customer satisfaction, and store loyalty within the retail department store context. Tests two complementary models that examine this interrelationship. Empirically examines the relative attitude construct put forth by Dick and Basu. The results indicate that service quality influences relative attitude and satisfaction with department stores. Satisfaction influences relative attitude, repurchase, and recommendation but has no direct effect on store loyalty. Fostering favorable relative attitude and getting customers to recommend the product or service holds key to fostering store loyalty. Results also indicate support for Oliver's four-stage cognitive-affective-conative-action model of loyalty(Sivadas & Baker-Prewitt, 2000).

- The authors investigate whether it is necessary to include disconfirmation as an intervening variable affecting satisfaction as is commonly argued, or whether the effect of disconfirmation is adequately captured by expectation and perceived performance. Further, they model the process for two types of products, a durable and a nondurable good, using experimental procedures in which three levels of expectations and three levels of performance are manipulated for each product in a factorial design. Each subject's perceived expectations, performance evaluations, disconfirmation, and satisfaction are subsequently measured by using multiple measures for each construct(*An Investigation into the Determinants of Customer Satisfaction - Gilbert A. Churchill, Carol Surprenant, 1982,* n.d.).

- This document is a report on how California community colleges can incorporate customer satisfaction models and theories from business to better serve students. Emphasis is given to two levels of customer satisfaction: macro- and micro-models. Macro-models look at how customer satisfaction relates to other elements or priorities of community colleges. They utilize techniques like comparing standards of performance of various community college services and products, which can positively or negatively affect customer satisfaction(**Hom, 2000**).

- This paper seeks to present an analysis of the literature examining objective information concerning the subject of customer service, as it applies to the current medical practice. Hopefully, this information will be synthesized to generate a cogent approach to correlate customer service with quality(**Vukmir, 2006**).

- This study aims to examine the relationships between customer satisfaction and a variety of company performance metrics at the firm-level of analysis. Numerous experts have noted that marketing needs to document the financial impact of marketing activities. Unlike most studies in this area, this study investigated these associations at the firm level, rather than at the aggregate or industry level where some relationships are potentially masked. The study also investigated the links between satisfaction and financial performance in the business-to-business services sector, rather than in business-to-customer services. Finally, the firm provided access to large samples of real customer attitude data over a five-year period, rather than from a cross-sectional study(**Williams & Naumann, 2011**).

- The focus of this article is on customer satisfaction and how it affects business performance by gauging how satisfied customers are with a company's goods and services. Research was done to identify the variables that affect customer happiness and the effectiveness of the company however, the company. We developed a model that clarifies the specific variables that affect customer happiness and affect a company's performance. This methodology can aid management in enhancing performance and improving how the company is run. The essay is based on research that concentrated on Czech Republic-based food industry businesses and their clients(**Suchánek & Králová, 2015**).

- The study helps to analyses empirical data on customer satisfaction and how it relates to quantitative measures of organizationalperformance. The company, a Flex company, is based in the Netherlands but also conducts business in other European nations. It is possible to find evidence for the hypothesis that there is a positive relationship between customer satisfaction and organizational performance indicators, though the relationship is not very strong, according to empirical data on customer satisfaction and business performance from 1998 and 1999. The lag between a change in customer satisfaction and the anticipated impact on the sales margin or other output metrics may be influenced by a number of reasons. Nevertheless, the analyses answer queries about the quality dimensions as underlying variables(**Boselie et al., 2001**).

- This study examines the relationships and the impacts of service quality, customer satisfaction and switching costs on customer loyalty of e-banking in commercial banks. This study uses questionnaires with 7-point Likert scale to collect data from 227 e-banking users, who are mainly students and paid employees in Hanoi City, Vietnam. The collected data are analyzed by using multivariate linear regression method. The results show that all five factors of service quality in e-banking – reliability, responsiveness, service capacity, empathy and tangibility –have positive correlations with customer satisfaction. Among these determinants, service capacity and tangibility have the strongest impact(NGUYEN et al., 2020).

- (Akbar & Parvez, 2009)This research has proposed a conceptual framework to investigate the effects of customers' perceived service quality, trust, and customer satisfaction on customer loyalty. To test the conceptual framework, structural equation modeling (SEM) has been used to analyze the data collected from 304 customers of a major private telecommunication company operating in Bangladesh. The results of the study indicate that trust and customer satisfaction are significantly and positively related to customer loyalty. Customer satisfaction has found to be an important mediator between perceived service quality and customer loyalty. A clear understanding of the postulated relationships among the studied variables might encourage the mobile service provider(s) to figure out appropriate course of action to win customers' trust by providing better services in order to create a loyal customer.

- The study Customer satisfaction is perhaps one of the most talked about challenges of organisations, both in the public and private sectors. Indeed, this represents every organisation's sole purpose, is at the heart of every mission statement, and is the ultimate goal of any strategies put in place. As such, this paper in continuation of the Best Practice series being so far covered, seeks to present this prominent topic as a total concept which encapsulates not only the measurement aspects of customer satisfaction *per se* but rather as a long-term pursuit of improvement, a culture change that can yield to competitive outcomes of the highest order. The paper includes some examples of best practice applications and concludes with a proposed audit tool that can help organisations assess their current approaches to customer satisfaction and thereby put forward targets and actions for improvement(*(10) Managing Customer Satisfaction: A Best Practice Perspective | Request PDF*, n.d.).

- This paper seeks to challenge researchers and business organizations to think about the measures they are using in their attempt to measure customer satisfaction and any subsequent decision-making and actions that may result. Specifically, the paper endeavours to raise awareness of the difficulties involved in measuring customer satisfaction and of using these measures for decision making(*Measuring Customer Satisfaction: Why, What and How? - UQ eSpace*, n.d.).

- This book examines the quality movement from a holistic perspective that is unique. It will serve as an invaluable handbook both for students and for those interested in enhancing quality in their own organizations. Practical illustrations are combined with a comprehensive and systemic overview of the extraordinary story of how Japanese industrialists adopted and developed the ideas of American quality gurus only to then find their own methodologies being exported to the USA and the rest of the world. The authors are leading Swedish academics with many years of experience in the quality field. The book is divided into five fairly independent parts. In Part I the quality concept and the evolution of the quality movement are examined(Bergman & Klefsjo, 2010).

- The main purpose of this research is to examine the relationship between customer satisfaction and business performance in Lloyds Bank UK. Moreover, it also examines the extent of customer satisfaction and the business performance of Lloyds Bank through examining various factors of customer satisfaction and business performance respectively. Design/ Methodology: The necessary data were collected from the customers and employees through structured questionnaires from 16 branches of Lloyds Bank United Kingdom(**Neupane, 2014**).

- The study extends the existing knowledge by taking a relationship perspective to study the effect of service quality on customer retention. We integrate business-to-business marketing literature with service quality literature to develop a model to capture relationship commitment and other influencing factors. The model is improved with help of semi-structured interviews which is later tested through a survey of 241 companies in the advertising sector. Findings indicate that service quality indeed contributes to the long-term relationships and customer retention(Venetis & Ghauri, 2004).

- This report is the outcome of a field research, which aimed to determine the quality of services offered by Sepah Bank, and also to study the relationship between the service quality, satisfaction and loyalty. In this research, the service quality standard model has been used for evaluation of service quality, Gremler and Brown (1996) model with some revision was used for evaluating the loyalty, and the instrument offered by Bitner and Hubbert (1994) was used for evaluation of customer satisfaction. The focus of this research is a Sepah Bank branch around Fatemi St., Tehran, Iran, and 147 customers of this bank were sampled. The results of this research show that in all aspects, customers' expectation, are higher than their perceptions of the Bank's operation, and in fact the quality of offered services is low. Besides, this research findings show that the customer satisfaction plays the role of a mediator in the effects of service quality on service loyalty. These findings are further explored((*10) (PDF) Service Quality, Customer Satisfaction and Loyalty: A Test of Mediation*, n.d.).

- This study seeks to investigate, through the development of an operationalized service quality construct in the context of a service factory, whether the typology to which a service belongs may explain the nature of the service quality (SQ) construct and its relationship to customer satisfaction (SAT) and behavioral intentions (BI)(*(10) Service Quality, Customer Satisfaction, and Behavioral Intentions in the Service Factory | Request PDF*, **n.d.**).

- The author proposes and tests an integrative model of service quality, customer value, and customer satisfaction. Using a sample from the luxury segment of the hotel industry, this study provides preliminary results supporting a holistic approach to hospitality customers' post purchase decision-making process. The model appears to possess practical validity as well as explanatory ability. Implications are discussed and suggestions are developed for both marketers and researchers(**Oh, 1999**).

- The aim of this study was to investigate the relationships between service quality, food quality, customer satisfaction and customer retention in limited service restaurants in Jordan. A questionnaire-based survey was distributed to 400 students served at 10 limited service restaurants in the neighbor-hood of universities in Amman, the capital city of Jordan. Service quality was measured in terms of SERVQUAL attributes. The key dimensions of food quality, customer satisfaction and customer retention were identified through literature. The data collected (283 valid questionnaires) were analyzed using SPSS 20.0(Wicaksono & Utami, n.d.).

- This paper aims to identify the influence of service quality on customer retention and the factors that affect this relationship using a systematic review and meta-analysis method to use in the second stage in examining the relationship of service quality on customer retention in higher educations. A systematic review method was conducted to select the studies that will assist in the current studies. This systematic review covered 32 research articles published in peer-reviewed journals from 1996 till 2018 and were reviews critically. The main findings of the study indicate that service quality-related factors is the most common factor, flowed by customer satisfaction, trust, commitment, and loyalty. Moreover, it has been noticed that the quantitative method using questionnaire was found to be the primary relied upon research methods for collecting data followed by a focus group. Furthermore, 75% of the analyzed studies recorded positive research outcomes(*(10) The Influence of Service Quality on Customer Retention: A Systematic Review in the Higher Education | Request PDF*, n.d.).

The hypotheses are then proposed and tested using confirmatory factor analysis (CFA) and the structural equation modelling technique (SME). The analysis reveals that service quality and customer satisfaction are important antecedents of customer loyalty and customer satisfaction mediates the effects of service quality on customer loyalty. These findings suggest that there are non-linear relationships between three constructs and emphasize the need to treat customer loyalty management as a process which includes plenty of factors interacting with each other(Tomas Bata University in Zlín et al., 2016).

- This study develops and empirically tests the interrelationships between service quality, customer satisfaction, and customer loyalty in a retail banking context. Increasingly intense competitiveness and fundamental changes in the business environment nowadays are forcing firms to implement a customer-focused strategy which raises the importance of customer-related constructs such as customer satisfaction, service quality, and customer loyalty in explaining a firm's performance. In particular, they are essential for competitiveness in industries where the exchanges are complex and customers are closely involved in the decision-making process, such as the banking industry. In this study, first, a research model about the interrelationships between service quality, customer satisfaction, and customer loyalty is suggested. Then a survey is conducted with retail banking customers about these constructs, which results in 261 valid respondents(Yang et al., 2023)

AI plays a significant part in marketing by efficiently meeting consumers' needs and wants, keeping customers satisfied and staff involved in their future relationships with the company. Despite its proficient value addition, there are still existing challenges with which organizations' employees are dissatisfied with the deployment of AIM in organizational operations, including the skill gap, reluctance to change, and job security threat(Eshiett et al., 2024).

RESEARCH METHODOLOGY

This problem suggests that the business is facing challenges related to customer satisfaction and wants to take action to improve it. The business needs to identify the reasons behind the increase in customer complaints and decline in retention rates and develop a strategy to address these issues effectively. By doing so, the business can improve customer satisfaction, increase customer loyalty, and ultimately enhance its bottom line.

Objective of Study

- To determine how satisfied customers are with the level of safety and comfort provided by Wonderland Holidays Ltd. is the primary objective of the study.

- To know whether customers will recommend Wonderland for others.
- To study about customer Revisiting Intention.

This is a primary data based study based on questionnaire design and data collection

The questionnaire framework was based on the attributes related to the variables of the study such as physical, emotional and cognitive and also related to the job performance and retention. The responses was received with the help satisfaction levels like strongly agree, agree, disagree etc. Through Five-point Likert scale and the questions were circulated in physical form.

- **Sample Size:** 100 Respondents
- **Software:** MS excel
- **Statistical tool:** Descriptive, correlation method, Regression Method
- **Sampling frame:** Visitors of Wonderland
- **Sampling method:** Convenience Sampling

HYPOTHESIS

H1 .H0: Dissatisfied Customers would not like to Revisit Wonderland Holidays Limited.

H1: Satisfied Customers like to revisit Wonderland Holidays Limited.

H2. H0: Dissatisfied customers would not recommend Wonderland Holidays Limited to Others.

H1: Satisfied customers would recommend Wonderland Holidays Limited to others.

LIMITATIONS OF STUDY

- The study was based on customer reviews, therefore it's possible that some of the good and trustworthy consumers were overlooked.
- Data is entirely dependent on the respondent's perspective, which may be skewed.
- The sample size was just 100, there were some difficulties with data validity and dependability.
- It is impossible to assume that the opinion expressed in research study represents the opinion of the entire population.

DISCUSSION AND FINDINGS

- According to the table and graph above, 52% of visitors are male and 48% are female.
- According to the above table and chart, 13% of visitors are between the ages of 10 and 20; 40% of employees are between the ages of 20 and 30; 30% are between the ages of 30 and 40; and 17% are above 40.
- According to the table and graph above, 36% of visitors are PG, 28% are UG, 24% are in the 12th position, and 12% are in the 10th position.
- According to the table and graph above, 33% of people are students, 16% are workers, 14% are employers, 22% are businessmen, and 15% are unemployed.
- According to the above table and chart, 46% of visitors make between 0 and 15 000 rupees, 14% make between 30 000 and 50 000, and 19% make between 50 000 and above. Employees make between 50 000 and above.
- According to the above table and figure, 63% of park visitors had previously been, while 37% had never been.
- According to the table and graph above, 28% of visits are made with friends, 28% with family, 22% with neighbors, 20% with people from institutions, and 2% are made by others.
- According to the above table and chart, 34% of people learned about Wonderland by word-of-mouth, 24% through social media, 29% through advertisements, and 13% from the staff.
- According to the above table and chart, 32% of summer vacationers, 41% of weekend visitors, 15% of occasional visitors, and 2% of other visitors would like to visit on other days.
- According to the table and graph above, 17% of visitors visited often each week, 36% did so each month, and 53% did so annually.
- According to the above table and chart, 38% of patrons strongly agreed that the quality of the food supplied in the park was good.7% of the consumers strongly disagreed, too.
- According to the above table and chart, 39% of consumers strongly agreed that the prices of the meals are reasonable. Additionally, 12% of customers strongly disagreed with the assertion.
- According to the above chart and table, 41% of customers strongly agreed that inside staff service is good and effective, while 5% strongly disagreed.
- According to the above table and chart, 42% of visitors strongly agreed that the staff service outside the park was extremely timely and effective. And 7% strongly disagreed with the preceding statement.
- According to the above table and chart, 52% of visitors strongly agreed that Land ride games were very nice at Wonderland, while 7% strongly disagreed.

- According to the above table and chart, 50% of customers strongly agreed that water games were enjoyable, while 6% strongly disagreed.
- According to the above chart and table, 50% of visitors strongly agree that cleanliness and hygiene in the park are well kept, while 7% strongly disagree that cleanliness and hygiene in the park are well maintained.
- According to the above table and chart, 42% of customers thought the restaurant's ambiance was nice. Furthermore, 8% of customers vehemently disagreed with it.
- According to the above table and data, 48% of consumers strongly think that Wonderland is worth the money. Furthermore, 6% of customers vehemently disagreed with it.
- According to the table and chart above, 58% of consumers strongly agreed that they will recommend Wonderland to others. And 6% strongly disagreed with the aforementioned claim.
- According to the table and graph above, 41% of the consumers plan to return to Wonderla.5% of respondents strongly disagreed and say they'll return.
- According to the above table and chart, 42% of customers strongly agreed that Wonder LA's cab service for client pick-up and drop-off is good. 6% of respondents strongly disagreed with the assertion.
- According to the accompanying table and chart, 39% of visitors strongly concur that their overall experience at the Wonderland Park was positive. Additionally, 27% strongly disagreed.
- According to the above chart and table, 33% strongly agreed that their whole experience at Wonderland Resort was very satisfactory, while 15% strongly disagreed.
- According to the above table and chart, 31% of visitors strongly agreed that overall safety precautions associated to the park's rides were sufficient, while 17% strongly disagreed.
- According to the above table and chart, 31% of customers strongly agreed that Wonderland is a nice place to have fun and spend time with friends, while 16% strongly disagreed.
- According to the above table and chart, 50% of the visitors strongly agreed that Wonderland satisfies the needs and wants of its customers, while just 6% strongly disagreed.

SUGGESTIONS

- Deliver outstanding client service: Develop the friendliness, awareness, and knowledge of your staff. Inquiries and concerns from customers should be handled quickly, and you should go above and beyond to satisfy them.

- Adapt the experience to you: Customer data should be gathered and used to customize interactions.
- Make a rewards scheme: Implement a loyalty programed that honors patrons for their continued support. Offer unique discounts, unique benefits, or freebies to entice clients to choose your company over rivals.
- Consistently ask for client response via surveys, comment cards, or online reviews and then act on it. Actively hear their comments and worries, then act on their advice to create changes. Inform others of the changes
- Track online reviews and ratings on sites like Google, Yelp, or TripAdvisor and respond as appropriate. Regard both good and negative reviews with promptness and professionalism. Show a sincere interest in customer satisfaction and publicly address any issues.
- Occasionally amuse and surprise your clients with unanticipated actions or rewards. It may be a tiny gift, a personal message of appreciation, or a free upgrade. These good deeds may leave a lasting impression and encourage repeat business.

CONCLUSION

Customer satisfaction is essential for building customer loyalty and enticing repeat business. You may create an atmosphere where consumers feel valued, respected, and ready to return by putting customer satisfaction improvement tactics into practice. Effective strategies to connect customers and make them feel special include personalizing the experience, offering outstanding customer service, and establishing a loyalty programed. Maintaining a neat and welcoming workplace, asking for and acting on client input, and providing convenience and comfort all help to increase customer satisfaction. A pleasant customer experience is facilitated by surprise and pleasure actions, remaining connected through digital channels, and ongoing training for your personnel. Your dedication to resolving client issues and fostering trust is seen by your attention to and response to internet evaluations. In the end, by continually outperforming customer.

REFERENCES

Akbar, M. M., & Parvez, N. (2009). Impact of Service Quality, Trust, and Customer Satisfaction on Customers Loyalty. *ABAC Journal*, 29(1), 1. http://www.assumptionjournal.au.edu/index.php/abacjournal/article/view/526

An Investigation into the Determinants of Customer Satisfaction—Gilbert A. Churchill, Carol Surprenant, 1982. (n.d.). Sage. https://journals.sagepub.com/doi/10.1177/002224378201900410

Bergman, B., & Klefsjo, B. (2010). *Quality from customer needs to customer Satisfaction,.*

Boselie, P., Hesselink, M., & van der Wiele, T. (2001). *Empirical Evidence for the Relation between Customer Satisfaction and Business Performance* (SSRN Scholarly Paper 370891). https://papers.ssrn.com/abstract=370891

Eshiett, I. O., Eshiett, O. E., Eshiett, I. O., & Eshiett, O. E. (2024). Artificial intelligence marketing and customer satisfaction: An employee job security threat review. *World Journal of Advanced Research and Reviews, 21*(1), 1. Advance online publication. doi:10.30574/wjarr.2024.21.1.2655

Hom, W. (2000). *An Overview of Customer Satisfaction Models.* ERIC. http://www. https://eric.ed.gov/?id=ED463825

Measuring customer satisfaction: Why, what and how? (n.d.). UQ eSpace. https://espace.library.uq.edu.au/view/UQ:127560

Neupane, R. (2014). Relationship between Customer Satisfaction and Business Performance: A Case Study of Lloyds Bank UK. *International Journal of Social Sciences and Management, 1*(2), 74–85. doi:10.3126/ijssm.v1i2.10019

Ngo, M. V., & Nguyen, H. H. Tomas Bata University in Zlín. (2016). The Relationship between Service Quality, Customer Satisfaction and Customer Loyalty: An Investigation in Vietnamese Retail Banking Sector. *Journal of Competitiveness, 8*(2), 103–116. doi:10.7441/joc.2016.02.08

Nguyen. D., Pham, V., Tran, M., & Pham, D. (2020). Impact of Service Quality, Customer Satisfaction and Switching Costs on Customer Loyalty. *The Journal of Asian Finance, Economics and Business, 7*, 395–405. 10.13106/jafeb.2020.vol7.no8.395

Oh, H. (1999). Service quality, customer satisfaction, and customer value: A holistic perspective. *International Journal of Hospitality Management, 18*(1), 67–82. doi:10.1016/S0278-4319(98)00047-4

Sivadas, E., & Baker-Prewitt, J. L. (2000). An examination of the relationship between service quality, customer satisfaction, and store loyalty. *International Journal of Retail & Distribution Management, 28*(2), 73–82. doi:10.1108/09590550010315223

Suchánek, P., & Králová, M. (2015). Effect of Customer Satisfaction on Company Performance. *Acta Universitatis Agriculturae et Silviculturae Mendelianae Brunensis, 63*(3), 1013–1021. doi:10.11118/actaun201563031013

Venetis, K., & Ghauri, P. (2004). *Service Quality and Customer Retention: Building Long-Term Relationships* (SSRN Scholarly Paper 2844589). https://papers.ssrn.com/abstract=2844589 doi:10.1108/03090560410560254

Vukmir, R. B. (2006). Customer satisfaction. *International Journal of Health Care Quality Assurance Incorporating Leadership in Health Services, 19*(1), 8–31. doi:10.1108/09526860610642573 PMID:16548396

Wicaksono, Y. M., & Utami, C. W. (n.d.). *THE EFFECT OF SERVICE QUALITY AND FOOD QUALITY ON CUSTOMER SATISFACTION AND CUSTOMER RETENTION AT PRIDE COFFEE AND KITCHEN*. Semantic Scholar.

Williams, P., & Naumann, E. (2011). Customer satisfaction and business performance: A firm-level analysis. *Journal of Services Marketing, 25*(1), 1. doi:10.1108/08876041111107032

Yang, T., Wu, J., & Zhang, J. (2023). Knowing how satisfied/dissatisfied is far from enough: A comprehensive customer satisfaction analysis framework based on hybrid text mining techniques. *International Journal of Contemporary Hospitality Management, 36*(3), 873–892. doi:10.1108/IJCHM-10-2022-1319

Chapter 2
Assessing the Utilization of Metaverse in Enhancing Marketing Practices:
Cases From an Emerging Market

Riza Ergün Arsal
Istanbul Bilgi University, Turkey

Asli Elif Aydin
Istanbul Bilgi University, Turkey

ABSTRACT

The purpose of this chapter is to explore the evolving landscape of marketing in the metaverse era. Metaverse applications of marketing activities from various industries are examined with cases from an emerging country. Beginning with an evaluation of marketing practices leading up to the metaverse, the chapter examines the transition from traditional methods to digital, social media, and mobile marketing strategies. It then delves into the myriad uses of the metaverse for marketing practices, highlighting immersive experiences, gamification, virtual commerce, and personalized engagement. Recent examples showcase how brands are leveraging virtual environments to connect with consumers in innovative ways. Last, expected challenges for companies are discussed. Concluding remarks offer recommendations for marketing practitioners, particularly in emerging countries, emphasizing the importance of embracing emerging technologies and adapting strategies to leverage the opportunities presented by the metaverse for effective brand engagement and consumer interaction.

DOI: 10.4018/979-8-3693-4167-4.ch002

INTRODUCTION

Metaverse has a pivotal prospect for boosting companies' marketing affairs. It is likely to influence every marketing domain, including new product development, brand communication, retail management, concept testing, and experience marketing (Dwivedi et al., 2022). Given such significance, understanding the role of the metaverse in triggering a revolution of marketing activities in the digital sphere becomes highly imperative.

In this chapter, we examine metaverse marketing practices across different industries in a developing country. Developing countries, which lack established market frameworks, provide a more fertile ground for the application and adoption of new technologies. Therefore, Turkey, with its dynamic market environment provides a stimulating playing field, which accelerates the development of metaverse marketing. As emphasized in a recent report by Deloitte, the successful development of the metaverse is expected to contribute up to US $37.5bn to the Turkish economy (Deloitte, 2022). This projection is an indicator of the potential economic impact of metaverse utilization for Turkey as well as an opportunity for firms to gain a sustainable competitive advantage over their rivals within their industries.

Even though it has not reached a stage of maturity, metaverse applications are employed ubiquitously in the marketing of various industries in Turkey. The industries where metaverse marketing applications are most seen are telecommunication (e.g. Turkcell, Vodafone), banking (e.g. Is Bank, Halkbank, Yapi Kredi), and apparel (e.g. LC Waikiki, Koton, Kigili, Damat Tween) industries which have undergone extensive digital transformation. The chapter will mainly focus on metaverse applications in these industries. In addition to them, sample practices of metaverse marketing in the fields of consumer durables (e.g. Vestel), furniture (e.g. Dogtas), food (e.g. Sagra), automotive (e.g. Ford, Toyota), entertainment (e.g. Kral Şakir, Muhteşem Yüzyıl) and airlines (e.g. THY) will also be examined.

This chapter aims to (1) determine the main marketing activities that will be altered by the metaverse and discuss the effect of the metaverse on these activities, and (2) present metaverse applications of companies from various industries in Turkey. As this book intends to provide an overview of the potential uses of the metaverse in enhancing marketing activities, we believe this chapter makes a valuable contribution.

The remainder of this chapter is organized as follows. First, the evaluation of marketing towards the metaverse era will be reviewed. Then, various uses of metaverse for marketing practices and recent examples will be presented. Lastly, concluding remarks will be made with recommendations for marketing practitioners, especially in emerging countries.

The Evolution of Marketing Towards the Metaverse Era

During the last two decades, there have been substantial changes within the business environment. These changes have been mainly driven by a shift to an information-based economy, which made intelligence the most valuable resource that every business needs to remain competitive, and the ICT revolution, which aims to provide access to technologies designed to handle information (Bourlakis et al., 2009). These breakthroughs affected consumers' behavior in the way how they communicated with brands and shared information with each other (Lamberton & Stephen, 2016). Consequently, this transformation prompted fundamental changes in the marketing sphere.

The metamorphosis in marketing initiated with the widespread use of the internet which enabled the emergence of digital marketing practices. Through the use of digital technologies, an online marketplace has been created where buyers and sellers interact with customers actively contributing value creation to better meet their demands (Wirtz et al., 2010). In addition to that, customers started to foster social ties as part of a virtual community Ginzarly & Teller, 2021).

Subsequently, the rise of social media accelerated the interactions within virtual communities (Ramadan, 2023). Customers started to share their own stories through various social media platforms, which enabled marketers to connect with the customers and impact their experiences (Ramadan and Farah 2020).

The following milestone has been the development of mobile marketing with the advent of personal mobile devices. Mobile marketing has offered distinct opportunities due to the widespread use of mobile phones, their capacity for private and personalized exchanges, and the facilitation of two-way interactions (Sunny & Anael, 2016). Mobile platforms enable marketers to have constant access to customers and enable them to gather valuable customer insight (Yadav et al., 2015).

As marketing has progressed beyond conventional methods to include digital, social media, and mobile marketing strategies, brands have always looked for creative ways to interact with consumers in an increasingly connected world. With the advent of the metaverse, marketers now have a unique opportunity to develop immersive, interactive experiences that go beyond the confines of the real world and the virtual world. The metaverse develops and continuously modifies the existing internet and social media structure rather than substituting them entirely (Hollensen et al., 2022). It generates an added 3D layer over the conventional 2D internet, offering a plethora of novel and captivating brand experiences. The metaverse offers marketers a vast testing ground where they may develop client experiences that improve the usability of their products or services (Hollensen et al., 2022).

Metaverse In Marketing

Many marketing experts recognize novel sets of opportunities presented by the emergence of the metaverse that help to improve the effectiveness of their marketing activities (Dwivedi et al., 2022). Accordingly, companies may employ the metaverse in multiple ways that enhance the relationships built with the customers.

Immersive Customer Experiences

Customer experience in the metaverse is mainly influenced by three elements, namely the extent of immersion, the degree of social interaction enabled for users, and the level of fidelity between the metaverse and the actual world (Barrera & Shah, 2023).

The immersive potential of the metaverse enables companies to design vivid and engaging interactions that provide greater value to customers (Nikhashemi et al., 2021). Similarly, enhanced sociability presented by the metaverse environment is instrumental in creating favorable customer attitudes and behavior (De Regt, Plangger, & Barnes, 2021). The degree of alignment between the representation of the virtual space with the real world is another factor affecting customer experiences. While high-fidelity, realistic environments yield more engagement for customers with functional motives (e.g., product purchase); low-fidelity, fantasy environments spark the interest of customers with hedonic motives (e.g., fun activities) (Barrera & Shah, 2023).

In addition to the representation of the surroundings, self-representation via the use of avatars also determines environmental fidelity (Barrera & Shah, 2023). In the metaverse, users employ avatars from a spectrum of lifelike and authentic to unrealistic and fantasy-based. Customers may choose between their true selves vs. their ideal selves via their user avatars. Through the avatars that users embody, interaction takes place with the virtual space, the products, and others (Kim, 2021). Consequently, avatars have a significant role in determining the experiences that customers will have in the metaverse.

Ford Turkey is one of the frontrunners in creating immersive experiences. Since car purchasing is largely a decision that takes place in the physical domain, the company prioritizes customer experience and communication over commercial efforts. The Ford Digital Studio application provides different experiences for current and potential customers who can create their own avatars before browsing through the studio (Mediacat, n.d.). For example, Ford owners can use the QR codes to access the AR-enhanced version of their vehicles. Others can visit the studio where each floor and room offer a different experience: They can join special virtual events, explore and test various Ford models, or interact with the customer service personnel for further questions about the products (Ford Company, 2024).

Still in the development stage, established Turkish brand Sagra has also announced the deployment of its metaverse premises, where the consumers will be able to visit the Sagra factory to learn about the manufacturing process as well as detailed information about its products (DHA, 2022).

In the entertainment industry, King Shakir (Turkish: Kral Şakir), a renowned cartoon character that is popular among children in Europe, the Middle East, and Africa, also has a presence in the metaverse. Along with an animated show streaming on Netflix, the franchise has a theme park, three feature films, 11 books, and nearly 350 licensed products. A King Shakir universe, which includes all the characters from the animation is built for the metaverse and a computer game in addition to NFTs is being developed that will further enhance children's engagement with the brand (Icozu, 2022).

Communication

The metaverse environment fosters a fluent line of communication between the source and the receiver. It is easier to get the attention of the customers and initiate dialogues on a captivating podium (Vargo, 2022). Moreover, the quality of the message is also improved since the metaverse allows customers to both create their own content and interact with the brands to co-create joint content (Hollensen, Kotler, & Opresnik, 2023).

The metaverse showcases interactivity abilities that transcend those of traditional media. Most businesses in the metaverse use anthropomorphism in the form of avatars to give human attributes to their brands (Miao et al., 2022). Avatars embodying more people-like characteristics improve the attractiveness, trustworthiness, and willingness to interact with the brand (Mull et al., 2015). Avatars are further utilized to express the brands' values and identity, which helps build stronger customer relationships.

Agent avatars that are representing brands address the lack of social interplay and individualized recommendations issues that most web-based environments fail to provide (Holzwarth, Janiszewski, & Neumann 2006). Providing prompt and helpful responses to customers through avatars in a natural conversation format is much more effective than using conventional CRM tools (Elsharnouby et al., 2022). In addition to goal-directed communication, avatars having the ability to incorporate social discourse in a dialogue improves both the level of authenticity of the communication and the level of connection with the customers (Miao et al., 2022).

Building fluid and continuous communication with consumers is particularly crucial for the banking industry where gaining the trust of customers is essential (Mukherjee & Nath, 2003). Accordingly, many of the leading banks in Turkey have established the metaverse as a complimentary digital channel of communication. Halkbank, the first bank in Turkey to do so, has created a "Metaverse Branch" where users can create their avatars, gain information about and apply for products through a 3-D enhanced reality platform supported by interactive customer service (Yurduneri, 2022). Isbank, which had already started to conduct internal meetings on the metaverse, also placed advertisements for its Maximum Gaming Card on ten different sites of Robox, a popular game on the metaverse (Yildiz, 2022).

Commerce

The utilization of the metaverse for e-commerce is estimated to have an effect of $2 trillion to $2.6 trillion by the year 2030 (McKinsey & Company, 2022a). The metaverse enables retailers to offer unique services that facilitate customer interaction with the retailer space such that the act of interaction is desired as much as the act of purchasing and consumption (Bourlakis, Papagiannidis, & Li, 2009). It is suggested that virtual retail environments that improve the level of telepresence positively influence customers' enjoyment of their experience and may generate purchasing intentions (Baker, Hubona & Srite, 2019; Kinzinger et al., 2022).

The metaverse not only generates increased returns on boosted sales of tangible goods but also a new line of returns on sales of virtual goods in the form of NFTs. Creating an alternate economy, the market for virtual goods now constitutes 40 percent of the transactions in the gaming industry worldwide (McKinsey & Company, 2022b). It is indicated that the unique characteristics of NFTs present novelties for traditional marketing in terms of promotion and distribution (Hofstetter et al. 2022).

In this regard, the retail apparel giant LCWaikiki has become one of the first major players in the metaverse with the launch of its MetaStore in 2022 (Aka, 2022). LCWaikiki has created an extended reality environment that aims to increase both customer engagement and enjoyment throughout the shopping experience. The store includes not only a variety of its standard goods in a 3D format but also customized products that are developed using its recommendation engines. MetaStore also demonstrates LCWaikiki's willingness to include various non-commerce activities to create customer enjoyment as well as increase social awareness. For instance, the store also exhibits a selection of NFTs whose sales are used to raise funds for TEGV, a non-profit educational foundation in Turkey. On the other hand, entertaining activities such as rollercoasters and whale riding in the sky make the whole customer experience more fun and immersive.

Leading companies in other industries also bring their commercial endeavors to the metaverse. For instance, Vodafone Turkey, a new entrant in 2023, does not limit its store to directly telco-related products but also aims to increase its revenues through the cross-sales of various technologies such as smart home appliances and personal electronic devices (Akbas, 2022).

Collaborations and Building Communities

The metaverse transforms marketing activities into collaborative efforts much more than ever before. Product development is decentralized because of multiple users enacting jointly as creators in the virtual space (Hofstetter et al. 2022). Moreover, crowdsourcing of branding practices occurs such as derivative collections that are inspired by blue chip NFTs and branded by the creators and supporting communities (NFT Culture, 2022; Hofstetter et al. 2022). The brands have the potential to transfer know-how and access complementary capabilities by cooperating with the communities of freelance designers and programmers that already gained some experience in the metaverse (McKinsey & Company, 2022b).

For instance, a collaboration between creators, developers, and game studios is set up to create a life-like representation of a touristic destination in Turkey named Cappadocia. It is expected that through such cooperation, the striking scenery of Cappadocia can be developed scrupulously and realistically. To incentivize the interest of talented partners, a contest is organized asking participants to design the most ravishing and creative hot air balloon, which is the trademark feature of Cappadocia coloring its skies.

Turkcell, the leading mobile phone operator in Turkey, has launched an application that allows employees to develop a familiarity with cutting-edge technologies as well as a sense of their future working environment and potential capabilities that would be crucial to develop. Turkcell also creates events for its employees from all functions to get together for the metaverse experience, which would create an informal social network within the company where employees can share their experiences and exchange ideas about what the future might convey in terms of both technology and work practices (Gunyol, 2022). Encouraged by the success of their internal use, Turkcell is planning to expand its marketing and sales activities for its customers on the metaverse. The company plans to collaborate with the consumers to develop personalized and additional offerings as well as sell their products in a highly immersive store.

The metaverse reconstructed the role of consumer brand communities from external stakeholders to partners that co-create value, manage the brand by making relevant decisions, and enhance brand equity (Costa & Helal, 2022). The brand communities not only deliver fruitful insight into unaddressed desires but also aid to nourish sensory, affective relations with the customers (Dos Remedios, 2023). Creating a more profound attachment will help brands to establish a loyal group of customers and support brand advocacy. Several strategies for thriving in community building in the metaverse are suggested (Henry, 2023). For instance, businesses may reward the community members (e.g., special access, NFTs), encourage branded creations (e.g., branded places, products, mascots), and engage with the community in an authentic way (e.g., sponsoring events relevant to target demographics).

To strengthen community bonds, a series of cultural experiences that celebrate Ramadan, is launched by Turkishverse. As part of the Ramadan event, users are invited to numerous activities such as visiting mosques like Hagia Sophia, attending virtual *iftar* meals after sunset, preparing *baklava*, and enjoying traditional such as traditional Turkish shadow play and *mehter* ceremony, a tribute to Ottoman military bands (Medium, 2023). These activities with a local touch help users to share the unique atmosphere of Ramadan with members of their community.

Virtual Events

The virtual space offers a convenient environment for businesses to sponsor events, host virtual meetings, start social responsibility activities, plan exhibitions, and organize virtual shows (Kshetri, 2022). The metaverse platform provides an opportunity to access worldwide audiences while enabling interactive encounters. Whereas virtual showrooms and interactive activities enable customers to explore new products and services, live events with Q&A sessions allow a personal touch (Khatri, 2022). Ultimately, the vibrant and personalized nature of events on the metaverse helps brands foster attraction and promote buzz.

It is stated that the true worth of the metaverse is attached to its social feature such that it provides the means to stand side-by-side with people elsewhere and creates a sense of social presence through this true-to-life togetherness (Hennig-Thurau & Ognibeni, 2022). Thus, enjoyment of the events held on the metaverse, and hence their influence on brand attitudes, is far more amplified. Events such as hanging out at a festival, visiting ana theme park, or attending a workshop may be utilized to offer customers a feeling of escapism and rejoicing that will intensify their connections with the brands (Cheahn & Shimul, 2023).

Since they do not necessarily require continuity, virtual events have acted as one-off opportunities for firms to demonstrate and even appraise their capabilities on the metaverse. In 2022, apparel companies such as Kigili and Koton conducted fashion shows that attracted high interest from both the public and the press. Koton, the first Turkish company to organize a fashion show on metaverse, used avatars, utilized 3D-optimized visualization, and embedded storytelling that involves consumers to catch on to the creation process of the presented collection (Buyukdumlu, 2022). Kigili followed a similar approach from a technological perspective, adding a live component that includes live models and presenters (Metin, 2022).

Turkish Airlines (THY) participates in metaverse-based activities with the largest basketball organization in Europe, the Euroleague (Kali, 2023). As the primary sponsor of the league, THY helps to create annual virtual events where basketball fans and even some of the players can get together in an interactive environment that integrates the use of avatars, provides a platform for an interactive get-together, and delivers users simplistic but fun basketball games that allow fans to challenge each other.

Another virtual event example was demonstrated by NFT Biennial Istanbul, which brought together artists from seven countries and gained exposure in front of a worldwide audience (Turkyilmaz, 2023). The exhibit with the theme "Cyber-Myth: Post-human Age Goddess", was the first Biennial held on the Metaverse, and prospered in bringing the digital space close to the real world while delivering a captivating showcase.

Gamification

While gamification is getting popular in the marketing domain, the enriched environment of the metaverse is providing an even more fertile venue for its implementation (Sveder & Lundbäck, 2023). Gamification is expected to enhance marketing practices, especially in the metaverse (Sharma et al., 2024). The immersive, novel, interactive, and vivid characteristics of the metaverse, provide a suitable platform for gamification (Bousba & Arya, 2022). The utilization of VR and AR tools allows a smooth way to incorporate games into our everyday lives through the metaverse (Jovanović and Milosavljević, 2022).

Gamification, the process of combining game mechanics to motivate users and accomplish a goal (Seaborn & Fels, 2015), is widely employed to maintain customer engagement with brands. Many gamification practices are employed to improve user experience within the metaverse environment, namely creating avatars, offering digital badges, awarding coupons and NFTs, providing leadership boards as well as other initiatives (Sangroya et al., 2021). It is suggested that gamification in the metaverse offers a more robust and scalable means of connecting with users (Tayal et al., 2022). It also improves consumer learning, by encouraging them to focus more on the brand in both the real and virtual worlds (Stefanic, 2022). Moreover, it is demonstrated that employing effective gamification applications in the metaverse generates positive outcomes such as strong emotional brand engagement, enhanced consumer-based brand equity, increased brand satisfaction, and stimulated purchase impulse (Arya et al., 2023; Bousba & Arya, 2022).

DBS Bank created a metaverse experience field named DBS BetterWorld, which is designed to demonstrate how the metaverse experience can be used for good with a gamification focus. The bank decided to address the global food waste problem. The goal was to raise awareness about the food waste issue and show inventive approaches of DBS-supported businesses in tackling the matter. Players of the game have to finish several tasks that are modeled after DBS-funded businesses with distinctive strategies for reducing food waste. Various rewards will probably be offered to those who complete the tasks. (Blockchain Türkiye, 2023).

Lacoste is one pioneer brand that developed a gamified experience for its global customers. This activity is mainly designed for customer loyalty and retention efforts. Inside the virtual store, as a part of the game, premium customers could find treasure chests filled with gifts, which encouraged them to return for more treats. This fostered a feeling of privilege and belonging within the branded area (Cakmak, 2022).

New Product Development

While organizations concentrate their efforts mostly on marketing efforts targeted to increase customer engagement, one area that provides unlimited opportunities is new product development in joint with the consumers. The contribution of consumers on new product development is well documented in innovation and knowledge management literatures (e.g. von Hippel, 1986; Prahalad & Ramaswamy, 2004). Previous studies indicate that innovation processes are more successful when the internal knowledge held within the organization is complemented by the external knowledge of consumers. This *co-creation* collaboration allows organizations to gain valuable insights about the consumer wants and needs at a rapid and cost-effective way while developing a common ground between the provider and the consumer (Piller & Walcher, 2006). Although the advent of the Internet delivered numerous web-based platforms where firms and consumers could interact directly and continuously, the consumer input has been bounded by guidelines or toolkits. On the other hand, metaverse can also act as a platform of co-creation of new products, only this time the interaction between the firm and consumer is enriched by advanced technologies such as virtual (VR) and augmented reality (AR) that allow "users to engage in immersive experiences to see, touch, meet, and travel beyond their physical environments" (Kim, 2023).

A recent industry report published by Ernst & Young (Peterson et al 2022) emphasizes the role of consumers in maximizing the value of metaverse. The report identifies co-creation as one of the core capabilities that would allow the development of products such as digital twins, NFTs and other digital assets through experiences that create immersive consumer engagement. However, firms also need to go through significant changes in their development processes where they need to share the driving wheel with the customers instead of simply leading them via pre-determined tools such as user toolkits or guidelines. In other words, co-creation of new products on metaverse requires the true democratization of the process for both the firm and the consumer (Peterson et al 2022). While traditional firm-customer relationships are built on customer trust, relationships built on metaverse will demand the trusting beliefs and behaviors of organizations on their customers. In return, not only more new products that meet the market needs will be developed but also the customer trust and loyalty will also be positively influenced by this collaborative process.

Therefore, it is not too surprising to observe that most of firms in the world and in Turkey are yet to take advantage of this co-creation opportunity despite its enormous potential. However, there are few companies from the sports apparel industry that demonstrate effective use of metaverse for new product development in collaboration with consumers. For instance, Adidas is utilizing the platform not only for marketing purposes but also for product development stage. The company presents various prototypes to customers and has them test these prototypes before they officially release them to the market. Adidas also provided the consumers with a PFP styling tool that allows the users to create their own digital apparel design. Similarly, Nike has created its. SWOOSH platform on metaverse in order to build a digital community where the members of the community can co-create product designs for shoes and jerseys. Puma has also followed the footsteps of Adidas and Nike, and created a similar environment where users can have access to exclusive products, try out prototypes and contribute to new designs.

Expected Challenges

This chapter presents an overview of various recent marketing activities in an emerging market, namely Turkey. While the organizations in Turkey seem to have some way to catch up with its contemporaries, we observe signals that indicate an increasing interest in utilizing the approaches, processes, and technologies that are essentials to gaining competitive advantage over their rivals. Nonetheless, there are several challenges that require attention. The first of these challenges is the legal and ethical aspect of metaverse. An insight report published on March 2024 by the World Economic Forum points out to the need for the close monitoring and controlling of the activities on the metaverse to make sure that all parties adhere to the laws and regulations and the integrity of the environment is protected (World Economic Forum, 2024). Since metaverse is at its infant stage in Turkey, there is a plethora of academic articles and training programs designed for organizational awareness. For example, The Banks Association of Turkey offers a full day seminar of "Metaverse Law" in which the legal aspects of metaverse, blockchain, and crypto currencies are covered (The Banks Association of Turkey, 2023). Istanbul Bar Association's IT Law Commission has published a document that focuses on the applicability of current law norms in the metaverse environment and discusses the personality rights of avatars as well as the crimes against the avatars (Istanbul Bar Association, 2023). In terms of law, there are a few critical areas for firms such as intellectual property rights, copyrights, privacy of the users and cybercrimes (Kalyvaki, 2023). Building a metaverse platform on legally and ethically reliable principles is perhaps the foundation stone of successful marketing activities. If the customer feels that her intellectual property rights would not be fully protected, how can the firm expect that individual to contribute to the innovation of a new product? If one is abused or harassed on metaverse even when she represents herself with an avatar, will the user ever find the courage or motivation to participate in a live event or visit a virtual store again? In a related matter, firms must also build adequate infrastructure and safeguards to implement the systems to prevent potential cyber security problems and data breaches (Cheah & Shimul, 2023). In emerging countries where a virtual platform like metaverse is yet to be adopted widely, finding the right answers and developing the right solution to such legal issues becomes as important as any business practice.

Another challenge for organizations is the diffusion of metaverse technology across the population. On one hand, there are promising signs from Zoomers (Gen Z). According to recent survey research (Retail Technology Show, 2023) more than 40% of Gen Z are already active users who actively engage with brands on the platform. On the other hand, as technology acceptance models indicate (e.g. Venkatesh et al., 2003), individuals from older generations may hesitate or have difficulty using the advanced technologies that are employed on the metaverse. Firms should think about innovative ways to engage older individuals to participate in their activities.

Even if the technology itself is well-understood and the customer shows a willingness to utilize it, she may still have difficulties adapting to the differences between the physical and virtual environments. Moreover, the customer may simply not be interested in building a bridge between the two environments, i.e. not make any purchases in the physical world (Lu & Mintz, 2023). Hence, companies should be aware that metaverse does not require adoption only on technological level but also on conceptual level, which involves the adoption of new business processes and products.

Finally, firms should acknowledge the fact that reaping the full benefits of their investments on metaverse is likely to take time. Research suggests that the full integration of metaverse into our daily lives would not be complete before 2040 (Anderson & Rainie, 2022). Still, capturing a significant portion of the population (e.g. Gen Z and Millennials) is an immense business opportunity on its own, which would also set the stage for the upcoming years as one of the first movers in the market.

CONCLUSION

Regardless of any location across the globe, the metaverse is still considered to be within the phase of infancy that is similar to the state of the internet in the 1990s

(Henry, 2023). Therefore, it is not surprising to see most Turkish companies that are present on the metaverse, are still at the stage of experimentation. This is akin to the development and introduction stages of the product lifecycle where the companies are investing in the required technologies, expanding their marketing and sales capabilities, and building the demand for their metaverse experiences for consumers. However, considering the metaverse ecosystem, the early signs are encouraging. On the technological end, several metaverse platforms are already developed in Türkiye, namely Atlas Space, Metapotamians, Turkishverse, GoArt, and MetaAge. These platforms contribute to the awareness of Turkish brands and consumers who realize the power of this universe where the opportunities and activities such as interactive games, art events, and NFT collections are nearly limitless. On the other hand, the consumer end seems to lack the power in terms of PCs and mobile devices that support the full capabilities of a well-developed metaverse environment. Also, the cost of the devices (e.g., headsets) required for the VR metaverses is still considerably high due to their limited diffusion (Hennig-Thurau & Ognibeni, 2022).

Figuring out impactful ways of utilizing the metaverse is an iterative process. While both the firms and the public are at the early stages of the adoption of this innovation, we believe that the economic and social returns look promising. Metaverse offers vast opportunities for companies to enhance their marketing activities, and many companies look eager to grab their share of the pie already.

REFERENCES

Aka, C. A. (2022). *LC Waikiki, metaverse mağazasını açtı!* Shiftdelete.net. https://shiftdelete.net/lc-waikiki-metaverse-magazasi-alisveris .

Akbas, Y. (2022, April 8). *Vodafone, Decentraland'de metaverse mağaza açıyor.* Doanimhaber. https://www.donanimhaber.com/vodafone-decentraland-de-metaverse-magaza-aciyor--147234 .

Anderson, J., & Rainie, L. (2022). *The metaverse in 2040*. Pew Research Centre.

Arya, V., Sambyal, R., Sharma, A., & Dwivedi, Y. K. (2024). Brands are calling your AVATAR in Metaverse–A study to explore XR-based gamification marketing activities & consumer-based brand equity in virtual world. *Journal of Consumer Behaviour*, *23*(2), 556–585. doi:10.1002/cb.2214

Baker, E. W., Hubona, G. S., & Srite, M. (2019). Does "being there" matter? The impact of web-based and virtual world's shopping experiences on consumer purchase attitudes. *Information & Management*, *56*(7), 103153. doi:10.1016/j.im.2019.02.008

Barrera, K. G., & Shah, D. (2023). Marketing in the Metaverse: Conceptual understanding, framework, and research agenda. *Journal of Business Research*, *155*, 113420. doi:10.1016/j.jbusres.2022.113420

Blockchain Türkiye. (2023). *Singapur'un en büyük bankasından sürpriz metaverse konsepti.* Blockchain Türkiye. https://bctr.org/singapurun-en-buyuk-bankasindan-surpriz-metaverse-konsepti-30121/

Bourlakis, M., Papagiannidis, S., & Li, F. (2009). Retail spatial evolution: Paving the way from traditional to metaverse retailing. *Electronic Commerce Research*, *9*(1-2), 135–148. doi:10.1007/s10660-009-9030-8

Bousba, Y., & Arya, V. (2022). Let's connect in metaverse. Brand's new destination to increase consumers' affective brand engagement & their satisfaction and advocacy. *Journal of Content Community Communication*, *14*(8), 276–293. doi:10.31620/JCCC.06.22/19

Buyukdumlu, S. (2022, August 22). *Türkiye'nin metaverse odaklı ilk defilesi.* Pazar Lamasyon. https://www.pazarlamasyon.com/turkiye-nin-metaverse-odakli-ilk-defilesi .

Cakmak, B. K. (2022). *Lacoste, Metaverse'de Oyunlaştırılmış Mağaza Açıyor.* https://www.bisektor.com/lacoste-metaversede-oyunlastirilmis-magaza/

Cheah, I., & Shimul, A. S. (2023). Marketing in the metaverse: Moving forward–What's next? *Journal of Global Scholars of Marketing Science*, *33*(1), 1–10. doi:10.1080/21639159.2022.2163908

Costa, T., & Helal, A. E. (2022). *Branding in the Metaverse.* [Master's Thesis, Lund University]. https://lup.lub.lu.se/student-papers/record/9096606

De Regt, A., Plangger, K., & Barnes, S. J. (2021). Virtual reality marketing and customer advocacy: Transforming experiences from story-telling to story-doing. *Journal of Business Research*, *136*, 513–522. doi:10.1016/j.jbusres.2021.08.004

DHA. (2022). *Çikolata markası Sagra, Metaverse'de fabrika açacak.* DHA. https://www.dha.com.tr/ekonomi/cikolata-markasi-sagra-metaversede-fabrika-acacak-2028834 .

Dos Remedios, L. (2023). The influence of the Metaverse on Brand Management: A study. *Communities*, *2*(2), 5.

Elsharnouby, M. H., Jayawardhena, C., Liu, H., & Elbedweihy, A. M. (2022). Strengthening consumer–brand relationships through avatars. *Journal of Research in Interactive Marketing*.

Ford Company. (2024). *Dijital Stüdyo Decentraland Klavuzu*. Ford Company. https://www.ford.com.tr/getmedia/c9a4bc41-fbc8-4d8b-b668-1677dd48f74c/Ford-Metaverse-Klavuz.pdf.aspx .

Ginzarly, M., & Teller, J. (2021). Online communities and their contribution to local heritage knowledge. *Journal of Cultural Heritage Management and Sustainable Development*, *11*(4), 361–380. doi:10.1108/JCHMSD-02-2020-0023

Gunyol, A. (2022). *Turkcell çalışanlarına "metaverse" dünyasının kapıları açıldı*. AA. https://www.aa.com.tr/tr/sirkethaberleri/bilisim/turkcell-calisanlarina-metaverse-dunyasinin-kapilari-acildi/675650 .

Hennig-Thurau, T., & Ognibeni, B. (2022). Metaverse marketing. *NIM Marketing Intelligence Review*, *14*(2), 43–47. doi:10.2478/nimmir-2022-0016

Henry, C. D. (2023). Six strategies to building successful communities in the Metaverse. *Journal of Brand Strategy*, *12*(1), 40–48.

Hofstetter, R., de Bellis, E., Brandes, L., Clegg, M., Lamberton, C., Reibstein, D., Rohlfsen, F., Schmitt, B., & Zhang, J. Z. (2022). Crypto-marketing: How non-fungible tokens (NFTs) challenge traditional marketing. *Marketing Letters*, *33*(4), 705–711. doi:10.1007/s11002-022-09639-2

Hollensen, S., Kotler, P., & Opresnik, M. O. (2023). Metaverse: The new marketing universe. *The Journal of Business Strategy*, *44*(3), 119–125. doi:10.1108/JBS-01-2022-0014

Holzwarth, M., Janiszewski, C., & Neumann, M. M. (2006). The influence of avatars on online consumer shopping behavior. *Journal of Marketing*, *70*(4), 19–36. doi:10.1509/jmkg.70.4.019

Icozu, T. (2022). *The Sandbox Kurucu Ortağı ve COO'su Sebastien Borget: "Türkiye önceki sezonda ilk 5'te yer aldı."* Webrazzi. https://webrazzi.com/2022/11/18/the-sandbox-kurucu-ortagi-ve-coo-su-sebastien-borget-turkiye-onceki-sezonda-ilk-5-te-yer-aldi/ Accessed, May 25, 2023.

Istanbul Bar Association. (2023). *Metaverse and Artificial Intelligence*. Istanbul Bar Association. https://www.istanbulbarosu.org.tr/files/komisyonlar/yzcg/metaverse_ve_hukuk.pdf

Jovanović, A., & Milosavljević, A. (2022). VoRtex Metaverse platform for gamified collaborative learning. *Electronics (Basel)*, *11*(3), 317. doi:10.3390/electronics11030317

Kali, Z. (2023, May 18). *The 2023 Turkish Airlines EuroLeague Final Four Kicks Off This Week with New Metaverse, EuroLeague Land*. Aeroportist. https://www. aeroportist.com/the-2023-turkish-airlines-euroleague-final/

Kalyvaki, M. (2023). Navigating the metaverse business and legal challenges: Intellectual property, privacy, and jurisdiction. *Journal of Metaverse, 3*(1), 87–92. doi:10.57019/jmv.1238344

Khatri, M. (2022). Revamping the marketing world with metaverse–The future of marketing. *International Journal of Computer Applications, 975*(29), 8887. doi:10.5120/ijca2022922361

Kim, J. (2021). Advertising in the metaverse: Research agenda. *Journal of Interactive Advertising, 21*(3), 141–144. doi:10.1080/15252019.2021.2001273

Kinzinger, A., Steiner, W., Tatzgern, M., & Vallaster, C. (2022). Comparing low sensory enabling (LSE) and high sensory enabling (HSE) virtual product presentation modes in e-commerce. *Information Systems Journal, 32*(5), 1034–1063. doi:10.1111/ isj.12382

Kshetri, N. (2022). Web 3.0 and the metaverse shaping organizations' brand and product strategies. *IT Professional, 24*(02), 11–15. doi:10.1109/MITP.2022.3157206

Lamberton, C., & Stephen, A. T. (2016). A thematic exploration of digital, social media, and mobile marketing: Research evolution from 2000 to 2015 and an agenda for future inquiry. *Journal of Marketing, 80*(6), 146–172. doi:10.1509/jm.15.0415

Lu, S., & Mintz, O. (2023). Marketing on the metaverse: Research opportunities and challenges. *AMS Review, 13*(1), 151–166. doi:10.1007/s13162-023-00255-5

McKinsey & Company. (2022a). *Value creation in the metaverse*. McKinsey & Company. https:// www.mckinsey.com/business-functions/growth-marketing-and-sales/ our-insights/value-creation-in-the-metaverse .

McKinsey & Company. (2022b). *Marketing in the metaverse: An opportunity for innovation and experimentation*. McKinsey & Company. https://www.mckinsey. com/business-functions/growth-marketing-and-sales/our-insights/marketing-in-the-metaverse-an-opportunity-for-innovation-and-experimentation .

Mediacat (n.d.). *Metaverse'ün Türkiye'deki ilk dijital otomotiv stüdyosu Ford Türkiye'den*. Mediacat. https://mediacat.com/metaverseun-turkiyedeki-ilk-dijital-otomotiv-studyosu-ford-turkiyeden/

Metin, U. (2022, September 30). *Kiğılı Türkiye'nin ilk canlı meta defilesini gerçekleştirdi*. Pazar Lamasyon. https://www.pazarlamasyon.com/kigili-turkiye-nin-ilk-canli-meta-defilesini-gerceklestirdi

Miao, F., Kozlenkova, I. V., Wang, H., Xie, T., & Palmatier, R. W. (2022). An emerging theory of avatar marketing. *Journal of Marketing, 86*(1), 67–90. doi:10.1177/0022242921996646

Mukherjee, A., & Nath, P. (2003). A model of trust in online relationship banking. *International Journal of Bank Marketing, 21*(1), 5–15. doi:10.1108/02652320310457767

Mull, I., Wyss, J., Moon, E., & Lee, S. E. (2015). An exploratory study of using 3D avatars as online salespeople: The effect of avatar type on credibility, homophily, attractiveness and intention to interact. *Journal of Fashion Marketing and Management, 19*(2), 154–168. doi:10.1108/JFMM-05-2014-0033

Nikhashemi, S. R., Knight, H. H., Nusair, K., & Liat, C. B. (2021). Augmented reality in smart retailing: A (n)(A) Symmetric Approach to continuous intention to use retail brands' mobile AR apps. *Journal of Retailing and Consumer Services, 60*, 102464. doi:10.1016/j.jretconser.2021.102464

Piller, F. T., & Walcher, D. (2006). Toolkits for idea competitions: A novel method to integrate users in new product development. *R & D Management, 36*(3), 307–318. doi:10.1111/j.1467-9310.2006.00432.x

Prahalad, C. K., & Ramaswamy, V. (2004). Co-creation experiences: The next practice in value creation. *Journal of Interactive Marketing, 18*(3), 5–14. doi:10.1002/dir.20015

Ramadan, Z. (2023). Marketing in the metaverse era: Toward an integrative channel approach. *Virtual Reality (Waltham Cross), 27*(3), 1905–1918. doi:10.1007/s10055-023-00783-2 PMID:37360809

Ramadan, Z. B., & Farah, M. F. (2020). Influencing the influencers: The case of retailers' social shopping platforms. *International Journal of Web Based Communities, 16*(3), 279–295. doi:10.1504/IJWBC.2020.108626

Sangroya, D., Yadav, R., & Joshi, Y. (2021). Does gamified interaction build a strong consumer-brand connection? A study of mobile applications. *AJIS. Australasian Journal of Information Systems, 25*, 25. doi:10.3127/ajis.v25i0.3105

Seaborn, K., & Fels, D. I. (2015). Gamification in theory and action: A survey. *International Journal of Human-Computer Studies, 74*, 14–31. doi:10.1016/j.ijhcs.2014.09.006

Sharma, W., Lim, W. M., Kumar, S., Verma, A., & Kumra, R. (2024). Game on! A state-of-the-art overview of doing business with gamification. *Technological Forecasting and Social Change*, *198*, 122988. doi:10.1016/j.techfore.2023.122988

Stefanic, D. (2022). *Gamification for Metaverse events: The ultimate guide + 8 examples*. Mootup. https://mootup.com/gamification-for-metaverse-eventsthe-ultimate-guide-8-examples/

Sunny, E. E., & Anael, O. (2016). Mobile marketing in a digital age: Application, challenges & opportunities. *British Journal of Economics. Management & Trade*, *11*(1), 1–13.

Sveder, M., & Lundbäck, E. (2023). *Gamification within the Metaverse: A quantitative study to understand how consumer engagement is influenced by gamification strategies in the Metaverse.*

Tayal, S., Rajagopal, K., & Mahajan, V. (2022, March). Virtual reality based metaverse of gamification. In *2022 6th International Conference on Computing Methodologies and Communication (ICCMC)* (pp. 1597-1604). IEEE. https://egitimkatalogu.tbb. org.tr/Seminer/Detay/2372/9436/metaverse-hukuku.

Turkyilmaz, F. (2023, January 6). *Yüzü aşkın eserin sergileneceği "NFT Biennial" Zorlu PSM'de başladı*. AA. https://www.aa.com.tr/tr/kultur/yuzu-askin-eserin-sergilenecegi-nft-biennial-zorlu-psmde-basladi/2781618

Vargo, L. (2022). *Council post: How the metaverse is shaping consumer behavior*. Forbes Business Development Council. com/sites/ forbesbusinessdevelopmentcouncil/2022/07/05/how-the- metaverse-is-shaping-consumer-behavior/?sh=572c5c493079 Accessed 4 July 2023.

Venkatesh, V., Morris, M. G., Davis, G. B., & Davis, F. D. (2003). User acceptance of information technology: Toward a unified view. *Management Information Systems Quarterly*, *27*(3), 425–478. doi:10.2307/30036540

Von Hippel, E. (1986). Lead users: A source of novel product concepts. *Management Science*, *32*(7), 791–805. doi:10.1287/mnsc.32.7.791

Wirtz, B. W., Schilke, O., & Ullrich, S. (2010). Strategic development of business models: Implications of the Web 2.0 for creating value on the internet. *Long Range Planning*, *43*(2–3), 272–290. doi:10.1016/j.lrp.2010.01.005

World Economic Forum. (2024) *Navigating the Industrial Metaverse: A Blueprint for Future Innovations*. WEF. https://www3.weforum.org/docs/WEF_Navigating_the_Industrial_Metaverse_A_Blueprint_2024.pdf

Yadav, M., Joshi, Y., & Rahman, Z. (2015). Mobile social media: The new hybrid element of digital marketing communications. *Procedia: Social and Behavioral Sciences, 189*, 335–343. doi:10.1016/j.sbspro.2015.03.229

Yildiz, G. (2022, January 27). *İş Bankası'nın reklamları Metaverse'te*. MarketingTürkiye. https://www.marketingturkiye.com.tr/kampanyalar/is-bankasi-roblox/

Yurduneri, D. (2022, November 8). Halkbank, yerli metaverse GoArt'ta şube açtı. *Coin Telegraph*. https://tr.cointelegraph.com/news/halkbank-partners-with-turkish-metaverse-goart

Chapter 3
Consumer Ethnocentrism and Buying Intentions on OTT Platforms

Praneet Poddar
School of Business and Management, Christ University, Bangalore, India

Karan Anand
School of Business and Management, Christ University, Bangalore, India

Babita
School of Business and Management, Christ University, Bangalore, India

ABSTRACT

This research delves into how OTT platforms are transforming media consumption patterns and explores the role of consumer ethnocentrism in shaping buying behaviors within this context. Through a literature review and quantitative research methodology using a Likert-scale questionnaire, the study investigates the relationship between consumer ethnocentrism, buying intentions, and various influencing factors on OTT platforms. Contrary to expectations, the findings show that consumer ethnocentrism has minimal impact on buying behavior. Instead, factors such as price, content variety, personalized recommendations, cultural alignment, ease of platform usage, familiarity with foreign content, and language preferences are crucial in determining viewers' buying intentions. The chapter concludes by recommending that OTT platforms integrate cultural sensitivities into their strategies to better cater to diverse viewer preferences, thereby enhancing market competitiveness and audience engagement.

DOI: 10.4018/979-8-3693-4167-4.ch003

INTRODUCTION

Over-the-top (OTT) platforms refer to video content providers that offer streaming services directly to viewers over the internet, bypassing traditional cable or satellite television providers. In recent years, the popularity of OTT platforms has grown significantly due to the convenience and flexibility they offer to viewers in terms of content consumption. Common examples of OTT platforms popular in India include Netflix, Amazon Prime Video, Jio Cinema, Disney+ Hotstar, SonyLIV, ZEE5, Voot, and ErosNow.

The Indian context is particularly interesting for studying the rise of OTT platforms. India is the world's most populous country and has a rapidly growing population of internet users, which has contributed to the growth of the OTT market. Additionally, India has a diverse culture and a large number of regional languages, which presents unique challenges and opportunities for OTT platforms in terms of catering to diverse audience preferences. The popularity of OTT platforms in India is also influenced by the availability of affordable mobile data plans, which has enabled more users to access streaming services on their mobile devices.

Despite the popularity of OTT platforms, the industry is also facing challenges such as intense competition, regulatory challenges, and monetization issues. Understanding consumer behavior and preferences is crucial for OTT platforms to survive and thrive in the Indian market. Factors such as consumer ethnocentrism, buying intentions, and customer satisfaction play a key role in determining the success of OTT platforms in India. In this context, it is important to examine the interplay between these factors and how they impact the decision-making process of Indian viewers when it comes to subscribing to and using OTT platforms. By studying these factors, OTT platforms can better understand the needs and preferences of their target audience and adapt their strategies accordingly.

Consumer ethnocentrism is a concept that has gained significant importance in recent years, especially in the context of globalisation and increasing cultural exchange. It refers to the tendency of consumers to prefer domestic products and services over foreign ones. It is the belief that products made in one's own country are superior to those made in foreign countries. This preference for domestic products is often based on cultural and nationalistic beliefs, and it can have a significant impact on the purchasing decisions of consumers.

Consumer ethnocentrism has been studied in various fields, including marketing, sociology, and psychology. Consumer ethnocentrism has been found to affect consumer attitudes towards foreign products and services, the willingness to pay a premium for domestic products, and the preference for domestically produced brands.

In the Indian context, consumer ethnocentrism has been a subject of study for researchers and marketers for many years. India is a country with a rich cultural heritage and a diverse population. Indian consumers are known to be highly value-conscious and price-sensitive. They tend to have a strong preference for domestic products and brands, and this preference is often based on cultural and nationalistic beliefs.

However, with the advent of the internet and the proliferation of global brands and products, Indian consumers are also exposed to foreign products and services. The increasing trend towards globalization and the rise of the digital economy have made it easier for consumers to access foreign products and services. This has led to a shift in consumer attitudes towards foreign products and services, and it is important for marketers to understand this shift and adapt their marketing strategies accordingly.

Overall, consumer ethnocentrism is an important concept that has significant implications for businesses. Understanding how consumer ethnocentrism influences the buying behavior of consumers is crucial for businesses to effectively target and cater to the needs and preferences of their target audience.

In the context of OTT platforms, it could influence the decision of subscribing to a domestic or foreign platform. Consumers with higher ethnocentric tendencies may prefer to subscribe to domestic platforms and avoid foreign content, while those with lower tendencies may be more open to exploring foreign platforms. This could have implications for the popularity and success of foreign OTT platforms in a given market. Therefore, understanding the impact of consumer ethnocentrism on subscription patterns and consumption of OTT content is crucial for OTT platform providers to tailor their content and marketing strategies effectively.

Features such as price, variety, recommendations, ease of use of platforms, foreign content, and language availability all impact the level of customer satisfaction towards an OTT platform.

This research paper aims to investigate the interplay between consumer ethnocentrism, buying intentions, customer satisfaction, and OTT platforms in the Indian context. The paper will provide insights into how these factors affect the decision-making process of subscribing to and continuing to use OTT platforms. By analyzing the data collected through questionnaires, this study will shed light on how viewers' preferences for domestic and foreign content, price sensitivity, and platform features impact their satisfaction levels. Overall, the paper will provide a comprehensive understanding of the complex and dynamic nature of the Indian OTT market and the factors that influence viewers' choices and satisfaction levels.

LITERATURE REVIEW

Several studies have shed light on the evolving landscape of over-the-top (OTT) platforms and their impact on consumer behavior in India. Park and Kwon (2019) found a significant shift in consumer preference towards OTT platforms over traditional television, attributing this trend to the lower subscription costs and convenience offered by OTT services.

Deloitte's report 'Digital Media: Rise of on-demand Content' further supports this notion by highlighting the increasing consumption of digital content, including audio-visual entertainment, among Indian youth. With 14% of their time and nearly 17% of their monthly income dedicated to entertainment, Indian consumers are embracing the accessibility and affordability of OTT platforms.

Nair's study (2021) emphasizes the importance of user-friendly interfaces in driving the adoption and retention of OTT platforms. The positive relationship between ease of use and platform adoption suggests that enhancing user experience could be a key strategy for OTT platforms to attract and retain users. Bhattacharyya et al. (2020) underscore the significance

of regional content development for OTT platforms in India. Recognizing the influence of cultural values on user engagement, platforms like Netflix and Amazon Prime have invested in developing regional content to cater to diverse linguistic and cultural preferences.

Consumer familiarity with foreign cultures also plays a crucial role in shaping their interaction with OTT platforms. Moochhala's findings (2018) suggest that the availability of localized foreign regional content and ease of use are primary factors driving user recommendations for platforms like Amazon Prime Video. However, Puthiyakath and Goswami (2021) highlight the dominance of English-language content preferences among Indian users, with only a minority preferring regional languages. This underscores the importance of offering a balanced mix of regional and English-language content to cater to diverse user preferences.

According to Luthra (2021), Zee5 and Amazon Prime Video saw a notable increase in membership during the COVID-19 epidemic because of their more reasonable prices when compared to Netflix. Due to the availability of female-centric material, women were shown to purchase memberships more frequently. This observation highlights the influence of both pricing and content on consumer behavior with regard to OTT platforms.

Dasgupta and Grover (2019) highlighted the increasing preference of Indian audiences for OTT content, emphasizing the inverse relationship between pricing strategies and platform popularity. They also noted challenges such as data consumption habits and preferences for traditional TV.

The research of Vahoniya et al. (2022), increasing the range of content selections available to OTT customers may improve their subscription and renewal rates. Various platforms such as Netflix, Amazon Prime, and Disney+Hotstar were favored due to their varied content classification and supplementary offerings; this underscores the need of accommodating customer inclinations to improve content pleasure and loyalty.

The importance of individualized recommendations in raising customer loyalty and retention rates was highlighted by Samriti and Sharma (2020). For the purpose of resolving user complaints and maximizing user satisfaction, they suggested controlling recommendation algorithms. These results highlight how crucial tailored recommendations are to improving customer satisfaction and retention in the cutthroat OTT market.

Overall, these studies provide valuable insights into the factors influencing consumer behavior and preferences in the OTT market in India. As OTT platforms continue to evolve, understanding these dynamics will be crucial for platforms to stay competitive and

effectively engage with their target audience. By focusing on user-friendly interfaces, investing in regional content development, and catering to diverse language preferences, OTT platforms can enhance user satisfaction and retention, ultimately driving their growth and success in the Indian market.

SCOPE OF THE STUDY

The scope of this study would be to investigate the relationship between consumer ethnocentrism and buying intentions for OTT content in India. Specifically, the study would aim to identify the factors that influence consumer ethnocentrism and buying intentions and to explore how these attitudes and behaviors impact the preferences of Indian viewers for OTT content. The study could use both qualitative and quantitative research methods, such as surveys, interviews, and focus groups, to collect data from a representative sample of Indian viewers. "Kumari, T. (2020)." research showing the growth of ott service in India.

Figure 1.

Data Interpretation

There were total 106 numbers of respondents selected as sample for data collection. Out of these 93 respondents were users of OTT services and 13 were non users. Among the user category approximately 81 percent of users used some kind of paid subscription for consuming OTT services were as 19 percent of the users did not opt for any paid subscription.

Table 1
Most preferred OTT Application

Preferred OTT Application	Percentage of Respondents
Amazon Prime	24
Hotstar	20
Netflix	44
Voot Select	5
Others	7

The third question of the questionnaire indicated about the most preferred OTT channel among Indian users. Approximately 44 percent viewer rate Netflix as the most used OTT channel for watching online video contents. Second preference was given to Amazon Prime (24%) followed by Hotstar (20%).

Table 2
Most preferred Device for OTT Consumption

Preferred Device	Percentage of Respondents
Computer	5
Firestick	25
Laptop	11
Smartphone	56
Tablet	3

The most preferred device among users for watching OTT content is smart phone. Approximately 56 percent of the users use smart phones. The second position was secured by firestick (25%) and the third rank in the list is of laptop users (11%).

RESEARCH OBJECTIVES

1. To examine the impact of consumer ethnocentrism on the subscription of OTT platforms among Indian viewers.
2. To identify the key factors influencing the buying intentions of Indian viewers towards OTT platforms, such as price, variety, recommendations, ease of use of platforms, and familiarity with foreign content and language.
3. To investigate the relationship between various features of OTT platforms, including price, variety, recommendations, ease of use of platforms, foreign content, and customer satisfaction levels among Indian viewers.

VARIABLES USED IN THE STUDY

Dependent Variable:

Consumer Ethnocentrism:

Definition: Consumer ethnocentrism refers to the degree to which individuals exhibit a preference for products or services originating from their own country over those from foreign countries.

Operationalization: Measured using a validated scale assessing respondents' agreement with statements reflecting ethnocentric beliefs, such as "I believe it is important to buy products made in my own country."

Customer Satisfaction:

Definition: Customer satisfaction denotes the level of contentment or satisfaction experienced by consumers with the OTT platforms they utilize.

Operationalization: Measured using a satisfaction scale comprising items assessing respondents' overall satisfaction with the platform's content, interface, and service quality.

Moderating Variables:

Demographic Factors:

Age: The age of respondents, categorized into distinct groups such as "18-24," "25-34," "35-44," and so forth.

Gender: The gender of respondents, typically categorized as "male" or "female."

Income: The annual income of respondents, categorized into income brackets such as "Below 20,000," "20,001-40,000," and so on.

Independent Variables:

Price (V1):

Definition: Price refers to how consumers perceive the price of OTT platforms relative to the value they receive.

Operationalization: Assessed using Likert-scale items measuring respondents' perceptions of the affordability and value-for-money offered by various OTT platforms.

Content Variety (V2):

Definition: Content variety denotes the range and diversity of content available on OTT platforms.

Operationalization: Measured through survey questions assessing respondents' perceptions of the breadth and depth of content offerings on their preferred OTT platforms.

Recommendations (V3):

Definition: Recommendations represent the influence of suggestions from acquaintances, family members, or the platform itself on consumers' preferences and buying intentions.

Operationalization: Assessed using items gauging the extent to which respondents consider recommendations as influential factors in their OTT platform choices.

Ease of Use (V4):

Definition: Ease of use refers to how user-friendly consumers perceive the interface and navigation of OTT platforms to be.

Operationalization: Evaluated using items measuring respondents' perceptions of the intuitiveness and simplicity of using various OTT platforms.

Familiarity with Foreign Content (V5):

Definition: Familiarity with foreign content denotes consumers' exposure to and familiarity with media content originating from foreign cultures.

Operationalization: Assessed through survey questions probing respondents' consumption habits and preferences regarding foreign-language or international content on OTT platforms.

Language Options (V6):

Definition: Language options refer to the availability of content in consumers' native languages on OTT platforms.

Operationalization: Measured by asking respondents to indicate their preference for consuming content in their preferred language(s) and assessing the availability of multilingual content on OTT platforms.

RESEARCH DESIGN

The research design of this study is a cross-sectional survey. The target population for this study is the youth aged between 18-30 years who are currently students and are also consumers of OTT platforms. A non-probability sampling technique, specifically convenience sampling, was employed to collect data from a sample of nearly 200 respondents through online questionnaires. The data collected was analyzed using statistical software, such as SPSS and Excel, to determine the relationship between consumer ethnocentrism, buying intentions, and customer satisfaction towards OTT platforms. This design allows for a comprehensive understanding of the factors influencing the decision-making process of subscribing to and continuing to use OTT platforms among the target population.

RESEARCH MODEL

The research model for this study includes features such as price, variety, recommendations, ease of use of platforms, and foreign content as independent variables, while customer satisfaction and consumer ethnocentrism are dependent variables. The study aims to investigate how these independent variables influence the two dependent variables.

The model suggests that the different features of OTT platforms influence customer satisfaction and consumer ethnocentrism. For instance, lower prices, a wider variety of content, personalized recommendations, and ease of use of the platform are likely to increase customer satisfaction, while unfamiliar foreign content and difficulty in navigating the platform may decrease it. On the other hand, higher levels of consumer ethnocentrism may result in a lower likelihood of subscribing to foreign OTT platforms, while lower levels may increase the likelihood

Overall, the research model aims to provide insights into the complex interplay between different features of OTT platforms, consumer ethnocentrism, and customer satisfaction, which can help OTT platform providers to improve their services and tailor them to the needs and preferences of viewers.

HYPOTHESIS

1. Hypothesis 1: The satisfaction levels of consumers towards OTT platforms are affected by various features such as price, variety, recommendations, ease of use of platforms, foreign content, etc.
2. Hypothesis 2: Higher consumer ethnocentrism will result in a lower likelihood of subscribing to foreign OTT platforms
3. Hypothesis 3: The features of OTT platforms have a significant impact on the viewership of the platform.
    H3(A): Price of the subscription will have a significant positive influence on the intention to watch OTT content.
    H3(B): Consumers will report higher levels of satisfaction with OTT platforms that offer a wider variety of content options
    H3(C): Customers will report higher levels of satisfaction with OTT platforms that provide customized and pertinent recommendations.
    H3(D): An easy-to-use OTT platform leads to higher user satisfaction and retention rates compared to a platform that is difficult to use.
    H3(E): Cultural valued have a significant impact on the types of content that users consume on OTT platforms
    H3(F): Users with higher levels of familiarity with foreign cultures are more likely to consume foreign content on OTT platforms compared to users with lower levels of familiarity with foreign cultures.
    H3(G): Users who speak multiple languages are more likely to consume content in different languages and explore diverse content offerings on the platform compared to users who speak only one language.

ANALYSIS AND RESULT

The primary data analysis involved analyzing responses from 200 survey participants using statistical methods. Descriptive statistics like means, standard deviations, and frequencies were used to characterize the sample and variables. Inferential statistics such as correlation and regression analyzed relationships between OTT platform features, consumer ethnocentrism, and customer satisfaction.

Gender Distribution:

Out of 200 respondents, 85 (42.5%) were female and 112 (56%) were male, indicating a fairly balanced gender distribution with slightly more male respondents.

Age Groups:

95.5% of respondents fell in the 16-25 age group, with only 2.5% in the 26-35 group and 2% in the 36 and above group, showing a predominant younger age demographic.

Occupational Status:

89% of respondents were students, with a small percentage self-employed (3%), employed (7.5%), or homemakers (0.5%), indicating a predominantly student respondent base.

NORMALITY TEST

In order to ensure the validity of statistical tests, it is important to determine if the data follows a normal distribution. This can be done through a normality test, which checks whether the data is normally distributed or not. If the data is not normally distributed, alternative tests may need to be used. In this study on consumer satisfaction and ethnocentrism towards OTT platforms, a normality test will be conducted to ensure the validity of subsequent statistical analyses.

Figure 2.

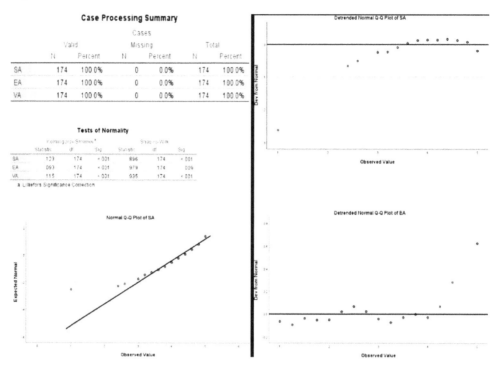

Figure 2 presents the outcomes of normality tests conducted on three variables, SA, EA, and VA, using the Kolmogorov-Smirnov (K-S) and Shapiro-Wilk tests, with the application of the Lilliefors Significance Correction to the K-S test. The null hypothesis for all tests is that the data follows a normal distribution. For SA, all tests reject this null hypothesis at the

0.05 significance level, indicating potential non-normality in the data. For EA, while the Shapiro-Wilk test rejects the null hypothesis, the K-S test does not, suggesting ambiguous results regarding the normality of the data. Conversely, both tests reject the null hypothesis for VA, indicating non-normality. In summary, the findings suggest that SA and VA data may not adhere to a normal distribution, while the distribution of EA data is less definitive. It's essential to acknowledge that disregarding the normality assumption can impact the accuracy of statistical analyses, necessitating alternative methods that do not rely on normality assumptions.

REGRESSION

In the model summary, the R-value represents the correlation coefficient between the dependent variable (SA) and the independent variables (V1, V2, V3, V4, V5, V6). The R-value, in this case, is 0.247, indicating a weak positive correlation between the variables.

In the ANOVA table, the R Square value represents the proportion of variance in the dependent variable (SA) that can be explained by the independent variables (V1, V2, V3, V4, V5, V6). The R Square value in this case is 0.061, indicating that only 6.1% of the variance in SA can be explained by the independent variables.

Both the R-value and R Square value suggest that there is not a strong relationship between the independent variables and the dependent variable in this linear regression model.

Coefficients^a

Model		Unstandardized Coefficients B	Std. Error	Standardized Coefficients Beta	t	Sig.
1	(Constant)	3.601	.244		14.785	<.001
	V1	-.014	.053	-.024	-.273	.785
	V2	.098	.065	.156	1.503	.135
	V3	-.009	.068	-.012	-.127	.899
	V4	.064	.070	.098	.917	.360
	V5	.022	.064	.035	.336	.738
	V6	.016	.054	.030	.304	.762

ANOVA^a

Model		Sum of Squares	df	Mean Square	F	Sig.
1	Regression	4.212	6	.702	1.809	.100^b
	Residual	64.830	167	.388		
	Total	69.042	173			

a. Dependent Variable: SA
b. Predictors: (Constant), V6, V2, V1, V3, V5, V4

		Coefficients^a				
		Unstandardized Coefficients		Standardized Coefficients		
Model		B	Std. Error	Beta	t	Sig.
1	(Constant)	3.601	.244		14.785	< .001
	V1	-.014	.053	-.024	-.273	.785
	V2	.098	.065	.156	1.503	.135
	V3	-.009	.068	-.012	-.127	.899
	V4	.064	.070	.098	.917	.360
	V5	.022	.064	.035	.336	.738
	V6	.016	.054	.030	.304	.762

Based on the provided information, it appears that a linear regression analysis was conducted to assess the relationship between "EA" (ethnocentrism level) and "VA" (variable level). The results indicate statistical significance (p = .006) for the regression model, with an R-squared value of .043, suggesting that approximately 4.3% of the variation in ethnocentrism level can be attributed to the variation in variable level.

The coefficient for the "VA" variable is .230, indicating that for every one-unit increase in variable level, there is a corresponding increase of .230 units in ethnocentrism level. This coefficient is statistically significant (t = 2.777, p = .006) at the .05 level, suggesting that the relationship between variable level and ethnocentrism level is unlikely to be a result of chance.

However, it's crucial to acknowledge the study's limitations, given its focus on consumer ethnocentrism and buying intention of OTT Platforms specifically in India. While the observed relationship between variable level and ethnocentrism level may be relevant within this context, its generalizability to other populations or contexts may be limited. Additionally, the low R-squared value implies that other factors beyond variable level likely influence ethnocentrism level in this particular context.

In conclusion, this analysis indicates a weak positive relationship between variable level and ethnocentrism level within the context of consumer ethnocentrism and buying intention of OTT Platforms in India. Further research is warranted to explore the specific factors influencing consumer ethnocentrism and buying intention comprehensively within this context.

CORRELATION TEST

Correlation analysis will also be conducted to determine the strength and direction of the relationship between consumer satisfaction, consumer ethnocentrism, and the features of OTT platforms. This analysis will help to identify whether there is a significant association between these variables. The correlation coefficients will be tested for significance to determine the strength and direction of the relationships. The correlation analysis will provide insights into the degree to which consumer satisfaction and consumer ethnocentrism are related to the features of OTT platforms.

Correlations

		SA	V1
SA	Pearson Correlation	1	.073
	Sig. (2-tailed)		.337
	N	174	174
V1	Pearson Correlation	.073	1
	Sig. (2-tailed)	.337	
	N	174	174

Price

The correlation analysis indicates that there is a weak positive correlation ($r = 0.073$) between the variables SA and V1. SA represents overall satisfaction with OTT platforms and V1 represents the influence of price and value on the decision to subscribe to an OTT platform. However, the correlation is not statistically significant ($p = 0.337$). This suggests that there may be other factors beyond price and value that influence overall satisfaction with OTT platforms.

Correlations

		SA	V2
SA	Pearson Correlation	1	.220**
	Sig. (2-tailed)		.004
	N	174	174
V2	Pearson Correlation	.220**	1
	Sig. (2-tailed)	.004	
	N	174	174

** Correlation is significant at the 0.01 level (2-tailed).

Variety

The correlation analysis shows that there is a significant positive correlation between SA (satisfaction) and V2 (variety) at the 0.01 level (2-tailed), with a Pearson correlation coefficient of .220. This suggests that as the variety of content available on an OTT platform increases, users are more likely to report higher levels of satisfaction.

Correlations

		SA	V3
SA	Pearson Correlation	1	.145
	Sig. (2-tailed)		.055
	N	174	174
V3	Pearson Correlation	.145	1
	Sig. (2-tailed)	.055	
	N	174	174

Recommendation

The correlation analysis suggests that there is a moderate positive correlation ($r = 0.145$, $p = 0.055$) between SA (satisfaction) and V3 (recommendations). However, the p-value is greater than 0.05, which indicates that this correlation is not statistically significant at the conventional level of significance (i.e., 0.05). Therefore, we cannot draw strong conclusions about the relationship between these variables based on this correlation analysis alone.

Table 7. Ease of use

Correlations		SA	V4
SA	Pearson Correlation	1	.207**
	Sig. (2-tailed)		.006
	N	174	174
V4	Pearson Correlation	.207**	1
	Sig. (2-tailed)	.006	
	N	174	174
** Correlation is significant at the 0.01 level (2-tailed).			

The analysis would show a significant positive correlation between SA (satisfaction) and V4 (ease of use) at the 0.01 level (2-tailed).

Table 8. Cultural values

Correlations		SA	V5
SA	Pearson Correlation	1	.168*
	Sig. (2-tailed)		.026
	N	174	174
V5	Pearson Correlation	.168*	1
	Sig. (2-tailed)	.026	
	N	174	174
* Correlation is significant at the 0.05 level (2-tailed).			

There is a positive correlation between SA (satisfaction) and V5 (cultural values), with a significant correlation coefficient of .168 at the 0.05 level (2-tailed). This suggests that viewers who place a high value on cultural values may be more satisfied with their OTT platform experience. However, correlation does not imply causation, so further analysis would be needed to establish a causal relationship.

Table 9. Familiarity with foreign languages

Correlations			SA	V6
SA	Pearson Correlation		1	.126
	Sig. (2-tailed)			.097
	N		174	174
V6	Pearson Correlation		.126	1
	Sig. (2-tailed)		.097	
	N		174	174

The given correlation analysis shows the Pearson correlation coefficient and significance level between two variables SA and V6. The correlation coefficient between SA and V6 is 0.126, which suggests a positive but weak correlation between the two variables. The significance level of the correlation is 0.097, which is greater than the typical alpha level of 0.05, indicating that the correlation is not statistically significant.

SECONDARY RESEARCH

1. Moochhala, Q. (2018). The future of online OTT entertainment services in India. Actionesque Consulting, Pune–India, research primary data analysis of the study revealed that Amazon Prime Video and Netflix were the most preferred OTT platforms among 280 respondents, followed by Hotstar, ErosNow, Alt-Balaji, Voot, SonyLiv, and JioCinema. However, it should be noted that different reports in India have shown varying results regarding the most popular OTT platforms, with Hotstar, Amazon Prime Video, and Voot being the leaders in various findings.

But now, it is worth mentioning that JioCinema has seen an increase in market share upto 7%, with one significant reason being that it is a free service and also telecasts major sports tournaments such as IPL.

Figure 3.

Which OTT Online Streaming Service brand would you recommend most to others?

		Frequency	Percent	Valid Percent	Cumulative Percent
Valid	Netflix	82	29.3	29.3	29.3
	Amazon Prime	108	38.6	38.6	67.9
	Hotstar	23	8.2	8.2	76.1
	Voot	12	4.3	4.3	80.4
	SonyLiv	11	3.9	3.9	84.3
	ErosNow	21	7.5	7.5	91.8
	Jio Cinema	3	1.1	1.1	92.9
	Alt_Balaji	20	7.1	7.1	100.0
	Total	280	100.0	100.0	

2. Vahoniya, et al(2022). Research on Awareness, Preferences, Perception, and Satisfaction about the Over-The-Top (OTT) Platforms/Players in Anand City, Gujarat, India, showed that the majority of respondents preferred OTT players based on multiple content categorizations, multiple user accounts, and multiple subtitles and video quality provided by the platforms. Additionally, some respondents preferred OTT players for downloading videos, supporting a number of devices, and watchlist facilities, but these were not the most important factors for most respondents.

Figure 4.

Reasons	Frequency	Percent
Multiple Content Categorization	66	33.50
Multiple User Accounts	47	23.86
Multiple Subtitles/ Language and Video Quality	36	18.27
Downloading Videos	29	14.72
Number of Devices Supported	14	7.11
Watch List	5	2.54
Total	197	100

Source: Field survey

DISCUSSION AND CONCLUSION

The study of consumer ethnocentrism and customer satisfaction towards OTT platforms in India is an interesting and relevant topic, given the increasing popularity of such platforms in recent years. The analysis conducted in this study aimed to investigate the relationship between variable level and ethnocentrism level, as well as the correlation between variable level and both SA and EA.

The results of the normality tests revealed that the data for SA and VA may not follow a normal distribution, while the distribution of data for EA was less clear. This is an important finding, as it suggests that alternative statistical methods that do not require normality assumptions may be necessary to accurately analyze the data.

The regression analysis showed a statistically significant relationship between variable level and ethnocentrism level, with a weak positive correlation between the two variables. The coefficient for the "VA" variable was statistically significant, indicating that the relationship between variable level and ethnocentrism level is unlikely to be due to chance. However, the low R-squared value suggests that other factors beyond variable level are likely to be influencing ethnocentrism level in this context.

The correlation analysis revealed a weak to moderate positive correlation between VA and both SA and EA. These findings suggest that variable level may play a role in shaping consumer ethnocentrism and customer satisfaction towards OTT platforms in India.

Overall, the analysis suggests that variable level is positively related to ethnocentrism level, and that there may be a weak to moderate positive correlation between variable level and both SA and EA. However, further research is needed to better understand the specific factors that are influencing consumer ethnocentrism and customer satisfaction towards OTT platforms in India, as well as to explore the potential impact of violating the assumption of normality on the accuracy of statistical analyses.

One potential limitation of this study is that it focused solely on the Indian market, and may not be generalizable to other populations or contexts. Additionally, the study did not explore other potential factors that may influence consumer behavior and satisfaction towards OTT platforms, such as cultural values, social norms, and personal preferences.

The acceptance or rejection of hypotheses in the study varies based on the specific relationships being tested. While consumer ethnocentrism was not found to significantly influence buying behavior on OTT platforms, factors like price, variety, recommendations, cultural values, ease of platform use, familiarity with foreign content, and language were identified as significant predictors of buying intentions.

These findings offer valuable insights for OTT platform providers to enhance customer satisfaction and usage. By focusing on improving platform usability, providing diverse content options, and tailoring marketing strategies to different consumer preferences, providers can boost customer satisfaction and retention.

However, the study has limitations, including its focus on the Indian context and reliance on self-reported data. Future research could address these limitations by employing larger, more diverse samples and objective measures of customer behavior.

Despite these limitations, the study contributes important insights into the factors shaping customer behavior in the OTT industry. As the industry continues to evolve, staying informed about research findings will be crucial for providers to remain competitive and meet the changing needs of their customers.

As the Indian market continues to grow and modernize, the demand for digital entertainment is likely to increase. OTT platforms are uniquely positioned to meet this demand by offering a wide range of content and flexible viewing options that cater to the diverse preferences of Indian audiences. With the increasing availability of high-speed internet and the adoption of smartphones and other connected devices, the potential for growth in the OTT market in India is significant.

Moreover, OTT platforms have the potential to create jobs and stimulate innovation in the Indian entertainment industry. By providing a platform for independent filmmakers, writers, and performers to showcase their work, OTT platforms can help to diversify the content available to audiences and foster new talent. This, in turn, can lead to the emergence of new genres and formats of content that are uniquely Indian and resonate with local audiences.

Finally, the growth of OTT platforms in India can also have a positive impact on the broader economy. As more consumers shift their entertainment spending to digital platforms, traditional media companies may need to adapt and innovate in order to remain competitive. This can create new opportunities for collaboration and investment between traditional and digital media companies, leading to greater efficiency and growth in the industry as a whole.

In summary, the future of OTT platforms in India looks bright, with significant potential for growth, innovation, and economic impact. As the market continues to evolve, it will be exciting to see how these platforms continue to shape the entertainment landscape and bring new voices and perspectives to audiences across the country.

REFERENCES

Bhattacharyya, S. S., Goswami, S., Mehta, R., & Nayak, B. (2022). Examining the factors influencing adoption of over the top (OTT) services among Indian consumers. *Journal of Science and Technology Policy Management, 13*(3), 652-682..

Dasgupta, D., & Grover, D. (2019). Understanding adoption factors of over-the-top video services among millennial consumers. *International Journal of Computer Engineering and Technology, 10*(1).

Ghalawat, S., Yadav, E., Kumar, M., Kumari, N., Goyal, M., Girdhar, A., & Agarwal, S. (2021). Factors influencing consumer's choice of streaming over the top (OTT) platforms. *Indian Journal of Extension Education, 57*(3), 99-101.

Luthra, S. (2021). The Impact of Covid-19 on Consumer Perception towards Subscription Based OTT Platforms. *International Journal of Management (IJM), 12*(3), 537-549.

Moochhala, Q. (2018). The future of online OTT entertainment services in India. *Actionesque Consulting, Pune–India, 4*, 2581-5792.

Park, S., & Kwon, Y. (2019). *Research on the Relationship between the Growth of OTT Service Market and the Change in the Structure of the Pay-TV Market.*

Platforms/Players in Anand City. (2020). Gujarat, India. Asian Journal of Agricultural Extension. *Economia e Sociologia, 40*(12), 254–264.

Puthiyakath, H. H., & Goswami, M. P. (2021). Is over the top video platform the game changer over traditional TV channels in India? A niche analysis. *Asia Pacific Media Educator, 31*(1), 133-150.

Samriti, D., & Sharma, P. (2020). OTT-existing censorship laws and recommendations. Available at SSRN 3735027. http://dspace.christcollegeijk.edu.in:8080/jspui/bitstream/123456789/1043/24/CC AS BCM023.pdf

Vahoniya, D. R., Darji, D. R., Baruri, S., & Halpati, J. R. (2022). Awareness, Preferences, Perception, and Satisfaction about the Over-The-Top (OTT) Platforms/Players in Anand City, Gujarat, India. *Asian Journal of Agricultural Extension, Economics & Sociology, 40*(12), 254-264.

Yousaf, A., Mishra, A., Taheri, B., & Kesgin, M. (2021). A cross-country analysis of the determinants of customer recommendation intentions for over-the-top (OTT) platforms. *Information & Management, 58*(8), 103543.

Chapter 4
Consumer Experience and Decision-Making in the Metaverse:
Marketing 2.0 Beyond Traditional Boundaries

Mani Tyagi

ⓘD https://orcid.org/0000-0002-6469-7041
Manav Rachna International Institute of Research and Studies, India

Shenki Tyagi
Kiet Group of Institutions, India

ABSTRACT

Traditional advertising channels are being reimagined and transformed in this virtual space, offering marketers unprecedented opportunities to connect with consumers on a deeper level. In this context, this chapter focuses specifically on uncovering the latest trends and strategies shaping advertising practices in the metaverse. From immersive brand experiences in virtual environments to targeted advertising campaigns using augmented reality overlays, the possibilities are vast and exciting. We will examine how brands are harnessing the power of virtual reality, augmented reality, and other emerging technologies to captivate audiences and drive meaningful engagement. Ultimately, this chapter serves as a roadmap for marketers navigating the complexities of advertising in the metaverse. By understanding the latest trends, technologies, and best practices, businesses can position themselves for success in this rapidly evolving landscape. Join us as we embark on this journey into the future of advertising in the metaverse.

DOI: 10.4018/979-8-3693-4167-4.ch004

INTRODUCTION TO MODERN ADVERTISING TRENDS

Personalization takes center stage as advertisers leverage data analytics and artificial intelligence to tailor messages to individual preferences. Social media platforms continue to dominate, with influencer marketing and user-generated content becoming integral components of brand promotion. Video advertising, powered by engaging storytelling and immersive experiences, captures the attention of audiences across diverse platforms. Programmatic advertising, fueled by automation and real-time bidding, enhances efficiency in campaign management. Ethical considerations gain prominence, challenging advertisers to balance transparency, authenticity, and societal values. As we navigate the future, emerging technologies like augmented reality, virtual reality, and the integration of blockchain promise to revolutionize advertising further. In this dynamic landscape, marketers must stay agile, embracing these trends to create compelling narratives that resonate with the modern consumer.

THE EVOLUTION OF ADVERTISING PLATFORMS

The evolution of advertising platforms has been shaped by technological advancements, changes in consumer behavior, and the growing influence of digital media. Here is an overview of the key stages in the evolution of advertising platforms:

1. **Print Advertising (Pre-20th Century):** The earliest form of advertising was in print, with businesses using newspapers, posters, and other print materials to promote their products or services. This era laid the foundation for visual communication and brand messaging.
2. **Radio Advertising (1920s-1930s):** The advent of radio brought a new dimension to advertising. Businesses began creating jingles and sponsored programs to reach a wider audience. This period marked the transition from print to audio-based advertising.
3. **Television Advertising (1940s-1950s):** The rise of television led to a significant shift in advertising. Brands embraced the visual and audio capabilities of TV to create compelling commercials. The "Golden Age of Television" saw the emergence of iconic ads and the use of storytelling to capture consumer attention.
4. **Internet and Banner Ads (1990s):** The proliferation of the internet introduced a revolutionary change in advertising. Banner ads appeared on websites, providing businesses with a new way to reach online audiences. The Internet also facilitated e-commerce, enabling direct transactions between consumers and brands.

5. **Search Engine Advertising (2000s):** As search engines like Google gained prominence, advertisers began to use pay-per-click (PPC) advertising to appear prominently in search results. Search engine optimization (SEO) became crucial for organic visibility, and businesses started to focus on keywords to improve their online presence.

6. **Social Media Advertising (2000s-2010s):** The rise of platforms like Facebook, Twitter, and Instagram transformed advertising by providing highly targeted and interactive options. Advertisers could leverage user data and engagement metrics to tailor campaigns to specific demographics. Influencer marketing also gained traction during this period.

7. **Mobile Advertising (2010s):** The widespread adoption of smartphones led to the emergence of mobile advertising. Brands began creating mobile-friendly content, and in-app ads became prevalent. Location-based targeting and push notifications allowed for personalized in addition, contextually relevant advertising.

8. **Video Advertising and Streaming Platforms (2010s-2020s):** With the popularity of online video content, platforms like YouTube, TikTok, and others became significant for video advertising. Streaming services like Netflix and Hulu also presented opportunities for brands to reach audiences through integrated and sponsored content.

9. **Programmatic Advertising (2010s-2020s):** Programmatic advertising, powered by algorithms and real-time bidding, automated the ad-buying process. This technology enabled advertisers to target specific audiences with greater efficiency, delivering personalized content in real time across various digital channels.

10. **Emergence of Augmented Reality (AR) and Virtual Reality (VR) Advertising (2020s and beyond):** The integration of AR and VR into advertising opened up new possibilities for immersive and interactive experiences. Brands started incorporating these technologies to engage audiences in unique and memorable ways.

11. **Voice Search and Smart Devices (2020s and beyond):** The rise of voice-activated devices and smart speakers introduced new challenges and opportunities for advertisers. Optimizing content for voice search became essential, and brands began exploring ways to integrate advertising into these voice-activated platforms.

The evolution of advertising platforms continues to be driven by technological innovation and shifts in consumer behavior. Advertisers need to stay adaptive and embrace emerging trends to effectively connect with their target audience in the ever-changing landscape of media and communication.

Marketing 2.0: Beyond Traditional Boundaries

In the realm of marketing, the emergence of Marketing 2.0 represents a paradigm shift from traditional strategies to a more dynamic and interactive approach. This literature review explores the concept of Marketing 2.0, its key characteristics, and its implications for businesses in the contemporary digital landscape.

Evolution of Marketing 2.0

Marketing 2.0 signifies a departure from one-way communication to a two-way dialogue between brands and consumers (Kotler & Keller, 2009). It builds upon Web 2.0 technologies, leveraging social media platforms, blogs, and user-generated content to engage with customers on a deeper level (Hanna et al., 2011). The evolution of Marketing 2.0 reflects the changing consumer behaviors and preferences, emphasizing the importance of authenticity, transparency, and customer-centricity (Mangold & Faulds, 2009).

Key Characteristics of Marketing 2.0

a. *Customer Engagement:* Marketing 2.0 focuses on fostering meaningful interactions with customers, allowing them to co-create value through active participation (Prahalad & Ramaswamy, 2004). Brands utilize social media channels to engage in conversations, solicit feedback, and build communities around their products or services (Kaplan & Haenlein, 2010).

b. *Content Marketing:* Content plays a central role in Marketing 2.0, with brands producing relevant and compelling content to attract and retain customers (Pulizzi & Barrett, 2008). Content marketing efforts aim to educate, entertain, or inspire audiences, rather than overtly selling products or services (Handley & Chapman, 2012).

c. *Data-Driven Insights:* The digital nature of Marketing 2.0 allows for the collection and analysis of vast amounts of data regarding customer preferences, behaviors, and interactions (Smith & Chaffey, 2005). Brands leverage data analytics to gain actionable insights, personalize marketing efforts, and measure the effectiveness of campaigns (Kaplan & Haenlein, 2010).

Implications for Businesses

a. **Brand Transparency:** Marketing 2.0 requires businesses to operate with transparency and authenticity, as consumers demand honesty and openness from brands (Fournier & Avery, 2011). Companies that embrace transparency build trust and credibility with their audience, fostering long-term relationships and loyalty (Mishra & Singh, 2019).

b. **Shift in Power Dynamics:** With Marketing 2.0, consumers wield greater influence and control over brand perceptions, often shaping the narrative through user-generated content and online reviews (Deighton & Kornfeld, 2009). Businesses must relinquish some control and embrace co-creation, collaborating with customers to enhance products, services, and experiences (Prahalad & Ramaswamy, 2004).

c. **Agility and Adaptability:** The dynamic nature of digital channels necessitates agility and adaptability in marketing strategies (Smith & Zook, 2011). Brands must continuously monitor and respond to changing trends, consumer feedback, and competitive pressures to remain relevant and effective in Marketing 2.0 landscape (Kaplan & Haenlein, 2010).

Marketing 2.0 represents a fundamental shift in how businesses approach marketing, emphasizing engagement, content, and data-driven insights. By embracing the principles of Marketing 2.0, organizations can foster deeper connections with customers, drive innovation, and remain competitive in an increasingly digital world.

SOCIAL MEDIA ADVERTISING STRATEGIES

Social media advertising has become a crucial component of marketing strategies, providing a powerful platform to reach and engage target audiences. Effective social media advertising strategies involve a combination of creativity, targeting precision, and continuous optimization. Here are some key strategies to consider:

1. **Define Clear Objectives:** Clearly define your advertising objectives. Whether it is increasing brand awareness, driving website traffic, generating leads, or boosting sales, having specific and measurable goals will guide your campaign.

2. **Know Your Audience:** Understand your target audience's demographics, interests, and online behavior. Social media platforms offer robust targeting options, allowing you to tailor your ads to reach the most relevant users.

3. **Choose the Right Platforms:** Each social media platform caters to a different audience and content format. Select platforms that align with your target demographic and the nature of your content. For example, Instagram and Pinterest are image-centric, while LinkedIn is more business-oriented.

4. **Create Compelling Content:** Develop visually appealing and engaging content. Use high-quality images, videos, and captions that resonate with your

audience. Ensure that your content aligns with the overall aesthetic and tone of the platform.

5. **Utilize Video Content:** Video content tends to capture attention more effectively than static images. Advantage short and captivating videos for your ads, as platforms like Facebook, Instagram, and TikTok prioritize video content.

6. **Craft Persuasive Ad Copy:** Write concise and compelling ad copy that communicates your value proposition. Highlight key benefits, use persuasive language, and include a strong call to action to encourage user engagement.

7. **Implement A/B Testing:** Test different ad variations to identify what resonates best with your audience. Experiment with various visuals, ad copy, and calls-to-action to optimize your campaigns based on performance data.

8. **Leverage Social Proof:** Incorporate social proof, such as customer testimonials, reviews, or user-generated content, into your ads. This builds credibility and trust, influencing potential customers to take action.

9. **Use Retargeting:** Implement retargeting strategies to re-engage users who have previously interacted with your brand. This can include those who visited your website, engaged with your social media profiles, or interacted with previous ads.

10. **Take Advantage of Ad Formats:** Each social media platform offers different ad formats, including carousel ads, slideshow ads, stories, and sponsored posts. Experiment with these formats to find the most effective way to display your products or services.

11. **Set a Budget and Schedule:** Define your advertising budget and schedule to ensure that your ads are displayed at optimal times. Use the ad platform's scheduling options to target specific days and times when your audience is most active.

12. **Monitor and Analyze Metrics:** Regularly monitor the performance of your ads using platform analytics. Track metrics such as click-through rates, conversion rates, and engagement. Use these insights to refine your strategy and improve future campaigns.

13. **Stay Updated on Platform Changes:** Social media platforms frequently update their algorithms, features, and ad policies. Stay informed about these changes to adapt your strategies and take advantage of new opportunities.

By combining these strategies and staying agile in response to evolving trends, businesses can create effective and impactful social media advertising campaigns that resonate with their target audience and drive desired outcomes.

INFLUENCER MARKETING: LEVERAGING DIGITAL CELEBRITIES

Influencer marketing has emerged as a dynamic and influential strategy for brands seeking to connect with their target audience in the digital era. The approach involves collaborating with digital celebrities, or influencers, who possess substantial followings on various online platforms. Leveraging the credibility and reach of these influencers, brands can effectively amplify their message, build brand awareness, and foster authentic connections with consumers. Whether collaborating with micro-influencers for niche engagement or macro-influencers for broader reach, the key lies in selecting influencers whose values align authentically with the brand. The collaborative content creation process allows influencers to display products or services in a relatable manner, ensuring resonance with their dedicated followers. By tracking and analyzing performance metrics, brands can measure the success of influencer campaigns, optimizing strategies for enhanced engagement and lasting impact. Influencer marketing not only provides a platform for creative storytelling but also capitalizes on the influencer's rapport with their audience, resulting in a potent avenue for digital brand promotion and consumer engagement.

AUGMENTED REALITY (AR) AND VIRTUAL REALITY (VR) IN ADVERTISING

Augmented Reality (AR) and Virtual Reality (VR) have emerged as transformative technologies in the realm of advertising, offering innovative ways to engage and captivate audiences. Here's an exploration of how AR and VR are making an impact in the advertising landscape:

1. **Immersive Brand Experiences:** AR and VR enable advertisers to create immersive brand experiences that go beyond traditional formats. Users can interact with products in virtual environments, enhancing their understanding and connection with the brand.
2. **Interactive Product Visualization:** AR allows consumers to visualize products in their real-world surroundings through their smartphones or AR glasses. VR, on the other hand, provides a complete virtual environment for users to explore products, contributing to a more informed purchasing decision.
3. **Try-Before-You-Buy Experiences:** Both AR and VR empower consumers to "try before they buy." AR applications enable virtual try-ons of clothing or accessories, while VR experiences can simulate real-world usage of products, allowing users to make more confident purchase decisions.

4. **Enhanced Print and Outdoor Advertising:** AR enhances traditional print and outdoor advertising by adding layers of interactivity. Users can point their smartphones at a print ad to unlock additional content, such as videos, 3D animations, or interactive elements, creating a more engaging experience.

5. **Virtual Showrooms and Test Drives:** VR is revolutionizing the automotive and retail industries by offering virtual showrooms and test drives. Users can explore the interior of a car or browse through a virtual store, providing a realistic and immersive preview of products.

6. **Location-Based AR Marketing:** AR can be integrated into location-based marketing strategies. Businesses can use location-aware AR experiences to deliver targeted promotions, information, or interactive content to users when they are in a specific geographic location.

7. **Brand Storytelling in VR:** VR provides a unique platform for immersive storytelling. Brands can create virtual experiences that transport users to different environments, allowing them to experience the brand narrative in a more emotionally resonant and memorable way.

8. **Gamification for Engagement:** AR and VR lend themselves well to gamification strategies. Brands can create interactive games or challenges that entertain users while subtly promoting products or services, fostering engagement and brand recall.

9. **Virtual Events and Experiential Marketing:** VR opens up possibilities for hosting virtual events and experiential marketing campaigns. Brands can engage with a global audience in a virtual space, providing a more inclusive and accessible way to connect with consumers.

AR and VR are redefining the advertising landscape, offering unprecedented opportunities for brands to connect with their audiences in more interactive and memorable ways. As these technologies continue to advance, advertisers who embrace AR and VR are likely to stay at the forefront of consumer engagement and innovation.

PROGRAMMATIC ADVERTISING: AUTOMATING CAMPAIGNS FOR EFFICIENCY

Programmatic advertising is a data-driven, automated approach to buying and optimizing digital advertising in real-time. This method relies on algorithms, artificial intelligence, and machine learning to make data-driven decisions on ad placements and targeting. Here is an exploration of programmatic advertising and its role in automating campaigns for efficiency:

1. **Automated Ad Buying:** Programmatic advertising automates the process of buying and placing digital ads. Advertisers use demand-side platforms (DSPs) to set criteria such as target audience demographics, ad placement preferences, and budget constraints. The system then autonomously bids for ad space across various digital channels.

2. **Real-Time Bidding (RTB):** A key feature of programmatic advertising is real-time bidding. In milliseconds, advertisers bid for available ad impressions based on predefined parameters. This ensures that ads are served to the most relevant audience at the optimal moment, maximizing the efficiency of ad spend.

3. **Precise Targeting:** Programmatic advertising allows for highly granular audience targeting. Advertisers can define their target audience based on demographics, behaviors, interests, and even contextual factors. This precision ensures that ads are delivered to users who are more likely to engage with the content.

4. **Cross-Channel Campaigns:** Programmatic advertising extends across various digital channels, including display, video, social media, and mobile. Advertisers can manage cross-channel campaigns seamlessly through a centralized platform, optimizing reach and engagement across different platforms.

5. **Dynamic Creative Optimization (DCO):** DCO is a feature that tailors ad creatives in real time based on user data. Programmatic advertising utilizes DCO to deliver personalized and relevant content to users, increasing the likelihood of engagement and conversion.

6. **Efficient Ad Placement:** Programmatic advertising optimizes ad placements by considering factors such as the user's browsing history, device, location, and online behavior. This ensures that ads are displayed in environments that align with the brand and are more likely to capture the user's attention.

7. **Data-Driven Decision-Making:** The automation in programmatic advertising is fueled by data. Advertisers leverage data analytics and machine learning algorithms to make informed decisions on targeting, bidding, and ad delivery. This data-driven approach enhances campaign efficiency and effectiveness.

8. **Improved Return on Investment (ROI):** Programmatic advertising's ability to target specific audiences, optimize in real-time, and analyze performance data contributes to improved ROI. Advertisers can allocate budgets more efficiently by focusing on the most effective channels and strategies.

9. **Ad Fraud Prevention:** Programmatic advertising platforms incorporate measures to combat ad fraud. The automated systems can detect and filter out fraudulent impressions, ensuring that advertisers get value for their investment and reducing the risk of ad fraud.

Programmatic advertising has revolutionized the digital advertising landscape by automating and optimizing the ad-buying process. As technology continues to advance, programmatic advertising is likely to play an increasingly central role in the efficient and data-driven execution of digital marketing campaigns.

NATIVE ADVERTISING: SEAMLESSLY INTEGRATING WITH CONTENT

Native advertising is a form of online advertising that seamlessly blends with the form and function of the platform on which it appears. Instead of appearing as a traditional display or banner ad, native ads match the visual design and user experience of the content surrounding them. Here's an exploration of native advertising and how it seamlessly integrates with content:

1. **Contextual Integration:** Native ads are designed to fit seamlessly into the overall look and feel of the platform and the surrounding content. They mimic the editorial style, font, and color scheme of the page, making them less disruptive and more integrated with the user experience.
2. **Platform Consistency:** Whether on social media feeds, news websites, or other digital platforms, native ads maintain consistency with the platform's content structure. This ensures that the ad appears natural within the user's browsing experience.
3. **Various Formats:** Native advertising comes in various formats, including in-feed ads on social media, promoted listings in search results, sponsored articles, and recommended content widgets. Each format is tailored to blend seamlessly with the specific platform and content type.
4. **Enhanced User Experience:** By aligning with the look and feel of the platform, native ads aim to enhance rather than interrupt the user experience. Users are more likely to engage with content that feels native, leading to higher click-through rates and improved overall campaign performance.
5. **Less Intrusive Design:** Native ads are less intrusive compared to traditional display ads. Their design avoids the abrupt interruption of the user's browsing experience, fostering a sense of cohesiveness between the ad and the surrounding content.
6. **Engaging Storytelling:** Native advertising often focuses on storytelling. Whether through articles, videos, or interactive content, native ads aim to tell a compelling story that resonates with the audience while maintaining the format and tone of the platform.

7. **Relevance and Targeting:** Native ads are often highly targeted and relevant to the specific audience on the platform. Advertisers can leverage data and audience insights to ensure that native ads align with the interests and preferences of the users.

8. **Disclosure and Transparency:** While blending with content, native ads include clear disclosure elements to distinguish them from organic content. This transparency helps build trust with users and ensures compliance with advertising regulations.

9. **Adaptable to Various Devices:** Native advertising is adaptable to different devices, providing a seamless experience across desktops, smartphones, and tablets. The responsive design ensures that the ads maintain their integration regardless of the user's device.

Native advertising's ability to seamlessly integrate with content while maintaining relevance and transparency has made it a popular choice for brands looking to engage audiences in a non-disruptive manner. As part of a well-rounded marketing strategy, native advertising can contribute to building brand awareness and fostering positive user experiences.

VIDEO ADVERTISING: ENGAGING AUDIENCES WITH VISUAL CONTENT

Video advertising has become a powerful tool for engaging audiences, delivering messages, and building brand awareness. With the rise of online platforms, social media, and streaming services, video ads offer a dynamic and immersive way to connect with viewers. Here's an exploration of video advertising and how it engages audiences with visual content:

1. **Visual Impact and Storytelling:** Video advertising enables brands to convey their messages through compelling visuals and storytelling. The combination of sight, sound, and motion creates a more immersive experience, allowing brands to evoke emotions and connect with audiences on a deeper level.

2. **Platform Diversity:** Video ads can be deployed across various platforms, including social media (e.g., Facebook, Instagram, TikTok), video-sharing platforms (e.g., YouTube), websites, and streaming services. This versatility ensures that brands can reach diverse audiences in their preferred digital spaces.

3. **Short-Form and Long-Form Content:** Video advertising accommodates both short-form content, suitable for quick engagement on platforms like Instagram and Twitter, and long-form content for in-depth storytelling on platforms like

YouTube. This flexibility allows advertisers to tailor their messages to different contexts.

4. **Engagement and Interactivity:** Video ads encourage higher levels of engagement compared to static content. Interactive elements, such as clickable links, polls, or shoppable features, enhance user participation and provide a seamless transition from viewer to potential customer.

5. **Mobile Optimization:** With the prevalence of mobile devices, video advertising is optimized for mobile consumption. Advertisers create visually appealing and concise video content that captures attention and delivers messages effectively on smaller screens.

6. **Live Streaming and Real-Time Interaction:** Live streaming video ads enable real-time interaction with audiences. Brands can host live events, product launches, or Q&A sessions, fostering a sense of immediacy and authenticity that resonates with viewers.

7. **In-Stream and Out-Stream Ads:** In-stream ads play within the content, often before or during online videos, while out-stream ads appear in non-video environments, such as social media feeds or articles. This variety allows advertisers to choose the most suitable format for their goals and target audience.

8. **Targeted Advertising:** Video advertising platforms often provide sophisticated targeting options. Advertisers can define their audience based on demographics, interests, behaviors, and online activities, ensuring that video ads are delivered to the most relevant viewers.

9. **Cross-Device Campaigns:** Video ads seamlessly transition across various devices, providing a consistent viewing experience. Advertisers can implement cross-device campaigns to reach audiences whether they are on desktops, smartphones, or connected TVs.

Video advertising's ability to combine visual storytelling with targeted delivery across diverse platforms positions it as a vital component of modern digital marketing strategies. As technology continues to evolve, video advertising will likely remain a dynamic and influential force in engaging audiences and driving brand impact.

DATA-DRIVEN ADVERTISING: HARNESSING THE POWER OF ANALYTICS

Data-driven advertising is a strategic approach that leverages the power of analytics and consumer insights to optimize the planning, execution, and assessment of advertising campaigns. By harnessing data, advertisers can make informed decisions, enhance targeting precision, and improve overall campaign effectiveness. Here's an exploration of data-driven advertising and its key components:

1. **Audience Segmentation:** Data-driven advertising begins with the segmentation of the target audience. Analyzing demographic data, online behaviors, and preferences allows advertisers to create specific audience segments, ensuring that content is tailored to the unique characteristics of each group.

2. **Behavioral Targeting:** Analyzing user behavior data enables advertisers to target audiences based on their online activities. This includes browsing history, search queries, and interactions with previous ads. Behavioral targeting ensures that ads are delivered to users with a demonstrated interest in relevant products or services.

3. **Personalization and Dynamic Content:** Data-driven advertising enables personalized messaging and dynamic content creation. Advertisers can use data to customize ad creatives based on user preferences, location, and past interactions, enhancing the relevance of the content to individual viewers.

4. **Predictive Analytics:** Predictive analytics involves using historical data to forecast future trends and behaviors. Advertisers leverage predictive models to anticipate consumer preferences, optimize campaign strategies, and allocate resources effectively, improving the overall efficiency of advertising efforts.

5. **A/B Testing and Optimization:** A/B testing, or split testing, involves comparing different versions of an ad to determine which performs better. Data-driven advertising uses A/B testing to optimize elements such as headlines, visuals, and calls to action, ensuring that campaigns are continually refined for maximum impact.

6. **Cross-Channel Integration:** Data-driven advertising is often integrated across multiple channels, including social media, display advertising, search engine marketing, and email campaigns. Data analytics facilitate a unified approach, allowing advertisers to coordinate messaging and targeting seamlessly across channels.

7. **Real-Time Bidding (RTB):** Real-time bidding relies on data to make instantaneous decisions on ad placements. Advertisers bid on ad space based on user data and predefined targeting criteria, ensuring that ads are delivered to the most relevant audience in real-time.

8. **Attribution Modeling:** Attribution modeling helps advertisers understand the contribution of each touchpoint in the customer journey. Data-driven attribution models analyze data from multiple channels to determine the most effective channels and touchpoints that lead to conversions.

ETHICS AND CHALLENGES IN CONTEMPORARY ADVERTISING

Contemporary advertising operates in a complex landscape shaped by technological advancements, cultural shifts, and heightened awareness of ethical considerations. While advertising plays a crucial role in driving economic activities, promoting products, and informing consumers, it also faces ethical challenges that require careful navigation. Here's an exploration of the ethics and challenges in contemporary advertising:

Ethical Considerations

- **Truthfulness and Transparency:** Advertisers face ethical dilemmas related to truthfulness and transparency. Presenting accurate information about products or services is essential to building trust with consumers.
- **Deceptive Practices:** The use of deceptive practices, such as misleading visuals or false claims, raises ethical concerns. Advertisers must avoid tactics that could potentially mislead or manipulate consumers.
- **Privacy Concerns:** Targeted advertising, data collection, and personalization raise privacy concerns. Advertisers must respect consumer privacy rights and comply with data protection regulations.
- **Stereotyping and Diversity:** Advertisements sometimes reinforce stereotypes or lack diversity. Ethical advertising promotes inclusivity, avoids harmful stereotypes, and reflects diverse perspectives.
- **Children and Vulnerable Audiences:** Marketing to children and vulnerable audiences requires careful ethical consideration. Advertisers should avoid exploiting the vulnerability of these groups and ensure that their messaging is appropriate.
- **Environmental Impact:** Sustainable and eco-friendly practices are becoming increasingly important. Advertisers must consider the environmental impact of their products and promote responsible consumption.
- **Consumer Manipulation:** Ethical concerns arise when advertising employs psychological tactics to manipulate consumer behavior. Advertisers should prioritize honest persuasion over manipulative techniques.
- **Native Advertising Disclosure:** Native advertising blurs the lines between content and advertising. Ethical considerations include disclosing when content is sponsored to maintain transparency with the audience.
- **Influencer Marketing Authenticity:** Authenticity in influencer marketing is critical. Advertisers should ensure that influencers disclose partnerships and that the content aligns with the influencer's genuine beliefs and experiences.

- **Corporate Social Responsibility (CSR):** Advertisers are increasingly expected to demonstrate commitment to CSR. Ethical advertising involves aligning brand messaging with socially responsible practices and contributing positively to society.
- **Public Health and Well-being:** Promoting products that can have adverse effects on public health or well-being raises ethical concerns. Advertisers should consider the potential impact of their messages on society.

Challenges in Contemporary Advertising

1. **Digital Ad Fraud:** Advertisers face challenges related to digital ad fraud, including click fraud, impression fraud, and ad stacking. Combatting these fraudulent activities requires ongoing vigilance and technological solutions.
2. **Ad Blockers:** The prevalence of ad blockers poses a challenge to advertisers seeking to reach online audiences. Advertisers must create compelling content that resonates with users and adds value to their online experience.
3. **Media Fragmentation:** The fragmentation of media channels and the rise of niche platforms make it challenging for advertisers to reach broad audiences. Targeting strategies need to adapt to the diverse media consumption habits of consumers.
4. **Data Security and Breaches:** With the increasing reliance on data for targeted advertising, data security is a significant challenge. Advertisers must implement robust security measures to protect consumer data from breaches.
5. **Ad View ability:** Ensuring that ads are viewable by the intended audience is a challenge, especially in programmatic advertising. Advertisers must address issues related to ad viewability to maximize campaign effectiveness.
6. **Navigating Social Media Algorithms:** Social media platforms' algorithms can affect the visibility of ads. Advertisers need to understand and adapt to algorithm changes to optimize their presence on these platforms.
7. **Brand Safety:** Advertisers face challenges related to brand safety in online environments. Ensuring that ads do not appear alongside inappropriate or harmful content requires continuous monitoring and adjustments.
8. **Adapting to Cultural Shifts:** Cultural shifts and changing consumer expectations pose challenges for advertisers. Staying relevant and culturally sensitive requires a deep understanding of evolving societal norms.
9. **Measuring Ad Effectiveness:** Measuring the effectiveness of advertising campaigns, especially in the digital space, is a constant challenge. Advertisers must employ accurate metrics and analytics to assess the impact of their efforts.

10. **Navigating Regulatory Changes:** Regulatory changes, such as data protection laws and privacy regulations, pose challenges for advertisers. Staying compliant with evolving legal frameworks requires continuous monitoring and adaptation.

FUTURE OUTLOOK: EMERGING TECHNOLOGIES AND TRENDS IN ADVERTISING

The future of advertising is intricately linked to the rapid evolution of technology and the dynamic shifts in consumer behavior. Emerging technologies are poised to reshape the advertising landscape, introducing new opportunities and challenges for marketers. Here's a glimpse into the future outlook, highlighting key emerging technologies and trends in advertising:

1. **Augmented Reality (AR) and Virtual Reality (VR):** AR and VR will play a significant role in creating immersive advertising experiences. From interactive product try-ons to virtual showrooms, advertisers will leverage AR and VR to engage audiences in innovative ways, providing highly immersive and personalized brand interactions.

2. **Artificial Intelligence (AI) and Machine Learning:** AI and machine learning will continue to revolutionize advertising by enabling advanced data analysis, personalization, and predictive modeling. Advertisers will use AI algorithms to optimize ad targeting, content creation, and customer interactions, enhancing the overall effectiveness of campaigns.

3. **Voice Search and Smart Speakers:** The rise of voice-activated technologies, like smart speakers and virtual assistants, will impact advertising strategies. Advertisers will need to optimize content for voice search and explore new avenues for reaching users in a voice-first environment.

4. **5G Technology:** The rollout of 5G technology will bring about faster internet speeds and lower latency, unlocking opportunities for more dynamic and data-intensive ad formats. Advertisers can leverage 5G to deliver high-quality video content, augmented reality experiences, and real-time interactions.

5. **Interactive Content and Shoppable Experiences:** Interactive content formats, such as polls, quizzes, and shoppable posts, will gain prominence. Advertisers will create more engaging and interactive experiences, allowing users to participate in the content and seamlessly make purchases directly from ads.

6. **Blockchain for Transparency and Security:** Blockchain technology will address issues related to transparency and security in advertising. Advertisers can use blockchain to verify ad delivery, combat ad fraud, and enhance transparency in the digital advertising ecosystem.

7. **Extended Reality (XR):** XR, encompassing AR, VR, and mixed reality, will enable advertisers to merge physical and digital worlds. Brands can create campaigns that extend beyond traditional screens, offering immersive experiences in both online and offline environments.

8. **Personalized and Contextual Advertising:** Advances in data analytics and AI will empower advertisers to deliver highly personalized and contextually relevant content. Advertisements will be tailored based on individual preferences, behaviors, and real-time contextual factors, enhancing user engagement.

9. **Privacy-Centric Marketing:** Increasing emphasis on privacy will reshape advertising strategies. Advertisers will prioritize transparency, consent-driven data collection, and compliance with evolving privacy regulations to build and maintain consumer trust.

10. **Green Advertising and Sustainability:** Sustainability and eco-conscious messaging will become integral to advertising campaigns. Advertisers will highlight environmentally friendly practices, corporate social responsibility, and sustainable product attributes to resonate with socially conscious consumers.

11. **Emphasis on Brand Purpose and Values:** Consumers are increasingly drawn to brands with a clear sense of purpose and strong values. Advertisers will focus on authentic storytelling that aligns with brand values, contributing to a deeper connection with socially aware audiences.

12. **Cross-Platform and Cross-Device Integration:** Advertisers will continue to prioritize seamless experiences across various platforms and devices. Cross-platform integration will allow brands to maintain consistency in messaging and user experience, irrespective of the user's chosen device or channel.

13. **NFTs and Digital Collectibles:** Non-fungible tokens (NFTs) and digital collectibles will open up new possibilities for advertising. Brands may explore tokenized campaigns, creating unique digital assets that users can collect or trade as part of engaging and memorable experiences.

14. **Emotional AI for Consumer Understanding:** Emotional AI, which analyzes facial expressions, voice tones, and other cues, will enable advertisers to better understand consumer emotions. This understanding will inform more emotionally resonant and empathetic advertising strategies.

15. **Adapting to New Social Platforms:** The emergence of new social media platforms and content-sharing channels will require advertisers to adapt quickly. Staying ahead of trends and understanding the preferences of diverse user demographics on emerging platforms will be crucial.

CONCLUSION

The future of advertising promises an exciting convergence of technological innovation, consumer-centric approaches, and ethical considerations. Advertisers who embrace these emerging technologies and trends will be well-positioned to create compelling, relevant, and memorable campaigns that resonate with the ever-evolving preferences of modern audiences.

Marketing 2.0 transcends traditional boundaries, offering a dynamic and adaptive approach to connect with the digital-savvy and ever-changing consumer. This chapter serves as a guide to navigating the complexities of this new marketing era, highlighting strategies that go beyond the ordinary to drive impactful and sustainable brand success.

Marketing has evolved significantly in recent years, transitioning from traditional methods to more dynamic and interactive approaches. This shift, often referred to as Marketing 2.0, emphasizes the importance of leveraging digital technologies, engaging with customers on multiple platforms, and fostering meaningful relationships. In this model, we explore the key principles and strategies of Marketing 2.0, illustrating how businesses can adapt and thrive in the digital age.

Suggested Model

1. **Customer-Centric Approach:** Understand the importance of putting the customer at the center of marketing efforts. Utilize data analytics and market research to gain insights into customer behavior, preferences, and needs. Develop personalized marketing strategies tailored to individual customers or target segments.
2. **Digital Marketing Channels:** Embrace a multi-channel approach, including social media, email marketing, search engine optimization (SEO), and content marketing. Optimize digital marketing efforts to reach target audiences across various platforms and devices. Leverage emerging technologies such as augmented reality (AR) and virtual reality (VR) to create immersive brand experiences.
3. **Content Creation and Distribution:** Create high-quality, relevant content that resonates with your target audience. Implement a content distribution strategy to ensure maximum reach and engagement. Encourage user-generated content and foster community participation to enhance brand authenticity and credibility.
4. **Building Brand Loyalty:** Focus on building long-term relationships with customers rather than one-time transactions. Offer personalized experiences, rewards, and incentives to foster brand loyalty. Implement loyalty programs

and customer feedback mechanisms to continuously improve the customer experience.

5. **Data-Driven Decision Making:** Harness the power of data analytics to make informed marketing decisions. Monitor key performance indicators (KPIs) and metrics to evaluate the effectiveness of marketing campaigns. Use A/B testing and experimentation to optimize marketing strategies and tactics.

6. **Agile Marketing:** Embrace agility and flexibility in marketing approaches to adapt to rapidly changing market conditions. Iterate and refine marketing strategies based on real-time feedback and insights. Collaborate across departments and teams to align marketing efforts with overall business goals.

7. **Ethical and Responsible Marketing:** Prioritize transparency, honesty, and integrity in all marketing communications. Respect consumer privacy and adhere to regulations such as GDPR and CCPA. Engage in socially responsible initiatives and support causes aligned with your brand values.

Marketing 2.0 represents a paradigm shift in the way businesses approach and engage with their customers. By adopting a customer-centric mindset, embracing digital technologies, and prioritizing authenticity and ethics, businesses can succeed in today's rapidly evolving marketplace. This model provides a framework for navigating the complexities of Marketing 2.0 and unlocking opportunities for growth and innovation.

Suggested Readings

- "The New Rules of Marketing & PR: How to Use Social Media, Online Video, Mobile Applications, Blogs, News Releases, and Viral Marketing to Reach Buyers Directly" by David Meerman Scott - This book provides insights into leveraging digital platforms and social media for effective marketing and public relations campaigns.

- "Influence: The Psychology of Persuasion" by Robert B. Cialdini - Understanding the psychology behind consumer behavior and decision-making is crucial in modern marketing. This book explores the principles of persuasion that can be applied in various marketing contexts.

- "Purple Cow: Transform Your Business by Being Remarkable" by Seth Godin - Seth Godin emphasizes the importance of standing out in a crowded marketplace by being remarkable. This book offers insights into creating remarkable products and marketing strategies that capture consumer attention.

- "Content Inc.: How Entrepreneurs Use Content to Build Massive Audiences and Create Radically Successful Businesses" by Joe Pulizzi - Content marketing is a key component of Marketing 2.0. This book provides a framework for creating valuable content that attracts and retains customers.

- "Hooked: How to Build Habit-Forming Products" by Nir Eyal - Understanding how to create products and marketing experiences that form habits can be transformative in modern marketing. This book delves into the psychology of habit formation and provides actionable strategies for building habit-forming products and experiences.
- "Social Media Marketing Workbook: How to Use Social Media for Business" by Jason McDonald - This workbook offers practical guidance on leveraging social media platforms for marketing purposes, including strategy development, content creation, and audience engagement.
- "Digital Marketing for Dummies" by Ryan Deiss and Russ Henneberry - For marketers new to the digital landscape, this book provides a comprehensive overview of digital marketing channels, tools, and strategies, helping marketers navigate the complexities of Marketing 2.0.
- "Contagious: How to Build Word of Mouth in the Digital Age" by Jonah Berger - Word-of-mouth marketing remains powerful in the digital age. This book explores the science behind why certain ideas, products, or content go viral and provides insights into creating contagious marketing campaigns.
- "The Lean Startup: How Today's Entrepreneurs Use Continuous Innovation to Create Radically Successful Businesses" by Eric Ries - The principles of the lean startup approach can be applied to marketing to enable rapid experimentation, iteration, and optimization of marketing strategies and tactics.
- "Hacking Growth: How Today's Fastest-Growing Companies Drive Breakout Success" by Sean Ellis and Morgan Brown - This book offers strategies and tactics for achieving rapid growth through data-driven experimentation and optimization across various marketing channels.

REFERENCES

Deighton, J., & Kornfeld, L. (2009). Interactivity's Unanticipated Consequences for Marketers and Marketing. *Journal of Interactive Marketing*, *23*(1), 4–10. doi:10.1016/j.intmar.2008.10.001

Fournier, S., & Avery, J. (2011). The Uninvited Brand. *Business Horizons*, *54*(3), 193–207. doi:10.1016/j.bushor.2011.01.001

Handley, A., & Chapman, C. (2012). *Content Rules: How to Create Killer Blogs, Podcasts, Videos, Ebooks, Webinars (and More) That Engage Customers and Ignite Your Business*. John Wiley & Sons.

Hanna, R., Rohm, A., & Crittenden, V. L. (2011). We're All Connected: The Power of the Social Media Ecosystem. *Business Horizons*, *54*(3), 265–273. doi:10.1016/j. bushor.2011.01.007

Kaplan, A. M., & Haenlein, M. (2010). Users of the World, Unite! The Challenges and Opportunities of Social Media. *Business Horizons*, *53*(1), 59–68. doi:10.1016/j. bushor.2009.09.003

Kotler, P., & Keller, K. L. (2009). *Marketing Management*. Pearson Prentice Hall.

Mangold, W. G., & Faulds, D. J. (2009). Social Media: The New Hybrid Element of the Promotion Mix. *Business Horizons*, *52*(4), 357–365. doi:10.1016/j. bushor.2009.03.002

Mishra, P., & Singh, A. (2019). Impact of Transparency on Consumer Trust and Purchase Intention: The Moderating Role of Brand Commitment. *Journal of Promotion Management*, *25*(3), 336–354.

Prahalad, C. K., & Ramaswamy, V. (2004). Co-Creation Experiences: The Next Practice in Value Creation. *Journal of Interactive Marketing*, *18*(3), 5–14. doi:10.1002/ dir.20015

Pulizzi, J., & Barrett, N. (2008). *Get Content Get Customers: Turn Prospects into Buyers with Content Marketing*. McGraw-Hill.

Smith, A. N., & Chaffey, D. (2005). *E-Marketing Excellence: Planning and Optimizing your Digital Marketing*. Butterworth-Heinemann.

Smith, W. K., & Zook, M. A. (2011). *The Wealth of Networks: How Social Production Transforms Markets and Freedom*. Yale University Press.

Chapter 5

Effect of Psychological Pricing on Consumer Buying Behaviour:
A Study on Indian Consumers

Srijaa Roy
Christ University, India

ABSTRACT

Consumer behaviour is a topic most sought after when it comes to creating successful marketing practices that affect consumers' psychology, acting as a stimulus and inducing them to make purchases. Evidence explains that the psychological pricing strategy communicates with the subconscious mind of consumers, creating a perceptual illusion. This makes the deal seem more appealing to them. This chapter entails a practical study examining the impact of psychological pricing strategies on consumers' buying behaviour. This study has used authentic primary data that has been collected directly from consumers in India based on their buying experiences when encountering psychological pricing. The findings of this research show how socio-demographic factors like age, income, education, gender and family size influence consumers' buying behaviour when encountered with psychological pricing and if psychological patterns such as the anchoring heuristics, recency bias, scarcity effect and halo effect can overpower the influence of psychological pricing strategies in consumer buying behaviour.

DOI: 10.4018/979-8-3693-4167-4.ch005

INTRODUCTION

Understanding and harnessing the intricacies of consumer behaviour is pivotal for businesses aiming to thrive and excel in the competitive marketplace (Kumar & Pandey, 2017; Adenigba & Akorede, 2023; Iwalewa, 2023). One of the powerful tools at the disposal of marketers is psychological pricing, a strategy that goes beyond mere monetary figures and taps into the psychological processes of consumers, influencing their perceptions and subsequent buying decisions (Kumar & Pandey, 2017). This pricing tactic is deeply rooted in human psychology, leveraging subtle alterations in pricing structure to evoke specific psychological responses from consumers.

In the context of India, a rapidly developing consumer market with a diverse and discerning consumer base, the influence of psychological pricing strategies on buying behavior holds immense significance (Kumar & Pandey, 2017). The pricing of a product, including the way it ends or is presented, can profoundly impact consumers' perception of value and affordability (Iwalewa, 2023). As a result, businesses operating in India's diverse market must carefully craft their pricing strategies, taking into account the psychological nuances that can significantly influence consumer purchasing choices.

This research will help understand the effect of psychological pricing strategies on consumer buying behavior, with a specific focus on the Indian consumer landscape. By conducting a comprehensive research, on the psychological mechanisms that underlie consumers' responses to various pricing strategies and other psychological factors that may overpower the psychological pricing strategy, shedding light on how these strategies influence purchasing decisions in the Indian market. Through this study, we seek to contribute valuable insights to marketers and businesses, aiding them in formulating effective pricing policies and marketing strategies tailored to the Indian context.

LITERATURE REVIEW

The pricing of products and services is a critical element influencing consumer purchasing decisions, and psychological pricing strategies hold a paramount position. The interplay between pricing strategies and consumer behaviour is a dynamic area of research, especially in diverse and competitive markets such as India. Understanding how psychological pricing impacts consumer choices and the subsequent implications for businesses is pivotal for effective marketing strategies.

Psychological Pricing Strategies

It encompasses a set of pricing approaches that strategically utilize human psychology to influence consumer behaviour and perceptions of value (Smith, 2012). These strategies are designed to exploit cognitive biases and consumer emotions, guiding them towards specific purchasing decisions (Thomas & Morwitz, 2005). These are some psychological pricing strategies that this study focuses on to understand their effect on the buying behaviour of Indian consumers.

- **Odd-Even Pricing:** This pricing approach involves setting prices just below a whole or round number (e.g., $9.99 instead of $10.00), creating a perception of lower cost despite a minimal difference (Schindler, 1989).
- **Prestige Pricing:** Luxury brands often employ this strategy by setting prices at a premium level to convey exclusivity and superior quality, leading consumers to associate higher prices with higher quality (Vigneron & Johnson, 2004).
- **Price Anchoring:** Presenting a higher-priced product alongside a lower-priced option to make the latter seem more attractive is a key aspect of this strategy (Ariely et al., 2003).
- **Bundling:** Combining products into a package and offering them at a reduced overall price creates a perception of value for consumers (Chen & Xie, 2008).
- **Decoy Pricing:** Introducing a third option priced similarly to a more expensive one but offering less value can steer consumers towards the original expensive option (Zhang & Krishna, 2009).
- **Loss Leader Pricing:** Selling a product at a minimal profit or even a loss to attract customers, with the expectation that they will purchase other higher-margin items, is a common approach (Bolton et al., 2003).

Consumer Perception and its Impact on Purchasing Behaviour

As outlined by Lindsay and Norman (1997), Sensation and perception are intertwined and constitute a continuous process, influencing how individuals perceive and respond to stimuli, such as pricing and advertising information. The way individuals perceive prices and advertising content is deeply linked to sensory experiences and mental interpretations. The perception of price as either cheap or expensive is subjective and varies among buyers, ultimately influencing their purchasing behaviour (Lindsay and Norman, 1997).

Psychological Patterns vs. Pricing Strategies

Psychological patterns such as anchoring heuristics, recency bias, scarcity effect, and halo effect play crucial roles in shaping consumer buying behaviour. These patterns can potentially overpower the influence of psychological pricing strategies, impacting consumers' perceptions and decisions regarding purchases, making it crucial for businesses to consider and understand the interplay of these cognitive biases when devising pricing strategies.

- **Anchoring Heuristics:** Anchoring involves relying heavily on the first piece of information encountered when making decisions. Consumers tend to use the initial price they see as an anchor and adjust their perception of subsequent prices accordingly (Tversky & Kahneman, 1974).
- **Recency Bias:** Recency bias refers to the tendency of individuals to give more weight to recent information or events when making decisions. In the context of pricing, consumers may be heavily influenced by the most recent price they encountered, ignoring past prices or the pricing strategy employed (Lichtenstein et al., 1993).
- **Scarcity Effect:** The scarcity effect occurs when consumers perceive a product or offer as more valuable due to its limited availability. This can lead consumers to make impulsive buying decisions, focusing more on the perceived scarcity than on the pricing strategy (Ariely & Wertenbroch, 2002).
- **Halo Effect:** The halo effect involves forming an overall positive or negative impression of a product or brand based on a single characteristic or experience. If consumers have a positive perception of a product based on factors like quality or brand image, they may overlook or rationalize higher prices (Nisbett & Wilson, 1977).

Psychological Pricing and Consumer Responses

Psychological pricing strategies aim to influence consumer behaviour by manipulating price points. Kumar and Pandey (2017) explored the connection between psychological pricing and consumer behaviour. Their research emphasized the role of socio-demographic factors, including education, income, and age, in shaping consumer responses to pricing strategies. Notably, the study highlighted that consumers sensitive to pricing often exhibit a propensity towards prices ending with the number nine, indicating a psychological influence on purchase decisions.

In the same manner, Schindler, Parse, and Naipaul (2011) found that consumers tend to pay lesser attention to the rightmost digits of a price, illustrating the psychological nuances that influence buying behaviour.

Extending Insights to Indian Consumers

Drawing insights from Adenigba and Akorede's study (2023) on the implications of psychological pricing in Islamic markets, it is essential to consider the cultural and religious context when analyzing similar strategies in diverse markets like India. India, with its unique cultural and socio-economic fabric, presents an interesting arena to study how psychological pricing strategies resonate with consumers, providing valuable insights into optimizing pricing strategies specifically tailored for the Indian market.

Psychological pricing strategies have been shown to significantly impact consumer perceptions and decisions in the Indian market. Understanding these dynamics is essential for businesses in India to design effective pricing strategies that resonate with consumers, maximize engagement, and ultimately drive purchase decisions.

OBJECTIVES OF THE STUDY

1. To examine the impact of psychological pricing strategies on consumer buying behavior within the Indian consumer market by investigating how different demographic factors such as age, income, education, gender, and family size influence and shape consumers' responses to these pricing strategies.
2. To explore how Indian consumers perceive prices, with a focus on the significance they attribute to price endings and the impact of psychological cues on their perception of product value.
3. To bring to light other psychological factors that induce consumer buying behaviour apart from psychological pricing strategies.

SIGNIFICANCE OF THE STUDY

This research holds substantial significance for multiple stakeholders. For businesses and marketers, insights from this study will guide the effective implementation of psychological pricing strategies, aiding in crafting pricing models that resonate with the Indian consumer psyche (Kumar & Pandey, 2017). Additionally, policymakers can benefit from this research to develop regulatory frameworks that ensure fair and ethical pricing practices, fostering a transparent market environment (Adenigba & Akorede, 2023). This study will also help researchers and provide as reference for further study. Lastly, consumers themselves will gain a deeper understanding of how psychological pricing affects their choices, empowering them to make informed purchasing decisions.

CONCEPTUAL FRAMEWORK

Figure 1. Showing the conceptual framework of the psychological pricing strategy and the consumers' buying behaviour

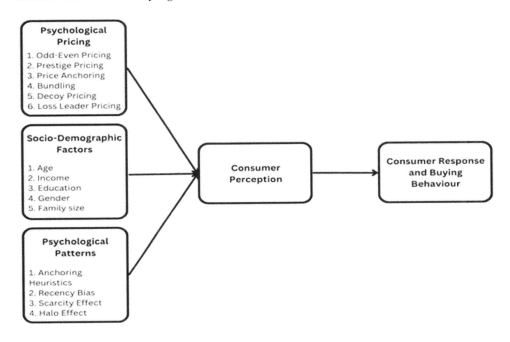

The conceptual framework illustrates the intricate relationships between psychological pricing strategies, socio-demographic factors, psychological patterns, and consumer behavior. The study explores how these elements collectively shape consumer perceptions and influence buying decisions in the context of the Indian market.

Psychological Pricing Strategies: encompass various pricing tactics such as Odd-Even Pricing, Prestige Pricing, Price Anchoring, Bundling, Decoy Pricing, and Loss Leader Pricing. These strategies are designed to influence consumer perceptions of value and affect purchasing decisions. They are the focal point of the study as highlighted by research (Schindler, 1989; Vigneron & Johnson, 2004; Ariely et al., 2003; Chen & Xie, 2008; Zhang & Krishna, 2009; Bolton et al., 2003).

Socio-demographic Factors: Include variables like age, income, education, gender, and family size, which play a crucial role in shaping consumer behavior. Different demographic groups may respond differently to psychological pricing strategies, thus impacting their buying decisions, as indicated by research (Kumar & Pandey, 2017).

Psychological Patterns: Encompass Anchoring Heuristics, Recency Bias, Scarcity Effect, and Halo Effect. These patterns significantly influence how consumers perceive prices and make decisions. Understanding these cognitive processes is essential for deciphering buying behavior, as supported by research (Tversky & Kahneman, 1974; Lichtenstein et al., 1993; Ariely & Wertenbroch, 2002; Nisbett & Wilson, 1977).

Consumer Perception and Buying Behaviour: Represent the ultimate outcome of the study, reflecting how the interplay of psychological pricing, socio-demographic factors, and psychological patterns influences consumer decision-making.

HYPOTHESIS OF THE STUDY

HO (Null Hypothesis): There is no significant difference in consumer buying behavior between products priced using psychological pricing strategies and products priced conventionally.

H1 (Alternative Hypothesis): Consumers are more likely to exhibit distinct buying behavior patterns when encountering products priced using psychological pricing strategies compared to products priced conventionally.

RESEARCH METHODOLOGY

The research targets Indian consumers aged 18 and above residing in Delhi NCR, Kolkata, and Mumbai. To ensure a comprehensive understanding across various age groups within these regions, a stratified random sampling technique has been implemented.

For data collection, a structured questionnaire has been meticulously designed to gather quantitative data. This questionnaire encompasses Likert-scale inquiries and demographic questions relating to age, income, education, and purchasing patterns influenced by psychological pricing strategies.

The distribution of the survey will be conducted both in person and electronically to guarantee a diverse representation of consumers within the specified regions.

In the subsequent phase of the study, data analysis will be undertaken. This will involve calculating descriptive statistics such as mean scores and frequency distributions to analyze demographic characteristics and consumer responses. Additionally, inferential statistics, including regression analysis, will be applied to identify relationships between demographic factors and the influence of psychological pricing on purchasing behavior. Furthermore, the analysis aims to discern whether psychological patterns play a dominant role in consumer behavior compared to psychological pricing strategies.

The variables under scrutiny encompass independent factors such as psychological pricing strategies, socio-demographic characteristics (e.g., age, income, education, gender, family size), and psychological patterns (e.g., Anchoring Heuristics, Recency Bias, Scarcity Effect, Halo Effect). These factors are not directly controlled by businesses but play a pivotal role in shaping consumer behavior.

The dependent variable in this research is consumer perception and buying behavior. It represents the ultimate outcomes influenced by the interplay of psychological pricing strategies, socio-demographic factors, and psychological patterns. Understanding these dynamics is crucial for comprehending consumer behavior and informing strategic business decisions.

DATA ANALYSIS AND FINDINGS

8.1.1 The age groups are represented by coded values (1 to 5)

- 18-24 age group (Old Value: 1)
- 25-34 age group (Old Value: 2)
- 35-44 age group (Old Value: 3)
- 45-54 age group (Old Value: 4)
- 55 and above age group (Old Value: 5)

The highest mean response is from the 55 and above age group, indicating a generally more positive response to attractive pricing. The 18-24 age group shows the most variability, while the 55 and above age group shows the least. The survey results suggest that the 55 and above age group tends to be more responsive to attractive pricing, as indicated by the highest mean response (2.58) and the least variability among all age groups. The 25-34 and 45-54 age groups also show moderate responsiveness, while the 18-24 and 35-44 age groups exhibit more variability in their responses to attractive prices. The findings imply that, overall, older age groups may be more positively influenced by attractive pricing strategies in terms of their buying behavior.

Table 1. Descriptives

		Would you as a consumer continue to respond to attractive pricing keeping aside other factors such as brand reputation, reviews etc?		Statistic	Std. Error
Age1					
	1 - Stro	Mean		2.00	.577
		95% Confidence Interval for Mean	Lower Bound	-.48	
			Upper Bound	4.48	
		5% Trimmed Mean		.	
		Median		2.00	
		Variance		1.000	
		Std. Deviation		1.000	
		Minimum		1	
		Maximum		3	
		Range		2	
		Interquartile Range		.	
		Skewness		.000	1.225
		Kurtosis		.	.
	2 - Disa	Mean		2.44	.205
		95% Confidence Interval for Mean	Lower Bound	2.02	
			Upper Bound	2.86	
		5% Trimmed Mean		2.43	
		Median		3.00	
		Variance		1.351	
		Std. Deviation		1.162	
		Minimum		1	
		Maximum		4	
		Range		3	
		Interquartile Range		2	
		Skewness		-.036	.414
		Kurtosis		-1.477	.809
	3 - Neut	Mean		2.47	.363
		95% Confidence Interval for Mean	Lower Bound	1.69	
			Upper Bound	3.25	
		5% Trimmed Mean		2.41	
		Median		2.00	
		Variance		1.981	
		Std. Deviation		1.407	
		Minimum		1	
		Maximum		5	
		Range		4	
		Interquartile Range		3	
		Skewness		.433	.580
		Kurtosis		-1.341	1.121

Continued on following page

Table 1. Continued

		Mean		2.43	.154
		95% Confidence Interval for Mean	Lower Bound	2.12	
			Upper Bound	2.74	
		5% Trimmed Mean		2.42	
		Median		2.00	
		Variance		1.042	
	4 - Agre	Std. Deviation		1.021	
		Minimum		1	
		Maximum		4	
		Range		3	
		Interquartile Range		1	
		Skewness		.262	.357
		Kurtosis		-1.013	.702
		Mean		2.58	.149
		95% Confidence Interval for Mean	Lower Bound	2.26	
			Upper Bound	2.91	
		5% Trimmed Mean		2.59	
		Median		3.00	
		Variance		.265	
	5 - Stro	Std. Deviation		.515	
		Minimum		2	
		Maximum		3	
		Range		1	
		Interquartile Range		1	
		Skewness		-.388	.637
		Kurtosis		-2.263	1.232

The chi-square test assesses whether there is a significant association between gender and the belief in the attractiveness of prices like 499 or 595.

The p-values (0.069 for Pearson, 0.041 for Likelihood Ratio) suggest that while there is some evidence of an association, it is not overwhelmingly strong.

The Cramer's V and Phi coefficients (both approximately 0.287) indicate a moderate degree of association between gender and the belief about attractive prices.

While the association is not highly significant, there seems to be a moderate relationship between gender and the perception of attractive pricing.

Table 2. Crosstab

Count					
			Gender		Total
			Female	Male	
Do you believe that prices such as 499 or 595 are more attractive than rounded numbers?		1 - Strongly Disagree	0	3	3
		2 - Disagree	9	12	21
		3 - Neutral	11	19	30
		4 - Agree	23	16	39
		5 - Strongly Agree	9	4	13
Total			52	54	106

Chi-Square Tests

	Value	df	Asymptotic Significance (2-sided)
Pearson Chi-Square	8.707[a]	4	.069
Likelihood Ratio	9.947	4	.041
N of Valid Cases	106		

a. 2 cells (20.0%) have expected count less than 5. The minimum expected count is 1.47.

The p-values (0.005 for Pearson, 0.003 for Likelihood Ratio) suggest a statistically significant association, indicating that education level and the tendency to purchase bundled products are likely related.

The Cramer's V and Phi coefficients (0.272 and 0.471, respectively) indicate a moderate degree of association between education level and the purchase of bundled products.

The results suggest that there is a statistically significant relationship between education level and the frequency of purchasing bundled products or services.

Most Likely to Purchase Bundled Products (Highest Frequency):

Education Level: Bachelor's degree

Least Likely to Purchase Bundled Products (Lowest Frequency):

Education Level: Doctoral or equivalent

Table 3. Crosstab

		Education Level				Total
		Bachelor's degree	Doctoral or equivalent	Highschool	Master's degree	
Do you purchase bundled products or services (e.g., combo meals, subscription bundles)?	2 - Rarely	6	2	7	3	18
	3 - Occasionally	11	1	0	14	26
	4 - Often	16	5	2	15	38
	5 - Very Often	10	4	5	5	24
Total		43	12	14	37	106

Chi-Square Tests

	Value	df	Asymptotic Significance (2-sided)
Pearson Chi-Square	23.555[a]	9	.005
Likelihood Ratio	24.887	9	.003
N of Valid Cases	106		

a. 7 cells (43.8%) have expected count less than 5. The minimum expected count is 2.04.

Symmetric Measures

		Value	Approximate Significance
Nominal by Nominal	**Phi**	**.471**	.005
	Cramer's V	**.272**	.005
N of Valid Cases		106	

The p-value (0.000) is less than the significance level (usually 0.05), indicating a statistically significant difference between income groups regarding whether the limited availability of a product makes it more appealing. Therefore, income significantly influences the perception of product availability.

The p-value (0.001) is less than the significance level, indicating a statistically significant difference between income groups regarding the preferred popcorn tub. Therefore, income significantly influences the choice of popcorn tub at the movies.

Table 4. ANOVA

		Sum of Squares	df	Mean Square	F	Sig.
Does the limited availability of a product make it more appealing to you?	Between Groups	25.278	4	6.320	6.917	.000
	Within Groups	92.278	101	.914		
	Total	117.557	105			
You are at the movies and you want to purchase popcorn. Which tub would you go for? (Price-INR)	Between Groups	10.215	4	2.554	5.338	.001
	Within Groups	48.323	101	.478		
	Total	58.538	105			

Individuals with higher monthly incomes, especially above 100,000 INR, show a significant preference for the Large-459 tub.

The Medium-349 tub is preferred across all income groups, with the highest preference from the above 100,000 INR group.

The Small-299 tub has some preference, particularly from individuals with monthly incomes above 20,000 INR.

Table 5. Crosstab

		Monthly income after tax (INR)					Total
		0-10000	0-20000	21000-50000	51000-100000	Above 100000	
You are at the movies and you want to purchase popcorn. Which tub would you go for? (Price-INR)	Large-459	0	3	3	5	22	33
	Medium-349	1	2	13	19	12	47
	Small-299	0	9	7	5	5	26
Total		1	14	23	29	39	106

Chi-Square Tests

	Value	df	Asymptotic Significance (2-sided)
Pearson Chi-Square	34.229[a]	8	.000
Likelihood Ratio	32.610	8	.000
N of Valid Cases	106		

a. 5 cells (33.3%) have expected count less than 5. The minimum expected count is .25.

Symmetric Measures

		Value	Approximate Significance
Nominal by Nominal	Phi	.568	.000
	Cramer's V	.402	.000
N of Valid Cases		106	

The psychological factor "Does the limited availability of a product make it more appealing to you?" has a significant positive impact on the likelihood of consumers responding to attractive pricing, keeping aside other factors.

The variable "You are at the movies and you want to purchase popcorn. Which tub would you go for? (Price-INR)" does not have a significant impact on the dependent variable.

Psychological patterns related to the limited availability of a product seem to have a stronger influence on consumer responses to attractive pricing compared to the specific pricing of popcorn tubs in a movie theater context, based on this analysis.

Table 6. Model Summary

Model	R	R Square	Adjusted R Square	Std. Error of the Estimate
1	.344[a]	.119	.102	1.045

a. Predictors: (Constant), Does the limited availability of a product make it more appealing to you?, You are at the movies and you want to purchase popcorn. Which tub would you go for? (Price-INR)

ANOVA[a]

Model		Sum of Squares	df	Mean Square	F	Sig.
1	Regression	15.128	2	7.564	6.933	.001[b]
	Residual	112.381	103	1.091		
	Total	127.509	105			

a. Dependent Variable: Would you as a consumer continue to respond to attractive pricing keeping aside other factors such as brand reputation, reviews etc?

b. Predictors: (Constant), Does the limited availability of a product make it more appealing to you?, You are at the movies and you want to purchase popcorn. Which tub would you go for? (Price-INR)

Coefficients[a]

Model		Unstandardized Coefficients		Standardized Coefficients	t	Sig.
		B	Std. Error	Beta		
1	(Constant)	2.344	.406		5.779	.000
	You are at the movies and you want to purchase popcorn. Which tub would you go for? (Price-INR)	.004	.138	.003	.029	.977
	Does the limited availability of a product make it more appealing to you?	.359	.097	.345	3.689	.000

a. Dependent Variable: Would you as a consumer continue to respond to attractive pricing keeping aside other factors such as brand reputation, reviews etc?

Considering the Pillai's Trace values, the "positive" variable has a stronger impact compared to "impulse." However, the interaction term ("positive * impulse") also contributes to the model's overall significance. Therefore, it seems that psychological patterns (represented by "positive") have a relatively stronger impact on consumers compared to psychological pricing patterns (represented by "impulse")

Table 7. Multivariate Tests[a]

Effect		Value	F	Hypothesis df	Error df	Sig.
Intercept	Pillai's Trace	.782	175.828[b]	2.000	98.000	.000
	Wilks' Lambda	.218	175.828[b]	2.000	98.000	.000
	Hotelling's Trace	3.588	175.828[b]	2.000	98.000	.000
	Roy's Largest Root	3.588	175.828[b]	2.000	98.000	.000
positive	Pillai's Trace	.265	5.033	6.000	198.000	.000
	Wilks' Lambda	.745	5.182[b]	6.000	196.000	.000
	Hotelling's Trace	.330	5.329	6.000	194.000	.000
	Roy's Largest Root	.285	9.392[c]	3.000	99.000	.000
impulse	Pillai's Trace	.063	3.311[b]	2.000	98.000	.041
	Wilks' Lambda	.937	3.311[b]	2.000	98.000	.041
	Hotelling's Trace	.068	3.311[b]	2.000	98.000	.041
	Roy's Largest Root	.068	3.311[b]	2.000	98.000	.041
positive * impulse	Pillai's Trace	.087	2.239	4.000	198.000	.066
	Wilks' Lambda	.913	2.268[b]	4.000	196.000	.063
	Hotelling's Trace	.095	2.296	4.000	194.000	.061
	Roy's Largest Root	.094	4.674[c]	2.000	99.000	.011

a. Design: Intercept + positive + impulse + positive * impulse

b. Exact statistic

c. The statistic is an upper bound on F that yields a lower bound on the significance level.

OVERALL FINDINGS

The analysis of age groups revealed that the 55 and above age group exhibited the highest mean response, suggesting a generally more positive attitude towards attractive pricing. The 18-24 age group showed the most variability in responses, implying that older age groups may be more positively influenced by attractive pricing strategies. The examination of gender-related responses indicated a moderate association between gender and the belief in the attractiveness of specific prices. While the association was not highly significant, there was a moderate relationship between gender and the perception of attractive pricing. A statistically significant relationship was found between education level and the frequency of purchasing bundled products. The results suggested that education level influences the tendency to purchase bundled products, with distinct preferences observed across different education levels.

Monthly income was identified as a significant factor influencing the perception of product availability. Individuals with higher incomes, especially above 100,000

INR, showed a significant preference for larger popcorn tubs. This income-dependent preference provided insights into consumer choices related to product availability. Analysis indicated that the limited availability of a product significantly influenced consumer responses, suggesting that the psychological factor of scarcity plays a crucial role. Additionally, psychological patterns related to limited availability had a stronger impact on consumer responses compared to the specific pricing of popcorn tubs. In the multivariate analysis, the variable representing positive psychological patterns demonstrated a stronger impact compared to impulse patterns. The interaction term ("positive * impulse") also contributed to the model's overall significance, indicating a combined influence of psychological patterns and pricing.

HYPOTHESIS EVALUATION

Null Hypothesis (H0): Rejected. There is a significant difference in consumer buying behavior, influenced by psychological factors, especially limited availability.

Alternative Hypothesis (H1): Accepted. Consumers exhibit distinct buying behavior patterns influenced more by psychological patterns than specific pricing strategies. Research

RESEARCH LIMITATIONS

Sample Size and Generalizability: The study was conducted with a sample size of [insert number] participants, which, while sufficient for the scope of this research, may limit the generalizability of the findings to the broader population. Future research with larger and more diverse samples is recommended for a more comprehensive understanding of the subject.

Geographical Scope: The research focused specifically on certain regions in India. Regional variations in consumer behaviour may exist, and caution should be exercised in extrapolating the findings to the entire country. Replicating the study in different geographical locations could provide a more nuanced understanding of psychological pricing effects.

Cultural Factors: The study acknowledges the influence of cultural factors on consumer behaviour. However, the depth of cultural analysis is limited, and a more in-depth exploration of cultural nuances and their impact on pricing perceptions could enhance the study's robustness.

Temporal Factors: Consumer behaviour is dynamic and subject to changes over time. This study represents a snapshot of consumer perceptions during the specific time frame of data collection. Longitudinal studies could capture the temporal dynamics of psychological pricing effects more comprehensively.

External Variables: External factors, such as economic conditions, marketing campaigns by specific companies, or changes in consumer trends, were not explicitly controlled for in the study. These variables could introduce confounding effects, and future research might consider a more controlled experimental design.

Self-Report Bias: The study relied on self-reported data from participants, introducing the possibility of response bias. Participants may not accurately recall or represent their actual purchasing behaviour, and future studies could explore alternative methods to validate reported responses.

CONCLUSION

In conclusion, this study aimed to shed light on the nuanced dynamics of psychological pricing and its impact on consumer buying behavior within the context of the Indian market.

One of the primary findings of this research is the significant influence of psychological pricing strategies on consumers' purchasing decisions. The experimental conditions, where subtle price manipulations were introduced, revealed notable shifts in consumer perceptions, preferences, and buying intentions. The results suggest that consumers in the Indian market are sensitive to pricing cues, and these cues can play a pivotal role in shaping their perceptions of product value and attractiveness.

Moreover, the study identified specific psychological patterns tactics that exhibited a more pronounced impact on consumer behaviour. This granularity in understanding the differential effects of various pricing cues provides actionable insights for marketers and businesses seeking to optimize their pricing strategies in the Indian consumer landscape.

However, it is crucial to interpret these findings within the context of the study's limitations. The sample size, geographical scope, and methodological approach, while appropriate for the study's objectives, introduce constraints on the generalizability of the results. Addressing these limitations in future research endeavours would further enhance the validity and applicability of the findings.

REFERENCES

Adenigba, S. A., & Akorede, H. Y. (2023). Implications of Psychological Pricing on Contemporary Muslim Retailers and Consumers in Nigeria. *Journal of Islamic Economic and Business Research*, *3*(1), 1–12. doi:10.18196/jiebr.v3i1.93

Ariely, D., Loewenstein, G., & Prelec, D. (2003). Coherent arbitrariness: Stable demand curves without stable preferences. *The Quarterly Journal of Economics*, *118*(1), 73–106. doi:10.1162/00335530360535153

Ariely, D., Loewenstein, G., & Prelec, D. (2003). "Coherent arbitrariness": Stable demand curves without stable preferences. *The Quarterly Journal of Economics*, *118*(1), 73–106. doi:10.1162/00335530360535153

Ariely, D., & Wertenbroch, K. (2002). Procrastination, deadlines, and performance: Self-control by precommitment. *Psychological Science*, *13*(3), 219–224. doi:10.1111/1467-9280.00441 PMID:12009041

Bolton, R. N., Kannan, P. K., & Bramlett, M. D. (2000). Implications of loyalty program membership and service experiences for customer retention and value. *Journal of the Academy of Marketing Science*, *28*(1), 95–108. doi:10.1177/0092070300281009

Bolton, R. N., Warlop, L., & Alba, J. (2003). Consumer Perceptions of Price (Un) fairness. *The Journal of Consumer Research*, *29*(4), 474–491. doi:10.1086/346244

Chen, Z., & Xie, J. (2008). Online consumer review: Word-of-mouth as a new element of marketing communication mix. *Management Science*, *54*(3), 477–491. doi:10.1287/mnsc.1070.0810

Chen, Z., & Xie, J. (2008). Online Consumer Review: Word-of-Mouth as a New Element of Marketing Communication Mix. *Management Science*, *54*(3), 477–491. doi:10.1287/mnsc.1070.0810

Dholakia, U. M. (2000). Temptation and resistance: An integrated model of consumption impulse formation and enactment. *Psychology and Marketing*, *17*(11), 955–982. doi:10.1002/1520-6793(200011)17:11<955::AID-MAR3>3.0.CO;2-J

Häubl, G., & Trifts, V. (2000). Consumer decision making in online shopping environments: The effects of interactive decision aids. *Marketing Science*, *19*(1), 4–21. doi:10.1287/mksc.19.1.4.15178

Kim, J., Natter, M., & Spann, M. (2009). Pay-what-you-want: A new participative pricing mechanism. *Journal of Marketing*, *73*(1), 44–58. doi:10.1509/jmkg.73.1.044

Kotler, P., & Armstrong, G. (2018). *Principles of Marketing*. Pearson.

Kumar, P., & Pandey, M. (2017). A review on the impact of psychological pricing on consumer perception. *International Journal of Management, IT, and Engineering*, *7*(3), 331–343.

Labrecque, L. I., Markos, E., & Milne, G. R. (2011). Online Personal Branding: Processes, Challenges, and Implications. *Journal of Interactive Marketing*, *25*(1), 37–50. doi:10.1016/j.intmar.2010.09.002

Lichtenstein, S., Burton, S., & Karson, M. J. (1993). The effect of semantic cues on consumer perceptions of reference price ads. *The Journal of Consumer Research*, *20*(4), 566–575.

Nagle, T. T., & Holden, R. K. (1994). *The strategy and tactics of pricing: A guide to growing more profitably*. Prentice Hall.

Nisbett, R. E., & Wilson, T. D. (1977). The halo effect: Evidence for unconscious alteration of judgments. *Journal of Personality and Social Psychology*, *35*(4), 250–256. doi:10.1037/0022-3514.35.4.250

Nisbett, R. E., & Wilson, T. D. (1977). Telling More Than We Can Know: Verbal Reports on Mental Processes. *Psychological Review*, *84*(3), 231–259. doi:10.1037/0033-295X.84.3.231

Roh, M. H., Oh, W. Y., & Shin, D. (2003). The Discount Heuristic: Simple Arithmetic vs. Complex Information in Making Numerical Estimates. *JMR, Journal of Marketing Research*, *40*(4), 399–414.

Schindler, R. M. (1989). The psychology of pricing. *Psychology and Marketing*, *6*(4), 307–324.

Schindler, R. M. (1989). The excitement of getting a bargain: Some hypotheses concerning the origins and effects of smart-shopper feelings. *Advances in Consumer Research. Association for Consumer Research (U. S.)*, *16*(1), 447–453.

Smith, R. (2012). Psychological Pricing: A Strategy for Maximizing Revenue. *Entrepreneurship & Organization Management*, *1*(2), 1–2.

Thomas, M., & Morwitz, V. G. (2005). Penny Wise and Pound Foolish: The Left-Digit Effect in Price Cognition. *The Journal of Consumer Research*, *32*(1), 54–64. doi:10.1086/429600

Tversky, A., & Kahneman, D. (1974). Judgment under uncertainty: Heuristics and biases. *Science*, *185*(4157), 1124–1131. doi:10.1126/science.185.4157.1124 PMID:17835457

Vigneron, F., & Johnson, L. W. (2004). Measuring perceptions of brand luxury. *Journal of Brand Management, 11*(6), 484–506. doi:10.1057/palgrave.bm.2540194

Zhang, J., & Krishna, A. (2009). The comprehensive assortment-as-variety hypothesis: How the interplay of per-option and per-category assortment influences perceived variety and choice. *The Journal of Consumer Research, 36*(6), 1006–1020.

Zhang, S., & Krishna, A. (2009). The Effect of Decoy Pricing on Consumer Choice: Understanding When a "Low-Price" Option Serves as a "Dominated Alternative.". *JMR, Journal of Marketing Research, 46*(6), 767–779.

Chapter 6
Ethical Considerations in the Metaverse and Augmented Retail Reality Era

Manjit Kour
https://orcid.org/0000-0003-1043-3187
Chandigarh University, India

ABSTRACT

Retail is changing as a result of the convergence of blockchain, virtual reality, and augmented reality technology. Since this is a dynamic setting, it is essential to address any ethical issues that come up. This study aims to provide practical guidance for the responsible adoption of VR, AR, and blockchain technologies in retail by synthesising case studies and existing ethical frameworks. It will also thoroughly examine the ethical challenges arising from the integration of these technologies, with a focus on consumer privacy and data security. The study employed a multifaceted approach, including a thorough review of the literature, a critical analysis of the state-of-the-art ethical frameworks, and an examination of real case studies. There are certain ethical issues with virtual and augmented reality that are discussed, along with some possible answers. The results highlight the importance of user education, strict data protection protocols, and international regulatory cooperation as crucial elements for tackling ethical dilemmas in the context of augmented retail reality.

DOI: 10.4018/979-8-3693-4167-4.ch006

INTRODUCTION

According to some, the metaverse is a new version of the internet that combines blockchain technology, virtual reality headsets, and avatars to create a seamless merging of the real and virtual worlds (Lee et al., 2021a; The Verge, 2021). According to Damar (2021), the metaverse is a "3D virtual shared environment where all activities may be carried out with the help of augmented and virtual reality technologies." It is also referred to as "the layer between you and reality." With the use of VR headsets, haptic gloves, AR, and Extended Reality (XR), which allows users to fully experience the high levels of engagement and immersive experience, the technology to enable the establishment of the metaverse is rapidly growing.

The retail industry has entered a transformational period as a result of the convergence of blockchain, virtual reality, and augmented reality in recent years. The result of this combination is a dynamic and engaging shopping experience that is revolutionising the way customers engage with goods and services (Kour & Rani, 2023). Examining the ethical implications of these new technologies is more important than ever as the retail industry changes due to technology breakthroughs.

The ethical issues raised by the combination of blockchain technology, augmented reality, and virtual reality in retail are covered in detail in this chapter. The way these technologies interact presents new issues that need to be carefully considered, especially when it comes to data security, consumer privacy, and general ethics. The aim is not only to identify and comprehend these moral dilemmas, but also to offer guidance for the conscientious integration of modern technologies in the retail sector.

Given the speed at which blockchain, augmented reality, and virtual reality are being incorporated into retail, this study is essential. It is critical to examine and resolve the ethical issues raised by retailers' increased use of these cutting-edge technology. In response to the growing ethical concerns about consumer privacy, data security, and general ethical behaviour in the use of immersive and data-driven technology, the study addresses these issues. The research seeks to establish responsible practises, build consumer trust, ensure legal compliance, and support the retail industry's sustainable growth in the augmented reality era by comprehending and proactively addressing these ethical problems. It can be said that this study is a useful tool for academics, politicians, and retailers managing the changing environment at the intersection of retail ethics and technology.

METHODOLOGY

This study uses an mixed approach to thoroughly examine the moral dilemmas raised by the combination of blockchain, augmented reality, and virtual reality technologies in the retail industry. The study includes a thorough analysis of the literature to lay the groundwork for understanding the present state of ethics in augmented retail reality. Furthermore, an evaluation of current ethical frameworks is carried out in order to pinpoint any shortcomings and potential topics for discussion. Analyses of real-world case studies are conducted in order to extract practical insights into ethical quandaries.

ETHICAL CONSIDERATION WITH VIRTUAL REALITY (VR) AND AUGMENTED REALITY (AR)

The ethical implications of Virtual Reality (VR) and Augmented Reality (AR) are multifaceted and impact people as well as society as a whole. With the increasing integration of these immersive technologies into our daily lives via retail industry, it is imperative that we comprehend and address these ethical considerations. The following (figure1) are some important moral questions around VR and AR:

Figure 1. Ethical considerations with VR and AR

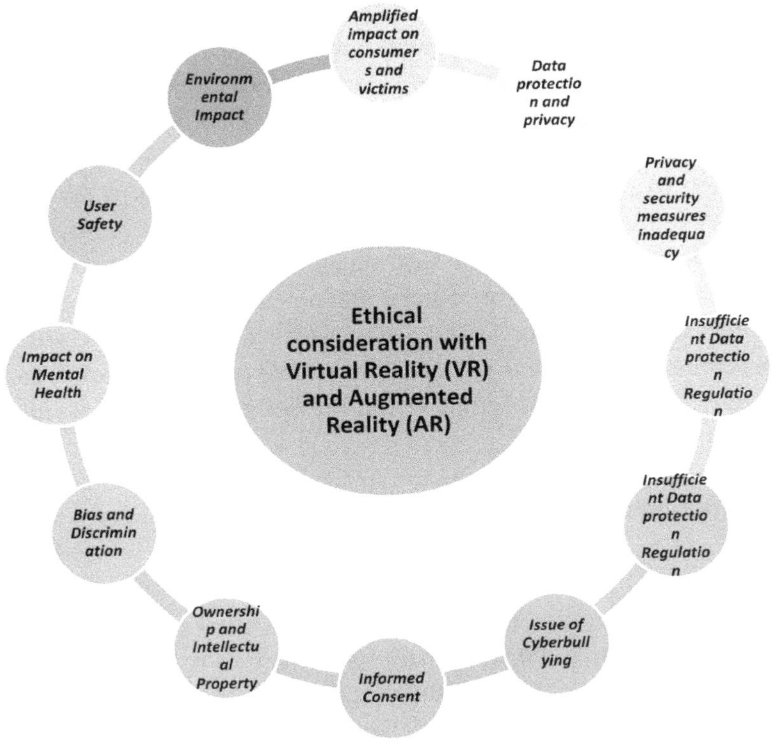

Amplified Impact on Consumers and Victims

There are multiple senses in the metaverse. When unwanted and privacy-invasive contents proliferate in the metaverse, they may be perceived as more intrusive and are likely to have a greater negative impact on the users or victims because of the metaverse's complex and sophisticated features, which include more graphic, 3D design, immersive visual and auditory experience, and so on. Therefore, what is known as an enhanced technological impact—that is, more serious consequences—are probably going to result from privacy infractions in the metaverse (ISACA, 2014; Kshetri, 2014). Additionally, users in the metaverse are more vulnerable to corporate exploitation. For example, in comparison to regular screens, VR headsets are able to gather more and richer user data. Businesses are therefore more motivated to gather user data and provide it to third parties. For instance, Meta (Facebook) revealed that it was developing Project Cambria, a high-end VR headset with features that are not achievable with the headsets that are being used today. The device's new sensors will enable the user's virtual avatar to mimic facial emotions and keep eye contact (Bonifacic, 2021). Project Cambria would be able to replicate a person's facial expressions and eye movements in virtual reality in this way. Advertisers and retailers may utilise this information from Meta to more precisely gauge consumers' attention spans (Dwivedi et al., 2022). By targeting people with adverts, the measurement can persuade them to purchase a product. According to Meta, the business does not currently give advertising access to eye-tracking information. However, the business hasn't promised that it won't gather and distribute this kind of information in the future (Hunter, 2022). Researchers discovered that they could physically relocate immersed users to a different location and manage their actions by taking use of VR technology. An attacker may, for example, manipulate a virtual reality platform and reset the physical boundaries of the hardware to coerce a user into taking activities that result in a fall down a flight of stairs and potentially fatal injuries. Even more dire outcomes may arise from AR-related security vulnerabilities. Users might, for example, be mistakenly led into a street, which could result in a hazardous situation. Wearers of AR headsets may become victims of violent crimes like assault, robbery, and mugging (Nichols, 2022).

Privacy and Security Measures Inadequacy

Nations and organisations are not entirely equipped to handle the security and privacy concerns that the metaverse presents. Lack of qualified personnel to handle the architecture's complexity and create safe solutions for the metaverse is one of the main problems (Vellante, 2022). Monitoring the metaverse and identifying assaults on these new platforms is more difficult than on existing platforms because of their novelty and complexity (Alspach, 2022). Regulations pertaining to cybersecurity and data privacy are behind the times when it comes to metaverse advancements. International laws like those of the European Union (EU). Due to the General Data Protection Regulation (GDPR) and other similar laws around the world, privacy compliance is now a top priority for all enterprises (Ghosh, 2018). Every attendee's biometric data, including their email address, phone number, location, gender, facial expressions, eye movements, hand gestures, and other data, would be accessible to metaverse platforms. Beyond the security and manipulation concerns with user data, the more important question is who controls this data and where it is housed. A compromise must be struck between the metaverse's handling of privacy issues and data tracking for improved consumer experience.

Data Protection and Privacy

The metaverse will give rise to new types of personal data that need to be processed in the areas of data protection and privacy. Given that businesses will be able to track biometric information, physiological reactions, and facial expressions, virtual reality platforms appear to be intrusive. As a result, the emergence of metaverse platforms presents a number of unresolved issues, including consent for data processing, accountability for lost or stolen data, and data processing responsibilities. One could argue that the metaverse is covered by the EU's General Data Protection Regulation (GDPR). Furthermore, by utilising 3D cameras, light detection and ranging sensors (LIDAR) sensors, and microphones, virtual reality (VR) glasses will analyse a variety of data regarding the private surroundings of their users in the real world, such as their home (Dwivedi et al., 2022). The metaverse will lead to new categories of personal data for processing in the realm of data protection and privacy. With businesses able to track physiological reactions, facial expressions, and biometric information, virtual reality platforms appear to be intrusive. The creation of metaverse platforms thus brings up a number of unresolved issues, including consent for data processing, accountability for lost or stolen data, and responsibility for data processing.

Insufficient Data Protection Regulation

The General Data Protection Regulation (GDPR) is not enough to control concerns about privacy in the metaverse (Creamer Media Engineering News, 2022). For example, it's unclear how the GDPR's provisions addressing the transfer and processing of data beyond the EU can be implemented because the metaverse is borderless and not separated into distinct nations. The location of the person at the time of data processing determines how the GDPR is applied. One question that may come up while processing an avatar's data is whether the location is based on the avatar itself or the person using it. In the latter instance, it is difficult to ascertain the avatar's location's jurisdiction (Lau, 2022).

Issue of Cyberbullying

Everyone can use the metaverse as an open platform. Users on metaverse platforms have occasionally been the victims of cyberbullying; one such occurrence occurred in Population One, which is currently controlled by Meta (Frenkel & Browning, 2021). Organizations such as Meta have implemented a personal space (safe zone) for every avatar in the Horizon Worlds game. This area prohibits any other avatar from entering without permission. Cyberbullying persists on metaverse platforms notwithstanding these commendable endeavours (Robertson, 2022).

Informed Consent

Users may be exposed to powerful, emotionally taxing, or even dangerous content or experiences through immersive VR and AR activities. It becomes imperative to ensure informed permission, particularly when working with vulnerable groups or when sensitive content is involved in the encounters. Users must to have the option to set boundaries or opt out, as well as sufficient information about the nature of the experience.

User Safety

Since users of VR may be completely absorbed in a virtual world and unaware of their actual surroundings, physical safety is a worry. This calls into question the moral obligations placed on developers and operators to prioritise user safety and reduce the likelihood of mishaps, injuries, or confusion (Dwivedi et al., 2022). Similar to how security lapses on the metaverse could have more negative effects than they do on the real Internet. For instance, criminals in the metaverse may target crypto-assets in addition to financial and personal information (Merre, 2022). Cyberattacks on metaverse systems have the potential to cause bodily harm in addition to financial losses. For example, it is possible to hack VR and AR headsets, which provide access to user data and put users at risk of bodily injury (Creamer Media Engineering News, 2022).

Impact on Mental Health

It is observed by psychologists that, prolonged use of VR and AR can have psychological effects on users. Ethical considerations include understanding the potential impact on mental health, such as issues related to addiction, anxiety, or the exacerbation of existing mental health conditions. Developers and content creators should consider these factors in the design and deployment of immersive experiences.

Bias and Discrimination

Applications for VR and AR could unintentionally reinforce prejudices that exist in the real world (Dwivedi et al., 2022) This may show up as exclusive design, discriminating content, or biassed algorithms. In order to guarantee that these technologies foster inclusivity and diversity rather than perpetuating societal preconceptions, ethical issues entail addressing and mitigating biases.

Ownership and Intellectual Property

Ownership and intellectual property rights are issues that arise in virtual and augmented environments. Determining the rights of users, content providers, and platform operators, assuring just pay, and prohibiting unauthorised use or manipulation of virtual assets are all ethical considerations.

Environmental Impact

Electronic waste and environmental damage may be caused by the manufacturing and disposal of VR and AR gear. Sustainable practises must be used in the development, production, and disposal of these technologies in order to reduce their environmental impact from an ethical standpoint.

POSSIBLE SOLUTIONS TO ETHICAL ISSUES IN THE AR AND VR

A comprehensive strategy encompassing developers, legislators, and industry stakeholders is needed to address the ethical issues surrounding virtual reality (VR) and augmented reality (AR). Here are some potential fixes to lessen the moral dilemmas:

Amplified Impact on Consumers and Victims

Because of its immersive qualities and cutting-edge graphic design and 3D elements, the metaverse presents a greater risk of invasive and private-invading content, which could have more dire effects for users. Programs for user awareness that emphasise the value of privacy settings and informed consent should be put in place to address this. Furthermore, in order to restrict data collecting and lessen any possible harm to users, it is imperative that metaverse platforms advocate for strict data privacy laws. This will help to provide a safer virtual environment.

Inadequate Privacy and Security Measures

In terms of privacy and security, the metaverse poses a new problem that organisations and countries are ill-equipped to address. A shortage of skilled workers and inadequate cybersecurity education make it more difficult to keep an eye out for and identify attacks in the metaverse. Investments in cybersecurity education and training initiatives are crucial in order to solve this, as is the creation and application of cutting-edge monitoring systems. Strengthening privacy and security safeguards can be achieved through industry certification programmes, regulatory revisions, and collaboration on security standards.

Insufficient Data Protection Regulation

It is believed that existing data protection laws, such as the General Data Protection Regulation (GDPR), are inadequate to address privacy concerns in the metaverse. Determining the jurisdiction for data processing presents issues due to the boundaryless nature of the metaverse. Global regulatory cooperation is required to create thorough data protection laws tailored to the metaverse in order to address this. To improve user control over their personal information in the virtual world and to assure clarity on data jurisdiction, it is possible to propose revisions to current rules and investigate user-centric data ownership models.

Privacy Protection

To secure user data, put strong data security mechanisms in place, such as encryption and anonymization. It is imperative to gain explicit agreement from consumers before to collecting or processing their personal information, and to clearly clarify data usage regulations. Create privacy-preserving technology that reduce the amount of sensitive data that central authorities store, such as decentralised identification solutions.

Informed Consent

Make clear communication a top priority to guarantee that consumers understand the nature of the VR or AR experience, any possible risks, and the scope of data gathering. Give consumers easy ways to opt-in and opt-out so they can manage how much and when they interact with potentially difficult content.

User Safety

Incorporate safety measures that stop users from unintentionally hurting themselves or other people, like boundary alerts and real-world object recognition. Set rules and specifications that put user safety first while developing VR and AR environments, especially in educational and medical contexts.

Mental Health Considerations

Investigate the psychological effects of VR and AR experiences, and apply the results to develop standards for content creation. Put in place elements that promote breaks, restrict extended exposure, and offer assistance to people who are uncomfortable or distressed.

Bias and Discrimination Mitigation

Audit content libraries and algorithms on a regular basis to find and fix biases in VR and AR applications. To guarantee a variety of viewpoints in content creation and lower the possibility of inadvertent bias, encourage diversity in development teams.

Ownership and Intellectual Property Rights

Provide precise rules and legislative frameworks for virtual property rights in order to safeguard authors' intellectual property and guarantee just recompense. Make use of distributed ledger or blockchain technology to build safe, open systems for tracking and administering virtual assets.

Security and Cybersecurity Measures

To guard against cyber dangers, unauthorised access, and data breaches, implement strong cybersecurity policies. Update firmware and software often to fix security flaws, and inform users about how to keep their VR and AR devices safe.

Environmental Sustainability

Encourage the use of eco-friendly materials and energy-efficient production techniques for producing VR and AR hardware, among other responsible manufacturing practises. Promote recycling initiatives and the creation of environmentally friendly substitutes for disposing of devices.

Industry Standards and Regulation

Establish and uphold industry norms for moral behaviour in VR and AR development by working with regulatory agencies. Encourage the creation of thorough moral standards that tackle new issues and encourage ethical innovation.

To ensure that VR and AR technologies obey ethical norms and have a good social impact, cooperation between technology developers, regulatory agencies, and user groups is necessary for the implementation of these solutions.

CONCLUSION

This study has examined the ethical issues, potential fixes, and future prospects surrounding the rapidly developing fields of virtual reality (VR) and augmented reality (AR). While integrating blockchain, virtual reality, and augmented reality into numerous industries presents disruptive prospects, it also raises ethical issues that need to be carefully considered.

The significance of protecting privacy, obtaining informed permission, putting user safety first, and addressing issues with bias, discrimination, and mental health were all brought to light by our investigation of ethical issues. The comprehensive remedies put forth—which include strong privacy protection laws, inclusive design principles, and industry standards—seek to direct stakeholders, legislators, and developers in the responsible mitigation of these ethical issues.

But as these technologies develop, the research emphasises how important it is to keep an eye out for ethical issues. Adopting VR and AR responsibly necessitates a persistent dedication to user safety, privacy, and diversity. To ensure that new technologies benefit society, it is imperative to acknowledge the possible influence on mental health and to rigorously eliminate biases.

In order to shape ethical principles, promote sustainable practises, and nurture innovation that is in accordance with society values, industry stakeholders, policymakers, and researchers must work together in the rapidly evolving field of virtual reality and augmented reality. By doing this, we may properly negotiate the morally complex landscape of immersive technologies and help to create a future in which VR and AR not only push the bounds of innovation but also improve our lives while respecting moral standards. As these technologies develop further, a promising and inclusive future in the field of augmented realities will depend on the synergy between technical advancement and ethical responsibility.

LIMITATIONS OF STUDY

The study acknowledges the lack of stakeholder or industry expert interviews. Instead, the research draws its ideas mostly from academic literature, ethical frameworks, and real-world instances, resulting in a thorough analysis of the ethical implications of augmented retail reality.

REFERENCES

Alspach, K. (2022) *Why the fate of the metaverse could hang on its security*. Venture Beat. https://venturebeat.com/2022/

Bonifacic, I. (2021). Project Cambria' is a high-end VR headset designed for Facebook's metaverse. TechCrunch. https://techcrunch.com/2021/10/28/project-cambria-is-a-high-end-vrheadset-designed-for-facebooks-metaverse

Casey, P., Baggili, I., & Yarramreddy, A. (2019). Immersive virtual reality attacks and the human joystick. *IEEE Transactions on Dependable and Secure Computing*, *18*(2), 550–562. doi:10.1109/TDSC.2019.2907942

Creamer Media Engineering News. (2022) *Meta safety Meta security*. Metaverse. https://www.engineeringnews

Damar, M. (2021). Metaverse shape of your life for future: A bibliometric snapshot. *Journal of Metaverse*, *1*(1), 1–8.

Dwivedi, Y. K., Hughes, L., Baabdullah, A. M., Ribeiro-Navarrete, S., Giannakis, M., Al-Debei, M. M., Dennehy, D., Metri, B., Buhalis, D., Cheung, C. M. K., Conboy, K., Doyle, R., Dubey, R., Dutot, V., Felix, R., Goyal, D. P., Gustafsson, A., Hinsch, C., Jebabli, I., & Wamba, S. F. (2022). Metaverse beyond the hype: Multidisciplinary perspectives on emerging challenges, opportunities, and agenda for research, practice and policy. *International Journal of Information Management*, *66*, 102542. doi:10.1016/j.ijinfomgt.2022.102542

Ghosh, D. (2018). How GDPR will transform digital marketing. *Harvard Business Review*, 2–4.

Hunter, T. (2022). *Surveillance will follow us into 'the metaverse,' and our bodies could be its new data source*.

ISACA. (2014). *Generating value from big data analytics* [White paper]. Information Systems Audit and Control Association. https://www.isaca.org/Knowledge-Center/ Research/ResearchDeliverables/Pages/Generating-Value-From-Big-Data-Analytics. aspx

Kour, M., & Rani, K. (2023). Challenges and Opportunities to the Media and Entertainment Industry in Metaverse. *Applications of Neuromarketing in the Metaverse,* 88-102.

Kshetri, N. (2014). Big data's impact on privacy, security and consumer welfare. *Telecommunications Policy*, *38*(11), 1134–1145. doi:10.1016/j.telpol.2014.10.002

Lau, P. L. (2022). The metaverse: three legal issues we need to address. *The conversation,* 1.

Lee, L. H., Braud, T., Zhou, P., Wang, L., Xu, D., Lin, Z., & Hui, P. (2021). All one needs to know about metaverse: A complete survey on technological singularity, virtual ecosystem, and research agenda. *arXiv preprint arXiv*:2110.05352.

Merre, R. (2022). *Security Will Make Or Break The Metaverse*. NASDAQ. https:// www.nasdaq.com/articles/security-will-make-or-break-themetaverse

The Verge. (2021). Mark in the Metaverse. *The Verge.* https://www.theverge. com/22588022/mark-zuckerberg-facebook-ceo-metaverse-interview

Chapter 7

Firm and Consumer Interactions in the Metaverse:
A Case Study of Indian Firms

Sonia Mukherjee
MIT World Peace University, India

ABSTRACT

Businesses are gradually shifting from the traditional models to newer business models with the adoption of metaverse. Consumers are expected to benefit immensely as a result of higher usage of metaverse technology in the different sectors such as healthcare, IT, travel and tourism, real estate, fashion brands and education, etc. India has a high potential of adopting the metaverse technology in the online gaming sector. However, numerous challenges such as dearth of investments, lack of infrastructure, dearth of rules and regulations, online fraud and harassment are part of the daily lives in today's world. Against this backdrop, the study examines the potential benefits and disadvantages of adopting the metaverse technology by business and brands and its interaction with consumers. Lastly, the study discusses the future of metaverse technology with emphasis on the gaming sector, its notable challenges associated with metaverse and the remedial measures and solutions which can be used for better integration of metaverse technology for business efficiency and consumer usage.

DOI: 10.4018/979-8-3693-4167-4.ch007

INTRODUCTION

The term Metaverse was invented by Neal Stephenson in the year 1992 in a novel. As per the novel, the term Metaverse is an all-inclusive computer-generated world that occurs in matching to the real world. In his fictional world, humans intermingle with each other in their incarnation form inside a three-dimensional computer-generated world. In the novel, operators get limitless autonomy when they perform real time communication and also build somewhat virtual environment they can perhaps visualize. Indeed, the term Metaverse has become part of today's reality. The Metaverse is a virtual 3D extension of the Internet. Metaverse is likely to revolutionize the growth of e-commerce. While creation of an google account, the user can take that account to numerous other notable websites like YouTube, Facebook and Instagram. Likewise, any avatar can be created on the Metaverse, which can be brought as the user visits different areas, podiums or worlds associated with the Metaverse link. A Metaverse avatar can also be created for work purposes. A Metaverse avatar to a work meeting held exclusively digital so individuals present anywhere in the global sphere can team up. The notion of the Metaverse denotes to the construction of computer-generated worlds which are centred from place to place to communal networks.

According to the report by **PWCs,** the Metaverse will restructure and reformulate the program of every single business and global leader. It is estimated that 82% of the Metaverse will be part of the business plans in the next coming three years and generate a need for newer skills, predominantly for the 3D entertainers and originators. Additional forecasts consist of that Artificial Intelligence could be transitional for the Metaverse as it might make it easier to generate immersive involvements and extract visions from vast quantities of data and replications, including following the action of incarnations. More than 60% of the commercial leaders surveyed by **PWC** in India confirmed that they have a thorough or good thoughtful of the Metaverse. Of the businesses surveyed, 22 percent represent Telecom, Media, and Technology (TMT), 19 percent FS, 16% pharma and healthcare, 15 percent in the retail and consumer sector, 12% industrial products, 9 percent in the government sector and 7% automotive and edtech. 79 percent of those in the TMT sector indicate that they either have a detailed or a good understanding of the domain. Globally, trades and industries have made in progress and are discovering and collaborating with some of the foremost companies in the Metaverse to discover commercial prospects. Nevertheless, the Metaverse network in India is still at a emerging stage and 25 percent of India's defendants say that their Metaverse strategies will be completely implanted in their actions within a year while 47 percent of the users say that this will take place within the time span of 2-3 years. (**PwC 2022 US Metaverse Survey, n.d.**)

According to the **reports based on the Financial Times**, the world's major fashion brands are testing in the Metaverse as they attempt to appeal to young consumers. Gucci, Burberry, Prada and Balenciaga are among the top brands involved in the process. All these notable brands are trying out all available in the Metaverse platform from using augmented reality to permit handlers to try on 3D versions of fashion before purchasing the actual object, and offering NFT proprietors the chance to purchase customized jewellery. According to the **news report,** approximately two-thirds (64 per cent) of the consumers located globally including those who are in India, have purchased a virtual good or have taken participation in a virtual experience in the previous years. The figure shows a rise of 83 per cent users showing keen interest in making their purchases through the applications of Metaverse. Furthermore, 42 per cent of respondents located globally, including in India, have visited a retailer in the virtual or digital world to get some form of advice and do some transactions or browse for a wide range of product for purchasing a physical item. Half (50 per cent) of consumers preferred buying a travel experience in the form of sightseeing tour or a hotel stay. For entertainment or leisure related experience, 54 per cent of consumers were interested in buying, tickets to a concert, or watching a show or attending a sporting event taking place in the digital world. (**Financial Times**)

According to the **global survey done by Accenture**, the increasing or rapid usage of the immersive technologies in various forms such as augmented and virtual reality will result in more usage of these applications by the companies working in the domain of the consumer sector. For example, business located in the retail sector, businesses and firms pertaining to consumer goods and travel sector will enhance their investment in the newer applications offered by Metaverse and provide an unique experience to blend both the physical and the virtual worlds. In other words, by embracing the latest form of technology in the form of Metaverse, the businesses have a higher chance to reinvent the consumer experiences and device newer ways of offering products and services. Nearly around half of the consumers agreed to the fact that with time they are gradually shifting their livelihoods towards the digital spaces. (*What is the metaverse?,* **2024**)

Deloitte's report, "**Metaverse: The Hype Possibilities and Beyond**" indicated that one of the main drivers driving the the Metaverse will be Web3.0's. It will have the ability to spur the digital transformation in the future. In addition to this, the Metaverse will be an enabling factor in boost the Indian Media and Entertainment sector. For example, newer avenues such as tapping the engineering graphics, video and animation will be done through the vast pool of Indian engineers. Newer emerging technologies will evolve over time and drive the digital transformation and redefine the customer experience of using these technologies. Firms and business will continue to adopt these numerous technologies for better and superior customer experience at a reasonable cost. (*Metaverse: The Hype Possibilities and Beyond,* **2022**)

Lastly, the **Nasscom** research titled " **Metaverse-Prepare to Win**" indicated that the IT sector has been working on the different Metaverse themes for performing internal business operations. This will assist in matters of customer-centric cases. Some IT companies are gradually developing internal use cases to serve the customer needs in the future time-period. For example, a prominent IT company Infosysis have started to see some good quality projects related to Augmented Reality and Virtual Reality. This caters to the different sectors including the manufacturing, retail, education training, and maintenance context. Lastly, the adoption level of the Metaverse may significantly vary across the Indian industries depending on demand and its benefits for consumers. (*Metaverse – Prepare to Win*, n.d.)

Application of Metaverse in Different Sectors

The adoption of Metaverse technology in the different sectors is offering its users an unique experience through technologies such as the virtual reality and augmented reality experience. For instance, the real estate sector can immensely profit from the usage of Metaverse technology. With the help of the Metaverse Technology, property tour options using virtual tour can help the the property owners and real estate owners to not travel to the original locations. For example, if the property is located in Delhi, the clients interested in purchasing or verifying the property will not waste time in travelling to the original location. Instead, the prospective client can take a Metaverse real estate tour in a digital environment. This is true for the other clients also. The virtual tour will be an alternative to physical tours and can be adopted according to the customer's scale, opinion, taste and design. The Real Estate sector is seriously looking forward to investing in the applications developed by the Metaverse technology. By catering to the needs of several clients, the virtual tour options offered through the Metaverse technology will further be economical for the consumers and property buyers and will in turn boost the sales and revenue of the real estate sector. This holds true for the health care sector too. In the domain of the Healthcare sector, the applications of Metaverse technology have opened newer avenues and channels for delivering treatments at an economical and cheaper rate. With enhanced usage of the new technology have led to improved outcomes for the customers. Furthermore, with the onset of the newer concept in the healthcare sector field such as "Tele-medicine" and "Tele-health" emerging over time, the usage of the Metaverse technology have increased manifold in the post pandemic era. Patients and doctors have simultaneously started interacting in a virtual 3D clinics for the purpose of medical consultation and treatment. Another prominent example of Metaverse application in the healthcare sector is the "**Application Therapy**". The advantage of this therapy is that the patients needing treatments need not come physically to the medical professional. However, in times of need they can transport themselves to a calmer and peaceful digital environment in special situations associated with severe panic, tension and anxiety. Newer and innovative Metaverse applications have evolved for patients and consumers as recommended from time to time by expert medical professionals. Prominent examples are different forms of digital workouts and exercises recommended by medical experts. Another notable and significant reference of Metaverse adoption in the health care sector is the application of the Digital Twin Technology. The application enables a patient's virtual or digital representation and thereafter performing treatments and providing medicines as per the needs.

In the **Banking and Finance sector**, the Metaverse technologies are gradually being integrated. The banking Metaverse technology is providing a 360 degree overview of the physical banks to the consumers. The consumer can be located in any place and can perform an endless number of banking services even if the consumer does not possess a Virtual Reality headset. The consumer can easily access the Metaverse banking through other notable devices in the form of laptops, iPad, tablets or mobile devices. Metaverse technology is evolving as one of the greatest advantage to the banking sector from the perspective of the Block Chain Technology, Non Functional Tokens (NFT), Other marketplace development and other DeFi crypto currency assets. The Metaverse banking is a crucial step and is found to be superior to the normal net banking experiences. The customers using the application can get the services with better experiences and data visualization.

For the **Media and Entertainment Industry**, the Metaverse technology have radically transformed the online entertainment for audiences. Users are communicating though digital modes using an appropriate digital avatars and virtual clones. Facebook have changed its name and now it is represented through Meta which denotes huge business opportunities and prospects in the virtual or digital media space. Similarly, Metaverse applications are gradually being adopted in some of the notable sectors such as sportswear, fashion and e-commerce industry. Many notable fashion brands are launching limited editions of virtual apparel for the customers to explore in the virtual world. In addition to this, it is complemented with the help of virtual try-on-features further provided by the e-commerce platforms and websites. Customers can envision how a particular merchandise would look on them before they are making the actual purchase

In the Travel and Tourism sector, Virtual tourism is gaining prominence. It has become of one the promising sector for the usage of Metaverse technology. The technology will allow the users to travel in a virtual environment. The consumers having health issues or having budgetary constraints or unable to travel to longer distance can use the virtual tour mode offered by the technology developed by Metaverse. In addition, sometimes consumers are unable to travel long distances due to paucity of time or not allowed to travel due to the location being declared a "hotspot" or environmentally vulnerable zone. In such cases, the virtual tourism option comes with an innovative solution. The immersive digital experience with the help of Augmented Reality and Virtual Reality and the 360 degree virtual tour, benefits the consumer present digitally in the desired location.The realistic experience gained by the consumers will be very much similar to the physical one. A prominent and famous travel and tourism firm, Thomas Cook have launched the Virtual Reality Holiday "*Try before you Fly*". The potential tourists can visit their desired destinations virtually before actually going the actual location.

In terms of delivering **quality education,** the Metaverse technology is not far behind. The technology is gaining prominence in the education sector. For example, in a New York, school students had a great learning experience in the subject astronomy using a virtual spaceship. Another notable example is Mesh created by the prominent IT firm Microsoft. It offers a mixed reality platform and there is social interaction among the faculty, staff and students using the 3D virtual avatars. Mesh is being used mainly to attend video conferences and other forms of live sessions.

The application of Metaverse technology is leading to a massive shift from the traditional business model to virtual business model. Many companies are already working towards the virtual business architecture. Examples include the virtual office enterprises such as the Nike, Intel, YouTube, McDonald's in addition to the latest emerging startups such as Gravity Sketch and Upland.

Application of Metaverse Since the Covid-19 Pandemic

The onset of the Covid-19 pandemic has necessitated a shift of business models. Fir instance, more and more businesses are gradually shifting towards using advanced e-commerce platforms as per the requirements of the consumers. There has been a speedy shift from the from brick-and-mortar stores to the internet or online mode of business. With increase in the adoption of the Metaverse technology, it is further adding to a third space. Marketers have a deep desire to develop an comprehensive, and well-planned strategy in the sphere of Metaverse retailing. It is expected to garner positive response and be more product-oriented in nature for the benefits received by the various businesses (**Bourlakis et al., 2009**). The research done in the field of Metaverse retailing has mainly focused on improving the quality of the virtual retail services (**Gadalla et al., 2013**) and identifying the factors leading to better services being provided to the users or customers (e.g., **Hassouneh & Brengman, 2015**).

Consumer habits, tastes and preferences are changing. The inclination has shifted more towards the digital world (**Shah and Murti, 2021**). Consumers located worldwide have indicated their preference for shopping via online channels. The interaction of brands become easier (**Elmasry et al., 2022, Wunderman Thompson, 2021**). There has been a rapid increase in the firms' investments in numerous digital platforms that is assisting and aiding the digital environments (Holmes, 2021). Combined all these factors are highly supportive and is expected to contribute to the growth of the *'metaverse'*. *The Metaverse* is expected *to* fundamentally change the way consumers, brands, and firms transact and interact with each other. Many consider that the Metaverse has the potency of radically changing the business and societal life on a level in comparison to the Internet (**Bobier et al., 2022, Elmasry et al., 2022, Foutty and Bechte, 2022, Hackl, 2021, Morino, 2022, Sullivan, 2021**). The promise delivered by the Metaverse Technology is gradually being accelerated with the increasing adoption, consumer usage and increase in the number of transactions in the digital world. Similarly, numerous business, brands and firms are also investing millions of dollars in developing newer Metaverse related technology with higher technological revolution. **Giang and Shah (2023)** in their study discussed how Metaverse would contribute to better marketing practices. The study further proposed a innovative research agenda for better marketing initiatives in the future time.

The Covid-19 pandemic has further augmented the need of Metaverse as it substitutes actual social communication with the digital world anywhere and customers can interact with each other. This motivated many companies and firms to grasp this chance to enlarge their goods and service into the Metaverse stage. For example, in November 2020, Roblox, an online gaming stage hosts its opening virtual show during the epidemic which involved 12.3 million simultaneous companies. Moreover, the upsurge in work-from-home values and social distancing rules that were fused during COVID-19 pandemic facilitated in promoting for higher demand for diverse Metaverse Podiums. It is projected that a quarter of the people will be in Metaverse for one hour a day in the coming time. Letting customers to imagine and intermingle with products in AR and VR will blur the borderline between computer-generated and in-person shopping involvements which makes the customers less probable to return goods that do not match the explanation provided in the product. As a result, less customers will be returning online purchases.

Various businesses and firms have started opting the latest technology to accomplish their goals and needs aligned with the demands and requirements of the businesses and clients. It is expected that the global Metaverse market will reach approximately **USD427.9 billion** by the year 2027 with a positive growth rate of 48.2 percent. The market was worth an amount of USD 62.8 billion in the year 2022. Many international and global firms have recognized the benefits of using the Metaverse technology. For example, in case of the business entity J.P. Morgan have established its branch through use of the Metaverse technology and started offering numerous forms of services to its customers since the year February 2022 (**Shevlin, 2022**). Prominent luxury brands such as Gucci and Ralph Lauren have also developed virtual stalls for selling their products. For example, digital clothes sold in Roblox (**Wong, 2022**). Different hotel groups including Citizen M and EV Hotel Corporation have started developing virtual hotels in the Sandbox app to engage and provide services with hotel customers (**Sheper & Speros, 2022**).

The Metaverse delivers adequately number of opportunities for firms to offer their products and attach with their clienteles and supporters and further involve them over virtual immersive involvements and understandings. Numerous brands can therefore use the Metaverse platforms in contributing an immersive experience which is alike to the experience already received while perusing a store in the physical presence of a person. For instance, real estate actions can use this kind of computer-generated models for customers to visit. The know-how can also promote the hybrid office model through inventive explanations, permitting individuals to team up and work via online mode.

Attractive marketing and improved customer experiences- Both technology intensive and non-technology intensive companies such as FMCG, clothing and other Apparel Firms can take advantage from use of the Metaverse platforms through numerous advertising, selling and distribution opportunities. The Metaverse will help in enormously personalized practices and collaborating engagement with clienteles. This will provide assistance to businesses for improved understanding of their clienteles and grow a permanent association with the customers. Further, the Metaverse applications can also play an enormous part in client retention and newer engagement for any commercial business.

The higher degree of immersion and interconnection will allow healthy buying patterns in the future. With time, many other forms of innovations are happening in the Metaverse, and is expected to enhance the rate of customers virtual involvements. Customers sections based on the dissemination of novelty and innovation theory will be willing to link the Metaverse as demonstrated by its increasing popularity in societal interacting opportunities, individual and specialized collaborations, the crossing point and interoperability of the platform, and the determined hard work in enhancing real-world understandings. Thus, as the Metaverse progresses and prominent firms and brands reinforce their advertising, selling and promotion strategies, many uncharted prospects will arise possibly helping both the notable global brands and customers. Consumers will buy a new range of virtual products in the Metaverse and further buy their avatar's outfits as per the requirements(**Belk et al. 2022**).

LEADING COMPANIES USING METAVERSE FOR CONSUMER INTERACTION

With the increase in the demand for the numerous Metaverse technology around the globe, many businesses and firms are converting projects with the assistance of Metaverse technology. Some potential Metaverse development companies in India are helping in this direction. The reason for higher collaboration with the Indian companies are many. Some notable factors are wider domestic markets, presence of a dynamic start-up ecosystem and availability of large pool of skilled labor in the future.

AWS is one of the prominent company and views the industrial Metaverse as changing the perception over people's relationship with the virtual or digital world. The users can incorporate the technology such as Augmented Reality and Virtual Reality to provide an immersive representation. All these potential solutions can help in improving the decision-making process, and further engage in fruitful collaboration . Its purpose-built cloud products include AWS, IoT Twin Maker to optimize operations with digital twins .

NVIDA is said to have a wide range of goods, products and services within the technology sector. The company is one of the world's leading graphics processing unit (GPU) developers. It is also one of the Metaverse 's largest investors. The company's platform provides a gamut of tools to make it easy for customers to create and customize their own virtual worlds.

Other prominent company such as **Google** has created several VR and AR products and launched in the market for numerous uses. The prominent examples include Google Glass, Google Cardboard and the Daydream VR headset. The company has also developed ARCore, an augmented reality application found on the Android devices. The focus of the company is developing and enhancing immersive technologies which allows customers to experience innovative and customized virtual environments. Google Starline, the most recent Metaverse project aims to use a combination of computer vision, machine learning and spatial audio to create an unique shared immersive experience for the customers.

The Apple mixed-reality (MR) headset was launched in the year 2023 and is expected to provide good MR experiences with more than half of consumers interested in using the latest technology.

Microsoft is one of the firms developing the Metaverse technology in collaboration with other firms. The firm has partnered with Meta to deliver future immersive experiences One of the firm's new Metaverse offering is Microsoft Mesh, which is a platform. It enables the users to connect and collaborate in mixed reality technology across different devices across numerous locations. The platform allows users to to interact with each other and with higher digital content in a intuitive way.

Meta have identified itself as a new brand in the year 2021. Furthermore, it has shifted its focus or target to development of newer technology and applications related to the Metaverse Technology. Presently, it is providing different information and services on different types of Metaverse applications such as the Virtual Reality, Augmented Reality and smart glasses, with imaginative ideas and interoperable applications being developed for the users for day to day purposes. The objective of the firm is to see that the Metaverse technology will work to transform the education sector, and other notable industries ranging from the healthcare, mechanics, and engineering etc.

Meta Horizon Worlds has a strong focus on the user-generated content and further encourages users to make and share their own experiences in the virtual world. Metaverse has the ability to duplicate the real-world using radical technologies in the forms of AR and VR. Metaverse is the next face to internet and social media and offers different business possibility to organization around the globe.

Companies and businesses such as **Target, Amazon**, and **Ikea** are pickings advantages of this opportunity. Other firms associated with the travel and tourism are offering numerous virtual tours of their goods or services to the customers in an rapid way. Other prominent examples include **Honda** collaborating a virtual agreement where clienteles can explore cars, get price quotes, take test drives and even schedule service. Other businesses such as Walmart have also created a custom-made 3D shopping participation that customer's can admittance from anywhere in the world. The luxury brand car "Audi" has launched a collaborating with the virtual showroom that have allowed customers to explore a wide range of cars and even go for a test-drive before the actual purchase. In the healthcare sector, companies including **Walgreens** have been offering some form of virtual doctor visits for their customers who needed some form of medical care and assistance but cannot physically visit their office. The business entity **Target** further launched the 3D experiences that allows for customers to explore various products and purchased them directly from the virtual store. Business firms **IKEA a**re using the Metaverse to provide customers with an immersive shopping experience by offering 3D models of their different forms of furniture that can be seen in a customer's home before making a purchase. These examples show how different industries influence and use the numerous applications of Metaverse to provide sole, appealing experience for their customers.

Indian companies such as **Mahindra and Mahindra**, **Tanishq,** and **MakeMyTrip** have ventured into the Metaverse space and are paving the road to the digital future.

Prominent Jewellery brand Tanishq have recently launched its wedding collection titled "**Romance of Polki**" in the 3D display zones where signature pieces from the collection has been displayed. The audience has the option to view the jewellery pieces in the 3D and the potential visitor could also try on the showstopper piece by scanning the QR code. Another notable example of business firm is **CEAT Limited**, It is one of India's largest tyre manufacturers and have created its own '**Ceat Shoppe**' in the Metaverse by integration with their e-commerce platform. Purchasers and clienteles will be able to view products of the company in 3D and book the orders at the same time. A pick-up facility from the physical stores is also planned for the purpose. **Mahindra & Mahindra** had auctioned four **Thar-themed NFTs,** costing around Rs 26 lakh. The Winners of the auction had got the chance to have off-road experience to drive the Thar. The travel firm **MakeMyTrip**, have recently launched its virtual vacation followed by **MG Motor India** who have future plans to launch a total of 1,110 NFTs starting at Rs 500. **IT giant Infosys** had launched the "**Infosys Metaverse Foundry**" helping companies and firms create their own Metaverse environment.

THE GAMING INDUSTRY AND THE USAGE OF METAVERSE

The Indian Metaverse industry have grown significantly in the recent years. Reports by **NASSCOM**, have predicted that the Indian gaming industry will increase at a steady pace in the coming years. The popularity of virtual reality devices have also contributed to the growth of Indian Metaverse Industry. The markets for VR and AR is expected to reach a figure of around $1.38 billion by the year 2025. Another major drivers of growth of Metaverse industry is the rise of startups that are providing and developing innovative solutions. Numerous Indian startups are working in creation of the virtual worlds and immersive experiences for its end users. These startups are attracting investment and contributing to the growth of this market (*Metaverse – Prepare to Win*, **n.d.**).

Video games are playing a vital role in the growth of the Indian Metaverse Industry This growth has driven by increasing popularity of video games and the rise of new gaming platforms in the form of mobile gaming. This has further given rise to new gaming technologies in the forms of virtual reality and games listings. Many video game developers are using the VR technology into their games with a target to provide immersive experience to the users or players. In the multiplayer online games using the Metaverse applications, users can interact with each other in virtual worlds. The gaming industry in India have transformed rapidly in the recent years through further technological advancement and rapid expansion of the digital infrastructure. In addition to this, the rise in internet connectivity from 2G to 5G including a high bandwidth have increased the growth of the gaming sector. Some estimates predict that by the year 2024, the market for video games will earn a revenue of $363.20 billion by 2027. Mobile gaming is believed to be the driving force behind the driving of the global video gaming market.

The future pace of gaming in India is driven by a combination of trends, technological advancement, introduction of Artificial Intelligence, government support and global integration to the growth of the gaming sector. Moreover the emergence of tech savvy population has fueled the demand for gaming and the rise of esports culture has contributed to gaming monetization in India. The gaming industry market size is estimated at $272.86 billion on 2024 and is predicted to reach $426.02 billion by 2029 with a CAGR of 9.32% between 2024 and 2029. Additionally,the growing investment in game development and the rise in gaming as a form of social interaction reshaped the industry because a growing number of Indians are now turning to casual games for entertainment accessing powerful gaming devices and improving internet connectivity with the merging affordable 5G network plan in India.

There seems to be major qualities and elements affected by Metaverse application in gaming.The Metaverse users will interact with the world in a way that fosters social connections, connect real world friends, form bonds with them, and will acquire a new dimension in the gaming sector. .The 3D universe that Metaverse provides for users will create a huge opportunity for the gaming industry and help the gaming world to be one of the major sectors using Metaverse. Metaverse, users can be immersed in a three-dimensional environment and can interact more personally with the elements available around them. This collaboration is a great technique to generate augmented reality when interacting in the games and taking part in the play-to-earn gaming with Non Functional Tokens, and will cater towards a deeper connection with the overall world.

However, there are few challenges within the gaming sector to shape the future of gaming in India. Firstly, India's transformation into a gaming powerhouse requires infrastructure development, improved internet connectivity and investment in data centers to maintain the future of gaming in India. Secondly, the policies and laws are essential steps to foster a favorable environment for the gaming industry in terms of game development, distribution and monetization. Thirdly, Indian gaming industry has grown internationally. Hence, developers should facilitate market expansion and partner with foreign gaming studios for maintaining the future of gaming in India.

Some of the **prominent international gaming businesse**s are rapidly using the Metaverse platform. For example, in the gaming sector, **Epic games is** one of the leading companies holding numerous virtual events with the help of the applications of Metaverse. The company have raised around US$2bn in the year 2022 to fund the other Metaverse projects including Unreal Engine to portray immersive experiences for players in the game in a simulated environment. **Unity Gaming Services** (UGS) is helping the developers to create, operate, and is now being widely used by industrial users for the digital twin solutions. After further acquisitions, of the **Weta Digital, Unity Firm** is relentlessly working to accelerate the growth and development of

3D technologies. **Decentraland** is a another prominent virtual reality platform, and users can access the platform by connecting the platform to a crypto wallet. 3D static scenes are generated and the users are engaged in an interactive gaming experiences **Tencent,** a notable technology-enabled company and have published some notable video games. In July 2023, Tencent had signed a Memorandum of Understanding (MoU) with the firm Morpheus Labs to drive **Web3gaming and Metaverse** innovation.()

NUMEROUS CHALLENGES BEHIND ADOPTION OF METAVERSE

The prominent emergence of the Metaverse technology has led to increasing levels of scholarly discourse and argument on the potential benefits and its impact at a social level. The numerous Metaverse applications are offering newer and active levels of interaction and offering newer opportunities, transformed and innovative business models (**Chayka, 2021**). However, the rapid adoption of Metaverse Technology and its applications poses numerous challenges related to the issues such as governance, ethics, safety, security, behaviour, privacy and mentality of sections of the people unable to use the Metaverse due to infrastructural deficiency (**Fernandez and Hui, 2022**; **Haimson and Hoffmann, 2016**). With the introduction of new technology comes all these challenges. The several technological, legal, and ethical issues must be addressed. One of the biggest and most prominent challenges is the need for advanced technology to support the Metaverse, As it currently stands, most existing hardware and software cannot support the high level of interactivity and immersion that Metaverse demands. Companies and individuals will need to invest in newer and more efficient technology to participate fully in the Metaverse. Another major challenge is the issue of privacy and security. With so much personal data being exchanged in the Metaverse, there is a risk of data breaches and other cyber threats. Companies and individuals will need to protect their information and ensure that they comply with all relevant data protection laws.

Firms that are presently active in the Metaverse domain has to ensure that they take care of the privacy issues in their own systems and examine the risk taken by the company in terms of Metaverse adoption and how to minimize the risks as per the needs of the company. Besides, there are tax treatment and different limits which are present while conducting different forms of financial transactions. With times, numerous forms of digital assets acquired through the help of Metaverse are also evolving over time. This raises some form of concern as there are newer possibilities of financial crimes evolving over time due to rise of newer dynamic technologies and their rapid adoption by the newer businesses. In the future, various cyber protocols, rules, regulations and newer guidelines have to be laid to gain the the customer's trust in matters of using and adopting the application of Metaverse. It is advisable to focus on publishing reports, constant sharing of information, experiences and knowledge of newer technology adoption to keep the consumers up-to-date with the current developments of the businesses and firms and the different risks associated with them.

Finally, there are some different ethical considerations while using the Metaverse applications. For instance, the Metaverse can create a newer type of digital divide in the forms of have and haves not. Some businesses and consumers may have the potential to use the Metaverse in their favor and be ahead in terms of competition. Accompanied by this, there might be a greater risk of addiction and negative impacts on the mental health of consumers using Metaverse for its greater benefits.

Metaverse adoption depends on the the level of economic and technological barriers present in the economy. Furthermore, the pace of adoption will be driven by the cost of devices used for the adoption of Metaverse such as Virtual Reality, different types of headsets, Smart wearable and the ability to nurture the latest technical skills and readiness to reskill and acquire knowledge. As different notable brands make forays into the Metaverse, the marketing strategies of the firms and businesses will be essential for their success in the future. The Metaverse will give access to unknown and positive opportunities to marketers to reach the tentative customers and give them an immersive experience. However, the marketing possibility in the Metaverse is highly experimental and is still at the nascent stage. Hence, it has different challenges for the marketers (**Hazan et al., 2022**). These further include technical and infrastructural considerations related to the accessibility and ability to afford different hardware and software, and other challenges. For the Indian firms, there are still numerous challenges for steady adoption of Metaverse which needs to be urgently addressed.

One of the biggest notable challenge is the deficiency of infrastructure and dearth of investment. For addressing such challenges,the Government of India needs to play a crucial role in the development of the infrastructure and provide necessary support to the business firms for a big time investment in the domain of Metaverse at a subsidized rate. There is also a need to address the regulatory issues in terms of privacy for the usage of data and ensure that the data is safe. Other important issues to be addressed are the issues related to cyber-crime, fraud, and online harassment which have increased at a rapid pace in this digital or virtual world. However, in spite of the barriers and obstacles faced from time to time, the Indian Metaverse industry holds a bigger promise for rapid growth and innovation.

CONCLUSION

The Metaverse is rapidly increasing its domain and its expansion is benefiting the numerous sector with the adoption of latest technology available in the market. Firms and businesses are experimenting with various Metaverse technology including augmented reality, digital 3D technologies. This is expected to help the industry or firms to increase its revenue to USD $615 billion by the year 2030. Metaverse can assist numerous business and industries through its usage and the virtual worlds holds the potential to become more immersive in the future period of time. (*Value creation in the metaverse*, 2022).

In case of the Indian Economy, the Metaverse industry have already made a good impact for the gaming industry. Other notable industries experiencing subsequent benefits from Metaverse are travel industry, health care sector, automobile sectors, jewellery sector, real estate sector and automobiles sectors. The growth of the Metaverse industry is expected to drive innovation and offer a new form of platform for businesses to reach out to the customers and display their brands in the domestic as well as international markets. One of the advantages given by the Metaverse industry is providing newer avenues for growth of digital commerce. As a result, this could further help boost the the Indian businesses and companies and give them further options to explore and reach to newer customers in the newer markets. Another potential of the adoption of the latest Metaverse technology is to enhance and boost growth in the promising Indian technology sector. Newer startups will emerge and help to develop newer forms of solutions in the coming time.

The success of the use of Metaverse and its penetration will depend on how much time the firms, organizations and businesses take to understand its importance in building its empire and future development. Newer technical skills and readiness have to be there in place with the increasing number of cyber-crimes, threats are there to thwart its adoption in the long run. With the growing awareness the different application possibilities, business will be likely to reorient their existing business models to take advantage of growing technology. Metaverse is currently offering the possibility of remote work potential for the business using the Metaverse technology. With the ability to create virtual offices and collaborate tools, the Metaverse offers an alternative to traditional office spaces. This can be especially valuable for companies looking to reduce their physical footprint or have employees working in different locations. The Metaverse offers entrepreneurs and startups a unique opportunity to create and test new products and services in a virtual environment. This can be a precious tool for companies looking to experiment with new ideas before investing in physical infrastructure or resources. Finally, the Metaverse has the potential to impact the gig economy significantly. With more companies and individuals working remotely, the Metaverse could become a hub for freelancers and independent contractors looking to connect with clients and collaborate on projects.

FUTURE OF THE METAVERSE TECHNOLOGY

Business firms have started taking the advantage offered by the Metaverse Technology. Metaverse has the potential to take the advertising done by the companies for displaying their product or brand to another level by using an unique form of storytelling experiences, that is, via using the 3D form of technology.The applications of Metaverse will help the businesses to conduct and enter into any event organized in a virtual mode. Different forms of Brands can have an interaction in the global forum with higher involvement of international audience. Metaverse is rapidly integrating with the e-commerce business framework despite the different challenges including territorial barriers. Metaverse is also supporting digital wallets and payments denoting that enterprises can conduct and monitor different forms of transactions performed in the digital ecosystem.

There are numerous benefits that businesses can reap by rapidly integrating with the applications of Metaverse. In the coming times, every notable business and firms will leverage Metaverse applications as per the needs of the business model and needs of the consumers. A recent survey conducted by **Statista** in March 2022 have revealed some promising statistics. It has been found that approximately 17% of the global IT enterprise and companies have already invested in the numerous applications of Metaverse. Meanwhile, the other promising industry sectors such as Education, Finance, Healthcare, and Marketing still in the process of adopting the Metaverse. The rate of adoption is between 9-12 percent. (**Clement, 2022**)

With the rise in the adoption rate of Metaverse technology, the Gaming industry is proving to be one of the major leading investors in terms of investing in the Metaverse technology. The Metaverse technology is providing an unique platform to the players to socially interact with the other users or players in the single interoperable environment. The most popular games which have evolved in the arena of Metaverse are games such as the Sandbox, Sorare and Axie Infinity. All these games are operating in the online gaming sector through the assistance of Metaverse Technology. Figures indicate that the game Axie Infinity is currently possessing over 350,000 average active daily players. In addition to this, it has crossed approximately 3 million monthly users. The main advantage of Metaverse games are that they have special features including a fully fledged social environment where every single user stays connected with each other. Metaverse application games are also having the ability and advantage to play and earn crypto -currency. Hence, the economic criteria gets fulfilled. Lastly, Metaverse is giving a mixed reality experiences where the players or users can switch between different formats or modes of communication within the digital world. (***Insights on the metaverse and the future of gaming, n.d.***).

REFERENCES

Barnes, S. J., & Mattsson, J. (2011). Exploring the Fit of Real Brands in the Second Life Virtual World. *Journal of Marketing Management, 27*(9-10), 934–958. doi:1 0.1080/0267257X.2011.565686

Belk, R., Humayun, M., & Brouard, M. (**2022**). Money, possessions, and ownership in the Metaverse: NFTs, cryptocurrencies, Web3 and Wild Markets. *Journal of Business Research, 153.*

Bobier, J., Mérey, T., Robnett, S., Grebe, M., Feng, J., Rehberg, B., Woolsey, K., & Hazan, J. (2022). *The Corporate Hitchhiker's Guide to the Metaverse.* BCG. https://on.bcg.com/3arrxsA

Bourlakis, M., Papagiannidis, S., & Li, F. (2009). Retail Spatial Evolution: Paving the Way from Traditional to Metaverse Retailing. *Electronic Commerce Research, 9*(1-2), 135–148. doi:10.1007/s10660-009-9030-8

Chayka, K. (**2021**). We already live in Facebook's metaverse. *The New Yorker.* https://www.newyorker.com/culture/infinite-scroll/we-alreadylive-in-facebooks-metaverse

Clement, J. (2022). *Leading business sectors already investing in the metaverse 2022.* Statista. https://www.statista.com/statistics/1302091/global-business-sectors-investing-in-the-metaverse/

Dwivedi, Y. K., Hughes, L., Baabdullah, A. M., Ribeiro-Navarrete, S., Giannakis, M., Al-Debei, M. M., Dennehy, D., Metri, B., Buhalis, D., Cheung, C. M. K., Conboy, K., Doyle, R., Dubey, R., Dutot, V., Felix, R., Goyal, D. P., Gustafsson, A., Hinsch, C., Jebabli, I., & Wamba, S. F. (2022). Metaverse beyond the hype: Multidisciplinary perspectives on emerging challenges, opportunities, and agenda for research, practice and policy. *International Journal of Information Management, 66,* 102542. doi:10.1016/j.ijinfomgt.2022.102542

Dwivedi, Y. K., Hughes, L., Wang, Y., Alalwan, A. A., Ahn, S. J., Balakrishnan, J., Barta, S., Belk, R., Buhalis, D., Dutot, V., Felix, R., Filieri, R., Flavián, C., Gustafsson, A., Hinsch, C., Hollensen, S., Jain, V., Kim, J., Krishen, A. S., & Wirtz, J. (2023). Metaverse marketing: How the metaverse will shape the future of consumer research andpractice. [AL.]. *Psychology and Marketing, 40*(4), 750776. doi:10.1002/mar.21767

Elmasry, T., Hazan, E., Hamza, K., Kelly, G., Srivastava, S., Yee, L. & Zemmel, R.W. (2022). *Value creation in the metaverse: The real business of the virtual world.*

Fernandez, C. B., & Hui, P. (2022). Life, the Metaverse and Everything: An Overview of Privacy. Ethics, and Governance in *Metaverse. arXiv preprint* arXiv.01480 doi:10.1109/ICDCSW56584.2022.00058

Foutty, J., & Bechte, M. (2022). *What's all the buzz about the metaverse?* https://bit.ly/3bRH313

Gadalla, E., Keeling, K., & Abosaq, I. (2013). Metaverse-Retail Service Quality: A Future Framework for Retail Service Quality in the 3D Internet. *Journal of Marketing Management*, *29*(13-14), 1493–1517. doi:10.1080/0267257X.2013.835742

Giang Barrera, K., & Shah, D. (2023). Marketing in the Metaverse: Conceptual understanding, framework, and research agenda. *Journal of Business Research, 155*(Part A). *Journal of Business Research*, *113420*, 113420. doi:10.1016/j.jbusres.2022.113420

Hackl, C. (2021). *Defining The Metaverse Today.* https://bit.ly/3NVvvHs

Haimson, O. L., & Hoffmann, A. L. (2016). Constructing and enforcing" authentic" identity online: Facebook, real names, and non-normative identities. *First Monday*. doi:10.5210/fm.v21i6.6791

Hassouneh, D., & Brengman, M. (2015). Metaverse Retailing: Are SVW Users Ready to Buy Real Products from Virtual World Stores? In P. Kommers, P. Isarias, & H. Fernandez Betancort (Eds.), *Proceedings of the 12th International IADIS Conference on e-Commerce and Digital Marketing (EC 2015): Multi Conference on Computer Science and Information Systems (MCCSI2015)* (pp. 104-110). IEEE.

Hazan, E., Kelly, G., Khan, H., Spillecke, D., & Yee, L. (2022). *Marketing in the metaverse: An opportunity for innovation and experimentation.*

Insights on the metaverse and the future of gaming. (n.d.). EY. https://www.ey.com/en_us/insights/media-entertainment/what-s-possible-for-the-gaming-industry-in-the-next-dimension/chapter-3-insights-on-the-metaverse-and-the-future-of-gaming

Metaverse – Prepare to Win. (n.d.). NASSCOM. https://www.nasscom.in/knowledge-center/publications/metaverse-prepare-win

Metaverse: The Hype Possibilities and Beyond. (2022, December). Deloitte. https://www2.deloitte.com/content/dam/Deloitte/in/Documents/technology/in-metaverse-2022-report-noexp.pdf

128

Morino, N. (2022). *Metaverse: 5 questions shaping the next frontier of human experience.* EY. https://www.ey.com/en_tw/digital/metaverse-5-questions-shaping-the-next-frontier-of-human-experience

PwC 2022 US Metaverse Survey. (n.d.). PwC. https://www.pwc.com/us/en/tech-effect/emerging-tech/metaverse-survey.html

Shah, D., & Murthi, B. P. S. (2021). Marketing in a data-driven digital world: Implications for the role and scope of marketing. *Journal of Business Research*, *125*(March), 772–779. doi:10.1016/j.jbusres.2020.06.062

Sheper, A., & Speros, W. (2022). *The hotel industry enters the Metaverse.* Hospitality Design. https://hospitalitydesign.com/news/development-destinations/hotel-industry-nfts -metaverse/

Shevlin, R. (2022). JP Morgan opens a bank branch in the metaverse. *Forbes.* https://www.forbes.com/sites/ronshevlin/2022/02/16/jpmorgan-opens-a-bank-bra nch-in-the-metaverse-but-its-not-for-what-you-think-its-for/?sh=9e1cf2c158d3

Sullivan, M. (2021). *What the metaverse will (and won't) be, according to 28 experts.* FastCompany. https://www.fastcompany.com/90678442/what-is-the-metaverse

Value creation in the metaverse. (2022, June). McKinsey. https://www.mckinsey.com/~/media/mckinsey/business%20functions/marketing%20and%20sales/our%20insights/value%20creation%20in%20the%20metaverse/Value-creation-in-the-metaverse.pdf

What is the metaverse? (2024). Accenture. https://www.accenture.com/in-en/insights/metaverse

Wong, Q. **(2022)**. Shopping in the Metaverse could be more fun than you think. Cnet. https://www.cnet.com/tech/computing/features/shopping-in-the-metaversecould-be-more-fun-than-you-think/

Wunderman Thompson Intelligence. (2021). *Into the Metaverse.* WTI. https://www.wundermanthompson.com/insight/new-trend-report-into-the-metaverse

Chapter 8
Influencer Marketing in the Age of Metaverse

Anuradha Yadav

https://orcid.org/0000-0001-5607-2343
Dayananda Sagar College of Engineering, India

Vijaya Kittu Manda

https://orcid.org/0000-0002-1680-8210
PBMEIT, India

Mallikharjuna Rao Jitta

https://orcid.org/0009-0001-4908-9646
GITAM University, India

ABSTRACT

The metaverse is an emerging virtual frontier that is becoming a new marketing channel for brands to showcase their products and services. Brands can now use the services of influencers (both human and virtual) to influence consumer decisions. The metaverse and other new-generation Web 3.0 technologies are used in marketing campaigns to take advantage of immersive and augmented reality environments. Influencers use strategies different from traditional e-commerce, B2B, and social media marketing. Virtual showrooms, events, and product launches engage with consumers to co-create products and give a memorable consumer experience. The metaverse provides opportunities for community building and user-generated content that is more social proof. As technologies improve, influencers get more engaged in the metaverse. Measuring and evaluating influencer campaigns, ethical considerations, legal and regulatory frameworks, and long-term implications of influencer campaigns are some areas of future study.

DOI: 10.4018/979-8-3693-4167-4.ch008

INTRODUCTION

The evolution of Web 2.0 and the upcoming Web 3.0 technologies have rescued marketers looking for fresh tools, methods, and strategies to market products and services. The Metaverse is a technology platform that promises a refreshed workplace and marketplace (Khan et al., 2022). Influencers have emerged as a new breed of marketing professionals in recent times. Their services were invaluable in both traditional social media and new-generation media, such as the Metaverse, because of their non-intrusive marketing methods (Bansal et al., 2023).

The Metaverse

The term "Metaverse" refers to a combination of the real and virtual worlds, promising a unique interaction that will benefit all parties involved in business, including producers, distributors, marketers, brand analysts, purchasers, investors, and many more. Since the Metaverse is still in its early stages, academics have much to consider and reconsider regarding its future. According to recent research, the Metaverse is predicted to be worth $5 trillion when active adopters from various industries, including gaming, entertainment, travel, social media, and commerce. Consumers also appear eager to explore this new realm of physical-virtual reality (McKinsey & Company, 2022). Markets are increasingly using customized digital assets Non-Fungible Tokens (NFTs) called Branded NFTs (BNFTs), considering some exciting features that they provide - scarcity, financial value, prestige, uniqueness, originality, and communication consistency). The result is that markets can generate a positive brand attitude and enhance brand commitment, purchasing intention, and active engagement (Lee et al., 2023).

"The most important thing in communication is to hear what isn't being said"

Peter Drucker - The Father of Management

Developing a brand is as much a full-time job for marketers as raising a child and providing them with good parenting. One essential component of good parenting is having appropriate and efficient communication: How often do you and your child connect? How well do you and your child connect? How easily is your child sharing anything with you, good or bad?" For brands, it is crucial to communicate with the appropriate consumers at the appropriate times and obtain the appropriate information. Metaverse is anticipated to be a one-stop shop since it provides consumers with numerous incentives to interact with brands while also serving as a valuable tool for tracking and evaluating the success of different marketing initiatives (Dwivedi *et. al.,* 2023).

Immersive Metaverse

Each penny spent on workplace technological infrastructure is purely to increase workplace productivity. Currently, technologies and their application of Metaverse are becoming more and more immersive, with consumers directly benefiting from being a part of it. Authenticity is essential for success in these times. This immersive feature of Metaverse will drive technological innovation in the future. By providing an augmented reality world to its staff, Metaverse is becoming an interactive tool for workplace training and brainstorming needs. Mixed reality workplaces accompanied by frog-leaping Avatar technologies significantly increase workplace efficiency day-by-day. The global virtual reality market will grow from $19 billion in 2022 to $166 billion by 2030, according to Fortune Business Insights. These immersive technologies can bring the business world from the physical to the remote, mixed-reality, and hybrid realm. These technologies are more immersive than teleconferencing and do not suffer from zoom fatigue. Even if it is a slow return, a goose can lay golden eggs (Javed, 2024). Being an immersive environment, the Metaverse can promote influencer-follower interactions. Telepresence continues to be necessary, significantly influences experiential value, and improves consumer satisfaction levels. Studies also showed that despite experiential value, the Metaverse still needs further development (Barta *et al.,* 2023).

Metaverse Influencers and Influencer Marketing Landscape

The landscape of influencer marketing is transforming, fueled by the emergence of Web 3.0 technologies and the immersive virtual world of the Metaverse.

Since its inception in 1992, the term "Metaverse" has recently gained popularity (Canavesi 2022). It is defined by Du (2022) as "a combination of spatial computing, augmented reality, virtual reality, and sensory technology, promises to provide humans with new experiences in the exciting virtual multiverse." The study went on to commend Metaverse for being both a virtual environment and a science fiction tale that spontaneously arises, allowing consumers to relish the experience of a novel, unique virtual encounter with virtual currency and non-fungible tokens. With their incredible user-engaging content, influencers on a variety of social media platforms (Corbitt, 2022) and in the Metaverse produce reels, films, videos, and interviews centered around their passions and hobbies in a range of areas, such as fitness, food, fashion, beauty, travel, finances, daily hacks, and much more (Chen, 2020). From a very ordinary, down-to-earth person to a knowledgeable, experienced professional, they can find their niche in the virtual world and have fun. Presenting an exceptional performance for consumers and employees, the Metaverse is something one should not ignore (Mengalli & Carvalho, 2023). Ten layers make up the four sections of the Metaverse. Primarily, the goal is to facilitate the Metaverse in the physical world by designating certain aspects as Enablers, such as "payment and monetization," "identity," "security, privacy, and governance." Second, Hardware and Infrastructure provide a more robust platform and foundation for correct operation. It comprises devices, operating system software, accessories, and "infrastructure." The third section consists of Platforms that expand the capabilities of Metaverse by providing "access and discovery" and "creators/3D development platform". The fourth section, "Virtual World," "Application," and "Content," focuses more on value by providing Content and Experience (McKinsey & Company, 2022).

Influencers and Influencer Marketing

A person with a large following on many social media platforms who is followed for advice or style regarding goods and services is known as an influencer or Social Media Influencer (SMI) (Vrontis, *et al.,* 2021). These influencers are active on several social media sites, such as Facebook, YouTube, Instagram pages, and TikTok (though blocked, banned, or restricted in several countries).

Influencer marketing has multiple definitions and is seen in different perspectives. One view is that it is seen as an approach to identifying and targeting influencers in the market. They are part of a decision-maker ecosystem, which revolves around a decision-maker (Brown & Hayes, 2008).

Influencer marketing has come a long way since the days of Aunt Jemima, African–the American model (1889), and Coca-Cola's Santa Claus campaigns (1931). The communication terrain and the place where prospects and potential buyers are located have changed. Because influencers come in different guises, their presence is as trivial as the buyers themselves. The Internet is the giant marketing playground created by Web 2.0 technologies. Instagram, YouTube, LinkedIn, Facebook, Snapchat, TikTok, Pinterest, and Twitch are the most popular social media platforms, and they are the digital playgrounds for influencers of the generation (Glenister, 2021). However, entering the Web 3.0 era, the platforms are changing. The Metaverse is a virtual cyber-social platform that blends virtual reality, augmented reality, sensorial technology, and spatial computing. Metaverse is creating a new consumer-first on-demand economy (Shavkatovna, 2023), extending the digital reach of the markets, and opening up doors to virtual supply chains. It is perceived to be the next big marketing playground. All major social media brands are expected to migrate to Metaverse. Influencers help create brand awareness and will be at the top of the sales funnel. They must establish good ties (preferably two-way and partly reciprocal) to develop a relationship.

As the *FE Lifestyle*, the most paid influencers in India are Bhuvan Bam, Prajakta Koli, Ranveer Allahbadia, Kusha Kapila, Ajey Nagar, and Masoom Minawala. Their net worth spans from Rs. 12 crores to Rs. 122 crores, and they have large subscriber bases ranging from 57.5k to 40.9 million (FE Lifestyle, 2023). According to the report released by Statista.com, the Indian influencer market is expected to increase at a compound annual growth rate of 25%. An additional estimate put the industry's market worth at 28 billion Indian rupees by 2026 from 12 billion Indian rupees in 2022. More than 55 million Indians living in cities are currently direct consumers of influencers of various kinds. As a result, influencer marketing has developed into an essential tool for businesses looking to draw in and keep Indian consumers in terms of their product research and purchase decisions. In addition to the personal care vertical, which is positioned to dominate the industry with a 25 percent market share by 2022, other significant industries that build relationships with their target consumers and enhance brand messaging include food, fashion, jewelry, mobile/electronics, and many more (Statista, 2023).

Therefore, selecting the right influencers is essential because (Glenister, 2021), for example, selecting people without knowledge will likely make mistakes and be disastrous at the product launch event. Too much focus should not be put on the number of followers alone. In some cases, more than quantity, the quality of followers turns out to be more critical. Setting the right goals for the influencers is essential. Similarly, the influencers can be from a diversified range that is good enough to fit the campaign. While freedom is to be given freedom, too much freedom might make the brand move away from the intended message it wishes to carry. It is essential to monitor the influencers promptly and ensure their tone and vocabulary fit the campaign.

To assess influencer marketing in Metaverse, Karabacak, Z. İ., & Güngör, İ. (2023) looked at the relationship between the influencer and the brand using a case study approach and the semiotic technique, focusing on just three brands: Superplastic, Boohoo, and Levi's. Avatars and gamification in the virtual world (Metaverse) are examples of add-on features that have made real-time engagement between the brand, influencer, and consumers more flexible and extensive. However, by utilizing Blockchain technology, Metaverse technology assists firms with digital sales and resolving payment problems and counterfeiting in influencer marketing. In parallel, brands can bridge two realms and improve the efficacy of their advertising campaign.

According to Du (2022), influencer marketing may be divided into five types based on the business's engagement and the freedom granted to the influencer: sponsored content, review content, competition and giveaway, content cooperation, and brand ambassador. However, again, excessive control can cause a firm to "influencer avoidance" and "anti-consumption," and excessive liberty can damage the brand's reputation. Studies showed that consumers with high neuroticism are less likely to enjoy or seek out experiences in the Metaverse, and such participants need professional support to overcome negative emotions towards digital technologies (Khan et al., 2022).

Social Media and Influencer Marketing

Influencer marketing is particularly effective on social media in bringing in new consumers and keeping hold of current ones. This is the platform where someone can be launched as an "influencer celebrity" depending on their popularity, number of views, and number of followers. The best-known platforms include Meta (formerly Facebook), X (formerly Twitter), Instagram, and WhatsApp, which are still evolving.

According to Barta *et al.* (2023), opinion leadership—closely related to influencer marketing in general—indirectly supports consumers' intentions to use the platform (such as TikTok) through perceived originality, the quality and quantity of the post or material, and humor. With its appealing user-generated material, it began with bloggers (Halvorsen *et al.,* 2013), progressed to vloggers, and eventually reached today's social media influencers –independent third-party endorser who has captured practically every industry section and clientele (Campbell and Farrell 2020). Building a trustworthy, engaging, reciprocal, and co-created relationship with people is just as important as selling. This concept is known as a "trans-parasocial relation," coined by Lou (2022). Hudders and Lou (2023) concurred on several advantages but cautioned marketers about unidentified possible risks when endorsing unhealthy foods or idealized body types. *Kidfluencers* are raising concerns about potential harm to children's privacy and identity development. As a result of this phenomenon, companies are now paying these reputable influencers to advertise their goods and services in online forums.

Social Proximity and Personal Space

Nothing comes without a price.

– Juliet Marillier

Brands use virtual and human influencers (VI and HI) in Metaverse to facilitate the branding experience for its consumers. In contrast, it is crucial to understand the effect of various dimensions of such brand experiences on social proximity and personal space in consumers' lives. For brands, therefore, it is crucial to understand the various factors matching the vibes of the consumer to design an optimal level of VI interaction (not too much; not too little).

E-Commerce and Influencer Marketing

Influencers can effortlessly express their opinions, tastes, and experiences about the goods and services through brief video snippets or reels, User Generated Content (UGC)/Brand Generated Content (BCG), photoshoots, and interviews. Therefore, influencer celebrities and e-commerce giants like Amazon, Flipkart, Nykaa, Myntra, and many more work together fruitfully (Basuroy, 2023).

B2B and Influencer Marketing

Influencer marketers mainly target consumers, as companies leverage the allure of influencer stars to expand their clientele. However, four forms of influencer marketing were introduced and addressed (Mero et al., 2023): reference-based, content-based, interaction-based, and purpose-based. These kinds of influencer marketing will be beneficial to B2B companies as well.

When viewers begin to shun influencers and the brands aligned with them, the old saying *"access to everything is harmful"* holds for marketers, too. Researchers take note of this rare characteristic of consumer behavior. Continuing along these lines, Pradhan *et al.* (2023) also established the concept of "influencer avoidance," which refers to a behavior in which consumers begin to avoid specific influencers and brands. The consumer's avoidance of these influencers results in anti-consumption. Furthermore, the researchers found that the brand—also referred to as a "scripted influence"—as well as viewer emotions—such as anger, rage, or irritation—and their relationship with the influencer—whether favorable or unfavorable—were significant factors in influencer avoidance or anti-brand consumption. Since *not all shoes fit every size,* businesses should exercise extreme caution when adding dishes to their menus.

UNDERSTANDING THE METAVERSE CONSUMER: A NEW BREED OF AUDIENCE

Demographics and Psychographics of Metaverse Consumers

Gen Z is perceived as being more engaged and likely to feed virtual influencers for various reasons, including hedonic functions like amusement and fun, as well as to consume them to reach their day-to-day buying decisions.

Consumer Behavior in the Metaverse: Expectations, Preferences, and Motivations

Traditional influencer campaigns depend on traditional metrics such as likes and shares. However, the social media campaign measurements and metrics have changed with the entry of Metaverse. Sentiment analysis focuses on the emotional undercurrents of online conversations, revealing brand perception and consumers' opinions beyond surface-level engagement. AI and machine learning models empower brands to predict campaign performance and identify the most effective influencer pairings, ensuring a targeted, ROI-driven approach.

Building Trust and Engagement in a Virtual World

The success of a Metaverse Marketing Strategy depends on trust and engagement with the consumers. Real-world trust-building strategies involve many face-to-face interactions and well-established and tested media channels. However, Metaverse strategies will differ, considering they happen in a virtual world. Building trust will be challenging because the consumer on the Metaverse does not know the influencer's identity or motive. So, the engagement should be authentic. This is why brands disclose specific identity details and be clear about their collaboration with the influencer right from the beginning. Influencers would livestream products, shape narratives, curate experiences, and allow some level of interaction with the consumer.

In some cases, user-generated content is included in the strategy. In this, the consumers can participate in an avatar co-creation, or perhaps the consumers can interact with product replicas. Because consumers can put their hands into the building process, a sense of trust is created. However, as is already established, trust is a two-way process. Influencers are expected to understand the brand and share their honest views and not merely promote or endorse it. Similarly, consumers too should be critical and share views after verification from credible sources.

THE RISE OF VIRTUAL INFLUENCERS: BEYOND HUMAN COLLABORATORS

Virtual Influencers

"She's the epitome of an aspirational Gen-Z: living her life to the full and paving her own way in the world, on her own terms."

Sarah Rotheram, CEO of Creed Fragrances

Virtual Influencers (VI), or digital influencers, are fictional social media characters entities operated by third parties (freelance creators, digital agencies, or brands) (Koles et al., 2024) with a sizable social media following. Some of these VIs are also called 'Avatar-based Virtual Influencers (AVIs)' because animated replacements are put in place for human social media influencers. They are also called 'virtual social robots' because they perform specific tasks on social media (Haikel-Elsabeh, 2023). VI can be an indispensable marketing tool and help in brand endorsement strategy (De Brito Silva et al., 2022). Figure 1 shows the level of various influencer marketing tools. The characters appear as a virtual 3D/4D digital model and are backed with technologies such as Computer-Generated Imagery (CGI) technology (Bansal & Pruthi, 2023), Web 3.0, Non-Fungible Tokens (NFTs), chatbots, avatars, or traditional video models. VIs like Lil Miquela, a Brazilian-American lifestyle influencer and singer from LA, already have millions of followers. Ayayi is a VI launched by the Alibaba Group's Alimama and Ranmai Technology as a part of their Lunar New Year campaign for the perfume brand Creed. Luxury brands like Prada, Louis Vuitton, and Burberry have queued to collaborate with Ayayi. Other popular Chinese VIs include Dong, launched for the Beijing Winter Olympics; Timo, a male digital idol who made his public debut on the Tmall Luxury Pavilion in 2022; and Noah, another digital creation launched by Alimama (Gemma, 2023).

Considering that it is crucial that markets carefully pick social media influencers with expertise in the product category (Khan et al., 2022), VIs come in handy because they can be trained by using appropriate programming.

While VIs are convenient digital abstractions, they are criticized for exploring labor conditions because they create a system of NDAs, job insecurity, and exploitation of worker passion, discouraging workers from discussing labor conditions (Hughes, 2023).

Figure 1. Various influencer marketing variants
Source: Literature Review

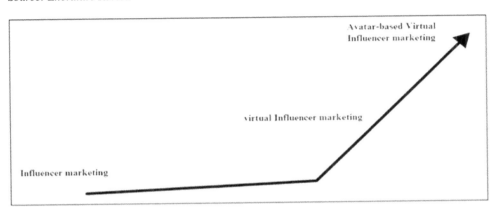

Design, Development, and Functionality

Influencer marketing benefits from the features and functionalities the Metaverse platform provides, which help create deeper connections with consumers. Influences thus require learning and fitting to the different designs, developments, and functionalities according to the marketing plan and the platform.

Design Process

As a part of the design process, influencers should carefully craft their avatars to reflect the digital persona, diverse identities, and resonate with the target consumer base. So, artistry work plays an important role. Apart from avatars, backstories and aesthetics also play a vital role. Advanced animation techniques, AI-powered chatbots, and deep fakes to generate realistic interactions are often used to generate them. The result is that the consumer can believe, relate, and connect well with the brand.

Development Process

As a part of the development process, influencers have sophisticated tools that can capture consumers' feedback much faster than existing modes, thanks to technological advancements. Artificial Intelligence (AI) algorithms are seamlessly integrated with Metaverse platforms and give inputs to steer and direct the influencers with their next steps. Traditional influencers collaborate with digital and virtual reality developers to create an immersive environment. This somewhat reduces the gap/blur between the physical and digital environments.

Functionality Process

The Metaverse provides much functionality because it provides a virtual environment while allowing interactive interfaces for the participants to express themselves. Thus, influencers must focus on many narratives and experiences to engage consumers with the brand. Influencers get support from digital tools to conduct virtual events and product demonstrations within interactive environments and facilitate *phygital* (physical-digital) purchases through integrated marketplaces. Sometimes, these happen instantly without pre-planning. Prolonged engagement with the brands helps consumers form and join the community as a part of the virtual ecosystem.

Innovation Process

Metaverse is still evolving and is open to innovation. Influencers can incentivize hardcore fans and loyal consumers on the Metaverse with virtual limited edition NFT goodies. A Blockchain in the background powers NFTs and facilitate peer-to-peer transactions on a distributed network.

Convergence: Influencer Marketing and Metaverse Revolution

Influencer marketing in the Metaverse goes beyond traditional product placements, promotions, and sponsored content. Because of simulated environments and immersive experiences, consumers will interact much more engagingly. The Metaverse allows interaction and consumption both physically and digitally. For example, a fashion influencer might showcase a new clothing line within a virtual store, allowing consumers to try the items virtually before facilitating a real-world purchase through an integrated platform. So, there is a convergence of physical and digital spaces, giving a multisensory brand experience to the consumer.

Convergence leads to redefining consumers' decision-making far above traditional endorsements. Interactive story-telling and gamified experiences are used to create a sense of community and shared value. Convergence allows influencers and companies to do segmentation and targeting more precisely, thanks to data analytics and algorithmic personalization. Campaigns are hence directed towards improved maximizing relevance and resonance.

Another dimension of convergence is in the form of co-creation and participatory engagement. Influencers can use this opportunity to cultivate brand advocates and evangelists.

Advantages of Utilizing Virtual Influencers

Using Virtual Influencers can help brands in several ways:

1. Unrestricted and Unlimited Creativity and Design
2. Precise Targeting, Niche Appeal, and Improved Reach
3. Scalability and Global Reach, often in a very short period
4. Enhanced Control and Consistent Brand Image
5. 24/7 and Perpetual Availability and Longevity
6. Reputation Risk Mitigation (which is prevalent with human influencers)
7. Data-Driven Optimization and Performance Tracking
8. Future-proof Brand Strategies
9. Integration with Metaverse Mechanics
10. Embodiment of Metaverse Aesthetic
11. Experimentation with Evolving Technologies (such as AI, deep fakes, amongst others)
12. Innovative Partnerships (between Artists, Marketers, Brand and Campaign Managers, and IT Developers)
13. Potential for Emotional Connection and Advocacy

Challenges for Virtual Influencers

While the Metaverse is a virtual platform and everything looks rosy, the concept of Virtual Influencers and their management comes with a few challenges.

1. Creating virtual influencers that are too realistic can trigger an "uncanny valley" effect and repel consumers. This highlights the need to balance between realism and relatability. On the other hand, sometimes, consumers may perceive them as artificial constructs with no genuine emotions or experiences.
2. The Metaverse influencers' space is expected to be crowded; hence, standing out becomes essential and challenging.
3. Building trust and authenticity for virtual influencers becomes complex and challenging because the consumers are also equipped with better tools that help in better decision-making.
4. Ethical concerns arise because of AI and deep fakes, which virtual influencers must handle carefully.
5. Virtual environments might pose unforeseen situations or unexpected consumer interactions. Sometimes, these become difficult for influencers to handle.
6. Metaverse may lack established legal and regulatory frameworks governing data privacy, consumer protection, advertising practices (such as advertising

disclosure), intellectual property rights, and digital asset ownership associated with virtual influencers.

7. Virtual influencers across diverse Metaverse platforms (interoperability) is a technical hurdle that needs addressing. Perhaps the upcoming technology upgrades would address this requirement. This requirement is also critical because Metaverse uses a complex mix of various digital technologies such as 3D modeling, animation, and AI programming.

8. Consumers' expectations within the Metaverse keep shifting according to industry trends. It is dynamic, requiring that virtual influencers regularly bring in quality, creativity, and sensational content.

9. Developing effective monetization strategies within the Metaverse is a problematic area. This is because the influencer job is more of a service quality-related activity with no specific tangible measurements, targets, and goals usually stated in the marketing campaign.

10. While virtual influencers offer unique advantages to the marketing field, they may never fully replace the power of human connection and the emotional resonance of real influencers. So, virtual influencers and human influencers co-exist, each dominating the other briefly until the other builds up the edge.

HUMAN INFLUENCERS IN THE METAVERSE

Not just virtual influencers but human influencers also have a vital role to play in Metaverse marketing. Human influencers form a dynamic link between traditional marketing systems and emergent virtual environments. They have cultivated authenticity, relatability, and aspirational lifestyles that help them to mingle and play in the virtual Metaverse quickly and smoothly. They have a considerable influence and impact on consumer behaviors and preferences. They understand and fit into virtual spaces with an understanding of digital social dynamics. They are an example of human-centric narratives in the digital age. The Metaverse might be a new environment for them regarding consumer engagement and marketing dynamics. However, over time, they can easily adjust and adapt to it. Ethically speaking, they will be burdened with the need to disclose digital manipulation and maintain transparency. The influencer's physical personification requirements are crucial for building trust within the Metaverse.

Adapting Influencer Strategies for the Metaverse Environment

Traditional influencer marketing strategies may not fit right away in the Metaverse. They must undergo substantial changes to engage with consumers and drive decision-making processes. The highest priority for influencers in the Metaverse is to establish credibility within the virtual communities. This can only be done with authentic engagement and expertise in specific niches. Influencers will have to cultivate a genuine presence to achieve this. They must actively participate in community activities to build trust and rapport with their consumer.

Influencers must take advantage of the virtual environments to create captivating experiences that closely align with the brand messaging and resonate with digital consumers. This can be done by incorporating augmented reality (AR) and virtual reality (VR) elements into content. Doing so will enhance consumer engagement and facilitate more meaningful interactions between influencers and their consumers. In addition, influencers need to build a network and collaborate with Metaverse platforms to use emerging technologies such as Blockchain. Technology does enhance the campaign's reach and effectiveness. They should be open to co-creation and co-innovation to drive brand and consumer value. Overall, those Influencers who can cultivate a strong avatar persona and use real-time engagement tools within the Metaverse are likely to build deeper connections with their consumers and thereby have an edge over the rest.

Skills Required for Metaverse Influencers

Metaverse influencers need to learn to embrace technology over and above traditional marketing and social media concepts. The skills include understanding the concepts of decentralization brought out by Blockchain, transacting with modern wallets such as *Metamask*, collaboration, working and immersive and 3D environments, virtual influencing, expanded scope of influencing by promoting NFTs and their issuers, and technical skills such as animations and game development. Interaction and engagement with peers (fellow influencers) are as important as communicating with the consumers. Studies emphasized that effective communication and collaboration among influencers, organizations, and competition venues in broadcasting within shared networks play an essential role (Kim & Chakraborty, 2023).

Steps in Becoming a Metaverse Influencer

Influencers typically get over 100 new followers every day, and reaching this level requires a lot of background home (Lane, 2023). To achieve this "target," influencers on the Metaverse must follow pretty much the same steps they would take on traditional social media, such as Instagram. The first step is to create an account. An important consideration here is to keep the account private (accessible only to friends) or a public account (content accessible to everyone but akin to opening windows will bring in dust and fresh air!). The profile picture will resemble an avatar in the Metaverse (Bansal & Pruthi, 2023).

The account description text requires careful consideration. The influencer should decide on the scope and nature of posts that will be posted on the account. Fresh content is to be posted regularly; hence, some homework and a queue are necessary. Each influencer has a unique communication style and often focuses on "niche products" that attract more consumers. Niche products and limited-edition avatars, collectibles, and memorabilia will become available as NFTs.

Content is tagged, categorized, and made discoverable with hashtags; hence, all Metaverse content (like on Instagram and X) must be tagged to reach the right targeted consumer. Captions and location information in the content are also important considerations. Getting quality and the right followers is essential; hence, influencers should refrain from crooked tactics of getting fake followers, such as *"follow for follow,"* spamming, and buying followers. Sentiment and perception studies showed that Metaverse is perceived as interrelated and integrated with finance, entertainment, and technology (Gündüz & Demirel, 2023).

Measuring Success and ROI for Metaverse Influencer Campaigns

Measuring the Return on Investment (ROI) for influencer marketing campaigns in the Metaverse is a different challenge. Traditional metrics such as website clicks, and coupon code redemption may not help. Some valuable methods and metrics for this include:

1. Brand awareness surveys and other qualitative feedback, monitoring brand perception, loyalty, and post-engagement activities within the Metaverse.
2. Social listening tools that track conversations within virtual spaces can reveal organic brand mentions and influencer campaign effectiveness.
3. Analyzing user-generated content, such as avatar selfies with branded items, can offer insights into brand integration and community sentiment.
4. Metrics like virtual foot traffic (virtual attendance) within branded experiences, dwell time spent interacting (interaction duration) with influencer content and click-through rates for virtual product trials can offer valuable insights.
5. Tracking conversions within the Metaverse environment itself is a challenge. Virtual currency purchases or redemptions of exclusive in-game items are often used.
6. Affiliate links embedded in NFTs or Metaverse wearables can track product ownership and usage, potentially leading to commission payouts based on virtual sales driven by influencer campaigns.

Creating Virtual Showrooms, Events, and Product Launches

Virtual showrooms act as digital representations of physical retail spaces. They allow consumers to explore and interact with products in a simulated setting. These virtual environments offer brands the opportunity to showcase their offerings dynamically and interactively and overcome the limitations of traditional retail channels. Consumers will be able to explore products in 3D, customize them on the fly, and even participate in virtual try-on experiences.

Virtual events allow brands to engage with consumers in real-time and offer them an immersive digital experience. These events can take various forms. Four popular models are:

1. Product demonstrations
2. Trivia Contests
3. Live Q&A sessions, and
4. Interactive presentations.

The brands can use the interactive capabilities of the Metaverse environment to create memorable experiences that captivate and resonate with consumers. They help make deeper connections and brand affinity.

Product launches in the Metaverse offer brands a unique opportunity to generate excitement and anticipation around the new offerings. By using the immersive nature of virtual environments, brands can create immersive story-telling experiences that captivate consumer engagement. Virtual product launches help brands to reach a global consumer base in a short period. This allows products and services to be announced globally beyond borders. Brands get increased visibility for new releases.

Consumers on the Metaverse need additional motivation to spend time in the new environment. Incentivizing the customer is a proven traditional method. Limited edition virtual merchandise in the form of NFTs or experiences tied to the influencer campaign can help in the incentivize process. This also improves consumer participation and stickiness with the brand. Influencers can host VIP events within the virtual showrooms and offer early access to products or behind-the-scenes glimpses at the design process.

Utilizing Gamification and Interactive Experiences

Influencer marketing strategies interconnect with gamification and interactive experiences. The final expected result is engaging consumers in novel and immersive ways. Using game-like elements is fundamental to using gamification into influencer marketing initiatives. Customers who participate and interact will be incentivized for their time and efforts. Influencers can integrate gamified features such as challenges, rewards, and virtual competitions into their content to encourage active engagement and foster a sense of enjoyment and achievement among their consumer base.

Some standard methods for achieving this are:

1. Organizing live streaming
2. Conducting Virtual events
3. interactive storytelling

Influencers can actively involve their consumer base in the brand narrative and create memorable experiences that resonate personally.

There are a few limiting factors to using gamification. Gamification should not be solely focused on extrinsic motivators. Influencers can design interactive experiences that tap into intrinsic desires for mastery and social connection. Virtual workshops, for example, can be led by influencers. Consumers benefit by learning new skills. Of course, the training will be related to the promoted product. These workshops create a sense of accomplishment and achievement for the consumer. At the same time, companies benefit from building brand affinity. Gamified experiences provide brands with the opportunity to gamify the influencer journey itself. The advantage of this is that collaboration and co-creation between influencers and their consumer base can be done. This helps in brand innovation and differentiation within virtual environments.

Community Building and User-Generated Content (UGC)

Community building and User-Generated Content (UGC) are two exciting aspects that help cultivate authentic brand engagement and promote consumer-driven interactions within virtual environments. Within the Metaverse, Community building involves creating spaces where consumers can connect, share experiences, and co-create content around shared interests and values. Influencers act as community moderators and facilitators. They promote meaningful interactions, create a vibe, and nurture a sense of belonging among their consumer bases. Influencers actively remind themselves to actively engage with the community members. So, they can cultivate trust and authenticity. This strengthens brand-consumer relationships and drives collective decision-making processes within virtual communities.

UGC is necessary to cultivate vibrant and inclusive virtual communities. UGC is the food that enables consumers to actively participate in shaping the brand narrative and co-creating value. Influencers can empower their consumers to contribute to UGC through contests, challenges, and collaborative campaigns, amplifying brand visibility. They create a sense of ownership and pride among community members.

By showcasing user-generated content, influencers validate consumer contributions and celebrate diverse perspectives. This reinforces brand authenticity and resonance within virtual communities. Live events are places where UGC can be created. It helps create organic brand exposure. They help extend the reach of the campaign. They also provide social proof and authenticity, influencing purchase decisions within the virtual world.

SCOPE FOR FURTHER STUDY

Marketing in the Metaverse has been a topic of research interest in recent times. Researchers focused on influencer marketing, sensory advertising, digital marketing, social media advertising, and brand engagement (Gupta et al., 2022). Considering the topic is still evolving, several opportunities and challenges have arisen. Some key topics being shortlisted for research include influencer marketing effectiveness, ethical considerations, societal implications, and the future development of influencer marketing (Aw & Agnihotri, 2023). Like other social media researchers, Metaverse researchers were seen using Cluster, semantic, and time series analyses. Programs such as NodeXL are used to analyze hashtag keyword networks.

1. **Metaverse Influencer Marketing Strategies**: Now, marketers are eager to investigate novel approaches for utilizing the Metaverse's special powers for influencer marketing efforts. In a similar vein, Eyice Başev, S. (2024) investigated the incorporation of influencer marketing into the Metaverse and discovered that certain brands, such as Beyman, are employing Computer-Generated Imagery (CGI) technology to provide consumers with distinctive virtual experiences and encourage them to interact with the brand for an extended period.

2. **Virtual Influencer Creation and Management**: This study aims to learn more about how virtual influencers are created and managed and how their engagement techniques, personality, and design affect their overall marketing efficacy. It will center on potential obstacles, openings, keys to success, and industry partnerships. While the younger generation is enjoying themselves while consuming it, Moustakas *et al.* (2020) noted a few obstacles, such as maintaining interest over an extended period, preferring the real world over the virtual, which highlights the significance of authenticity, credibility, and reliability, lacking a human touch, and not being appropriate for commercial objectives. According to the researcher, virtual influencers should prioritize problem-solving above indiscriminate application everywhere. Virtual influencers can also take advantage of this field's prospects for creativity and storytelling. In response to concerns about sustainability, Arsenyan, J.,

& Mirowska, A. (2021) proposed *"virtual agents"* as a workable alternative that could resolve moral and practical dilemmas. Furthermore, Kim, et al. (2023) distinguished between two types of virtual influencers: Human Virtual Influencers and Animal Virtual Influencers. This further bolstered the findings of earlier studies that emphasized the significance of message credibility in sustaining consumer engagement over the long haul.

3. **Measurement and Evaluation of Metaverse Influencer Campaigns**: Developing metrics and techniques to assess the overall efficacy of influencer marketing campaigns in the Metaverse is necessary, despite the many benefits that virtual influencers offer, such as their availability, controllability, never-aging, superiority over traditional PR, adaptability, customization, vast potential for community building, storytelling, creativity, amongst others. (Bernadett Koles, *et al.,* 2024; Sands, *et al.,* 2022; Drenten, & Brooks, 2020; Moustakas, *et al.,* 2020; Robinson, 2020; Duffy & Hund, 2019).

4. **Ethical Considerations in Metaverse Influencer Marketing**: This involves addressing ethical concerns related to privacy, data protection, and the potential impact of virtual influencers on society. Virtual influencers are non-human characters, and their interaction with humans (consumers) could lead to a non-level playing field and potential issues such as data vulnerability, cybercrime, and the creation of fake profiles surrounding it (Liyanaarachchi et al., 2024).

Though technology is created to make human living more manageable, it is vital to comprehend ethical issues about data protection, privacy, and the possible effects of virtual influencers on society. The fact that 30% of the content that people consume on X (formerly known as Twitter) is generated by technology serves as a sobering reminder of how serious the subject is. This could lead to hyper-reality, in which readers react without being able to distinguish between reality and simulations, or it could result in anthropomorphism, in which technology can easily display expressions based on human emotions (Marwick, 2018; Epley *et al.,* 2007; Baudrillard & Glaser, 1994). As technology continues to improve, the distinction between the genuine and the fake becomes increasingly hazy, opening new possibilities for privacy concerns, data security, and the potential impact of virtual influences on society. Digital ethics should, therefore, be essential. Some social issues, such as skin color and body shape, must be addressed, from traditional media commercials to the latest virtual influencers. It may lead to dissatisfaction and body shaming in many real humans. Technology development happens much faster than changes in a nation's legal system. Therefore, it is critical to establish and uphold a certain standard of morality or ethics to combat misidentification (Kim, & Wang, 2023), sensationalism, algorithmic cues, perfect realism, and unachievable beauty standards (El-Deeb, 2022).

Concerns about data are yet another nightmare. The author investigated three data-related issues: cybercrime, fake profiles, and data vulnerability. Each of the three has unique difficulties when it comes to protecting the privacy of data. According to Martin and Murphy (2017), data vulnerability refers to the exploitation of data through unlawful access that does not align with the original purposes of data collection, placing individuals at increased risk associated with data. Businesses frequently purchase and sell people's personal information without their consent, which is a severe breach of the data protection industry. Second, any illicit conduct in cyberspace that results in data loss or destruction, unlawful access to data, or a breach of privacy affecting data at the individual or organizational level is considered cybercrime. There have been a lot of documented instances of cybercrime, hacking, internet fraud, etc., recently. Third, there has been a discussion about phony profiles lately. To purposely fulfill some criminal wants, such as data vulnerability and cybercrime, or to satiate their illusionary need to be like that fictional identity, people frequently create fake profiles that are either entirely or partially false (Liyanaarachchi, *et al.*, 2024).

5. **Legal and Regulatory Frameworks for Metaverse Influencer Marketing**: Metaverse owes us a great deal of experience bridging the virtual and physical worlds, and most enterprises highly value it. However, because of its intricacy and abrupt adoption everywhere, it raises several potential modifications from a variety of perspectives, including "governance & infrastructure framework", "safety, privacy, & security", "behavioral & societal", and "ethical, legal, & moral". It is becoming increasingly necessary to investigate the necessity of legal and regulatory frameworks to control influencer marketing in the Metaverse. Current research has revealed a number of user-generated negative concerns, including lifestyle disorders (such as addiction), psychological risks and harms, data misuse, false information and disinformation, deviant behaviors (such as sexual harassment), support for terrorism and crime, identity problems, forging, cloning, distraction/poor concentration, anonymity & cyberbullying, disconnection from reality, anxiety, and relationship problems (Cheung, *et al.*, 2021; Pandey, *et al.*, 2020; Rauschnabel, *et al.*, 2019; Dwivedi, *et al.*, 2022).

6. **Integration of Metaverse Influencer Marketing with Traditional Marketing Channels**: This topic is an extension of ongoing research in traditional marketing. Researchers need to consider and acknowledge the future of social interactions with Metaverse. Research work must leapfrog to emerging areas. The transition from traditional to Metaverse marketing will create a research gap that some budding researchers can fill. Their studies would focus on the synergies between Metaverse influencer marketing and traditional marketing channels to maximize reach and impact.

7. **Long-Term Implications of Metaverse Influencer Marketing**: This area largely focuses on analyzing the potential long-term effects of Metaverse influencer marketing. Some critical areas that will remain important despite the new environment or platform are consumer behavior, brand loyalty, and the evolution of marketing.

CONCLUSION

The Metaverse presents a revolutionary platform for influencer marketing. It offers a more immersive and interactive experience than traditional social media channels. This new platform provides virtual worlds that give rise to virtual influencers (VIs) alongside human influencers. Metaverse brings more dynamics into the marketing environment. Key advantages include deeper consumer engagement, enhanced marketing campaigns and targeting, virtual influencers who can be deployed anytime, and the convergence of physical and digital experiences.

Despite the advantages, influencer marketing in the Metaverse comes with some challenges. Building trust, ethical concerns, and monetization strategies are some of them. Influencer marketing strategies will evolve as the Metaverse evolves, making the influencers continuously adapt to the changed circumstances and environments. Influencers who embrace new technologies, cultivate strong avatar personas, and prioritize authentic engagement will be well-positioned for success in this transformative landscape. By understanding these opportunities and challenges, brands and influencers can use the power of the Metaverse to build deeper connections with consumers and shape the future of marketing.

REFERENCES

Arsenyan, J., & Mirowska, A. (2021). Almost human? A comparative case study on the social media presence of virtual influencers. *International Journal of Human-Computer Studies*, *155*, 102694. doi:10.1016/j.ijhcs.2021.102694

Aw, E. C.-X., & Agnihotri, R. (2023). Influencer marketing research: Review and future research agenda. *Journal of Marketing Theory and Practice*, 1–14. doi:10.1 080/10696679.2023.2235883

Bansal, R., & Pruthi, N. (2023). Avatar-Based Influencer Marketing: Demystifying the Benefits and Risks of Marketing Through Virtual Influencers. In R. Bansal, S. A. Qalati, & A. Chakir (Eds.), (pp. 78–86). Advances in Marketing, Customer Relationship Management, and E-Services. IGI Global. doi:10.4018/978-1-6684-8898-0.ch005

Bansal, R., & Pruthi, N. (2023). Avatar-Based Influencer Marketing: Demystifying the Benefits and Risks of Marketing through Virtual Influencers. In *Influencer Marketing Applications Within the Metaverse* (pp. 78–86). IGI Global. doi:10.4018/978-1-6684-8898-0.ch005

Bansal, R., Qalati, S. A., & Chakir, A. (Eds.). (2023). *Influencer marketing applications within the Metaverse*. IGI Global. doi:10.4018/978-1-6684-8898-0

Barta, S., Belanche, D., Fernández, A., & Flavián, M. (2023). Influencer marketing on TikTok: The effectiveness of humor and followers' hedonic experience. *Journal of Retailing and Consumer Services*, *70*, 103149. doi:10.1016/j.jretconser.2022.103149

Barta, S., Gurrea, R., & Flavián, C. (2023). Telepresence in live-stream shopping: An experimental study comparing Instagram and the Metaverse. *Electronic Markets*, *33*(1), 29. doi:10.1007/s12525-023-00643-6

Baudrillard, J., & Glaser, S. F. (1994). *Simulacra and Simulation*. University of Michigan Press.

Brown, D., & Hayes, N. (2008). *Influencer marketing: Who really influences your customers?* Elsevier/Butterworth-Heinemann. doi:10.4324/9780080557700

Campbell, C., & Farrell, J. R. (2020). More than meets the eye: The functional components underlying influencer marketing. *Business Horizons*, *63*(4), 469–479. doi:10.1016/j.bushor.2020.03.003

Canavesi, B. (2022). *What Is the Metaverse: Where We Are and Where We're Headed*. Association for Talent Development. https://www. td. org/atd-blog/whatis-the-metaverse-where-we-are-and-where-were-headed

Chen, J. (2020). *What is influencer marketing: How to develop your strategy*. Sprout Social. https://sproutsocial. com/insights/influencer-marketing/(дата звернення: 25.04. 2020).

Cheung, C. M., Wong, R. Y. M., & Chan, T. K. H. (2021). Online disinhibition: Conceptualization, measurement, and implications for online deviant behavior. *Industrial Management & Data Systems*, *121*(1), 48–64. doi:10.1108/IMDS-08-2020-0509

Corbitt, L. (2022). Influencer marketing in 2022: Strategies + examples. *The BigCommerce Blog.* https://www.bigcommerce.com/blog/influencer-marketing/#what-is-influencer-market-ing.

De Brito Silva, M. J., De Oliveira Ramos Delfino, L., Alves Cerqueira, K., & De Oliveira Campos, P. (2022). Avatar marketing: A study on the engagement and authenticity of virtual influencers on Instagram. *Social Network Analysis and Mining, 12*(1), 130. doi:10.1007/s13278-022-00966-w

Drenten, J., & Brooks, G. (2020). Celebrity 2.0: Lil Miquela and the rise of a virtual star system. *Feminist Media Studies, 20*(8), 1319–1323. doi:10.1080/14680777.2020.1830927

Du, T. (2022). *Virtual influencers in Metaverse: Discussion and research on the impacts of the purchasing decisions of Generation Z.*

Duffy, B. E., & Hund, E. (2019). Gendered Visibility on Social Media: Navigating Instagram's Authenticity Bind [social media, visibility, gender, authenticity, Instagram, influencers]. *International Journal of Communication, 13*, 4983–5002. https://ijoc.org/index.php/ijoc/article/view/11729/2821. doi:10.32376/3f8575cb.3f03db0e

Dwivedi, Y. K., Hughes, L., Baabdullah, A. M., Ribeiro-Navarrete, S., Giannakis, M., Al-Debei, M. M., & Wamba, S. F. (2022). Metaverse beyond the hype: Multidisciplinary perspectives on emerging challenges, opportunities, and agenda for research, practice and policy. *International Journal of Information Management, 66*, 102542. doi:10.1016/j.ijinfomgt.2022.102542

Dwivedi, Y. K., Hughes, L., Wang, Y., Alalwan, A. A., Ahn, S. J., Balakrishnan, J., Barta, S., Belk, R., Buhalis, D., Dutot, V., Felix, R., Filieri, R., Flavián, C., Gustafsson, A., Hinsch, C., Hollensen, S., Jain, V., Kim, J., Krishen, A. S., & Wirtz, J. (2023). Metaverse marketing: How the Metaverse will shape the future of consumer research and practice. *Psychology and Marketing, 40*(4), 750–776. doi:10.1002/mar.21767

El-Deeb, S. (2022, December). Computer-Generated Imagery Influencer Marketing—Which Ends of the Continuum Will Prevail? Humans or Avatars? *In International Conference on Marketing and Technologies* (pp. 3-15). Singapore: Springer Nature Singapore.

Epley, N., Waytz, A., & Cacioppo, J. T. (2007). On seeing human: A three-factor theory of anthropomorphism. *Psychological Review, 114*(4), 864–886. doi:10.1037/0033-295X.114.4.864 PMID:17907867

Eyice Başev, S. (2024). Influencer marketing in the age of Metaverse: Beymenverse and meta-influencer Bella. *International Journal of Eurasian Education and Culture*, 9(25), 29–41. doi:10.35826/ijoecc.1820

Gemma, W. A. (2023, February 14). *Should Brands Use Virtual Influencers in China?* Business of Fashion. https://www.businessoffashion.com/briefings/china/should-brands-use-virtual-influencers-in-china/

Glenister, G. (2021). *Influencer Marketing Strategy: How to create successful influencer marketing*. Kogan Page.

Gündüz, U., & Demirel, S. (2023). Metaverse-related perceptions and sentiments on Twitter: Evidence from text mining and network analysis. *Electronic Commerce Research*. doi:10.1007/s10660-023-09745-x

Gupta, G., Gupta, A., & Joshi, M. C. (2022). A Conceptual and Bibliometric Study to Understand Marketing in Metaverse: A new Paradigm. *2022 5th International Conference on Contemporary Computing and Informatics (IC3I)*, (pp. 1486–1491). IEEE. 10.1109/IC3I56241.2022.10073455

Haikel-Elsabeh, M. (2023). Virtual Influencers versus Real Influencers Advertising in the Metaverse, Understanding the Perceptions, and Interactions with Users. *Journal of Current Issues and Research in Advertising*, 44(3), 252–273. doi:10.1080/10641734.2023.2218420

Halvorsen, K., Hoffmann, J., Coste-Manière, I., & Stankeviciute, R. (2013). Can fashion blogs function as a marketing tool to influence consumer behavior? Evidence from Norway. *Journal of Global Fashion Marketing*, 4(3), 211–224. doi:10.1080/20932685.2013.790707

Hudders, L., & Lou, C. (2023). The rosy world of influencer marketing? Its bright and dark sides, and future research recommendations. *International Journal of Advertising*, 42(1), 151–161. doi:10.1080/02650487.2022.2137318

Hughes, C. (2023). *Virtual Influencers and the New Wave of Digital Labour Exploitation* [Thesis for the Degree of Master of Arts, Graduate Program in Communications and Culture, York University]. https://yorkspace.library.yorku.ca/server/api/core/bitstreams/e6cdf2e9-ea96-4e38-964e-92d6cb825d29/content

Karabacak, Z. İ., & Güngör, İ. (2023). The Metaverse as Influencer Marketing Platform: Influencer-Brand Collaborations of Parıs Hilton with 'Superplastic', 'Bohoo', and 'Levi's'. *Etkileşim*, 6(11), 176–199. doi:10.32739/etkilesim.2023.6.11.194

Khan, S. W., Raza, S. H., & Zaman, U. (2022). Remodeling digital marketplace through Metaverse: A multi-path model of consumer neuroticism, parasocial relationships, social media influencers credibility, and ppenness to Metaverse experience. *Pakistan Journal of Commerce and Social Sciences, 16*(3), 337–365.

Kim, D., & Wang, Z. (2023). The ethics of virtuality: Navigating the complexities of human-like virtual influencers in the social media marketing realm. *Frontiers in Communication, 8*, 1205610. doi:10.3389/fcomm.2023.1205610

Kim, E., Kim, D. E. Z., & Shoenberger, H. (2023). The next hype in social media advertising: Examining virtual influencers' brand endorsement effectiveness. *Frontiers in Psychology, 14*, 1089051. doi:10.3389/fpsyg.2023.1089051 PMID:36949930

Kim, H. M., & Chakraborty, S. (2023). Exploring the diffusion of digital fashion and influencers' social roles in the Metaverse: An analysis of Twitter hashtag networks. *Internet Research*. Advance online publication. doi:10.1108/INTR-09-2022-0727

Koles, B. (2024). The authentic virtual influencer: Authenticity manifestations in the Metaverse. *Journal of Business Research, 170*, 114325. . Hal-04298734 doi:10.1016/j.jbusres.2023.114325

Koles, B., Audrezet, A., Moulard, J. G., Ameen, N., & McKenna, B. (2024). The authentic virtual influencer: Authenticity manifestations in the metaverse. *Journal of Business Research, 170*, 114325. doi:10.1016/j.jbusres.2023.114325

Lane, M. (2023). Social Media Marketing: Learn how to build a great brand. *Master the secrets of influencing.*

Lee, C. T., Ho, T.-Y., & Xie, H.-H. (2023). Building brand engagement in metaverse commerce: The role of branded non-fungible tokens (BNFTs). *Electronic Commerce Research and Applications, 58*, 101248. doi:10.1016/j.elerap.2023.101248

Lifestyle, F. E. (2023, 06 28). Prajakta Koli to Bhuvan Bam: Here are the highest-paid Indian Influencers. *Financial Express*. https://www.financialexpress.com/lifestyle/prajakta-koli-to-bhuvan-bam-here-are-the-highest-paid-indian-influencers-know-about-their-net-worth-and-more/3145723/

Liyanaarachchi, G., Mifsud, M., & Viglia, G. (2024). Virtual influencers and data privacy: Introducing the multi-privacy paradox. *Journal of Business Research, 176*, 114584. doi:10.1016/j.jbusres.2024.114584

Lou, C. (2022). Social media influencers and followers: Theorization of a trans-parasocial relation and explication of its implications for influencer advertising. *Journal of Advertising, 51*(1), 4–21. doi:10.1080/00913367.2021.1880345

Marwick, A. E. (2018). The algorithmic celebrity. In C. Abidin & M. L. Brown (Eds.), *Microcelebrity Around the Globe* (pp. 161–169). Emerald Publishing Limited. doi:10.1108/978-1-78756-749-820181015

McKinsey & Company. (2022, June 1). *road to change Value creation in the Metaverse*. McKinsey & Company. https://www.mckinsey.com/capabilities/growth-marketing-and-sales/our-insights/value-creation-in-the-metaverse

Mengalli, N. M., & Carvalho, A. A. (2023). The Intrinsic Property of a Representation in the Phygital Transformation: A (Meta) Influence as a Force With Magnitude and Direction in the Metaverse. In S. Teixeira, S. Teixeira, Z. Oliveira, & E. Souza (Eds.), (pp. 147–162). Advances in Marketing, Customer Relationship Management, and E-Services. IGI Global. doi:10.4018/979-8-3693-0551-5.ch007

Mero, J., Vanninen, H., & Keränen, J. (2023). B2B influencer marketing: Conceptualization and four managerial strategies. *Industrial Marketing Management*, *108*, 79–93. doi:10.1016/j.indmarman.2022.10.017

Moustakas, E., Lamba, N., Mahmoud, D., & Ranganathan, C. (2020, June). Blurring lines between fiction and reality: Perspectives of experts on marketing effectiveness of virtual influencers. In *2020 International Conference on Cyber Security and Protection of Digital Services (Cyber Security)* (pp. 1-6). IEEE. DOI: 10.1109/CyberSecurity49315.2020.9138861

Pandey, N., Nayal, P., & Rathore, A. S. (2020). Digital marketing for B2B organizations: Structured literature review and future research directions. *Journal of Business and Industrial Marketing*, *35*(7), 1191–1204. doi:10.1108/JBIM-06-2019-0283

Pradhan, D., Kuanr, A., Anupurba Pahi, S., & Akram, M. S. (2023). Influencer marketing: When and why gen Z consumers avoid influencers and endorsed brands. *Psychology and Marketing*, *40*(1), 27–47. doi:10.1002/mar.21749

Rauschnabel, P. A., Felix, R., & Hinsch, C. (2019). Augmented reality marketing: How mobile AR-apps can improve brands through inspiration. *Journal of Retailing and Consumer Services*, *49*, 43–53. doi:10.1016/j.jretconser.2019.03.004

Robinson, B. (2020). Towards an Ontology and Ethics of Virtual Influencers. *AJIS. Australasian Journal of Information Systems*, *23*, 333–345. doi:10.3127/ajis.v24i0.2807

Sands, S., Campbell, C., Plangger, K., & Ferraro, C. (2022). Unreal influence: Leveraging AI in influencer marketing. *European Journal of Marketing*, *56*(6), 1721–1747. doi:10.1108/EJM-12-2019-0949

Shavkatovna, R. D. (2023). A new tendency of Virtual Economics and its influence on the social life. *Scientific Impulse, 15*(100). http://nauchniyimpuls.ru/index.php/ni/article/download/12940/8928

Statista. (2023). *Value of influencer marketing industry in India from 2021 to 2022, with projections until 2026.* Statista. https://www.statista.com: https://www.statista.com/statistics/1294803/india-influencer-marketing-industry-value/

Vrontis, D., Makrides, A., Christofi, M., & Thrassou, A. (2021). Social media influencer marketing: A systematic review, integrative framework and future research agenda. *International Journal of Consumer Studies, 45*(4), 617–644. doi:10.1111/ijcs.12647

KEY TERMS AND DEFINITIONS

Augmented Reality (AR): A technology that superimposes a computer-generated text, image, or graphic on a user's real-world view. AR is used in gaming, education and learning, machine maintenance and repair, shopping, and navigation.

Influencer Marketing: A marketing strategy, usually on social media, that involves collaborating with influencers to reach a target audience. Influencers address the target audience, provide brand awareness engagement, and help brands get sales.

Metaverse Avatar: A 3D digital representation of a user in the Metaverse. Many Metaverse platforms offer users to customize their avatar for facial features, body types, clothing, accessories, and even animation styles. Avatar has functionality allowing the user to move around, pick up objects, and perform actions specific to the platform.

Metaverse: A next-level internet (virtual world) that combines virtual reality, augmented reality, and other technologies to provide a new and superior user experience. The Metaverse is accessed through special headgear through which virtual worlds are explored. Virtual meetings, Virtual events, and social gatherings happen in this virtual world.

Non-Fungible Token (NFT): NFTs are digital assets representing ownership of a unique virtual item. NFTs are used in digital art, collectibles, gaming, supply chain management, ticketing, and merchandise.

Social Media Influencer: A person with a large following on social media who uses their platform to promote products or services. They typically focus on a specific niche, like fashion, beauty, fitness, gaming, or travel, and share their knowledge and passions with their audience. They partner with brands to promote products and services.

User-Generated Content: (UGC): Content created by users, such as text (reviews, discussions, blog posts), images (photos), or videos. UGC often reflects individual users' genuine experiences, opinions, and perspectives, providing authentic insights and engagement. UGC has become integral to digital marketing strategies, brand engagement initiatives, and online content ecosystems.

Virtual Influencer (VI): A computer-generated character (persona) used for influencer marketing within the Metaverse. These are usually AI-generated characters, 3D models, or animations that do not have physical form but have distinct personalities and aesthetics to engage audiences across platforms.

Virtual Reality (VR): A technology that creates an immersive, computer-generated simulation of a three-dimensional environment. Unlike augmented reality (AR), which overlays digital elements in the real world, VR completely replaces your surroundings with a virtual one. VR uses Head-Mounted Display (HMD), Input Devices, and Motion Tracking.

Web 3.0: A collection of next-generation technologies that form the basis of the future Internet. Technologies include Blockchain and Cryptocurrencies, Non-Fungible Tokens (NFTs), Decentralized Applications (dApps), Decentralized Autonomous Organizations (DAOs), Semantic Web, Artificial Intelligence, Edge Computing, Spatial Web, Metaverse, and others.

Chapter 9
Leveraging Marketing Strategies to Help Consumers Make Decisions Using Metaverse Technologies

Theodore Tarnanidis
https://orcid.org/0000-0002-4836-3906
International Hellenic University, Greece

Lampros Gkiouzepas
Hellenic Open University, Greece

ABSTRACT

Metaverse technologies have become ground-breaking tools, changing the way businesses interact with consumers and analyze their behavior. This research examines innovative Metaverse marketing strategies that focus on enhancing customer experiences and comprehending consumer behavior through cutting-edge technologies, platforms, and models. Businesses can create interactive and realistic experiences for their clients in a vibrant and immersive setting provided by the Metaverse. Companies can create virtual storefronts by utilizing VR and AR technologies, allowing customers to explore products and services in visually compelling ways. The chapter provides a summary of the origins of the metaverse in marketing, with further explanations about the immersive technologies employed in the creation of marketing strategies. The main trends and their implications are presented, along with a discussion of the current state of the art research in marketing, which was originally developed by the 'father of modern marketing,' Philip Kotler.

DOI: 10.4018/979-8-3693-4167-4.ch009

INTRODUCTION

Businesses are now using metaverse technologies to change how they interact with consumers and analyze their behavior, making them groundbreaking tools. In this study, we explore innovative marketing strategies in the Metaverse that put emphasis on enriching customer experiences and understanding consumer behavior through cutting-edge technologies, platforms, and models. By using the Metaverse, businesses can create interactive, realistic experiences for their clients in a vibrant, immersive setting. With the help of virtual reality (VR) and augmented reality (AR) technologies, companies can establish virtual storefronts that allow customers to explore products and services in visually captivating ways. Personalized interactions between physical and digital realms can be bridged through interactive 3D models, simulations, and gamified experiences that enhance customer engagement. Businesses have the ability to create branded spaces, host virtual events, and foster meaningful connections with their audience through the use of Metaverse platforms such as Decentraland, Roblox, and VRChat. Real-time analysis of consumer behavior is now possible through the use of metaverse technologies. Businesses can monitor customer interactions, preferences, and purchasing patterns through Metaverse platforms' advanced AI algorithms, machine learning, and data analytics. By focusing on data, marketers can gain valuable insights into consumer behavior, which enables them to make informed decisions, optimize product offerings, and tailor marketing campaigns.

METALVERSE ORIGINS AND MEANING

The term 'metaverse' was introduced by science fiction author Neal Stephenson in his 1992 novel 'Snow Crash' (Stephenson, 1992). Through avatars, users interact with each other and digital environments in a virtual reality space depicted in the novel. Stephenson's depictions of the metaverse as a vast, immersive virtual realm caught the imagination of readers and promoted the concept of virtual reality and online virtual communities. Stephenson's novel played a significant role in popularizing and shaping the meaning of the term 'metaverse' within the context of virtual reality and digital environments (Evans et al., 2022). Moreover, the concept of the metaverse has been further explored and developed in various fields, including technology, gaming, and marketing, with companies like Facebook and other tech giants actively working towards creating immersive virtual spaces that resemble the vision of the metaverse depicted in Stephenson's novel (Chakraborty, 2024). Critical examination of the concept, its potential implications, and potential challenges is necessary to conduct a skeptical analysis of the metaverse (Ioannıdıs & Kontıs, 2023).

While the concept of the metaverse holds promise for creating immersive virtual experiences and connecting people in new ways, skeptics rightly point out the potential challenges and risks that must be addressed to realize this vision in a responsible and sustainable manner (Gauttier et al., 2024). A balanced and critical analysis of the metaverse is essential to navigate the complexities and uncertainties surrounding this emerging technology.

METAVERSE TECHNOLOGIES AND MARKETING

The metaverse utilizes a range of technologies to generate immersive virtual environments and facilitate user interaction. Examples of virtual and augmented reality environments that enable users to explore and interact with virtual worlds experiences (Alabau et al., 2024). The metaverse is the place where avatars and AI agents interact with users through digital representations and virtual assistants. Through avatars, users can navigate virtual environments and express themselves, while AI agents offer help, guidance, and automation (Israfilzade, 2022).

The overall immersion and realism of the virtual environment is enhanced by the use of cloud computing technology, 3D modeling and animation, and artificial intelligence to simulate realistic behaviors. Collaborating, socializing, and engaging in virtual activities with others around the world is made possible through high-speed, low-latency networks (Seok, 2021). Together, these technologies create virtual environments that are immersive, interactive, and interconnected, and they are the foundation of the metaverse. The metaverse's capabilities and possibilities will expand as technology advances, determining the future of digital experiences and interactions.

Brands can engage with consumers in new and immersive ways when the metaverse is integrated into marketing, opening up exciting possibilities (Keegan et al., 2024). Various digital platforms can be seamlessly integrated through the metaverse. Creating unified experiences that span social media, gaming, and e-commerce platforms allows brands to guarantee consistent and cohesive consumer engagement. Rich data analytics opportunities are made possible by the digital nature of the metaverse. Real-time strategy adjustments can be made by brands to optimize engagement and conversion rates by tracking how consumers interact with their virtual environments. Virtual spaces on Roblox have already been implemented by businesses like Gucci and Nike where users can explore and purchase virtual Gucci items. Despite the metaverse's vast potential, brands are confronted with obstacles such as ensuring data privacy, maintaining brand authenticity, and avoiding overcommercialization, which can alienate consumers. Furthermore, the technical and financial expenditures necessary to create high-quality metaverse experiences are significant. Table 1 gives an overview of the primary marketing trends in the metaverse and their implications.

Table 1. Summary of principal trends and their implications

Marketing trends	Implications	Key notes	Authors
Branding strategies	Immersive virtual environments can be created by brands to allow consumers to interact with products and services in a lifelike manner	Brand engagement can be enhanced by this immersive experience and consumers can leave a lasting impression.	Arya et al. (2024); Payal et al. (2024); SanMiguel et al. (2024); Aydın & Nalbant (2023); Wanick, & Stallwood, 2023); Tarnanidis & Sklavounos (2024)
Virtual events and experiences	Virtual events, conferences, and experiences can be hosted by brands in the metaverse, allowing them to reach a global audience without the constraints of physical space.	Attendees can interact at these events by networking, participating in activities, and engaging with brand content in real-time.	Arya et al. (2024); Anand & Jindal (2024); Wongkitrungrueng and Suprawan (2023); Mittal et al. (2023)
Personalized Storefronts	Communications that are customized to fit the preferences and interests of each consumer.	Virtual showrooms or storefronts can be utilized by these spaces to provide personalized product recommendations and allow consumers to explore and interact with products in a personalized environment.	Taneja & Shukla, (2024); Özkan & Özkan (2024); Chakraborty et al. (2024); Warden et al. (2024); Eggenschwiler et al. (2024); Yoo et al. (2023)
Social engagement and community	Establish communities and promote social interaction among consumers	In a social context, consumers can engage with brand content through virtual hangout spaces, social hubs, and interactive experiences that brands can create	Lee et al. (2023); Wanick et al. (2023); Bousba, & Arya (2022); Arya et al. (2024); Singh et al. (2023); Riva et al. (2024)
Virtual marketing through influencers	Reaching target audiences in the virtual space is possible for brands to collaborate with virtual influencers and avatars	In the metaverse environment, virtual influencers can advertise brand messages, endorse products, and interact with consumers in a way that is authentic and relatable	Tarnanidis & Sklavounos (2024); Sands et al. (2022); Koles et al. (2024); Aw & Agnihotri (2023)
Seamless integration with eCommerce.	Consumers can make purchases directly within virtual environments through the metaverse's seamless integration with e-commerce platforms	This integration makes it possible for brands to capitalize on consumer interest and engagement in real-time while simplifying the purchasing process.	Bratu & Sabău (2022); Idrees et al. (2023); Tariq (2024); Özkan & Özkan (2024); Tarnanidis (2024); Singla et al. (2024); Chen et al. (2024)

Source: The authors

Although there is still a lot of literature on the metaverse in marketing, there are already some key themes and studies that have emerged. Researchers have initiated an investigation into how consumers interact with brands and make purchasing decisions in virtual environments. Immersion and presence have been found to have a significant impact on consumer behavior in the metaverse, with consumers frequently exhibiting high levels of engagement and emotional attachment to virtual experiences (Ko et al., 2021). The effectiveness of virtual brand experiences and product demonstrations in the metaverse has been examined by other scholars. Research suggests that immersive and interactive experiences can enhance brand recall, improve product understanding, and increase purchase intentions among consumers (Shi et al., 2020; Rathore, 2018; Yoo et al., 2023). Research has been conducted on the use of personalization and targeting strategies within the metaverse to deliver personalized content and recommendations to virtual consumers. Studies have found that personalized marketing experiences can lead to higher levels of consumer satisfaction and engagement, ultimately driving conversion rates and brand loyalty (Kim et al. 2023), suggests that enhancing brand visibility, driving engagement, and increasing sales can be achieved through synergies between virtual and physical touchpoints (based on research). Using augmented reality, virtual reality, and gamification techniques are innovative approaches to marketing within the metaverse. Research highlights the importance of creativity and novelty in capturing consumer attention and creating memorable brand experiences in virtual environments (Choi, 2022; Lee et al. 2021).

METAVERSE EXAMPLES IN MARKETING

Metaverse concepts are being experimented with by several brands in their marketing efforts. Figure 1 shows a few examples

Figure 1. How brands are exploiting the metaverse

Brands	Virtual examples	Description
Nike's Virtual Sneaker Drops (www.nike.com)	Nike has organized virtual sneaker drops in virtual environments.	Users can purchase limited-edition virtual sneakers for their avatars during these events, which leads to buzz and engagement among sneaker enthusiasts.
Gucci's Virtual Fashion Shows (www.gucci.com)	Virtual fashion shows and events are being hosted by Gucci and Zepeto as a partnership.	Attending these shows with Zepeto avatars, interacting with digital versions of Gucci products, and even purchasing virtual items for their avatars are all possible for users.
Budweiser's Virtual Bars (www. budweiser.com)	Virtual bars have been launched by Budweiser on social media platforms.	The use of virtual bars allows users to socialize, play games, and participate in branded events and promotions while consuming virtual Budweiser products.
Mercedes-Benz's Virtual Test Drives (www. group.mercedes-benz.com)	Virtual reality experiences have been developed by Mercedes-Benz that enable users to take virtual test drives of their latest vehicles.	The features and performance of Mercedes-Benz cars can be explored by users in the comfort of their homes through immersive experiences.

In these examples, we can see how brands are using the metaverse and virtual environments to create immersive, interactive, and engaging marketing experiences that connect with customers in novel and innovative ways. With the advancement of technology, we can expect to see even more innovative marketing strategies using the metaverse. The metaverse in marketing is still being researched and explored by researchers, who are looking at consumer behavior, brand experiences, ethical considerations, and innovation in virtual environments. Future research will likely explore these areas deeper to uncover new insights into the role of the metaverse in shaping the future of marketing as the field continues to develop.

This emerging field of study is examining consumer purchase behavior in the metaverse, which examines how individuals make purchasing decisions in virtual environments. Consumers in the metaverse have the option to interact with virtual product representations before making any purchases. This entails trying on virtual clothes, test-driving virtual cars, and exploring virtual homes. By understanding how consumers interact with these virtual products, we can gain insights into their preferences and purchase intentions. In the metaverse, consumers make purchases based on a combination of factors, such as virtual product engagement, social influence, personalization, brand engagement, and rewards. By examining these factors, marketers can acquire insights on how to effectively engage consumers and drive sales in virtual environments.

PHIILIP KOTLER AND METAVERSE

The metaverse has not been specifically addressed by Philip Kotler, who is widely recognized as the 'father of modern marketing (Kotler et al., 2023). We can speculate on Kotler's approach to the topic based on his marketing principles and insights.

- Kotler emphasizes the significance of comprehending and meeting customer needs and desires (Kotler et al., 2021). Kotler's focus on the metaverse could be on how brands can use virtual environments to create personalized and immersive experiences that appeal to consumers and engage them.
- Kotler places value creation as a central tenet of marketing. In the metaverse, Kotler may contemplate how brands can generate value by implementing innovative virtual experiences, such as virtual product demonstrations, interactive storytelling, or virtual events and activations.
- Relationship marketing stresses the significance of developing long-term relationships with customers. In the metaverse, Kotler may suggest that brands concentrate on developing meaningful connections and communities

in virtual environments, which will promote loyalty and advocacy among virtual consumers.

- Kotler stresses the significance of ethical marketing practices and corporate social responsibility. In the metaverse, Kotler may suggest that marketing tactics should not be exploitative or manipulative and support transparency, authenticity, and respect for consumer privacy and rights.

Philip Kotler's marketing principles and insights are a foundation for understanding how brands might approach marketing in virtual environments, even though he hasn't specifically addressed the metaverse in his writings or statements (Kotler et al., 2024). The metaverse's evolution makes it interesting to observe how Kotler's principles are applied and adapted to this new digital frontier. In general, the metaverse has the capacity to promote economic expansion, foster social cohesion, and lessen environmental impact. Nevertheless, it also presents difficulties in terms of economic inequality, digital divide, and environmental sustainability (Inder, 2023). The digital age can be a better place for marketers to develop more inclusive, sustainable, and impactful marketing strategies by addressing these challenges and harnessing the potential benefits of the metaverse (Tarnanidis & Manaf, 2024).

CONCLUSION AND AVENUES FOR FUTURE RESEARCH

Overall, the metaverse offers consumers a range of benefits that enhance their purchasing behavior, including virtual try-on and product visualization, personalization and customization, social recommendations, access to virtual markets, convenience and accessibility, immersive brand experiences, rewards and incentives, and access to information and education. By leveraging these benefits, consumers can make more informed, personalized, and satisfying purchasing decisions within virtual environments. The metaverse holds tremendous potential to transform consumer research and practice by offering new avenues for data collection, experimentation, personalization, and collaboration. Brands can create more engaging and satisfying experiences for their customers when they embrace the opportunities presented by the metaverse and gain deeper insights into consumer behavior. Although there are challenges, the metaverse offers marketers exciting opportunities to create immersive, interactive, and personalized experiences that engage consumers in new and innovative ways.

Marketers can unlock new avenues for brand growth and customer engagement in the digital age by proactive addressing these challenges and utilizing the unique capabilities of the metaverse. While the metaverse presents exciting opportunities for marketing, it also comes with its own set of challenges. Building and navigating virtual environments within the metaverse can be technically complex, requiring specialized skills and expertise. Marketers may face challenges in understanding and mastering the tools and technologies needed to create immersive experiences and engage with consumers effectively. The metaverse may not be equally accessible to all consumers, particularly those who lack access to high-speed internet connections or advanced hardware devices required for virtual reality experiences. Marketers must consider how to ensure inclusivity and accessibility in their metaverse marketing efforts to reach a diverse audience.

Exploring the potential of the metaverse in marketing presents a rich area for future research. Marketing managers and academic researchers can investigate how consumers behave within virtual environments, including their interactions with brands, purchase decisions, and engagement patterns. Also, the metaverse can help to evaluate the effectiveness of various marketing strategies, including virtual product demonstrations, interactive experiences, and virtual events. Research could examine metrics such as brand awareness, engagement, and conversion rates to assess the impact of metaverse marketing efforts. By addressing these research topics, scholars can contribute to a deeper understanding of the role of the metaverse in marketing and help shape future practices and strategies in this emerging field. Finally, the potentials of the metaverse in marketing can be enriched through the use of different MCDM methods (Tarnanidis et al., 2025; Tarnanidis et al., 2023) as they can handle big data analytics with improved visualization.

REFERENCES

Alabau, A., Fabra, L., Martí-Testón, A., Muñoz, A., Solanes, J. E., & Gracia, L. (2024). Enriching User-Visitor Experiences in Digital Museology: Combining Social and Virtual Interaction within a Metaverse Environment. *Applied Sciences (Basel, Switzerland)*, *14*(9), 3769. doi:10.3390/app14093769

Anand, A., & Jindal, P. (2024). Brand Building in the Metaverse. In Creator's Economy in Metaverse Platforms: Empowering Stakeholders Through Omnichannel Approach (pp. 58-70). IGI Global. doi:10.4018/979-8-3693-3358-7.ch004

Arya, V., Sambyal, R., Sharma, A., & Dwivedi, Y. K. (2024). Brands are calling your AVATAR in Metaverse–A study to explore XR-based gamification marketing activities & consumer-based brand equity in virtual world. *Journal of Consumer Behaviour*, *23*(2), 556–585. doi:10.1002/cb.2214

Aw, E. C. X., & Agnihotri, R. (2023). Influencer marketing research: Review and future research agenda. *Journal of Marketing Theory and Practice*, 1–14. doi:10.1 080/10696679.2023.2235883

Aydın, S., & Nalbant, K. G. (2023). The significance of artificial intelligence in the realms of marketing, advertising, and branding inside the metaverse. *JOEEP: Journal of Emerging Economies and Policy*, *8*(2), 301–316.

Bousba, Y., & Arya, V. (2022). Let's connect in metaverse. Brand's new destination to increase consumers' affective brand engagement & their satisfaction and advocacy. *Journal of Content Community Communication*, *14*(8), 276–293. doi:10.31620/ JCCC.06.22/19

Bratu, S., & Sabău, R. I. (2022). Digital commerce in the immersive metaverse environment: Cognitive analytics management, real-time purchasing data, and seamless connected shopping experiences. *Linguistic and Philosophical Investigations*, *21*(0), 170–186. doi:10.22381/lpi21202211

Chakraborty, D., Polisetty, A., & Rana, N. P. (2024). Consumers' continuance intention towards metaverse-based virtual stores: A multi-study perspective. *Technological Forecasting and Social Change*, *203*, 123405. doi:10.1016/j.techfore.2024.123405

Chakraborty, O. (2024). Introduction to Metaverse: Concept and Evolution. In New Business Frontiers in the Metaverse (pp. 14-33). IGI Global.

Chen, C., Zhang, K. Z., Chu, Z., & Lee, M. (2024). Augmented reality in the metaverse market: The role of multimodal sensory interaction. *Internet Research*, *34*(1), 9–38. doi:10.1108/INTR-08-2022-0670

Choi, H. Y. (2022). Working in the metaverse: Does telework in a metaverse office have the potential to reduce population pressure in megacities? Evidence from young adults in Seoul, South Korea. *Sustainability (Basel)*, *14*(6), 3629. doi:10.3390/ su14063629

Eggenschwiler, M., Linzmajer, M., Roggeveen, A. L., & Rudolph, T. (2024). Retailing in the metaverse: A framework of managerial considerations for success. *Journal of Retailing and Consumer Services*, *79*, 103791. doi:10.1016/j.jretconser.2024.103791

Evans, L., Frith, J., & Saker, M. (2022). The roots of the metaverse. In *From Microverse to Metaverse: Modelling the Future through Today's Virtual Worlds* (pp. 15–24). Emerald Publishing Limited. doi:10.1108/978-1-80455-021-220221002

Gauttier, S., Simouri, W., & Milliat, A. (2024). When to enter the metaverse: Business leaders offer perspectives. *The Journal of Business Strategy*, *45*(1), 2–9. doi:10.1108/JBS-08-2022-0149

Idrees, S., Vignali, G., & Gill, S. (2023). Interactive marketing with virtual commerce tools: Purchasing right size and fitted garment in fashion metaverse. In *The Palgrave Handbook of interactive marketing* (pp. 329–351). Springer International Publishing. doi:10.1007/978-3-031-14961-0_15

Inder, S. (2023). Entrepreneurial opportunities in metaverse. In *Promoting Consumer Engagement Through Emotional Branding and Sensory Marketing* (pp. 52–62). IGI Global.

Ioannıdıs, S., & Kontıs, A. P. (2023). The 4 Epochs of the Metaverse. *Journal of Metaverse*, *3*(2), 152–165. doi:10.57019/jmv.1294970

Israfilzade, K. (2022). Marketing in the metaverse: A sceptical viewpoint of opportunities and future research directions. [EPESS]. *The Eurasia Proceedings of Educational & Social Sciences*, *24*, 53–60. doi:10.55549/epess.1179349

Keegan, B. J., McCarthy, I. P., Kietzmann, J., & Canhoto, A. I. (2024). On your marks, headset, go! Understanding the building blocks of metaverse realms. *Business Horizons*, *67*(1), 107–119. doi:10.1016/j.bushor.2023.09.002

Kim, D. Y., Lee, H. K., & Chung, K. (2023). Avatar-mediated experience in the metaverse: The impact of avatar realism on user-avatar relationship. *Journal of Retailing and Consumer Services*, *73*, 103382. doi:10.1016/j.jretconser.2023.103382

Ko, S. Y., Chung, H. K., Kim, J. I., & Shin, Y. (2021). A study on the typology and advancement of cultural leisure-based metaverse. *KIPS Transactions on Software and Data Engineering*, *10*(8), 331–338.

Koles, B., Audrezet, A., Moulard, J. G., Ameen, N., & McKenna, B. (2024). The authentic virtual influencer: Authenticity manifestations in the metaverse. *Journal of Business Research*, *170*, 114325. doi:10.1016/j.jbusres.2023.114325

Kotler, P., Kartajaya, H., & Setiawan, I. (2023). *Marketing 6.0: The Future Is Immersive*. John Wiley & Sons.

Kotler, P., Pfoertsch, W., & Sponholz, U. (2021). *H2H marketing: The genesis of human-to-human marketing* (M. Haas, Ed.). Springer. doi:10.1007/978-3-030-59531-9

Kotler, P., Pfoertsch, W., Sponholz, U., & Haas, M. (Eds.). (2024). *H2H Marketing: Case Studies on Human-to-Human Marketing*. Springer Nature.

Lee, H., & Han, J. Y. (2021). A study on classification and charact eristics of metaverse platforms according to experience type s. *Journal of the Korea Institute of the Spatial Design*, *16*(8), 427–436.

Lee, H. W., Chang, K., Uhm, J. P., & Owiro, E. (2023). How avatar identification affects enjoyment in the metaverse: The roles of avatar customization and social engagement. *Cyberpsychology, Behavior, and Social Networking*, *26*(4), 255–262. doi:10.1089/cyber.2022.0257 PMID:37001178

Mittal, G., & Bansal, R. (2023). Driving force behind consumer brand engagement: the metaverse. In *Cultural Marketing and Metaverse for Consumer Engagement* (pp. 164–181). IGI Global. doi:10.4018/978-1-6684-8312-1.ch012

Özkan, A., & Özkan, H. (2024). Meta: XR-AR-MR and Mirror World Technologies Business Impact of Metaverse. *Journal of Metaverse*, *4*(1), 21–32.

Payal, R., Sharma, N., & Dwivedi, Y. K. (2024). Unlocking the impact of brand engagement in the metaverse on Real-World purchase intentions: Analyzing Pre-Adoption behavior in a futuristic technology platform. *Electronic Commerce Research and Applications*, *65*, 101381. doi:10.1016/j.elerap.2024.101381

Rathore, B. (2018). Metaverse marketing: Novel challenges, opportunities, and strategic approaches. *Eduzone: International Peer Reviewed/Refereed Multidisciplinary Journal, 7*(2), 72-82.

Riva, G., Wiederhold, B. K., & Mantovani, F. (2024). Searching for the metaverse: Neuroscience of physical and digital communities. *Cyberpsychology, Behavior, and Social Networking*, *27*(1), 9–18. doi:10.1089/cyber.2023.0040 PMID:37057986

Sands, S., Ferraro, C., Demsar, V., & Chandler, G. (2022). False idols: Unpacking the opportunities and challenges of falsity in the context of virtual influencers. *Business Horizons*, *65*(6), 777–788. doi:10.1016/j.bushor.2022.08.002

SanMiguel, P., Sádaba, T., & Sayeed, N. (2024). Fashion brands in the metaverse: Achievements from a marketing perspective. *Journal of Global Fashion Marketing*, 1-21.

Seok, W. H. (2021). Analysis of metaverse business model and ecosystem. *Electronics and Telecommunications Trends*, *36*(4), 81–91.

Shi, H., Liu, G., Zhang, K., Zhou, Z., & Wang, J. (2022). Marl sim2real transfer: Merging physical reality with digital virtuality in metaverse. *IEEE Transactions on Systems, Man, and Cybernetics. Systems*, *53*(4), 2107–2117. doi:10.1109/TSMC.2022.3229213

Singh, A., Sharma, S., Singh, A., Unanoglu, M., & Taneja, S. (Eds.). (2023). *Cultural marketing and metaverse for consumer engagement.* IGI Global. doi:10.4018/978-1-6684-8312-1

Singla, B., Shalender, K., & Singh, N. (Eds.). (2024). *Omnichannel Approach to Co-Creating Customer Experiences Through Metaverse Platforms.* IGI Global. doi:10.4018/979-8-3693-1866-9

Stephenson, N. (1992). *Snow Crash.* Bantam Books.

Taneja, S., & Shukla, R. P. (2024). Omnichannel Retailing: A Comprehensive Exploration of Integration, Customer Engagement, and Market Share in Today's Retail. In Omnichannel Approach to Co-Creating Customer Experiences Through Metaverse Platforms (pp. 60-76). IGI Global.

Tariq, M. U. (2024). Metaverse in Business and Commerce. In *Exploring the Use of Metaverse in Business and Education* (pp. 47–72). IGI Global. doi:10.4018/979-8-3693-5868-9.ch004

Tarnanidis, T., & Manaf, A. H. (2024). Research Notes on the Future of Marketing and Consumer Insights. In T. Tarnanidis & N. Sklavounos (Eds.), *New Trends in Marketing and Consumer Science* (pp. 324–336). IGI Global. doi:10.4018/979-8-3693-2754-8.ch017

Tarnanidis, T., Papathanasiou, J., Mareschal, B., & Vlachopoulou, M. (2025). MCDM Review in marketing and managerial decisions: Practical implications and Future research. *Management Science Letters, 15*(1), 45–54. doi:10.5267/j.msl.2024.3.004

Tarnanidis, T., Papathanasiou, J., Vlachopoulou, M., & Mareschal, B. (2023). Review and the Use of PROMETHEE Methods in Marketing (Problems). In T. Tarnanidis, M. Vlachopoulou, & J. Papathanasiou (Eds.), *Influences of Social Media on Consumer Decision-Making Processes in the Food and Grocery Industry* (pp. 196–212). IGI Global. doi:10.4018/978-1-6684-8868-3.ch009

Tarnanidis, T. K. (Ed.). (2024). *Consumer Experience and Decision-Making in the Metaverse.* IGI Global.

Tarnanidis, T. K., & Sklavounos, N. (Eds.). (2024). *New Trends in Marketing and Consumer Science.* IGI Global. doi:10.4018/979-8-3693-2754-8

Wanick, V., & Stallwood, J. (2023). Brand storytelling, gamification and social media marketing in the "metaverse": A case study of the Ralph Lauren winter escape. In *Reinventing fashion retailing: Digitalising, gamifying, entrepreneuring* (pp. 35–54). Springer International Publishing. doi:10.1007/978-3-031-11185-3_3

Warden, C. A., Chen, J. F., & Yen, W. H. (2024). Metaverse Servicescape: Emotional Response to Virtual Retail Design. *International Journal of Human-Computer Interaction*, 1–14. doi:10.1080/10447318.2024.2322200

Wongkitrungrueng, A., & Suprawan, L. (2023). Metaverse meets branding: Examining consumer responses to immersive brand experiences. *International Journal of Human-Computer Interaction*, 1–20. doi:10.1080/10447318.2023.2175162

Yoo, K., Welden, R., Hewett, K., & Haenlein, M. (2023). The merchants of meta: A research agenda to understand the future of retailing in the metaverse. *Journal of Retailing*, *99*(2), 173–192. doi:10.1016/j.jretai.2023.02.002

KEY TERMS AND DEFINITIONS

Augmented Reality: Augmented reality (AR) is the practice of overlaying digital information, such as images, videos, or sounds, on the real world through devices.

Avatars: Users' digital representations of themselves in virtual spaces are called avatars. In the metaverse and augmented reality applications, they are a crucial component of social interactions. The appearance and movements of the user can be duplicated by avatars, whether they are simple 2D images or complex 3D models.

Influencer Marketing: Strategic approach in which brands collaborate with individuals who have a significant following and influence on social media platforms to promote their products or services.

Metaverse Marketing: Marketing strategies and initiatives conducted within virtual, interconnected, and immersive digital environments known as the metaverse. The metaverse is a collective virtual shared space, created by the convergence of virtual reality (VR), augmented reality (AR), the internet, and other emerging technologies.

Chapter 10

Management of Customer Relationships:
Strategies and Initiatives

Pratap Chandra Mandal
ⓘ https://orcid.org/0000-0002-0300-4002
Indian Institute of Management, Shillong, India

ABSTRACT

It is imperative for companies to develop and manage customer relationships effectively. The objective of the study is to analyze the effective management of customer relationships by companies. The methodology adopted is a conceptual analysis of the various strategies and initiatives adopted by companies for managing customer relationships. Companies customize and personalize their offerings with the help of permission marketing and engagement marketing. They empower their customers, manage customer word of mouth, and deal with customer complaints effectively. Academicians may analyze the existing strategies and initiatives and suggest effective strategies and initiatives for management of customer relationships. Practicing managers may evaluate the existing strategies and initiatives and implement effective strategies and initiatives in future. All these will enable companies to develop strong bondage with their customers, to manage customer relationships effectively, and to achieve business excellence in the long run.

DOI: 10.4018/979-8-3693-4167-4.ch010

BACKGROUND

It is imperative for companies and businesses to understand customer requirements and preferences (Oey, Puspitasari, Fransiska, & Polla, 2023). Companies collect information about customers to understand their requirements and preferences and to build long-term relationships (Mandal, 2022). Customer relationship management (CRM) is the process of carefully managing detailed information about individual customers and all customer touch points to maximize customer loyalty (Kumar & Reinartz, 2018). It is important for companies to develop and manage customer relationships because company profitability increases as the life of the customers with the company increases (Erlangga, 2023). Companies will not be able to develop and manage customer relationships unless they collect and maintain relevant information about customers. Consequently, companies also require maintaining records of their customers and require increasing the aggregate value of customers. Companies aim to optimize the value of their customer base with the help of customer value management (Kotler, 2017). Customer value management focuses on the analysis of individual data on prospects and customers to develop marketing strategies for acquiring and retaining customers and to drive customer behavior (Verhoef & Lemon, 2013).

Customer relationship management allows companies to streamline their processes. It helps companies to understand customer requirements better. Companies are able to provide excellent real-time customer service through the effective use of individual account information (Anabila & Awunyo-Vitor, 2013). Companies are also able to infer various characteristics about their valued customers. Based on the understanding, companies can customize their market offerings, services, programs, messages, and media. Companies adopt a number of strategies to enhance customer relationship management. These strategies include customization, customer empowerment, managing customer word of mouth, and dealing with customer complaints.

The discussions indicate the importance of customer relationship management. Companies require developing, building, and maintaining relationships with customers. Companies will not succeed unless they formulate strategies for effective customer relationship. Companies and businesses require focusing on the evolving trends in the field of customer relationship management to succeed in the long run. Although it is important for companies to develop and maintain effective customer relationships, few studies have focused on the topic. The study aims at addressing this research gap.

The objective of the study is to analyze the various and evolving aspects of customer relationship management and the various strategies and initiatives adopted by companies for effective customer relationship management.

The methodology adopted is a conceptual analysis of the various and evolving aspects of customer relationship management. Companies adopt a number of strategies and initiatives for effective customer relationship management. A conceptual analysis of such strategies is done. Research studies published in reputed academic journals on the topic are studied and analyzed. Primary data is not collected and empirical analysis is not done.

The novelty and the contributions of the study lie in the fact that an in-depth conceptual analysis of various and evolving strategies and initiatives adopted by companies for managing customer relationships effectively, is done. Companies require developing and managing customer relationships effectively to sustain and to grow in the competitive business environment. Academicians may study and analyze the various strategies and initiatives adopted by companies and suggest strategies and initiatives which are effective in managing customer relationships. Practicing managers will appreciate the importance of customer relationship management and of managing customer relationships effectively. They may analyze the strategies and initiatives adopted by their companies at present and may suggest strategies and initiatives which are effective in managing customer relationships and which can be implemented in future.

CUSTOMIZATION

Customization refers to the process of personalizing products and services based on the requirements and preferences of customers (Kumari, Zhang, Zhang, Shechtman, & Zhu, 2023). Customization can encompass adopting the actual physical product and modifying the service experience. Companies can make their offerings personally relevant to as many customers as possible (Tang & Chan, 2023). This may become a challenge for companies because the requirements and preferences of different customers are different. Customization requires that marketers should abandon the mass market practices that built brand powerhouses in the 20th century for new approaches. Previously, marketers literally knew their customers individually by names. Companies could design unique offerings for their customers (Thaichon, Surachartkumtonkun, Quach, Weaven, & Palmatier, 2018).

Companies aim at customizing the customer experience. Companies use call centers, along with online, digital, and mobile tools complemented by artificial intelligence and data analytics to ensure seamless contact between company and customers (Nuseir, El Refae, Aljumah, Alshurideh, Urabi, & Kurdi, 2023). However, companies should realize that customer relationship management is not only about employing technology or about rolling out too many automated-response phone systems or social networking tools in order to satisfy customer service requests

(Kumar & Reinartz, 2018). Many customers prefer personal interactions with company representatives. They prefer to receive more personal services. Companies should provide personalized services to such customers for building lasting customer relationships (Wang & Groth, 2014).

Companies understand and recognize the roles and importance of maintaining personal contacts with customers. Personal contacts are important once customers start interacting with the company (Thakur, 2022). Employees have a definitive role to play in the process. Employees can interact with customers and create strong bonds with customers by individualizing and personalizing relationships (Lu, Liu, & Yang, 2022). For example, British Airways maintains direct contacts at all phases to satisfy its valued customers. The company tries to personalize its service experiences (Taneja, 2016).

BMW conducts in-depth research to personalize its products. The personalization in products includes 500 side-mirror combinations, 1300 front-bumper combinations, and 9000 center-console combinations (Siby & George, 2022). The company also allows new buyers to experience their new cars being manufactured till the time of delivery with the help of a video link (Reimer, 2023). The detailed manufacturing and procurement system takes the slack out of the production process, reduces inventory carrying costs, and avoids rebates on slow-moving sellers. Loyal customers of BMW like the process. Consequently, this results in more profitability for BMW and its dealers (Reimer, 2023). Coca-Cola is another company which has a strong focus on customization. The Coca-Cola Freestyle dispensing machine can dispense 125 sparkling and still brands that customers can mix with the help of a touchscreen. This helps customers to prepare a beverage as per their individual tastes and preferences (Coelho, Corona, ten Klooster, & Worrell, 2020).

Companies will be able to develop and maintain effective customer relationship management programs only when they know their customers very well (Herman, Sulhaini, & Farida, 2021). Maintenance of customer databases forms the foundation of an effective customer relationship management program. A customer database is an organized collection of comprehensive information about individual customers or prospects that is current, accessible, and actionable for lead generation, lead qualification, sale of a product or service, or maintenance of customer relationships (Kumar & Reinartz, 2006). Consequently, customer relationship management may be viewed as a process of building, maintaining, and using customer-related data to contact customers, transact with them, and to build customer relationships in the long run (Kumar & Reinartz, 2006).

Online retailers try to understand customer preferences. Based on such preferences, they add their own recommendations to consumer selections or purchases e.g. "If you like that black handbag, you'll love this red top." Such recommendations are beneficial for retailers because research suggests that such recommendation systems contribute 10 percent to 30 percent of sales for an online retailer (Ngah, Thurasamy, & Han, 2023). Retailers apply specialized software tools to *discover* customers and to understand their unplanned purchases. However, online retailers should ensure that online tracking of customers to create relationships do not backfire. Customers may be bombarded by computer-generated recommendations which they may dislike. For example, when a customer buys a few baby gifts on Amazon.com, the personalized recommendations for the individual may not look that much personal (Wang, 2021). Online retailers should understand and appreciate the limitations of technology in predicting personalization. Retailers should adopt those practices that really work (Shen, Wan, & Li, 2023). Companies should consider permission marketing and engagement marketing when formulating customer relationship strategies.

Permission Marketing

Companies should understand the desire of customers for personalization and should learn to adapt to it. Companies should realize and appreciate the fact that not all customers wish to build relationships. Customers may have privacy concerns. So, marketers now-a-days are wise enough to embrace permission marketing (Abashidze, 2023). Permission marketing is the practice of marketing to customers only after getting their expressed permission. Permission marketing is based on the premise that marketers can no longer employ mass media campaigns to do *interruption marketing* (Abashidze, 2023). Companies send newsletters only to those readers who have chosen to subscribe. This means that such readers have granted permission to the publisher to send them relevant information. This is one of the examples of permission marketing (Abashidze, 2023).

Permission marketing requires that companies should communicate with customers and should develop customer relationships only after obtaining their explicit consent. Companies should send communications and messages to those customers who have expressed willingness to become more engaged with the brand (Krafft, Arden, & Verhoef, 2017). Both companies and customers are benefited in the process because the communications happen based on mutual consent (Jones, 2021).

The basic assumptions of permission marketing include that customers are aware about their requirements and preferences, even though such requirements and preferences may often be undefined, ambiguous, or conflicting (Nigam, Behl, Pereira, & Sangal, 2023).

Engagement Marketing

Engagement marketing happens when customers are aware about their requirements and preferences and when they are willing to share those requirements and preferences with companies (Blut, Kulikovskaja, Hubert, Brock, & Grewal, 2023). Engagement marketing happens when companies and customers work together to find out how the firm can best satisfy customers and also when both companies and customers benefit from each other (Bag, Srivastava, Bashir, Kumari, Giannakis, & Chowdhury, 2022). In other words, permission marketing is a pre-requisite for engagement marketing to be effective. In engagement marketing, customers become a part of the entire process and help companies to deliver the offering (Hoang, Kousi, Martinez, & Kumar, 2023).

CUSTOMER EMPOWERMENT

In the recent times, customers have higher control in the manner in which they interact with companies (Smith, 2022). Previously, consumers were passive receivers of marketing messages. However, at present, consumers can decide whether they want to respond to marketing messages. Also, they will decide the manner in which they wish to interact with companies. Companies should realize and acknowledge that customers are empowered at present (Lambillotte & Poncin, 2023). Customer empowerment requires that companies must strengthen their relationships with customers and engage with them in newer and innovative ways (Mishra & Singh, 2023). Company empowerment needs to be mapped with customer empowerment. Consequently, companies require modifying the ways in which they interact with customers (Morrongiello, N'Goala, & Kreziak, 2017). Marketers motivate customers to become evangelists for brands. Customers are provided with resources and opportunities to demonstrate their passion. For example, Doritos held a contest to understand the opinions of customers and to name its next flavor (Acar & Puntoni, 2016). Converse asked amateur filmmakers to submit a 30-second film that demonstrated how the iconic sneaker brand inspired them. Converse showcased the best submissions in the Converse Gallery website. Also, Converse finalized its television commercials from the best of the best submissions (Acar & Puntoni, 2016).

New technologies allow customers to be empowered and to be involved in the marketing of a brand. At the same time, technological developments allow customers to avoid marketing promotions. For example, many web browsers feature ad-blocking and popup-blocking software, e-mail servers offer spam filters, and mobile phones offer call-blocking options (Lambillotte & Poncin, 2023).

Companies try to empower customers to get involved in brand-building processes and how the brands are marketed. However, only some consumers want to get involved with some of the brands they use, and even then, only some of the time (Lahtinen, Pulkka, Karjaluoto, & Mero, 2023). Consumers have other priorities in their lives. Those priorities may be more important to them than the brands which they purchase and consume. It is important for companies to understand about how they should market a brand given that consumer interests and preferences are diverse (Hu, 2023).

It is difficult to understand when and why consumers decide to engage with a brand. Many factors govern the process. However, one study revealed that "… most do not engage with companies via social media simply to feel connected … To successfully exploit the potential of social media, companies need to design experiences that potential of social media, companies need to design experiences that deliver tangible value in return for customers' time, attention, endorsement and data" (Baird & Parasnis, 2011). Customers look for various tangible values viz. information, coupons, discount, price while making a purchase. Many businesses overlook social media's capabilities for delivering customer value while capturing customer insights, monitoring the brand, conducting research, and soliciting new-product ideas (Mandal, 2023).

MANAGING CUSTOMER WORD OF MOUTH

Consumers are mainly influenced by the recommendations and viewpoints of friends and relatives. However, at present, individuals are getting influenced by recommendations from other consumers (Azhari, bin S Senathirajah, & Haque, 2023). In an atmosphere of heightening mistrust of some companies and their advertising, online customer ratings and reviews are playing an important role in the customer buying process (Oetarjo, Rohim, Firdaus, & Togayev, 2023).

A Forrester research study reveals that individuals hesitate to book hotel rooms unless online reviews are available for such hotel rooms (Yang, Wang, & Zhao, 2023). Consequently, hotels are launching their own programs through which they can collect customer reviews. For example, Starwood places independent and authenticated reviews on individual hotel sites (Acciarini, Cappa, Boccardelli, & Oriani, 2023). Similarly for travel reviews, Wyndham streams its five most recent reviews from TripAdvisor (Jeong, Shin, Lee, & Lee, 2023). Such reviews are valuable and authentic resources for travelers.

Brick-and-mortar retailers have started understanding the importance of customer reviews. Retailers like Best Buy, Staples, and Baas Pro Shops display consumer reviews in their stores. However, despite consumer acceptance of such reviews, their quality and integrity can be in question (Huang, Gao, & Gao, 2023). The cofounder and CEO of Whole Foods Market posted more than 1100 entries on Yahoo! Finance's online bulletin board under a pseudonym for seven continuous years. The cofounder praised the efforts of his company and criticized that of competitors (Zhang, Lu, & Prombutr, 2022). Such cases of fraud should not be entertained. Companies apply computer-recognition technology to monitor and to prevent such frauds. Bazaarvoice applies a process called device fingerprinting which helps companies like Walmart and Best Buy to manage and monitor online reviews. Bazaarvoice detected one firm which posted hundreds of positive reviews of one of its products and negative reviews of its competitors' products (König, Hein, & Nimsgern, 2022).

It is challenging for companies to keep a track of comments made by customers through online reviews and blogging sites (Shi & Chen, 2021). Companies should try to ensure that the reviews are provided by individuals who disclose their identities and are unbiased. To address this issue, Angie's List allowed only paid and registered subscribers to access its website (Ponathil, Bhanu, Piratla, Sharma, & Chalil Madathil, 2022). Users rate providers on price, quality, responsiveness, professionalism, and punctuality, using a report card – style scale of A to F. There are various websites which offer summaries of professional third-party reviews. Leading critics from multiple publications provide music, games, television, and movie reviews. Metacritic aggregates such reviews and converts them into a single 1-to-100 score. In the gaming industry, some game companies tie bonuses for their developers to game scores on the more popular websites. Stock prices of publishers may drop when a major new release does not make the 85-plus cut-off based on user reviews (Ponathil, Bhanu, Piratla, Sharma, & Chalil Madathil, 2022).

Marketers may keep a track of personal and public blogs by tracking the social media. Bloggers who review products or services are influential individuals. They may have thousands of followers. Also, online searches for brands or product categories result in finding the most popular blogs. Companies also look out for popular bloggers to promote their offerings via free samples and advanced information. Many bloggers disclose their special treatment from the companies they write about (Lepkowska-White & Kortright, 2018).

Online word of mouth is crucial and critical for companies with smaller brands and limited media budgets (You, He, Chen, & Hu, 2021). For example, organic food maker, Amy's Kitchen shipped out samples before its release to several of more than fifty vegan, glutton-free, or vegetarian food bloggers that the company tracks. This was done to generate prelaunch buzz for one of its new hot cereals (Rogers, 2023). The initiative was a success. Favorable reviews appeared on the blogs. Individuals approached the company asking where to buy the cereal (Rogers, 2023).

Negative reviews may sometimes be beneficial for companies (Yang, Li, Chen, & Li, 2020). Negative reviews may hurt an established brand. However, such reviews can also create awareness about unknown or overlooked brands. Such reviews can provide valuable insights (Tan, Cherapanukorn, Kim, & Chon, 2014). A Forrester study of 10000 consumers of Amazon.com's electronics and home and garden products revealed that 50 percent found negative reviews to be helpful (Yao, 2023). Negative reviews help consumers to better learn the advantages and disadvantages of products. Consequently, there may be fewer product returns which may save substantial amount of money for retailers and producers (Li, Zhao, & Srinivas, 2023).

DEALING WITH CUSTOMER COMPLAINTS

Companies have a perception that analysis of customer complaints will provide an idea about customer satisfaction (Kunathikornkit, Piriyakul, & Piriyakul, 2023). However, studies reveal that even when individuals are dissatisfied with their purchases about 25 percent of the time, only about 5 percent of dissatisfied customers complain. The rest 95 percent of the dissatisfied customers either feel that filing complaints is not worth the effort or they do not know to whom and where to complain. They just stop buying (Kunathikornkit, Piriyakul, & Piriyakul, 2023).

Customers decide whether to continue buying or not depending on the responses which they receive to their complaints. Fifty percent to 70 percent of customers might do business with the company if they feel that the complaint was resolved quickly (Kunathikornkit, Piriyakul, & Piriyakul, 2023). Customers who are satisfied with the complaints being resolved, tell an average of five individuals about the treatment which they receive. However, a dissatisfied customer talks about the experience to at least 11 individuals on an average. Again, the individuals who hear about the bad experiences with other individuals, get influenced. The chain may grow exponentially (Kunathikornkit, Piriyakul, & Piriyakul, 2023).

Companies will commit mistakes even after they have designed and implemented an effective marketing program (Wang & Karmina, 2023). Companies can try to minimize the chances of mistakes happening in the first place. They should also try to ensure that customers find it easy to complain. Companies may arrange for suggestion forms, toll-free numbers, websites, apps, and e-mail addresses for quick and effective two-way communications (Wang & Karmina, 2023). Customers feel that companies are serious about addressing complaints when they are allowed to provide customer feedback. The process also helps companies to improve its products and services (Ming, 2023). The 3M Company claims that more than two-thirds of its product-improvement ideas come from listening to customer complaints (Na, Choi, & Kwon, 2019).

Companies are aware that a majority of dissatisfied and frustrated customers prefer not to complain. Consequently, companies should proactively monitor social media and other places where customer complaints and feedback may be posted (Wang, Lai, & Lin, 2023). For example, the customer service team of Jet Blue keeps a track of the airline's social media presence. It monitors the Twitter account and the Facebook account regularly. Jet Blue received a complaint from a customer regarding a fee for bringing a folded bike on board. The complaint started circulating online. Jet

Blue was prompt in responding to the complaint. The company decided that it was a service for which fees should not be charged (Gunarathne, Rui, & Seidmann, 2018).

A dissatisfied customer may cause substantial harm to the reputation of a company (Arruda Filho & Barcelos, 2021). It makes sense for companies to address negative customer experiences properly and promptly. Companies may adopt a number of practices which can help them to recover customer goodwill (Nyrhinen, Kemppainen, Grénman, Frank, Makkonen, & Wilska, 2021).

1. Companies may make it easier for customers to register complaints by setting up a seven-day, 24-hour toll-free hotline through e-mail, online chat, phone, or fax. This may also make it easier for companies to track and to act on complaints (Anwar, 2023).
2. Once a complaint has been registered, companies should contact the complaining customer at the earliest. The slower the company is to respond; the more dissatisfaction may grow. This may lead to negative word of mouth (Garding & Bruns, 2015).
3. Companies should investigate and try to find out the true source of customer dissatisfaction. They should try to solve the issue only after a thorough investigation. Some complaining customers are not looking for compensation so much as for a sign that the company cares (Anwar, 2023).
4. Companies cannot blame customers for any of the failures. They should accept the responsibility for the customer's disappointment (Istanbulluoglu & Oz, 2023).
5. Companies should strive to resolve customer complaints promptly and to the customer's satisfaction. Companies should take into account the costs of resolving the complaint and the lifetime value of the customer (Japutra, Loureiro, Molinillo, & Primanti, 2023).

Companies may not be always at fault when customers register complaints related to the products and services provided by them (Chen, Li, Chiu, & Chen, 2021). Customers may be opportunistic and may target big companies. Customers may try to capitalize on even minor transgressions or generous compensation policies (Chen, Li, Chiu, & Chen, 2021). Many companies fight back when they feel that the criticism or complaint is unjustified. Some other companies may seek ways to find a silver lining in customer complaints and use them to improve the image and performance of the company (Uusitalo, Hakala, & Kautonen, 2011).

Taco Bell received negative buzz online when rumors and a consumer lawsuit alleged that its taco mixture contained more filler than meat (Mandel, 2003). The company responded with a full-page newspaper advertisement headlined, "Thank you for suing us." The complaint allowed Taco Bell to strengthen its brand image by communicating that its taco mixtures were 88 percent beef, with ingredients such as water, oats, spices, and cocoa powder added only for flavor, texture, and moisture. These communications were posted on Facebook and YouTube. Taco Bell marketers also bought the key words *taco*, *bell*, and *lawsuit* so that the official responses of the company appeared as the first link on Google and other search engines (Duhon, Ellison, & Ragas, 2016).

It is challenging for companies to achieve zero level of complaints. There are customers who will never be satisfied however hard companies may try. So, companies should try to balance customer satisfaction with their own strategic and monetary goals. In this way, companies will be able to create value for both their customers and their stakeholders.

Critics are worried about social media and the negative effects created by customers who communicate online. However, companies argue that the benefits received from the usage of social media outweigh the harmful effects. They also claim that measures can be adopted to minimize the extent of damage created. Companies, now-a-days, are active in corporate social responsibility. Such companies try to build their public image during quiet times and then leverage the goodwill in paid or other media during difficult times. Internet-savvy critics once skillfully used search engine optimization to populate unflattering portraits of Nike. At present, searches for Nike yield links to sites that describe in many environmental and community initiatives such as shoe recycling (Jhunjhunwala, 2023).

INITIATIVES BY COMPANIES

Companies adopt a number of initiatives for managing customer relationships. Some of the companies include Dunnhumby, British Airways, and TripAdvisor.

Initiatives by Dunnhumby

Dunnhumby is a British customer data science company which was founded by husband-and-wife team, Clive Humby and Edwina Dunn (Chakravorti, 2023). The company has helped retailers and other firms to increase their profitabilities by generating insights from their loyalty program data and credit card transactions. The company also helps the British supermarket giant, Tesco to manage its various aspects of business. These include creating new shop formats, arranging store layouts, developing private-label products, and tailoring coupons and special discounts to its loyalty shoppers (Beattie, 2023). Tesco was thinking of dropping a poor-selling type of bread from its product portfolio. However, finally Tesco decided against dropping it when the analysis performed by Dunnhumby revealed that it was a *destination product* for a loyal cohort that would shop elsewhere if the product is taken off (Chakravorti, 2023). Dunnhumby has conducted analysis based on data from over 350 million individuals across the globe. The analysis has helped to take decisions related to product ranges, availability, space planning, and new-product innovations (Beattie, 2023). Dunnhumby conducted data analysis for a major European catalog company. The analysis revealed that individuals with different body types not only prefer different clothing styles, but also shop at different times of the year. Slimmer consumers tended to buy early in a new season. Larger folks tended to take fewer risks and wait until later in the season to see which styles proved popular (Beattie, 2023).

Initiatives by British Airways

British Airways is a company which focuses on personalization. It started its *Know Me* campaign to centralize information about frequent fliers from all the service channels of the company into a single and centralized database. These service channels include website, call center, e-mail, on-board planes, and inside airports (Johnston, 2016). This initiative allowed British Airways to track the current seating location, previous flights and meal choices, and even previous complaint history for all passengers who book its flight. British Airways distributes iPads to crew members and ground staff. Crew members and ground staff are able to access the centralized database and to receive personal recognition messages about passengers on any flight. The company identifies and facilitates its VIP passengers with the help of stored photos of fliers which are downloaded from Google Image searches (Karaağaoğlu & Çiçek, 2019). One company representative commented that the program aimed to "recreate the feeling of recognition you get in a favorite restaurant when you're welcomed there, but in our case, it will be delivered by thousands of staff to millions of customers" (Karaağaoğlu & Çiçek, 2019). Some critics raised privacy and security concerns and called it *creepy*. However, British Airways noted that the passenger information was already available or was viewed as helpful by its most valuable fliers (Johnston, 2016).

Initiatives by TripAdvisor

TripAdvisor was founded by Stephen Kaufer in 2001. He founded the company after he was frustrated by the lack of detailed, reliable, and up-to-date information available to help him decide where to go on a Mexican holiday (Juteau, 2023). TripAdvisor is a pioneer in online consumer travel reviews. The rise of the company is phenomenal and at present, it is the world's largest website. The company allows customers to collect and share information. Customers can make bookings for a wide variety of hotels, vacation rentals, airlines, restaurants, and other travel-related locations or businesses through its hotel and air booking partners (Sann & Lai, 2023). Customers can post reviews, photos, and opinions. They can also participate in discussions on a variety of different topics. TripAdvisor aims to improve the quality and accuracy of its content by reviewing content both manually and with advanced computer algorithms. TripAdvisor has a verification and fraud detection system that monitors the IP and e-mail addresses of reviewers. Other review attributes are monitored as well. The system also tracks suspicious patterns of postings as well as inappropriate language (Mukherjee, Debnath, Chakraborty, Jena, & Hasan, 2023). More than 490 million unique visitors visit the website of TripAdvisor on a monthly basis. The website features over 700 million reviews. Every month, hundreds of millions of individuals view its content on hundreds of other sites, including Hotels.com and Expedia (Sann & Lai, 2023). TripAdvisor focuses on innovation to personalize the social nature of its services. TripAdvisor was one of the initial launch partners with Facebook for its *Instant Personalization* project. The initiative allows users to personalize their TripAdvisor experience. Users can see their TripAdvisor content posted by their Facebook friends, subject to the friends' privacy selections (Kim, Best, & Choi, 2023). Local Picks is a Facebook app that allows users to localize TripAdvisor restaurant reviews and auto-share user reviews on Facebook (Alaimo, Kallinikos, & Valderrama, 2020).

DISCUSSIONS

It is imperative for companies to develop and manage customer relationships. Companies adopt various and innovative strategies to manage customer relationships viz. customization, customer empowerment, word of mouth, and dealing with customer complaints. Companies will be able to customize and personalize offerings if they adopt permission marketing and engagement marketing. Customers should be empowered so that they understand the importance of their involvement in the process of customer relationship management. Word of mouth is important for developing customer relationships. Companies should be able to manage customer word of mouth properly. They should also deal with customer complaints efficiently and effectively. All these will help companies to develop and manage customer relationships effectively. The discussions have both theoretical and managerial implications.

Theoretical Implications

Academicians may study and analyze the various strategies and initiatives adopted by companies for developing and managing customer relationships. Based on the analysis, academicians may suggest better and effective ways of managing customer relationships. They may suggest more effective ways of understanding customers and may formulate models for customer relationships which can be implemented by companies.

Managerial Implications

The success of companies is determined by how effectively they are able to develop and manage relationships with their customers. They require analyzing the business environment and their customers to develop strategies and initiatives which are oriented towards their customers. They should customize and personalize their offerings as per customer requirements and preferences. They require empowering their customers. They should manage customer word of mouth and deal with customer complaints effectively. All these will help companies to develop and manage customer relationships effectively.

CONCLUSION

Companies function in a competitive business environment. Companies will not succeed unless they develop effective customer relationships and unless they manage such relationships effectively. Companies customize and personalize their offerings with the help of permission marketing and engagement marketing. They empower their customers, manage customer word of mouth, and deal with customer complaints effectively. All these strategies and initiatives allow companies to develop and manage customer relationships effectively.

Limitations

The study conducted a conceptual analysis of various strategies and initiatives adopted by companies for managing customer relationships effectively. Primary data is not collected and empirical analysis is not done. Also, the analysis is performed mainly with a focus on the markets in the United States.

Avenues of Future Research

It is imperative for companies to develop and manage customer relationships effectively to sustain and to grow in the competitive business environment. The study conducted a conceptual analysis of the various aspects of managing customer relationships. Researchers may collect primary data and conduct an empirical analysis to understand the effectiveness of various strategies and initiatives better. Also, analysis should be conducted in markets other than that of the United States to understand the scenario in other markets. All these will allow companies to develop and manage customer relationships more effectively and to achieve business excellence.

REFERENCES

Abashidze, I. (2023). Permission Marketing Strategy Shaping Consumer Behaviour Through Online Communication Channels. *Baltic Journal of Economic Studies*, *9*(2), 8–18. doi:10.30525/2256-0742/2023-9-2-8-18

Acar, O. A., & Puntoni, S. (2016). Customer empowerment in the digital age. *Journal of Advertising Research*, *56*(1), 4–8. doi:10.2501/JAR-2016-007

Acciarini, C., Cappa, F., Boccardelli, P., & Oriani, R. (2023). How can organizations leverage big data to innovate their business models? A systematic literature review. *Technovation*, *123*, 102713. doi:10.1016/j.technovation.2023.102713

Alaimo, C., Kallinikos, J., & Valderrama, E. (2020). Platforms as service ecosystems: Lessons from social media. *Journal of Information Technology*, *35*(1), 25–48. doi:10.1177/0268396219881462

Anabila, P., & Awunyo-Vitor, D. (2013). Customer relationship management: A key to organisational survival and customer loyalty in Ghana's banking industry. *International Journal of Marketing Studies*, *5*(1), 107–117. doi:10.5539/ijms.v5n1p107

Anwar, S. (2023). Understanding the conceptualisation and strategies of service recovery processes in service organisations. *International Journal of Services. Economics and Management*, *14*(2), 175–197.

Arruda Filho, E. J. M., & Barcelos, A. D. A. (2021). Negative online word-of-mouth: Consumers' retaliation in the digital world. *Journal of Global Marketing*, *34*(1), 19–37. doi:10.1080/08911762.2020.1775919

Azhari, N. F. B., bin S Senathirajah, A. R., & Haque, R. (2023). The role of customer satisfaction, trust, word of mouth, and service quality in enhancing customers' loyalty toward e-commerce. *Transnational Marketing Journal*, *11*(1), 31–43.

Bag, S., Srivastava, G., Bashir, M. M. A., Kumari, S., Giannakis, M., & Chowdhury, A. H. (2022). Journey of customers in this digital era: Understanding the role of artificial intelligence technologies in user engagement and conversion. *Benchmarking*, *29*(7), 2074–2098. doi:10.1108/BIJ-07-2021-0415

Baird, C. H., & Parasnis, G. (2011). From social media to social customer relationship management. *Strategy and Leadership*, *39*(5), 30–37. doi:10.1108/10878571111161507

Beattie, R. (2023). *Bringing Loyalty to Life: How to earn, build and leverage enduring customer loyalty*. SRA Books.

Blut, M., Kulikovskaja, V., Hubert, M., Brock, C., & Grewal, D. (2023). Effectiveness of engagement initiatives across engagement platforms: A meta-analysis. *Journal of the Academy of Marketing Science*, *51*(5), 1–25. doi:10.1007/s11747-023-00925-7 PMID:37359266

Chakravorti, S. (2023). Customer Relationship Management: A Global Approach. *Sage (Atlanta, Ga.)*.

Chen, H., Li, X., Chiu, T. S., & Chen, F. (2021). The impact of perceived justice on behavioral intentions of Cantonese Yum Cha consumers: The mediation role of psychological contract violation. *Journal of Hospitality and Tourism Management*, *49*, 178–188. doi:10.1016/j.jhtm.2021.09.009

Coelho, P. M., Corona, B., ten Klooster, R., & Worrell, E. (2020). Sustainability of reusable packaging–Current situation and trends. *Resources, Conservation and Recycling. X*, *6*, 100037. doi:10.1016/j.rcrx.2020.100037

Duhon, S., Ellison, K., & Ragas, M. W. (2016). A whale of a problem: A strategic communication analysis of SeaWorld Entertainment's multi-year Blackfish crisis. *Case Studies in Strategic Communication*, *5*(1), 2–37.

Erlangga, A. W. (2023). The Effect of Digitalization and Customer Relationship Management on Member Loyalty. *Journal of Digital Business and Data Science*, *1*(1), 1–12.

Garding, S., & Bruns, A. (2015). *Complaint management and channel choice: An analysis of customer perceptions*. Springer. doi:10.1007/978-3-319-18179-0

Gunarathne, P., Rui, H., & Seidmann, A. (2018). When social media delivers customer service: Differential customer treatment in the airline industry. *Management Information Systems Quarterly*, *42*(2), 489–520. doi:10.25300/MISQ/2018/14290

Herman, L. E., Sulhaini, S., & Farida, N. (2021). Electronic customer relationship management and company performance: Exploring the product innovativeness development. *Journal of Relationship Marketing*, *20*(1), 1–19. doi:10.1080/15332 667.2019.1688600

Hoang, D., Kousi, S., Martinez, L. F., & Kumar, S. (2023). Revisiting a model of customer engagement cycle: A systematic review. *Service Industries Journal*, *43*(9-10), 579–617. doi:10.1080/02642069.2023.2202912

Hu, Y. (2023). Research on Brand Marketing Model of Perfect Diary of Beauty Enterprises based on 4P Theory Framework. *Highlights in Business. Economics and Management*, *6*, 29–35.

Huang, L., Gao, B., & Gao, M. (2023). Comparison of E-Commerce Retail Between China and Japan. In *Value Realization in the Phygital Reality Market: Consumption and Service Under Conflation of the Physical, Digital, and Virtual Worlds* (pp. 151–184). Springer Nature Singapore. doi:10.1007/978-981-99-4129-2_8

Istanbulluoglu, D., & Oz, S. (2023). Service Recovery via Twitter: An Exploration of Responses to Consumer Complaints. *Accounting Perspectives*, *22*(4), 1–26. doi:10.1111/1911-3838.12339

Japutra, A., Loureiro, S. M. C., Molinillo, S., & Primanti, H. (2023). Influence of individual and social values on customer engagement in luxury thermal spa hotels: The mediating roles of perceived justice and brand experience. *Tourism and Hospitality Research*, 14673584231188847. doi:10.1177/14673584231188847

Jeong, M., Shin, H. H., Lee, M., & Lee, J. (2023). Assessing brand performance consistency from consumer-generated media: The US hotel industry. *International Journal of Contemporary Hospitality Management*, *35*(6), 2056–2083. doi:10.1108/IJCHM-12-2021-1516

Jhunjhunwala, S. (2023). Corporate Social Responsibility: Making a Difference. In *Corporate Governance: Creating Value for Stakeholders* (pp. 145–169). Springer Nature Singapore. doi:10.1007/978-981-99-2707-4_7

Johnston, A. (2016). Creepiness Is in the Eye of the Beholder [Opinion]. *IEEE Technology and Society Magazine*, *35*(1), 27–28. doi:10.1109/MTS.2016.2518254

Jones, W. (2021). *Email Marketing*. Editora Bibliomundi.

Juteau, S. (2023). TheFork by TripAdvisor: A French success story. *Journal of Information Technology Teaching Cases*, 20438869231179989.

Karaağaoğlu, N., & Çiçek, M. (2019). An evaluation of digital marketing applications in airline sector. *International Journal of Human Sciences*, *16*(2), 606–619. doi:10.14687/jhs.v16i2.5661

Kim, E., Best, A. R., & Choi, K. (2023). Mapping the research trends on social media in the hospitality sector from 2010 to 2020. *Tourism and Hospitality Management*, *29*(2), 167–181. doi:10.20867/thm.29.2.2

König, T. M., Hein, N., & Nimsgern, V. (2022). A value perspective on online review platforms: Profiling preference structures of online shops and traditional companies. *Journal of Business Research*, *145*, 387–401. doi:10.1016/j.jbusres.2022.02.080

Kotler, P. (2017). Customer value management. *Journal of Creating Value*, *3*(2), 170–172. doi:10.1177/2394964317706879

Krafft, M., Arden, C. M., & Verhoef, P. C. (2017). Permission marketing and privacy concerns—Why do customers (not) grant permissions? *Journal of Interactive Marketing*, *39*(1), 39–54. doi:10.1016/j.intmar.2017.03.001

Kumar, V., & Reinartz, W. (2018). *Customer relationship management*. Springer-Verlag GmbH Germany.

Kumar, V., & Reinartz, W. J. (2006). *Customer relationship management: A databased approach*. Wiley.

Kumari, N., Zhang, B., Zhang, R., Shechtman, E., & Zhu, J. Y. (2023). Multi-concept customization of text-to-image diffusion. In *Proceedings of the IEEE/CVF Conference on Computer Vision and Pattern Recognition* (pp. 1931-1941). IEEE.

Kunathikornkit, S., Piriyakul, I., & Piriyakul, R. (2023). One-to-one marketing management via customer complaint. *Social Network Analysis and Mining*, *13*(1), 83. doi:10.1007/s13278-023-01082-z

Lahtinen, N., Pulkka, K., Karjaluoto, H., & Mero, J. (2023). *Digital Marketing Strategy: Create Strategy, Put It Into Practice, Sell More*. Edward Elgar Publishing. doi:10.4337/9781035311316

Lambillotte, L., & Poncin, I. (2023). Customers facing companies' content personalisation attempts: Paradoxical tensions, strategies and managerial insights. *Journal of Marketing Management*, *39*(3-4), 213–243. doi:10.1080/026725 7X.2022.2105384

Lepkowska-White, E., & Kortright, E. (2018). The business of blogging: Effective approaches of women food bloggers. *Journal of Foodservice Business Research*, *21*(3), 257–279. doi:10.1080/15378020.2017.1399046

Li, M., Zhao, L., & Srinivas, S. (2023). It is about inclusion! Mining online reviews to understand the needs of adaptive clothing customers. *International Journal of Consumer Studies*, *47*(3), 1157–1172. doi:10.1111/ijcs.12895

Lu, X., Liu, Z., & Yang, C. (2022, June). Research on Touchpoint Management in the Catering Industry——Taking Haidilao as an Example. In *International Conference on Human-Computer Interaction* (pp. 443-454). Cham: Springer International Publishing. 10.1007/978-3-031-05900-1_31

Mandal, P. C. (2022). Generation of customer insights–roles of marketing information and marketing intelligence. *International Journal of Business and Data Analytics*, *2*(2), 111–124. doi:10.1504/IJBDA.2022.126794

Mandal, P. C. (2023). Engaging Customers and Managing Customer Relationships: Strategies and Initiatives. [JBE]. *Journal of Business Ecosystems*, *4*(1), 1–14. doi:10.4018/JBE.322405

Mandel, G. N. (2003). Gaps, inexperience, inconsistencies, and overlaps: Crisis in the regulation of genetically modified plants and animals. *SSRN*, *45*, 2167. doi:10.2139/ssrn.418221

Ming, F. (2023). Total Quality Management (TQM) Influence on the Service Quality of Services Companies in China. *Journal of Digitainability* [DREAM]. *Realism & Mastery*, *2*(01), 28–33.

Mishra, M. K., & Singh, L. (2023). Customer Empowerment, Customer Retention, and Performance of Firms: Role of Innovation and Customer Delight as Mediators Through Satisfaction. In Handbook of Research on the Interplay Between Service Quality and Customer Delight (pp. 112-132). IGI Global.

Morrongiello, C., N'Goala, G., & Kreziak, D. (2017). Customer psychological empowerment as a critical source of customer engagement. *International Studies of Management & Organization*, *47*(1), 61–87. doi:10.1080/00208825.2017.1241089

Mukherjee, D., Debnath, R., Chakraborty, S., Jena, L. K., & Hasan, K. K. (2023). Performance Improvement in Budget Hotels Through Consumer Sentiment Analysis Using Text Mining. In *Smart Analytics, Artificial Intelligence and Sustainable Performance Management in a Global Digitalised Economy* (pp. 67–85). Emerald Publishing Limited. doi:10.1108/S1569-37592023000110A004

Na, H. J., Choi, S., & Kwon, O. (2019). The association of institutional information on websites with present and future financial performance. *Journal of Society for E-business Studies*, *23*(4), 63–85.

Ngah, A. H., Thurasamy, R., & Han, H. (2023). If you don't care, I will switch: Online retailers' behaviour on third-party logistics services. *International Journal of Physical Distribution & Logistics Management*, *53*(7/8), 813–837. doi:10.1108/IJPDLM-04-2022-0124

Nigam, A., Behl, A., Pereira, V., & Sangal, S. (2023). Impulse purchases during emergency situations: Exploring permission marketing and the role of blockchain. *Industrial Management & Data Systems*, *123*(1), 155–187. doi:10.1108/IMDS-12-2021-0799

Nuseir, M. T., El Refae, G. A., Aljumah, A., Alshurideh, M., Urabi, S., & Kurdi, B. A. (2023). Digital Marketing Strategies and the Impact on Customer Experience: A Systematic Review. *The Effect of Information Technology on Business and Marketing Intelligence Systems*, 21-44.

Nyrhinen, J., Kemppainen, T., Grénman, M., Frank, L., Makkonen, M., & Wilska, T. A. (2021, December). Positive Online Customer Experience as an Antecedent of the Willingness to Share Information with an E-Commerce Retailer. In *European, Mediterranean, and Middle Eastern Conference on Information Systems* (pp. 376-383). Cham: Springer International Publishing.

Oetarjo, M., Rohim, D. A. G., Firdaus, V., & Togayev, S. S. (2023, May). Online Reviews and Ratings Shape Purchasing Decisions in Indonesian E-Commerce. In *International Conference on Intellectuals' Global Responsibility (ICIGR 2022)* (pp. 557-566). Atlantis Press. 10.2991/978-2-38476-052-7_61

Oey, E., Puspitasari, P. P. M., Fransiska, F., & Polla, J. R. (2023). Identifying and improving customer preferences of frozen tuna for the export market. *International Journal of Productivity and Quality Management*, *39*(4), 512–535. doi:10.1504/IJPQM.2023.132831

Ponathil, A., Bhanu, A., Piratla, K., Sharma, V., & Chalil Madathil, K. (2022). Investigation of the factors influencing the online consumer's choice of a service provider for home improvement. *Electronic Commerce Research*, 1–28. doi:10.1007/s10660-022-09621-0

Reimer, T. (2023). Environmental factors to maximize social media engagement: A comprehensive framework. *Journal of Retailing and Consumer Services*, *75*, 103458. doi:10.1016/j.jretconser.2023.103458

Rogers, E. (2023). Impossible Foods: Growing the Plant-Based Meat Sector at Home and Abroad. *Journal for Global Business and Community*, *14*(1). doi:10.56020/001c.71493

Sann, R., & Lai, P. C. (2023). Topic modeling of the quality of guest's experience using latent Dirichlet allocation: Western versus eastern perspectives. *Consumer Behavior in Tourism and Hospitality*, *18*(1), 17–34. doi:10.1108/CBTH-04-2022-0084

Shen, P., Wan, D., & Li, J. (2023). How human–computer interaction perception affects consumer well-being in the context of online retail: From the perspective of autonomy. *Nankai Business Review International*, *14*(1), 102–127. doi:10.1108/NBRI-03-2022-0034

Shi, X., & Chen, Z. (2021). Listening to your employees: Analyzing opinions from online reviews of hotel companies. *International Journal of Contemporary Hospitality Management*, *33*(6), 2091–2116. doi:10.1108/IJCHM-06-2020-0576

Siby, A., & George, J. P. (2022). Influence of customer relationship management for the success of E-business. In Information and Communication Technology for Competitive Strategies (ICTCS 2020) ICT: Applications and Social Interfaces (pp. 473-481). Springer Singapore. doi:10.1007/978-981-16-0739-4_45

Smith, T. A. (2022). A Qualitative Inquiry into Marketing Effectiveness of SMEs. In *Marketing Effectiveness and Accountability in SMEs: A Multimethodological Approach* (pp. 81–106). Springer International Publishing. doi:10.1007/978-3-031-09861-1_4

Tan, E., Cherapanukorn, V., Kim, H. H., & Chon, K. (2014). The art of service in Asia: A conceptual framework through a case study of hospitality industry in Thailand. In *Proceedings of the Global Tourism and Hospitality Conference and 11th Asia Tourism Forum* (pp. 1217-1244). Research Gate.

Taneja, N. K. (2016). *The Passenger Has Gone Digital and Mobile: Accessing and Connecting Through Information and Technology*. Routledge. doi:10.4324/9781315554792

Tang, Y., & Chan, E. Y. (2023). Name reminders and customization preferences: The role of perceived control. *International Journal of Hospitality Management*, *109*, 103425. doi:10.1016/j.ijhm.2022.103425

Thaichon, P., Surachartkumtonkun, J., Quach, S., Weaven, S., & Palmatier, R. W. (2018). Hybrid sales structures in the age of e-commerce. *Journal of Personal Selling & Sales Management*, *38*(3), 277–302. doi:10.1080/08853134.2018.1441718

Thakur, A. (2022). Technological Innovations in the Hospitality and Tourism Industry. In *Mobile Computing and Technology Applications in Tourism and Hospitality* (pp. 72–97). IGI Global. doi:10.4018/978-1-7998-6904-7.ch004

Uusitalo, K., Hakala, H., & Kautonen, T. (2011). Customer complaints as a source of customer-focused process improvement: A constructive case study. *Operations Management: A Modern Approach, 29*(2), 107-133.

Verhoef, P. C., & Lemon, K. N. (2013). Successful customer value management: Key lessons and emerging trends. *European Management Journal, 31*(1), 1–15. doi:10.1016/j.emj.2012.08.001

Wang, J. (2021). Genre change in the online context: Responding to negative online reviews and redefining an effective genre construct on Amazon. Com. *Journal of Business and Technical Communication, 35*(3), 297–332. doi:10.1177/10506519211001113

Wang, J., Lai, J. Y., & Lin, Y. H. (2023). Social media analytics for mining customer complaints to explore product opportunities. *Computers & Industrial Engineering, 178*, 109104. doi:10.1016/j.cie.2023.109104

Wang, K. L., & Groth, M. (2014). Buffering the negative effects of employee surface acting: The moderating role of employee–customer relationship strength and personalized services. *The Journal of Applied Psychology, 99*(2), 341–350. doi:10.1037/a0034428 PMID:24079672

Wang, X., & Karmina, N. (2023, February). *Theoretical Approaches to the Concept of Marketing Strategies*. In 4th International Conference on Economic Management and Model Engineering, ICEMME 2022, November 18-20, 2022, Nanjing, China. 10.4108/eai.18-11-2022.2327135

Yang, S., Li, T., Chen, S., & Li, B. (2020). When and why do negative reviews have positive effects? An empirical study on the movie industry. *Nankai Business Review International, 11*(1), 87–101. doi:10.1108/NBRI-11-2018-0063

Yang, Y., Wang, Y., & Zhao, J. (2023). Effect of user-generated image on review helpfulness: Perspectives from object detection. *Electronic Commerce Research and Applications, 57*, 101232. doi:10.1016/j.elerap.2022.101232

Yao, Q. (2023). When in Rome, Do as the Romans Do: Differences of Interactive Behaviors Across Social Media Networks. In *The Palgrave Handbook of Interactive Marketing* (pp. 451–473). Springer International Publishing. doi:10.1007/978-3-031-14961-0_20

You, Y., He, Y., Chen, Q., & Hu, M. (2021). The interplay between brand relationship norms and ease of sharing on electronic word-of-mouth and willingness to pay. *Information & Management, 58*(2), 103410. doi:10.1016/j.im.2020.103410

Zhang, Y., Lu, X., & Prombutr, W. (2022). The asymmetric online talk effect. *Review of Behavioral Finance, 14*(2), 157–182. doi:10.1108/RBF-05-2020-0117

KEY TERMS AND DEFINITIONS

Customer Complaints: Customer complaints refer to when a business does not deliver on its commitment and does not meet customer expectations in terms of the products or services. The vital aspect of every business is its clients. For greater success, businesses need more satisfied clients.

Customer Empowerment: Customer empowerment is when companies provide their customers the information and the tools for making effective decisions.

Customization: Customization refers to the action of altering a product or service to suit a person's or company's preferences or requirements.

Engagement Marketing: Engagement marketing is the strategy and the content required to create meaningful customer interactions and build brand loyalty.

Permission Marketing: Permission marketing is a form of advertising where the audience is given the choice to opt-in to receiving promotional messages.

Word of Mouth: Word-of-mouth marketing (or WOM marketing) is when a consumer's interest in a company's product or service is reflected in their daily dialogues.

Chapter 11

Navigating Consumer Choices in the Metaverse:
Virtual and Augmented Reality's Impact on Purchasing Decisions and Experiences

Naboshree Bhattacharya
iD https://orcid.org/0000-0001-5572-4098
Amity University, India

Divya Bansal
iD https://orcid.org/0000-0001-6268-5402
Amity University, India

ABSTRACT

The chapter explores how VR and AR technologies influence consumer behavior in the metaverse, emphasizing the need for businesses to understand these dynamics. It delves into cognitive processes, emotional responses, and socio-cultural influences shaping purchasing decisions in virtual environments. The research analyzes user interactions, interface design, sensory immersion, and social interactions to uncover factors driving consumer engagement and decision-making. It highlights the importance of user-centered design, personalized marketing, and immersive storytelling for creating compelling virtual experiences. The study also identifies challenges and opportunities for businesses leveraging VR and AR technologies to enhance consumer engagement and drive sales in the metaverse, offering practical recommendations for success in the digital marketplace of the future.

DOI: 10.4018/979-8-3693-4167-4.ch011

INTRODUCTION

The intricate interplay between perception, emotion, and cognition shapes our daily behaviors and choices, ranging from meticulously planned actions to spontaneous, impulsive decisions. This distinction has been consistently observed in rigorously controlled studies within the fields of psychological and cognitive neuroscience. The categorization of decisions as either cognitive or emotional responses has been explored across various disciplines, including neuroscience, philosophy, psychology, and commercial studies (Schall, 2001). Notably, behavioral studies have long posited a dichotomy between an emotional, impulsive system and a more cognitively driven, deliberative system (Frankish, 2010).

The advent of digital transformation has paved the way for new realities, with a heightened emphasis on immersive experiences and how brands can engage consumers through personalized and entertaining interactions to drive product purchases in this decentralized landscape. However, consumer behaviors are not uniform, and in these novel contexts, it is imperative to investigate their behaviors and purchasing predispositions. As e-commerce has become increasingly prevalent in consumers' lives, understanding the distinction between this new concept of reality and traditional commerce is crucial (Neves et al., 2022).

Virtual commerce, defined as commercial activity conducted within immersive virtual environments, represents one of the latest advancements in e-commerce, a transformative business tool propelled by technological progress, business innovation, and societal adoption over the past two decades (Grupac, 2022). Consumer behaviors have undergone a shift from physical, brick-and-mortar stores to online platforms (Cheung et al., 2005), and are now on the cusp of fully transitioning into mixed reality (MR) (Shen et al., 2021).

Recent research in Virtual Reality (VR) has explored the integration of VR and supermarkets as a research tool (Peschel et al., 2022) and as an educational application for individuals with autism (Thomsen and Adjorlu, 2021). VR supermarkets have also been employed to examine consumers' behavior in selecting healthy food (Eichhorn et al., 2021; Melendrez-Ruiz et al., 2021), and with the assistance of artificial intelligence, virtual supermarkets have been studied as a "shopping at home" solution (Shravani et al., 2021). Recently, the diverse effects of VR on brain responses have been assessed using electroencephalography (EEG) (D'Errico et al., 2020; Dini et al., 2022). The immersive nature of VR and the semi-realistic environments these technologies offer could facilitate the examination of neural responses in a more authentic manner. Schaefer et al. (2016) conducted a VR shopping task to investigate the impact of price expectation violation on the P300 component of EEG, while Rosenlacher et al. (2018) studied the effects of a VR store on human shopping behavior.

Beyond consumer neuroscience, VR and MR have been utilized as treatment tools (Tran et al., 2022) and educational avenues (Makransky et al., 2019) in neuroscientific studies. As interest in implementing MR worlds as a solution for everyday situations surges (Bazzani et al., 2020), often referred to as the "metaverse," our understanding of attentional, emotional, and cognitive responses remains limited. Although we can assume a priori that the responses observed within MR mirror those seen outside MR, few studies have been conducted to validate this assumption. Despite numerous neuroscientific studies attempting to investigate the neural mechanisms underlying consumers' decision-making processes, the validity of their findings has not been thoroughly tested in real-life scenarios.

Virtual Reality (VR) experience escapes allow individuals to immerse themselves for extended periods in virtual environments, interacting with content in a world that offers shelter and the illusion of an alternative reality – the metaverse (Han et al., 2022). As this new frontier of consumer interaction and commerce evolves, it is crucial for researchers and businesses to deepen their understanding of the cognitive, emotional, and behavioral implications of these immersive environments on consumer decision-making and overall well-being.

UNDERSTANDING THE METAVERSE

The Metaverse: The Next Evolution of the Internet

The metaverse is envisioned as the next stage in the development of the internet, representing a network of persistent, shared, and three-dimensional virtual spaces that are interconnected to form a perceived virtual universe. This immersive and embodied version of the internet offers users the experience of being inside the digital realm rather than merely observing it from the outside.

The metaverse will harness the power of various immersive technologies, including:

1. Virtual Reality (VR)
2. Augmented Reality (AR)
3. Mixed Reality (MR)

These technologies will enable the creation of more engaging and immersive digital experiences that seamlessly blend with the physical world, blurring the boundaries between the real and the virtual. As the metaverse continues to evolve and take shape, it holds the potential to revolutionize the way we interact, work, and engage with digital content. This new frontier of human interaction and experience will likely have far-reaching implications across various sectors, including education, entertainment, commerce, and social networking.

By leveraging the capabilities of immersive technologies, the metaverse aims to create a more intuitive, natural, and engaging way for users to navigate and interact with digital environments, ultimately redefining our relationship with technology and the internet as we know it.

Key Characteristics of the Metaverse

- Always-on virtual environments that continue to exist even when you're not engaged
- Shared spaces where many people can interact with each other and with digital objects
- Users are represented by virtual avatars
- Highly interoperable - virtual items/assets can move between different metaverse platforms
- Bridges the gap between the virtual and physical, with virtual objects representing real-world ones

Current State and Future Potential

The metaverse, as a singular, unified entity, has not yet come into existence. However, metaverse-like elements can be observed in various online games, such as Roblox, Fortnite, and Minecraft, as well as in VR social platforms. Major technology companies, including Meta (Facebook), Microsoft, Epic Games, and Nvidia, are making significant investments in developing the foundational technologies necessary for the metaverse's realization.

Currently, the metaverse remains in its early stages of development, comparable to the state of the internet in the 1970s and 1980s. The ultimate form and impact of the metaverse are yet to be determined, as the underlying technologies continue to mature and creative visions come to life. Understanding and exploring this space will be crucial for shaping its future potential and ensuring that its development aligns with the needs and values of its users.

Impacts of Metaverse

The metaverse is transforming the landscape of digital commerce, emerging as a buzzword among tech giants and business leaders. It represents a fusion of the physical and digital realms, made possible by the convergence of 3D graphics, web technology, and Extended Reality (XR). The metaverse allows individuals to inhabit and interact within a virtual environment that offers unique social experiences in persistent multi-user spaces. As defined by Zhao et al. (2022), "the metaverse refers to a virtual world created using software code that allows users to create an avatar that looks like them and interact with other avatars in various virtual platforms." The metaverse has enhanced user functionality and interactivity while addressing the limitations of traditional web-based e-commerce, such as the absence of face-to-face interaction and product engagement (P. Kowalczuk et al., 2010; A. Mollen et al., 2010). Consequently, numerous high-tech companies have invested in the metaverse, recognizing its immense potential and advantages for the digital realm (A. Mollen et al., 2010).

Businesses embracing the metaverse can establish 3D virtual stores where customers can virtually try on products using lifelike avatars. The Unreal Engine's Meta-Human Creator enables users to create a realistic avatar of themselves, allowing them to enter a virtual store and gain a clear understanding of the products offered. Additionally, metaverse companies operate within an omnichannel framework, enabling consumers to enter a virtual store, purchase digital sneakers for their avatar, and have the physical product delivered to their doorstep (Yim et al., 2017). Selfridges, Charli Cohen, and Pokémon collaborated to create a fashion city in the metaverse called an E-fashion city, where customers could browse and purchase digital garments for their avatars (Algharabat et al., 2018). Similarly, Adidas acquired digital property in the Sandbox, allowing customers to purchase digital products and have them physically delivered (Cowan et al., 2019). The Spanish global fashion brand ZARA has also launched its first collection of designs for both humans and avatars, hosted by the South Korean tech firm 'ZEPETO.' These actual and virtual models can be purchased at any of ZARA's outlets worldwide (Ye et al., 2020).

In contrast to traditional online shopping, where consumers spend hours scrolling through websites, reading conflicting reviews, or watching endless advertisements, shopping in the metaverse offers an optimal blend of the physical and digital worlds. Shoppers can browse and interact with products as if they were real, and digital assistants will be available to guide consumers through the purchasing process (Fischer et al., 2011). As a result, the unique characteristics of the metaverse can serve as a focal point for developing new theories, techniques, and phenomena. Researchers studying interactive marketing who are interested in the business aspects of the metaverse may find it particularly valuable to understand and explore the effects of these distinctive features.

Despite the growing interest in the metaverse, research on metaverse retailing and purchasing behaviors remains limited. Existing studies have primarily explored the virtual world from the perspectives of online games (Zhao et al., 2022), transportation in the metaverse (Liu et al., 2016), or metaverse tourism (Mosteller et al., 2014). The present study offers a research model to investigate how user interactions and organismic experiences influence metaverse users' shopping intentions. The purchasing experiences and purchase intentions within the metaverse have yet to be thoroughly examined in the retailing and marketing literature, presenting an opportunity for further exploration and understanding of this emerging domain.

The Metaverse: Transforming Digital Interaction and Experiences

The metaverse, envisioned as the next evolution of the internet, is poised to transform the way we interact, work, and play in the digital realm. It represents a convergence of multiple maturing technologies, including:

1. Virtual Reality (VR)
2. Augmented Reality (AR)
3. Blockchain
4. 5G
5. Artificial Intelligence (AI)
6. Internet of Things (IoT)

As these technologies integrate and evolve, they will enable the creation of immersive, persistent, and interconnected virtual environments that blend seamlessly with the physical world. The metaverse will offer users unprecedented opportunities for engagement, collaboration, and creativity, redefining the boundaries of digital experiences.

For the metaverse to reach its full potential, interoperability and open standards will be crucial. The development and adoption of protocols that allow avatars, virtual items, and data to move seamlessly between different platforms will be essential to avoid a fragmented ecosystem controlled by a few dominant players. Initiatives like the Metaverse Standards Forum and the evolution of web3 technologies will play a key role in enabling an open and user-centric metaverse. These efforts aim to establish a common framework for developers, businesses, and users, ensuring that the metaverse remains accessible, inclusive, and decentralized.

The economic landscape of the metaverse is already taking shape, with virtual goods and digital assets becoming major revenue streams in gaming platforms like Roblox and Fortnite. As the metaverse grows, we can expect to see the emergence of new business models centered around creating, selling, and trading unique digital assets, represented by non-fungible tokens (NFTs). The ability to earn real economic value from virtual activities could drive significant growth and innovation in the metaverse economy.

Beyond its economic implications, the metaverse has the potential to profoundly impact social interactions, culture, and society as a whole. It could enable new forms of expression, creativity, and community-building that transcend physical barriers. However, it also raises important questions around identity, privacy, security, addiction, and inequality that will need to be addressed as the metaverse becomes more integrated into daily life.

Enterprises across various industries are also beginning to explore the potential applications of metaverse technologies. From training and collaboration to product design and customer engagement, industry-specific metaverses could revolutionize how businesses operate. Digital twins, virtual models that replicate real-world assets and systems, will be a key building block for industrial metaverse applications, enabling powerful new capabilities for optimization and innovation.

The design artifacts identified barely cover any general design requirement except for scalability and accessibility of a client. In terms of Virtual World (VW) design, Shen et al. (2020) identified the emerging requirements of sufficiency, reliability, persistency, and credibility. Particularly, persistency and credibility can be highly relevant to consumer purchases in a VW. For persistency, user content persistency is directly related to the permanent existence of a user's digital asset in a VW. Presumably, a low level of content persistency can reduce a user's willingness to buy high-value products in a VW. Similar results can be expected with a low level of credibility, which stresses the trust of users on a VW to securely manage and legally protect their data.

The metaverse, which has been perceived as the next generation of the Internet, is where interconnected, shared, and persistent 3D virtual spaces co-exist. Immersive technology applied in virtual commerce can sufficiently create the visually immersive virtual spaces for a metaverse. Nevertheless, utilization of other emerging technologies, such as faster communication infrastructures (e.g., 5G), secure distributed ledgers (e.g., blockchain), and innovative computing paradigms (e.g., mobile, edge, and cloud computing), is essential to achieve the interconnectivity, persistency, and other features of the metaverse, which is likely to establish a new form of electronic commerce.

Figure 1. Designs of virtual commerce system
Source: *Shen, B.; Tan, W.; Guo, J.; Zhao, L.; Qin, P. How to Promote User Purchase in Metaverse? A Systematic Literature Review on Consumer Behavior Research and Virtual Commerce Application Design. Appl. Sci. 2021, 11, 11087*

Category	Design Artifact	Definition
AR	Direct product information presentation	In AR applications, display product information at appropriate positions of the graphical user interface.
	Fashionable facial accessories try-on	In AR applications, use algorithms to track the position and movements of a human face to accurately display virtual facial accessories.
	Feature matching accuracy improvement	In AR applications, improve the accuracy of virtual object positioning
	Marker-free	The design of AR applications without using markers for tracking.
	Mobile AR	The design of mobile platform AR applications.
	Stand-alone AR	AR technologies that integrate tracking, displays, calculation, and other AR-related tasks in a single device.
Client design	3D representation of a multi-agent system	The design of 3D VWs populated by agents that are either autonomous or human-controlled
	Accessibility	The use of standard protocols, software, procedures, and so on to deliver the designed artifact to a broad audience.
	Combining virtual environment and Sociality	The design of a 3D virtual shopping mall for collaborative shopping.
	Intuitive virtual shop interface	The design of the user interface that provides natural interaction with the virtual objects.
	Scalability	The capability of an application to handle large-scale concurrent access to its services.
	Social commerce system design framework	The design principles and practices that consider multi-user activities
	Virtual mall	An integrated solution to 3D virtual mall creation, operation, and navigation.
	VR Shopping experience enhancement	Design principles and practices that generate an enjoyable shopping experience in a VR shop.
Customization	Product customization	The capability to dynamically display products based on a user's characteristics and inputs.
	Product searchability and recommendation	The capability to accurately provide or recommend products based on user inputs or activities
	User-designed virtual environments for product visualization	A framework that allows customers to personalize a 3D virtual room and certain properties of the pre-defined products.
	Virtual shop personalization, customization, or consumer adaption	Dynamic generation of 3D virtual shop based on a user's characteristics and preferences.
Software agent	Navigation agent	The design of software agents for navigation in 3D virtual environment.
	Sales agent for price negotiation	Software agents that users can interact with to negotiate price.
	Semantic agent for information query	The use of semantic technologies to develop virtual retailing environments that support information query.
	VR-driven shopping agent for decision support	A combination of VR avatars and decision support system for VR shopping.
Function design	Navigability	The design of functions to navigate the users to a specific product in a 3D virtual environment.
	Realistic product modeling	Methods to render a product such that it is perceived to be real by users.
	Reputation mechanism	A method to objectively evaluate a seller's reputation based on user reviews using VR.
	Trust-building interaction design	The design principles and practices of a VR-based e-commerce environment using an empirically-tested trust-building model.

CONSUMER BEHAVIOUR IN VIRTUAL ENVIRONMENTS

Consumer behavior in virtual environments is a fascinating and rapidly evolving area of study, as the rise of immersive technologies like virtual reality (VR) and the growing prominence of metaverse platforms are reshaping how people interact with digital content and make purchasing decisions. In virtual environments, consumers are represented by digital avatars, which can serve as an extension of their real-world identity or allow them to explore new identities and personas. This ability to express oneself in new ways can influence consumer preferences and decision-making, as people may be more inclined to experiment with styles, products, or experiences that they might not pursue in the physical world.

Virtual environments also offer unique opportunities for brands to engage with consumers through immersive experiences, interactive product demonstrations, and personalized content. Brands can create virtual storefronts, host events, and offer exclusive digital products or collectibles, tapping into the growing demand for virtual goods and experiences. The ability to create scarcity and exclusivity around digital items, such as through the use of non-fungible tokens (NFTs), can drive consumer desire and willingness to pay.

Social influence and community play a significant role in shaping consumer behavior in virtual environments. People can connect with like-minded individuals from around the world, forming communities based on shared interests, values, or experiences. These virtual communities can serve as powerful sources of product recommendations, reviews, and user-generated content, influencing consumer opinions and purchase decisions. The gamification of virtual environments, through rewards, challenges, and competitive elements, can also drive consumer engagement and loyalty. By offering incentives for exploration, participation, and achievement, brands can encourage consumers to spend more time in virtual environments and develop deeper connections with their products or services.

However, consumer behavior in virtual environments also raises important considerations around privacy, data protection, and ethical marketing practices. As people spend more time in immersive digital spaces, they generate vast amounts of data about their preferences, behaviors, and social interactions. Brands must be transparent about their data collection and usage practices, and ensure that they respect consumer privacy and consent. Additionally, the blurring of boundaries between the virtual and physical worlds can create new challenges for consumer protection and regulation. Issues such as virtual asset ownership, fraud prevention, and content moderation will require ongoing attention and collaboration between businesses, policymakers, and consumer advocates.

As virtual environments continue to evolve and become more integrated into daily life, understanding and adapting to changing consumer behaviors will be essential for businesses looking to succeed in the metaverse economy. By creating engaging, personalized, and socially connected experiences, while prioritizing privacy, safety, and ethical practices, brands can build lasting relationships with consumers in the virtual world.

Consumer Purchase Model

Classical Model of Consumer Purchase Decisions

Consumer purchase decisions can be described by the five-stage classical model (see Figure 1), which serves as a well-established theoretical foundation. Although this model has undergone refinements over time (Karimi, 2013), it remains a valuable framework for understanding consumer behavior. The five-stage classical model has been widely adopted in the information system discipline to study consumer behaviors in the context of e-commerce (Zhang, 2016).

Figure 2. The five-stage classical model of consumer purchase decisions
Source: *Shen, B.; Tan, W.; Guo, J.; Zhao, L.; Qin, P. How to Promote User Purchase in Metaverse? A Systematic Literature Review on Consumer Behavior Research and Virtual Commerce Application Design. Appl. Sci. 2021, 11, 11087*

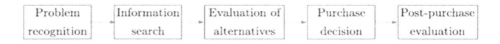

The five stages of the classical model are as follows:

1. Problem Recognition: The consumer identifies a need or desire that requires fulfilment.
2. Information Search: The consumer seeks out relevant information about potential solutions to their problem or need.
3. Evaluation of Alternatives: The consumer compares and assesses the available options based on their criteria and preferences.
4. Purchase Decision: The consumer selects the most suitable option and makes the purchase.
5. Post-Purchase Behavior: The consumer evaluates their purchase decision and experiences satisfaction or dissatisfaction, which can influence future purchase decisions.

This model provides a structured approach to understanding the various stages consumers go through when making purchase decisions. By applying this framework to the study of consumer behavior in e-commerce, researchers can gain valuable insights into how consumers navigate the online purchasing process and identify factors that influence their decision-making at each stage.

As the landscape of e-commerce continues to evolve, particularly with the emergence of immersive technologies and virtual environments, the five-stage classical model remains a relevant and adaptable framework for investigating consumer purchase decisions in new contexts. By understanding the unique challenges and opportunities presented by these new digital spaces, researchers can refine and extend the model to better capture the complexities of consumer behavior in the modern era.

The five stages of the classical model of consumer purchase decisions encompass various aspects of the decision-making process, with the purchase decision stage being particularly significant. This stage refers to a consumer's willingness to fulfill a purchase (Kardes et al., 2011) and is perceived as the most relevant factor to the actual purchase (Ajzen, 1985; Morrison, 1979). In most cases, purchase decision is measured by purchase intention, which is defined as the strength of a consumer's willingness to buy a particular product, service, or products and services from a specific brand (Chang et al., 1994; Chen et al., 2008; Mirabi, 2015).

It is important to note that a purchase decision can be influenced by the activities and factors present in all the stages of the classical model. Consumers may not always strictly follow the sequential order of the stages during a purchase, as they may engage in activities from different stages simultaneously or revisit certain stages based on their individual needs and experiences. This flexibility in the decision-making process highlights the complex nature of consumer behavior and the importance of considering the interplay between the various stages when studying purchase decisions.

By understanding the factors that influence consumer behavior at each stage of the classical model, businesses and researchers can develop targeted strategies to effectively guide consumers through the decision-making process and ultimately drive purchase decisions.

The Stimulus-Response Model and the "Buyer's Black Box"

In marketing research, a stimulus-response model was adopted, giving rise to the "buyer's black box" model (Sandhusen, 2008). This model incorporates several key components:

1. Stimuli: The marketing mix (Borden, 1964) and the marketing environment (Duncan, 1979) are considered as stimuli that influence consumer behavior.
2. Buyer's Black Box: The classical model of consumer purchase decisions, along with buyer characteristics, is merged into the "buyer's black box." This black box represents the internal processes and factors that shape a consumer's decision-making process.

3.   Buyer's Responses: The outputs of the "buyer's black box" are the buyer's responses, which are measures of the purchase decision process. These responses can include actions such as product choice, brand choice, purchase timing, and purchase amount.

The stimulus-response model and the "buyer's black box" concept provide a framework for understanding how external factors (stimuli) interact with internal factors (buyer characteristics and the classical model) to influence consumer behavior and ultimately lead to purchase decisions (buyer's responses).

By considering the marketing mix and the marketing environment as stimuli, researchers can examine how various elements, such as product, price, promotion, and place (Borden, 1964), as well as environmental factors like economic, technological, and cultural influences (Duncan, 1979), impact consumer behavior. The "buyer's black box" represents the complex interplay between these external stimuli and the internal processes and characteristics of the consumer, which are captured by the classical model of consumer purchase decisions and individual buyer characteristics.

The buyer's responses, as measures of the purchase decision process, provide valuable insights into the effectiveness of marketing strategies and the impact of various stimuli on consumer behavior. By analyzing these responses, businesses can refine their marketing efforts and tailor their approaches to better meet the needs and preferences of their target consumers.

As the field of marketing continues to evolve, the stimulus-response model and the "buyer's black box" concept remain relevant frameworks for understanding and predicting consumer behavior. However, it is important to recognize the increasing complexity of the modern marketing landscape, particularly with the rise of digital technologies and changing consumer expectations. Researchers and practitioners must continually adapt and expand these models to incorporate new stimuli, buyer characteristics, and response measures that reflect the dynamic nature of consumer behavior in the contemporary marketplace.

Table 1. The black box model in marketing

Environmental Factors		Buyer's Black Box		Buyer's Responses
Marketing Stimuli	Environmental Stimuli	Buyer's Characteristics	Decision Process	
Product	Economic	Attitudes	Problem recognition	Product
Price	Technical	Motivation	Information search	Brand
Place	Political	Perceptions	Evaluation of alternatives	Dealer
Promotion	Cultural	Personality	Purchase decision	Purchase amount
		Lifestyle	Post-purchase evaluation	Purchase timing

Source: Shen, B.; Tan, W.; Guo, J.; Zhao, L.; Qin, P. How to Promote User Purchase in Metaverse? A Systematic Literature Review on Consumer Behavior Research and Virtual Commerce Application Design. Appl. Sci. 2021, 11, 11087

User Satisfaction With Virtual Reality

The Role of Trust in Virtual Shopping Environments

The user's trust in the virtual shopping environment has been a subject of interest in several studies (Baker et al., 2019; Teoh et al., 2008). Trust, in this context, refers to the psychological state of consumers who are willing to further interact with the shopping environment to achieve a planned goal. This trust is crucial for fostering positive consumer attitudes and encouraging continued engagement with the virtual shopping platform.

Baker et al. (2019) investigated the relationship between shopping attitudes and consumer trust cultivated during the shopping experience. They argued that consumer trust is dually influenced by two key factors: perceived telepresence and social presence.

1. Perceived Telepresence: Telepresence refers to the sense of "being there" in a virtual environment, where users feel as if they are physically present in the simulated space. The higher the level of perceived telepresence, the more likely consumers are to develop trust in the virtual shopping environment.
2. Social Presence: Social presence is the extent to which users feel connected to other individuals within the virtual environment. This can include interactions with virtual sales assistants, other shoppers, or even the perception of a human touch in the design of the virtual space. Strong social presence has been shown to contribute to the development of consumer trust.

Teoh et al. (2008) further explored the constructs of perceived telepresence and social presence in relation to trust outcomes in virtual shopping environments. Their research aimed to provide a deeper understanding of how these factors influence consumer behavior and decision-making processes.

Implications for Virtual Shopping Platforms

The findings from these studies have important implications for the design and development of virtual shopping platforms. To foster consumer trust and encourage positive shopping attitudes, virtual shopping environments should prioritize the following:

1. Enhancing Telepresence: Virtual shopping platforms should strive to create immersive experiences that make users feel as if they are physically present in

the virtual space. This can be achieved through high-quality graphics, realistic product representations, and intuitive navigation.

2. Promoting Social Presence: Incorporating elements of social interaction, such as virtual sales assistants or real-time customer support, can help to create a sense of human connection within the virtual environment. Additionally, enabling user-to-user interactions, such as product reviews or social sharing, can further enhance social presence.

3. Ensuring Security and Privacy: Consumer trust is also heavily influenced by the perceived security and privacy of the virtual shopping environment. Platforms must prioritize robust data protection measures, secure payment systems, and transparent privacy policies to maintain user confidence.

By understanding and leveraging the constructs of perceived telepresence and social presence, virtual shopping platforms can create environments that foster consumer trust and drive positive shopping attitudes. As the virtual shopping landscape continues to evolve, ongoing research into the factors influencing consumer trust will be essential for developing effective strategies and technologies that meet the changing needs and expectations of online shoppers.

Figure 3. Conceptual framework of user satisfaction with a VR shopping site
Source: Shen, B.; Tan, W.; Guo, J.; Zhao, L.; Qin, P. How to Promote User Purchase in Metaverse? A Systematic Literature Review on Consumer Behavior Research and Virtual Commerce Application Design. Appl. Sci. 2021, 11, 11087

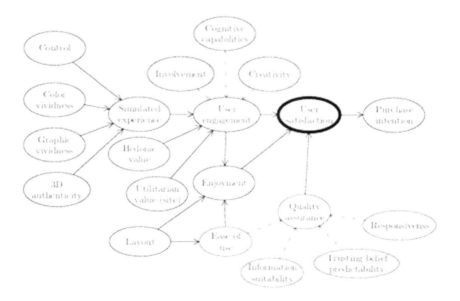

Retailing in Social Virtual Worlds

Social virtual worlds (SVWs), such as Second Life (SL), have attracted numerous entrepreneurs seeking to sell both virtual and real products to the growing number of in-world residents. Many of these entrepreneurs consider their in-world revenues as a primary source of income for their real lives, with some even amassing significant wealth from their virtual businesses (Au, 2009a; Au, 2009b; Chiang, 2010; Tiffany, 2007). Real-world brands, such as Toyota and L'Oreal, have also utilized SVWs for various business purposes by establishing virtual stores within these platforms (Arakji and Lang, 2008). The retailing business is particularly active in SVWs, as evidenced by the fact that during the first decade of SL's existence, 2.1 million user-created virtual goods were offered for sale, with resident-to-resident transactions totaling over $3.2 billion USD (Linden Lab, 2013).

However, despite the initial enthusiasm, many big brands have struggled to maintain successful virtual stores in SVWs and have subsequently left SL, the most developed SVW (Kuntze et al., 2013). Store design appears to be a crucial factor in this regard, with some retailers simply transferring an exact copy of a traditional store into the SVW, while others are more considerate of the specific characteristics and opportunities offered by this new channel. For example, American Apparel's failure in SL was partially attributed to their 'traditional' store design, which was perceived as disrespectful to the unique culture of the virtual world (DMD, Combined Story, and Market Truths, 2007). Conversely, the virtual store environment was identified as one of the main factors contributing to users' positive perceptions of shopping in SVWs (Hassouneh and Brengman, 2011a).

The current research aims to set a foundation for understanding virtual store design principles by exploring current practices in the application of atmospherics in SVW stores and proposing a new typology for three-dimensional (3D) virtual store atmospherics.

Virtual environments are considered an evolution of the traditional web, offering retailers advantages and an enhanced shopping experience for customers. By utilizing virtual environments, online retailers can increase the entertainment value offered to shoppers, enhance their in-store enjoyment, and consequently improve their shopping satisfaction (Kim and Forsythe, 2008; Lee and Chung, 2008; Papadopoulou, 2007). SVWs bridge the gap between offline and online spaces by reintroducing store atmospherics into online retailing, providing online shoppers with an experience similar to that of traditional stores (Papagiannidis et al., 2013). As a result, several researchers view virtual worlds as the future of e-commerce, succeeding traditional 2D web stores, or as an additional/complementary channel to the web (Bourlakis et al., 2009; Mackenzie et al., 2013; Papagiannidis et al., 2013; Park et al., 2008).

Although studies concerning retailing and store design in SVWs are emerging (Tran et al., 2011), only one study thus far has specifically addressed virtual store atmospherics. While Krasonikolakis et al. (2011) demonstrated that atmospherics are applicable in virtual stores, they did not specify the different elements that constitute these atmospheric factors or describe how they are being used in SVW stores. The current paper aims to fill this gap by investigating the atmospherics in 27 virtual stores in SL. Through deductive content analysis and building upon atmospheric classifications in traditional and online stores, this paper seeks to (1) identify and categorize atmospheric elements in SVWs to propose a typology of SVW/3D store atmospherics, and (2) describe how atmospherics are being employed by SVW retailers.

'Store atmospherics' has been shown to be of strategic importance for retailers in both traditional and online stores (Liang and Lai, 2000; Turley and Milliman, 2000). Thus, it can be assumed that atmospherics will also be of major importance in metaverse retailing (i.e., in the virtual world), influencing shopper behavior and retailer performance. The proposed virtual store atmospherics typology can provide a framework for further investigating the impact of specific virtual store atmospherics on in-world consumer behavior and the performance of SVW retailers, thereby guiding future research on metaverse retailing.

The Role of Virtual Reality in Consumer Decision Making

Virtual Reality (VR) is rapidly emerging as a powerful tool for influencing consumer decision-making, offering brands and retailers new opportunities to engage with customers and drive sales. By immersing consumers in realistic, interactive digital environments, VR can transform the way people explore products, gather information, and ultimately make purchasing decisions.

One of the key advantages of VR in consumer decision-making is its ability to provide a more tangible and experiential product understanding. Through VR simulations, consumers can interact with products in a way that closely mimics real-world experiences, allowing them to test features, explore different configurations, and get a sense of scale and spatial relationships. This hands-on, immersive experience can help consumers feel more confident in their product choices and reduce the uncertainty often associated with online shopping (Suh and Lee, 2005; Van Kerrebroeck et al., 2017).

VR can also enable consumers to visualize and personalize products in ways that are not possible through traditional e-commerce interfaces. For example, home furnishing retailers can use VR to allow customers to place virtual furniture in a digital representation of their own living space, helping them to envision how different pieces would look and fit in their homes (Javornik, 2016). Similarly, fashion and beauty brands can use VR to let customers virtually try on clothing, accessories, or makeup, providing a more engaging and personalized shopping experience (Smink et al., 2019).

In addition to enhancing product exploration, VR can also influence consumer decision-making by providing immersive access to product information and reviews. Brands can create VR experiences that guide consumers through product features, specifications, and benefits in an interactive and visually compelling way. By integrating user-generated content, such as customer reviews or social media posts, into these VR experiences, brands can leverage social proof to build trust and credibility with potential buyers (Hilken et al., 2020).

VR can also play a role in driving impulse purchases and reducing decision friction. By creating immersive, emotionally engaging experiences that showcase products in exciting or aspirational contexts, brands can tap into consumers' desires and encourage spontaneous buying decisions (Martínez-Navarro et al., 2019). VR can also streamline the decision-making process by allowing consumers to seamlessly move from product exploration to purchase within a single, cohesive virtual environment.

However, the use of VR in consumer decision-making also raises important considerations around data privacy and manipulation. As VR experiences become more sophisticated in tracking user behavior and preferences, brands must be transparent about their data collection practices and ensure that they respect consumer consent (Bailenson, 2018). There is also a risk that VR could be used to manipulate consumer perceptions or choices, such as by presenting products in an overly idealized or misleading manner (Cowan and Ketron, 2019).

As VR technologies continue to advance and become more widely adopted, their role in consumer decision-making is set to grow. By leveraging the immersive, interactive, and personalized capabilities of VR, brands can create more engaging and informative shopping experiences that drive sales and build long-term customer relationships. However, it will be important for businesses to use VR responsibly and ethically, prioritizing transparency, fairness, and consumer well-being in their virtual reality marketing strategies.

AUGMENTED REALITY AND PURCHASING DECISIONS

Augmented Reality (AR) is increasingly influencing consumer purchasing decisions by transforming the way people interact with products and make buying choices. AR technology overlays digital information onto the real world, allowing consumers to visualize and engage with products in more immersive and personalized ways.

1. Enhanced Product Visualization: AR enables consumers to see how products would look in their own environment before making a purchase. For example, furniture retailers like IKEA use AR apps that let customers virtually place furniture in their homes to assess fit, style, and colour. This reduces uncertainty and increases confidence in purchase decisions. Interactive Product Exploration: AR allows consumers to interact with products in more engaging ways. They can rotate, zoom, and manipulate virtual 3D models to examine products from all angles. AR can also provide additional information, animations, or simulations to highlight key features and benefits. This interactive experience aids in product understanding and evaluation.

2. Virtual Try-Ons: For products like clothing, accessories, and cosmetics, AR enables virtual try-ons. Consumers can see how items would look on them without physically trying them on. This convenience and personalization enhance the shopping experience and helps consumers make more informed choices. Increased Engagement and Conversion: The immersive and interactive nature of AR keeps consumers engaged for longer. Studies show AR experiences lead to increased product interest, brand recall, and purchase intent compared to traditional media. The ability to virtually experience product bridge the gap between online and in-store shopping, driving conversions.

3. Reduced Perceived Risk: By providing more information and interactive visualization, AR helps mitigate perceived risks associated with purchases. Consumers feel more assured about factors like quality, fit, and suitability for their needs. This is especially valuable for high-involvement or expensive purchases where decision-making is more complex.

4. Social Sharing and Validation: Many AR shopping experiences allow consumers to capture and share photos or videos of their virtual product interactions. This user-generated content serves as social proof, influencing the purchase decisions of others in the shopper's network.

However, retailers must consider factors like ease of use, quality of experience, and privacy when implementing AR. Poor execution or intrusive data collection can negatively impact consumer perceptions. Additionally, while AR aids decision-making, it is ultimately one component in the broader customer journey that leads to a purchase.

As AR technologies advance and become more accessible, their impact on consumer decision-making will continue to grow. By enabling more engaging, personalized, and informed shopping experiences, AR empowers consumers and influences their path to purchase. Retailers that strategically leverage AR can differentiate themselves, build consumer confidence, and drive conversions in an increasingly competitive landscape.

Effectiveness of Augmented Reality

Augmented Reality (AR) is a technology that integrates virtual content into a user's perception of the real world, creating a composite view that enhances the user's experience (Azuma, 1997). AR has been gaining traction in various fields, including marketing, where it has the potential to revolutionize the way businesses interact with their customers. AR Marketing represents a novel and potentially disruptive subdiscipline within the broader field of marketing (Saffari, 2023). This emerging area of marketing focuses on leveraging AR technology to create immersive and engaging experiences for consumers, ultimately influencing their purchasing decisions and brand loyalty.

The emergence of AR Marketing can be compared to the advent of the World Wide Web and its impact on traditional marketing practices. Just as the internet gave rise to online marketing, search engine optimization, and social media marketing, AR technology is now paving the way for a new set of marketing strategies and tactics (Saffari, 2023). AR-infused marketing activities, such as virtual product trials, interactive advertising, and gamified brand experiences, are becoming increasingly popular among businesses looking to differentiate themselves in a competitive market (Javornik, 2016). These innovative approaches to marketing fall under the umbrella of AR Marketing, which is poised to become a significant subdiscipline within the marketing field.

As AR technology continues to advance and become more accessible to consumers, the potential impact of AR Marketing on business outcomes is expected to grow (Hilken et al., 2017). By providing customers with immersive and personalized experiences, AR Marketing can help businesses to increase brand engagement and loyalty, drive product sales and revenue, enhance customer understanding of complex products or services, and differentiate themselves from competitors. However, the success of AR Marketing initiatives will depend on businesses' ability to develop compelling and user-friendly AR experiences that align with their brand values and customer needs (Scholz and Smith, 2016).

While the extant research on AR Marketing has provided a foundation for understanding this emerging subdiscipline, there is still much to be explored. Future research should focus on identifying best practices for designing and implementing AR Marketing campaigns, examining the factors that influence consumer adoption and acceptance of AR technology, investigating the long-term effects of AR Marketing on customer relationships and brand perception, and exploring the ethical implications of AR Marketing, such as data privacy and user manipulation.

Figure 4. Conceptual framework of a consumer's attitudes toward innovative technology
Source: Shen, B.; Tan, W.; Guo, J.; Zhao, L.; Qin, P. How to Promote User Purchase in Metaverse? A Systematic Literature Review on Consumer Behavior Research and Virtual Commerce Application Design. Appl. Sci. 2021, 11, 11087

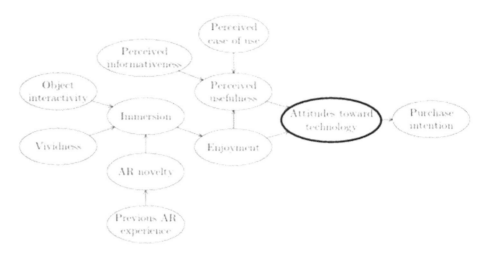

The effectiveness of Augmented Reality (AR) on purchase intention has been evaluated through comparisons with conventional online e-commerce sites in several studies (Yim et al., 2017; Rese et al., 2017). Yim et al. (2017) investigated consumers' attitudes toward AR from the perspective of the enjoyment experience generated by AR's immersion effect. Their findings suggest that the immersive nature of AR technology can enhance the overall shopping experience, leading to more positive attitudes toward the product and a higher likelihood of purchase.

Similarly, Rese et al. (2017) examined the factors influencing a consumer's perceived usefulness of AR using an extended Technology Acceptance Model (TAM). Their results not only confirmed the role of perceived enjoyment, as found in Yim et al. (2017), but also discovered that perceived informativeness, which refers to the extent to which users feel the product information is relevant and useful, influenced AR attitudes through the perceived usefulness of AR. This suggests that the effectiveness of AR in driving purchase intention is not solely dependent on the enjoyment factor but also on the quality and relevance of the information provided through the AR experience.

In a related study, Plotkina et al. (2019) applied the TAM to investigate AR-based mobile Virtual Try-on, yielding results consistent with those of Rese et al. (2017). This further emphasizes the importance of perceived usefulness and informativeness in shaping consumer attitudes toward AR technology in the context of online shopping.

It is worth noting that the adoption of innovative technologies, such as Virtual Try-on, has been a topic of interest in consumer behavior research even before the widespread use of AR. Kim et al. (2008) studied consumer adoption of Virtual Try-on when it was still considered an innovative tool. Their findings contribute to the understanding of consumer attitudes toward innovative technology in general, which can be applied to the context of AR adoption in e-commerce.

Therefore, the effectiveness of AR on purchase intention has been demonstrated through various studies that highlight the importance of factors such as perceived enjoyment, usefulness, and informativeness. As AR technology continues to evolve and become more integrated into the online shopping experience, understanding consumer attitudes and the factors that influence their adoption of AR will be crucial for businesses looking to leverage this technology to drive sales and enhance customer engagement. As businesses continue to experiment with AR technology and researchers delve deeper into the dynamics of AR Marketing, this subdiscipline is expected to evolve and mature, ultimately shaping the future of marketing practice. The potential for AR Marketing to transform the way businesses engage with their customers is vast, and it will be exciting to see how this emerging field develops in the coming years.

Bridging the Gap Between Digital and Physical Environments

The rapid advancement of technologies like virtual reality (VR), augmented reality (AR), and the Internet of Things (IoT) is blurring the boundaries between digital and physical environments, creating new opportunities for seamless, integrated experiences that span both realms. This convergence, often referred to as the "phygital" space, is transforming industries, reshaping consumer behavior, and unlocking innovative ways to interact with the world around us.

One of the key areas where the bridging of digital and physical environments is making a significant impact is in retail and commerce. By leveraging AR and VR technologies, retailers can create immersive, personalized shopping experiences that combine the best of online and in-store browsing. For example, AR apps can allow customers to virtually try on clothes, visualize furniture in their homes, or access product information and reviews by scanning physical items with their smartphones. This blending of digital and physical elements enhances the shopping journey, provides more informed decision-making, and creates a seamless transition between online and offline channels.

The physical approach is also transforming the way we work and collaborate. As remote work becomes more prevalent, VR and AR technologies are enabling new forms of virtual collaboration that feel more engaging and immersive than traditional video conferencing. Colleagues can meet in shared virtual spaces, interact with 3D models and data visualizations, and collaborate on projects in real-time, regardless of their physical location. This bridging of digital and physical workspaces can boost productivity, foster innovation, and create a sense of presence and connection among distributed teams.

In the realm of entertainment and media, the convergence of digital and physical is creating new forms of interactive, multi-sensory experiences. Theme parks, museums, and live events are incorporating AR and VR elements to enhance visitor engagement and storytelling. For example, visitors can use AR apps to access additional information about exhibits, participate in interactive games, or see historical sites and artifacts come to life through digital overlays. In the gaming industry, the rise of location-based AR games like Pokémon Go has demonstrated the potential for blending digital content with the physical world, encouraging players to explore their surroundings and interact with others in new ways.

As the boundaries between digital and physical continue to dissolve, it's important to consider the implications for privacy, security, and social interaction. The ubiquity of sensors and digital interfaces in physical spaces raises concerns about data collection, surveillance, and the potential for manipulation. Ensuring transparent and ethical data practices, as well as robust security measures, will be critical to building trust and acceptance of phygital technologies. Additionally, as people spend more time in blended digital-physical environments, it will be important to strike a balance between the benefits of enhanced experiences and the need for human connection and presence in the physical world.

Bridging the gap between digital and physical environments represents a transformative shift in how we live, work, and play. By leveraging technologies like VR, AR, and IoT, we can create more immersive, personalized, and intelligent experiences that span both realms. As these technologies continue to evolve and become more integrated into our daily lives, they will reshape industries, redefine social interactions, and unlock new possibilities for innovation and growth. Navigating this phygital future will require a thoughtful, human-centered approach that balances the benefits of technological advancement with the preservation of our fundamental human values and connections.

ENHANCING CONSUMER EXPERIENCES IN THE METAVERSE

The metaverse, a term used to describe a collective virtual shared space, is rapidly evolving and presenting new opportunities for businesses to engage with consumers in innovative ways. As this virtual landscape continues to grow, it's crucial for companies to focus on enhancing consumer experiences to build brand loyalty, drive engagement, and create memorable interactions. By focusing on user-centered design, personalized marketing, interactive storytelling, and community building, businesses can create immersive and engaging experiences that captivate audiences and foster long-term relationships.

To create effective consumer experiences in the metaverse, companies must prioritize user-centered design principles. This involves understanding the needs, preferences, and behaviors of target audiences and designing virtual experiences that cater to those factors. Intuitive navigation, accessibility, consistency, and regular feedback and iteration are key considerations in creating user-friendly and engaging virtual environments.

Personalized marketing strategies are another essential component of enhancing consumer experiences in the metaverse. By leveraging data and interactivity, companies can tailor experiences to individual users, delivering targeted content, recommendations, and promotions that resonate with their interests and preferences. Techniques such as avatar-based targeting, contextual advertising, gamification, and user-generated content can help create personalized and memorable experiences that drive engagement and loyalty.

Interactive storytelling and engagement techniques are also crucial for capturing and maintaining consumer attention in the metaverse. By creating immersive, multi-sensory experiences that incorporate branching narratives, collaborative challenges, and hidden surprises, companies can create memorable and emotionally resonant experiences that keep users coming back for more. These techniques can help foster a sense of adventure, discovery, and shared experience that sets brands apart in the virtual landscape.

Finally, building community and facilitating social interaction is a key strength of the metaverse that companies should leverage to enhance consumer experiences. By creating virtual spaces that serve as social hubs, fostering interest-based communities, empowering user-led events, and collaborating with influencers, businesses can create vibrant and engaged communities that extend beyond traditional brand-consumer relationships. These communities can serve as powerful sources of user-generated content, advocacy, and loyalty, driving long-term growth and success in the metaverse.

CHALLENGES AND OPPORTUNITIES

As businesses and consumers increasingly engage with the metaverse, it's important to consider the various challenges and opportunities that this new frontier presents. From privacy and security concerns to technological limitations and market fragmentation, companies must navigate a complex landscape to successfully leverage the potential of the metaverse. At the same time, the metaverse offers significant opportunities for innovation, growth, and the creation of new business models and revenue streams.

Privacy and Security Concerns

One of the primary challenges in the metaverse is ensuring the privacy and security of user data. As virtual experiences become more immersive and personalized, they often require the collection and processing of sensitive user information, such as biometric data, location data, and behavioral patterns. Companies must implement robust data protection measures and be transparent about their data practices to build trust with users. Additionally, the decentralized nature of the metaverse can make it more difficult to regulate and enforce privacy standards, requiring collaboration and consensus among stakeholders.

Technological Limitations and Accessibility Issues

Another challenge in the metaverse is the current technological limitations and accessibility issues. While advances in virtual and augmented reality have made immersive experiences more feasible, there are still barriers to entry in terms of hardware costs, network infrastructure, and user comfort with these technologies. Moreover, ensuring that virtual experiences are accessible to users with different abilities and devices is crucial for inclusivity and widespread adoption. As the metaverse evolves, it will be important to address these technological and accessibility challenges to create more seamless and equitable experiences for all users.

Market Fragmentation and Competition

The metaverse is still a relatively nascent and fragmented market, with multiple platforms, standards, and ecosystems competing for users and market share. This fragmentation can make it difficult for businesses to reach and engage with their target audiences effectively. Companies must navigate the complexities of different virtual environments, interoperability challenges, and shifting consumer preferences to succeed in the metaverse. As the market matures, it's likely that some consolidation and standardization will occur, but in the meantime, businesses must be agile and adaptable to thrive in this dynamic landscape.

Innovation and Growth Opportunities

Despite these challenges, the metaverse presents significant opportunities for innovation and growth. The immersive and interactive nature of virtual experiences opens up new possibilities for storytelling, education, entertainment, and commerce. Companies can experiment with new business models, such as virtual product sales, subscriptions, and experiences, to diversify their revenue streams. The metaverse also offers opportunities for brand building, customer engagement, and community development, allowing businesses to forge deeper and more meaningful connections with their audiences.

Moreover, the metaverse has the potential to drive significant economic growth and job creation, as new industries and professions emerge to support the development and management of virtual experiences. From virtual architects and designers to community managers and event planners, the metaverse will require a diverse range of skills and expertise, creating new opportunities for workers and entrepreneurs alike.

REFERENCES

Ajzen, I. (1985). From intentions to actions: A theory of planned behavior. In *Action Control* (pp. 11–39). Springer. doi:10.1007/978-3-642-69746-3_2

Algharabat, R., Rana, N. P., Dwivedi, Y. K., Alalwan, A. A., & Qasem, Z. (2018). The effect of telepresence, social presence and involvement on consumer brand engagement: An empirical study of non-profit organizations. *Journal of Retailing and Consumer Services*, *40*, 139–149. doi:10.1016/j.jretconser.2017.09.011

Arakji, R. Y., & Lang, K. R. (2008). Avatar Business Value Analysis: A Method for the Evaluation of Business Value Creation in Virtual Commerce. *Journal of Electronic Commerce Research*, *9*(3), 207–218.

Au, W. J. (2009a, March 24). *Top Second Life Entrepreneur Cashing Out US$1.7 Million Yearly; Furnishings, Events Management Among Top Earners.* New World Notes. http://nwn.blogs.com/nwn/2009/03/million.html#more

Au, W. J. (2009b, April 23). How's the Second Life Economy Doing? M. and T. Linden (eds.) *Talk Earnings, Land Owning, L$ Transactions, More.* New World Notes. https://nwn.blogs.com/nwn/2009/04/hows-the-second-life-economy-doing.html

Bailenson, J. N. (2018). *Experience on demand: What virtual reality is, how it works, and what it can do.* WW Norton & Company.

Borden, N. H. (1964). The concept of the marketing mix. *Journal of Advertising Research*, *4*, 2–7.

Bourlakis, M., Papagiannidis, S., & Li, F. (2009). Retail Spatial Evolution: Paving the Way from Traditional to Metaverse Retailing. *Electronic Commerce Research*, *9*(1-2), 135–148. doi:10.1007/s10660-009-9030-8

Chang, H. H., & Chen, S. W. (2008). The impact of online store environment cues on purchase intention. *Online Information Review*, *32*(6), 818–841. doi:10.1108/14684520810923953

Chang, T. Z., & Wildt, A. R. (1994). Price, product information, and purchase intention: An empirical study. *Journal of the Academy of Marketing Science*, *22*(1), 16–27. doi:10.1177/0092070394221002

Chiang, O. (2010, October 27). Creating a $1M Virtual Goods Brand in Second Life. *Forbes*.

Cowan, K., & Ketron, S. (2019). A dual model of product involvement for effective virtual reality: The roles of imagination, co-creation, telepresence, and interactivity. *Journal of Business Research*, *100*, 483–492. doi:10.1016/j.jbusres.2018.10.063

DMD. (2007). *The Virtual Brand Footprint: the Marketing Opportunity in Second Life [Report]*. DMD. http://www.dmdinsight.com/research/

Duncan, R. B. (1972). Characteristics of organizational environments and perceived environmental uncertainty. *Administrative Science Quarterly*, *17*(3), 313–327. doi:10.2307/2392145

Fischer, E., & Reuber, A. R. (2011). Social interaction via new social media: (How) can interactions on Twitter affect effectual thinking and behavior? *Journal of Business Venturing*, *26*(1), 1–18. doi:10.1016/j.jbusvent.2010.09.002

Frankish, K. (2010). Dual-process and dual-system theories of reasoning. *Philosophy Compass*, *5*(10), 914–926. doi:10.1111/j.1747-9991.2010.00330.x

Grupac, M., Husakova, K., & Balica, R. Ş. (2022). Virtual navigation and augmented reality shopping tools, immersive and cognitive technologies, and image processing computational and object tracking algorithms in the metaverse commerce. *Analysis and Metaphysics*, *21*(0), 210–226. doi:10.22381/am21202213

Habil, S. G. M., El-Deeb, S., & El-Bassiouny, N. (2024). The metaverse era: Leveraging augmented reality in the creation of novel customer experience. Management & Sustainability. *An Arab Review*, *3*(1), 1–15.

Han, D. I. D., Bergs, Y., & Moorhouse, N. (2022). Virtual reality consumer experience escapes: Preparing for the metaverse. *Virtual Reality (Waltham Cross)*, *26*(4), 1443–1458. doi:10.1007/s10055-022-00641-7

Hassouneh, D., & Brengman, M. (2011b). Virtual Worlds: A Gateway for SMEs Toward Internationalization. *Journal of Brand Management*, *19*(1), 72–90. doi:10.1057/bm.2011.24

Hassouneh, D., & Brengman, M. (2014). *Shopping for Virtual Products in Social Virtual Worlds: Does Users' Gender Matter?* [Working paper].

Hilken, T., Heller, J., Chylinski, M., Keeling, D. I., Mahr, D., & de Ruyter, K. (2020). Making omnichannel an augmented reality: The current and future state of the art. *Journal of Research in Interactive Marketing*, *14*(1), 55–79.

Javornik, A. (2016). Augmented reality: Research agenda for studying the impact of its media characteristics on consumer behaviour. *Journal of Retailing and Consumer Services*, *30*, 252–261. doi:10.1016/j.jretconser.2016.02.004

Kardes, F. R., Cline, T. W., & Cronley, M. L. (2011). *Consumer Behavior: Science and Practice*. South-Western Cengage Learning.

Karimi, S. (2013). A Purchase Decision-Making Process Model of Online Consumers and Its Influential Factora Cross Sector Analysis (Doctoral dissertation, The University of Manchester, Manchester, UK].

Kim, J., & Forsythe, S. (2008). Adoption of Virtual Try-on Technology for Online Apparel Shopping. *Journal of Interactive Marketing*, *22*(2), 45–59. doi:10.1002/dir.20113

Koohang, A., Nord, J. H., Ooi, K. B., Tan, G. W. H., Al-Emran, M., Aw, E. C. X., Baabdullah, A. M., Buhalis, D., Cham, T.-H., Dennis, C., Dutot, V., Dwivedi, Y. K., Hughes, L., Mogaji, E., Pandey, N., Phau, I., Raman, R., Sharma, A., Sigala, M., & Wong, L. W. (2023). Shaping the Metaverse into Reality: A Holistic Multidisciplinary Understanding of Opportunities, Challenges, and Avenues for Future Investigation. *Journal of Computer Information Systems*, *63*(3), 735–765. doi:10.1080/0887441 7.2023.2165197

Kowalczuk, P., & Siepmann, C. (2021). Cognitive, affective, and behavioral consumer responses to augmented reality in e-commerce: A comparative study. *Journal of Business Research*, *124*, 357–373. doi:10.1016/j.jbusres.2020.10.050

Krasonikolakis, I. G., Vrechopoulos, A., & Pouloudi, A. (2011). Defining, Applying and Customizing Store Atmosphere in Virtual Reality Commerce: Back to Basics? *International Journal of E-Services and Mobile Applications*, *3*(2), 14. doi:10.4018/jesma.2011040104

Kuntze, R., Crudele, T. R., Reynolds, D., & Matulich, E. (2013). The Rise and Fall of Virtual Reality Retailing in Second Life: An Avatar's Perspective. *Journal of Management and Marketing Research*, 13.

Laudon, K. C., & Traver, C. G. (2016). *E-Commerce: Business, Technology, Society*. Pearson.

Lee, K. C., & Chung, N. (2008). Empirical Analysis of Consumer Reaction to the Virtual Reality Shopping Mall. *Computers in Human Behavior*, *24*(1), 88–104. doi:10.1016/j.chb.2007.01.018

Liang, T. P., & Lai, T. P. (2000). Electronic Store Design and Consumer Choice: an Empirical Study. *Proceedings the 33rd Hawaii International Conference on System Sciences, (vol. 6*, pp. 60-42). IEEE.

Liang, T. P., & Lai, T. P. (2002). Effect of Store Design on Consumer Purchases: Van Empirical Study of Online Bookstores. *Information & Management*, *39*(6), 431–444. doi:10.1016/S0378-7206(01)00129-X

Linden Lab. (2013, June 20). *Infographic: 10 Years of Second Life*. Linden Lab. https://www.lindenlab.com/releases/infographic-10-years-of-second-life

Liu, H., Chu, H., Huang, Q., & Chen, X. (2016). Enhancing the flow experience of consumers in China through interpersonal interaction in social commerce. *Computers in Human Behavior*, *58*, 306–314. doi:10.1016/j.chb.2016.01.012

MacKenzie, K., Buckby, S., & Irvine, H. J. (2013). Business Research in Virtual Worlds: Possibilities and Practicalities. *Accounting, Auditing & Accountability Journal*, *26*(3), 352–373. doi:10.1108/09513571311311856

Martínez-Navarro, J., Bigné, E., Guixeres, J., Alcañiz, M., & Torrecilla, C. (2019). The influence of virtual reality in e-commerce. *Journal of Business Research*, *100*, 475–482. doi:10.1016/j.jbusres.2018.10.054

Mirabi, V., Akbariyeh, H., & Tahmasebifard, H. (2015). A study of factors affecting on customers purchase intention. [JMEST]. *Journal of Multidisciplinary Engineering Science and Technology*, *2*, 267–273.

Mollen, A., & Wilson, H. (2010). Engagement, telepresence and interactivity in online consumer experience: Reconciling scholastic and managerial perspectives. *Journal of Business Research*, *63*(9-10), 919–925. doi:10.1016/j.jbusres.2009.05.014

Morrison, D. G. (1979). Purchase intentions and purchase behavior. *Journal of Marketing*, *43*(2), 65–74. doi:10.1177/002224297904300207

Neves, J., Bacalhau, L. M., & Santos, V. (2022, December). A Systematic Review on the Customer Journey Between Two Worlds: Reality and Immersive World. In *International Conference on Marketing and Technologies* (pp. 401-416). Singapore: Springer Nature Singapore.

Papadopoulou, P. (2007). Applying Virtual Reality for Trust-building E-commerce Environments. *Virtual Reality (Waltham Cross), 11*(2), 107–127. doi:10.1007/s10055-006-0059-x

Papagiannidis, S., & Bourlakis, M. (2010). Staging the New Retail Drama: At a Metaverse Near You! *Journal of Virtual Worlds Research, 2*(5). doi:10.4101/jvwr.v2i5.808

Papagiannidis, S., Pantano, E., See-To, E. W. K., & Bourlakis, M. (2013). Modelling the Determinants of a Simulated Experience in a Virtual Retail Store and Users' Product Purchasing Intentions. *Journal of Marketing Management, 29*(13-14), 1462–1492. doi:10.1080/0267257X.2013.821150

Park, J., Stoel, L., & Lennon, S. J. (2008). Cognitive, Affective and Cognitive Responses to Visual Simulation: The Effects of Rotation in Online Product Presentation. *Journal of Consumer Behaviour, 7*(1), 72–87. doi:10.1002/cb.237

Park, S. R., Nah, F. F., & Dewester, D., & Eschenbrenner. (2008). Virtual World Affordances: Enhancing Brand Value. *Journal of Virtual Worlds Research, 1*(2), 1–18.

Plotkina, D., & Saurel, H. (2019). Me or just like me? The role of virtual try-on and physical appearance in apparel M-retailing. *Journal of Retailing and Consumer Services, 51*, 362–377. doi:10.1016/j.jretconser.2019.07.002

Rauschnabel, P. A., Babin, B. J., tom Dieck, M. C., Krey, N., & Jung, T. (2022). What is augmented reality marketing? Its definition, complexity, and future. *Journal of Business Research, 142*, 1140–1150. doi:10.1016/j.jbusres.2021.12.084

Rese, A., Baier, D., Geyer-Schulz, A., & Schreiber, S. (2017). How augmented reality apps are accepted by consumers: A comparative analysis using scales and opinions. *Technological Forecasting and Social Change, 124*, 306–319. doi:10.1016/j.techfore.2016.10.010

Saffari, F., Kakaria, S., Bigné, E., Bruni, L. E., Zarei, S., & Ramsøy, T. Z. (2023). Motivation in the metaverse: A dual-process approach to consumer choices in a virtual reality supermarket. *Frontiers in Neuroscience, 17*, 1062980. doi:10.3389/fnins.2023.1062980 PMID:36875641

Sandhusen, R. (2008). *Marketing.* Barrons.

Schall, J. D. (2001). Neural basis of deciding, choosing and acting. *Nature Reviews. Neuroscience, 2*(1), 33–42. doi:10.1038/35049054 PMID:11253357

Shen, B., Tan, W., Guo, J., Cai, H., Wang, B., & Zhuo, S. (2020). A Study on Design Requirement Development and Satisfaction for Future Virtual World Systems. *Future Internet*, *12*(7), 112. doi:10.3390/fi12070112

Shen, B., Tan, W., Guo, J., Zhao, L., & Qin, P. (2021). How to promote user purchase in metaverse? A systematic literature review on consumer behavior research and virtual commerce application design. *Applied Sciences (Basel, Switzerland)*, *11*(23), 11087. doi:10.3390/app112311087

Smink, A. R., Frowijn, S., van Reijmersdal, E. A., van Noort, G., & Neijens, P. C. (2019). Try online before you buy: How does shopping with augmented reality affect brand responses and personal data disclosure. Electronic Commerce Research and Applications, 35, 100854.

Suh, K. S., & Lee, Y. E. (2005). The effects of virtual reality on consumer learning: An empirical investigation. *Management Information Systems Quarterly*, *29*(4), 673–697. doi:10.2307/25148705

Teoh, K. K., & Cyril, E. U. (2008). The role of presence and para social presence on trust in online virtual electronic commerce. *Journal of Applied Sciences (Faisalabad)*, *8*(16), 2834–2842. doi:10.3923/jas.2008.2834.2842

Tiffany, L. (2007, January 9). *Starting a Second Life Business*. Entrepreneur.

Van Kerrebroeck, H., Brengman, M., & Willems, K. (2017). When brands come to life: Experimental research on the vividness effect of Virtual Reality in transformational marketing communications. *Virtual Reality (Waltham Cross)*, *21*(4), 177–191. doi:10.1007/s10055-017-0306-3

Yim, M. Y. C., Chu, S. C., & Sauer, P. L. (2017). Is augmented reality technology an effective tool for e-commerce? An interactivity and vividness perspective. *Journal of Interactive Marketing*, *39*, 89–103. doi:10.1016/j.intmar.2017.04.001

Zarantonello, L., & Schmitt, B. H. (2023). Experiential AR/VR: A consumer and service framework and research agenda. *Journal of Service Management*, *34*(1), 34–55. doi:10.1108/JOSM-12-2021-0479

Zhang, K. Z., & Benyoucef, M. (2016). Consumer behavior in social commerce: A literature review. *Decision Support Systems*, *86*, 95–108. doi:10.1016/j.dss.2016.04.001

KEY TERMS AND DEFINITIONS

Augmented Reality: Augmented reality (AR) is a technology that overlays digital information onto the real world, enhancing the user's perception of reality by adding computer-generated elements such as graphics, sounds, or haptic feedback.

Consumer Behaviour: Consumer behavior is the study of how individuals, groups, and organizations select, buy, use, and dispose of goods, services, ideas, or experiences to satisfy their needs and wants.

Decision Making: Decision making is the cognitive process of selecting a course of action among multiple alternatives.

Metaverse: The metaverse is a collective virtual shared space, created by the convergence of virtually enhanced physical reality and physically persistent virtual space, including the sum of all virtual worlds, augmented reality, and the internet.

Purchasing Goods: Purchasing goods refers to the act of buying products or services. It involves the exchange of money or other forms of payment for the ownership or use of a particular item or service.

User Experience: User experience (UX) is the overall experience of a person using a product, system, or service. It includes the practical, experiential, affective, meaningful, and valuable aspects of human-computer interaction and product ownership.

Virtual Reality: Virtual reality (VR) is a simulated experience that can be similar to or completely different from the real world. VR allows users to interact with and navigate through the virtual environment as if they were physically present in it.

Chapter 12
Role of Youtube and Instagram Advertising in Attracting Gen–Z Consumers in Delhi–NCR

Sarthak Kumar Dutta
Christ University, India

Supriyo Manna
Christ University, India

ABSTRACT

Similar to a rising global trend, Gen-Z consumers in Delhi-NCR are spending more time on social media sites such as YouTube and Instagram. Understanding how advertising on these sites affects their purchasing decisions is critical. This study investigates the influence of YouTube and Instagram advertising in recruiting Generation Z customers. Based on a recent study that highlighted entertainment, informativeness, customization, and irritation as important elements impacting advertising value on YouTube, this chapter analyzes how these features influence brand awareness and purchase intention among Gen-Z consumers in Delhi-NCR. The study predicts that, like YouTube, Instagram commercials that are entertaining, informative, and personalized will be more effective in attracting Gen-Z customers. In contrast, irritating advertisements will have a negative influence. By evaluating these aspects, the study provides useful insights for marketers looking to use YouTube and Instagram advertising to effectively attract Gen-Z consumers in Delhi-NCR.

DOI: 10.4018/979-8-3693-4167-4.ch012

INTRODUCTION

The evolution of consumer behavior is in a constant state of flux, and the emergence of Generation Z (Gen-Z), a cohort deeply ingrained in digital platforms, born from the late 1990s to the early 2010s, poses a distinct challenge for marketers. In contrast to previous cohorts, Generation Z consumers are bombarded with advertisements from a young age, leading them to approach traditional marketing tactics with a sense of doubt, and instead, prioritize genuineness, social responsibility, and brand principles in their buying choices. This shift necessitates a revision of marketing approaches, focusing on actively engaging Generation Z through their preferred channels and fostering genuine relationships.

Conventional marketing strategies, such slick advertisements and celebrity endorsements, frequently fall flat with Generation Z. They see these approaches as impersonal, sales-oriented, and devoid of the interpersonal interaction they long for. Gen-Z places a high importance on social responsibility and authentic brand narratives. They are drawn to companies that support issues close to their hearts, encourage diversity, and push for constructive change. According to studies, 73% of Gen-Z buyers are prepared to pay more for environmentally friendly goods. This demonstrates their willingness to work with companies that share their beliefs and represent something more significant than just financial gain.

Moreover, while making selections about what to buy, Gen-Z customers actively search out user-generated content (UGC). More than traditional advertising messages, they believe the opinions and experiences of their peers. Gen-Z is able to investigate items, compare pricing, and find new businesses through the eyes of real people thanks to social media platforms like YouTube and Instagram, which serve as a fertile ground for user-generated content.

For Generation Z, YouTube and Instagram have become the main social media channels. Every channel has unique benefits for marketers looking to reach this audience.

YouTube has approximately 2 billion monthly users, most of whom are Generation Z. The platform specializes in providing a wide variety of content, from in-depth tutorials and product reviews to engaging videos, blogs, and entertainment skits. This differentiation allows businesses to tailor messaging to an individual's unique interests and capture the ongoing interest of Gen Z. Additionally, creating long-form content on YouTube is more interactive, giving marketers the opportunity to share their values, goals, and the human element within them.

Instagram has captured the interest of Generation Z with its emphasis on visually stunning material. The platform facilitates the utilization of influencer marketing, short-form films (Reels and Stories), and high-quality photos by marketers to provide an immersive and interactive visual experience. Visual communication is highly valued by Generation Z, and Instagram gives marketers the opportunity to present their goods in an enticing and inspiring way.

This research paper evaluates the influence of YouTube and Instagram advertising in attracting Generation Z customers. These platforms, which are central to Gen-Z's digital experience, provide fertile ground for companies to build meaningful interactions with this important cohort. Marketers may create customized advertisements that resonate with Gen-Z's beliefs and attract their attention by exploiting each platform's distinct features.

In recent times, there has been a notable focus on online social media platforms such as Facebook, Twitter, YouTube, and Instagram (Dwivedi et al., 2018). The development of a robust online presence has become a crucial element of marketing tactics. The efficiency of using company accounts to promote products online via social media platforms for advertising (Earl, 2023). Users of social networking sites regularly produce and distribute user-generated multimedia material in addition to sponsored postings and fan pages. User reviews of products and brands are a typical feature of this kind of content. When it comes to popularity and effectiveness, user-generated material has outperformed professional advertisements. Vân Riel, 2023). According to statistical data, a projection indicates that the global Internet user population will exceed 5.3 billion individuals by August 2023. The utilization of social media platforms has experienced a significant surge across various demographic segments in recent times. Likewise, there has been a substantial rise in the quantity of individual accounts established on social networking platforms like YouTube and Instagram. On these platforms, individuals not only share their own original material but also interact with brands and products (Utomo et al., 2023) and offer and receive feedback on goods (Ausat, 2023). Customers can talk to strangers and acquaintances about the products (Dong & Saini, 2023). Social media tools facilitate communication, particularly between peers, and exert a major influence on consumers' marketing strategies and purchase decisions (Dong & Saini, 2023). Consequently, social media has profoundly changed how consumers and brands communicate by enabling direct and reciprocal communication (Dong & Saini, 2023). People may now react to brand content instead of just consuming it, as was the case in the past. In addition, they actively create material that is relevant to their brand. They engage in brand marketing, which is influenced by more knowledgeable consumers (Rixom & Rixom, 2023).

Therefore, the purpose of this study is to provide and examine a comprehensive integrated model for YouTube and Instagram advertising by overcoming the limitations of previous studies on social media. To this aim, our research questions are:

1.   In what ways do customers view YouTube and Instagram advertisements as reliable sources of information when making judgements about what to buy?

2. What is the effect of entertainment, informativeness and customization on brand awareness?
3. Does brand awareness eventually lead to purchase decisions?

The paper proceeds as follows: it briefly reviews the literature on our variables, then develops research hypotheses and describes our methods. Finally, it presents the results of the data analysis and a discussion of findings.

LITERATURE REVIEW

Online video advertising is a recently established format that shares some qualities with social media and television, but also differs from more traditional forms of advertising in some ways (Dehghani, Nourani, & Choubtarash, 2012). Social media advertising is believed to be more reliable and educational, which has an impact on conventional evaluations of advertising effectiveness (i.e., the information and entertainment value) and influences the advertising value more than the ad's ability to influence consumer choices. Recent studies show that advertising spending allocated to social media is always rising, suggesting that brands are becoming more and more interested in engaging with their followers, influencing their experiences, and leveraging their opinions to demand more impact from advertising (Lipsman, Mudd, Rich, & Bruich, 2012). Although YouTube offers a variety of video formats that might theoretically highlight the brand more prominently, some research indicates that consumers find it difficult to remember watching product-related content on the platform, suggesting that companies frequently take on a more lateral position.

However, the elements influencing the advertising value and its consequent effects on brand awareness and consumer purchase intention have never been taken into account in the prior literature on YouTube advertising. Furthermore, prior research on social media advertising has demonstrated a relationship between advertising attitude and three variables: informativeness, amusement, and annoyance; however, the direct impact of customizing ads in conjunction with other elements has never been examined. Thus, this study delves into the literature by establishing a connection between consumers' perceptions of advertising value, brand awareness, and buy intention, and by using the customization of commercials as a determining factor for ad value.

Some of the factors that are crucial for social media advertising are:

Entertainment

Media channels' level of entertainment determines how engaging they are for viewers. Higher entertainment value is likely to benefit media consumers and encourage them to use the medium more frequently, according to prior research. Advertising entertainment denotes the potential of an advertisement as well as the pleasure and enjoyment that consumers derive from it. It is likely that advertisements will be used to fulfill the hedonic needs of consumers. Consequently, increasing likeability of pleasure and enjoyment. The hedonic needs of consumers can be enhanced by the social media environment advertising through the presentation of enjoyable entertainment. Entertainment's value is found in its capacity to satisfy users' needs for amusement, emotional release, and distraction by enabling them to interact with, share, and even exchange images and videos with their social media networks.

Many advertisers have subscribed to the Madison & Vine YouTube channel, which combines entertainment and advertising, in an effort to attract a larger audience by displaying brands on props and in entertaining content. According to Kotler and Armstrong (2013), product placements are the most popular type of branded entertainment because they cut through the noise and open up new channels for attracting more customers' attention.

Informativeness

The degree to which a resource offers users useful and inventive information is known as its informativeness. According to Clancy, Maura, media consumers should evaluate if an advertisement's ability to enlighten consumers is the primary factor in their decision to accept it. According to Ducoffe (Ducoffe, 1995a), informativeness is defined as "consensus exists regarding the ability of advertising to inform consumers of product alternatives," meaning that it may influence consumers to make satisfied purchasing decisions. Consumers are more likely to look for product information and are more likely to obtain knowledge through unrestricted, face-to-face interactions (De Mooij & Hofstede, 2010). Additionally, the idea is expanded upon, and numerous academics have demonstrated the significance of informativeness on opinions regarding social media advertisements (Aswad). Due to its format, which shows additional product information, social media thus offers an appropriate instrument for such a goal.

Customization

When commercials are tailored to their individual needs and interests, consumers are more receptive to them. Advertisers must thus monitor consumer demands, profiles, and consumption trends (Rao & Minakakis, 2003). According to Ducoffe, advertising is most successful when it results in a value exchange between the advertised messages and the consumers. Put another way, people are probably going to notice advertisements that are clearly more personalized and ignore those that are thought to be less so (Liu, Li, Mizerski, & Soh, 2012). Social media's ability to personalize content can revolutionize the way that advertising is done. This includes profiling and tracking consumer behavior according to each user's location and demographics. As one of the most powerful social media channels, YouTube offers a platform to help the organization achieve its goal of sharing and creating video content that caters to the individual needs and tastes of each user.

Brand Awareness

Strong ties with consumers can be efficiently enhanced by brands (Tsimonis & Dimitriadis, 2014). A brand's recognition or recollection is referred to as brand awareness (Huang & Sarigo€llü, 2012). In addition to strengthening current relationships between businesses and their customers, new media also offers new opportunities for conventional options. This enhances businesses' capacity to engage in customer dialogue and, as a result, fortifies their communications tool (Tsimonis & Dimitriadis, 2014). Brand recognition can be increased and built through social media. A brand name that is widely disseminated over social media can assist inform people about it and become widely associated with the company, generating brand awareness, as a large number of people already use these platforms (Golding).

Consumer Attraction

Consumer attraction, which can be influenced by factors including attitude towards the advertisement, is the most notable measure of advertising efficacy, according to prior study (Wu, 2006). discovered that brand awareness and Consumer attraction are influenced by the attitude towards the advertisement. Furthermore, behavior intention in the social media environment is positively correlated with consumer attraction. To be more precise, advertising value in social media advertising is a leading indicator of consumer attraction. Dehghani and Tumer (Dehghani & Tumer, 2015) examined how much consumers attraction to make a purchase were influenced by the recommendations and brand value that other users had provided on social media.

Figure 1. Conceptual framework

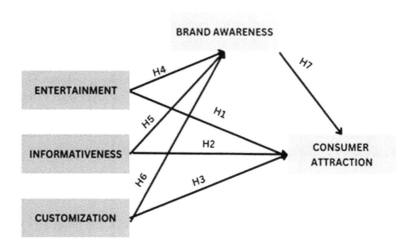

On the basis of the above framework, following hypotheses for our empirical research:

H1: Consumer has perceived entertainment through YouTube and Instagram advertising, which is positively affecting on consumer attraction.
H2: Consumer has perceived informativeness through YouTube and Instagram advertising, which is positively affecting on consumer attraction.
H3: Consumer has perceived customization through YouTube and Instagram advertising, which is positively affecting on consumer attraction.
H4: Consumer has perceived entertainment through YouTube and Instagram advertising, which is positively affecting on Brand awareness.
H5: Consumer has perceived informativeness through YouTube and Instagram advertising, which is positively affecting on Brand awareness.
H6: Consumer has perceived customization through YouTube and Instagram advertising, which is positively affecting on Brand awareness.
H7: Perceived entertainment, informativeness and customization in YouTube and Instagram advertising mediates the relationship between brand awareness and consumer attraction.

Our Independent variables were entertainment, informativeness and customization and all these variables have an effect on brand awareness and customer attraction.

RESEARCH METHODOLOGY

Sample and Data Collection

Data for the present study was collected in March, 2024.The participants in this study were recruited from various social media platforms, including YouTube and Instagram. A convenience sampling technique was employed, with a total of approximately 149 students from the Christ Deemed to be University (Delhi), participated in this study via a questionnaire. Participants were selected based on their active engagement with social media platforms.

Out of the 159 responses, approximately **96.6%** of respondents are between the age group of 15-25. Approximately 66% of respondents use YouTube daily, in which About 56% of respondents often see ads in YouTube. Approximately 70% of respondents use Instagram daily, in which About 60% of respondents often see ads in Instagram.

Figure 2. Age group

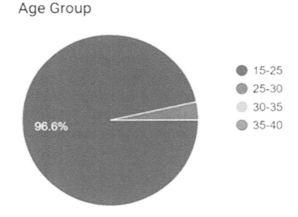

Figure 3. Gender

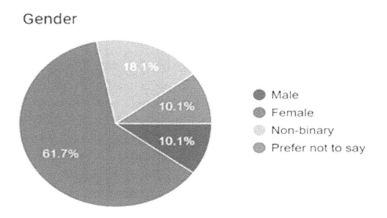

Measurement

The relationships between variables have been measured instead of measuring the variables itself. All measurement scales are Likert-type with 4- point format, anchoring at "1"–Daily and "4"–Less than Monthly. Descriptive statistics were used to summarize the demographic characteristics of the participants and provide an overview of the key variables under investigation. Measures such as means, standard deviations, frequencies, and percentages were computed to describe the sample and variables of interest. Correlation analysis was performed to examine the relationships between different variables, such as the correlation between influencer credibility and purchase intention, as well as the correlation between social media usage and consumer behavior.

RESULTS

Descriptive Statistics

Table 1. Descriptive statistics

	N	Minimum	Maximum	Mean	Std. Deviation
Entertainment	159	1	143	70.09	44.883
Customer attraction	159	1	116	37.46	34.179
customization	159	1	130	30.53	29.166
Brand Awareness	159	1	83	38.13	31.585
informativeness	159	1	106	20.01	25.124
Valid N (listwise)	159				

· Interpretation:

The mean value for entertainment is 70.09, which suggests that advertising content on both YouTube and Instagram is perceived as moderately entertaining by Gen-Z consumers in Delhi-NCR. The mean value for customer attraction is 37.46, indicating that advertising efforts on these platforms have a moderate impact on attracting Gen-Z consumers. With a mean value of 30.53, customization seems to be a strong suit in advertising. This implies that personalized content resonates well with Gen-Z consumers. The mean value for brand awareness is 38.13, indicating that advertising efforts contribute to brand visibility among Gen-Z consumers. The mean value for informativeness is 20.01, suggesting that advertising content provides useful information but could be improved to better engage Gen-Z consumers.

Ads on YouTube and Instagram slightly entertain and raise brand awareness among Generation Z in Delhi-NCR. Personalization is crucial, with customization rating best. However, informativeness and customer attraction require improvement. Brands may increase the impact of their advertising on these channels by generating more engaging and useful content.

Correlation

Table 2. Correlations

			Entertainment	Customer attraction
Spearman's rho	Entertainment	Correlation Coefficient	1.000	.232**
		Sig. (2-tailed)	.	.003
		N	159	159
	Customer attraction	Correlation Coefficient	.232**	1.000
		Sig. (2-tailed)	.003	.
		N	159	159

**. Correlation is significant at the 0.01 level (2-tailed).
(entertainment and customer)

· Interpretation:

The correlation coefficient between Entertainment and Customer attraction is 0.232 (significant at the 0.01 level, two-tailed). This indicates a positive correlation between entertainment and customer attraction. In other words, as entertainment increases, customer attraction tends to increase as well. However, the strength of this correlation is moderate, not very strong.

Table 3. Correlations

			Customer attraction	informativeness
Spearman's rho	Customer attraction	Correlation Coefficient	1.000	.815**
		Sig. (2-tailed)	.	.000
		N	159	159
	informativeness	Correlation Coefficient	.815**	1.000
		Sig. (2-tailed)	.000	.
		N	159	159

**. Correlation is significant at the 0.01 level (2-tailed).
(customer and informativeness)

Interpretation:

The correlation coefficient between Customer attraction and Informativeness is 0.815 (significant at the 0.01 level, two-tailed). This indicates a strong positive correlation between customer attraction and informativeness. In other words, as the informativeness of advertising content increases, customer attraction tends to increase as well.

Table 4. Correlations

			Customer attraction	customization
Spearman's rho	Customer attraction	Correlation Coefficient	1.000	.846**
		Sig. (2-tailed)	.	.000
		N	159	159
	customization	Correlation Coefficient	.846**	1.000
		Sig. (2-tailed)	.000	.
		N	159	159

**. Correlation is significant at the 0.01 level (2-tailed).
(attraction and customization)

· Interpretation:

The correlation coefficient between Customer attraction and Customization is 0.846 (significant at the 0.01 level, two-tailed). This indicates a strong positive correlation between customer attraction and customization. In other words, as the level of customization in advertising increases, customer attraction tends to increase as well.

Table 5. Correlations

			customization	Brand Awareness
Spearman's rho	customization	Correlation Coefficient	1.000	.680**
		Sig. (2-tailed)	.	.000
		N	159	159
	Brand Awareness	Correlation Coefficient	.680**	1.000
		Sig. (2-tailed)	.000	.
		N	159	159

**. Correlation is significant at the 0.01 level (2-tailed).
(customization and brand awareness)

· Interpretation:

The correlation coefficient between Customization and Brand Awareness is 0.680 (significant at the 0.01 level, two-tailed). This indicates a strong positive correlation between customization and brand awareness. In other words, as the level of customization in advertising increases, brand awareness tends to increase as well.

Table 6. Correlations

			Brand Awareness	informativeness
Spearman's rho	Brand Awareness	Correlation Coefficient	1.000	.542**
		Sig. (2-tailed)	.	.000
		N	159	159
	informativeness	Correlation Coefficient	.542**	1.000
		Sig. (2-tailed)	.000	.
		N	159	159

**. Correlation is significant at the 0.01 level (2-tailed).
(informativeness and brand awareness)

· Interpretation:

The Spearman's rho correlation coefficient between Brand Awareness and Informativeness is 0.542 (significant at the 0.01 level, two-tailed). This indicates a positive moderate correlation between these two variables. In simpler terms, as brand awareness increases, so does the perceived informativeness of the advertising content.

Table 7. Correlations

			Brand Awareness	customization
Spearman's rho	Brand Awareness	Correlation Coefficient	1.000	.680**
		Sig. (2-tailed)	.	.000
		N	159	159
	customization	Correlation Coefficient	.680**	1.000
		Sig. (2-tailed)	.000	.
		N	159	159

**. Correlation is significant at the 0.01 level (2-tailed).
(brand awareness and customization)

· Interpretation:

The Spearman's rho correlation coefficient between Brand Awareness and Customization is 0.680 (significant at the 0.01 level, two-tailed). This indicates a strong positive correlation between these two variables.

When we did the correlation test, we found out that all the variables are having a positive relationship. Our Independent variables were entertainment, informativeness and customization and all these variables have an effect on brand awareness and customer attraction.

Table 8.

Hypothesis	Accepted/ Rejected	Reason
H1(Entertainment and consumer attraction)	Accepted	There is positive relation between entertainment and consumer attraction through correlation test.
H2(Informativeness and consumer attraction)	Accepted	There is positive relation between Informativeness and consumer attraction through correlation test.
H3(Customization and consumer attraction)	Accepted	There is positive relation between customization and consumer attraction through correlation test.
H4(Entertainment and Brand awareness)	Accepted	There is positive relation between entertainment and Brand awareness through correlation test.
H5(Informativeness and brand awareness)	Accepted	There is positive relation between informativeness and Brand awareness through correlation test.
H6(Customization and Brand awareness)	Accepted	There is positive relation between Customization and Brand awareness through correlation test.
H7(Consumer attraction and Brand awareness)	Accepted	There is positive relation between Consumer attraction and Brand awareness through correlation test.

Regression

Figure 4.

SUMMARY OUTPUT

Regression Statistics	
Multiple R	0.842189023
R Square	0.70928235
Adjusted R Square	0.703655557
Standard Error	0.390457255
Observations	159

ANOVA

	df	SS	MS	F	Significance F
Regression	3	57.65360198	19.21786733	126.0544547	2.21193E-41
Residual	155	23.63081451	0.152456868		
Total	158	81.28441649			

	Coefficients	Standard Error	t Stat	P-value	Lower 95%	Upper 95%	Lower 95.0%	Upper 95.0%
Intercept	0.141720508	0.129410631	1.095122608	0.275161688	-0.113915588	0.397356604	-0.113915588	0.397356604
Entertainment	0.478080646	0.05268455	9.074399323	4.89411E-16	0.374008263	0.582153028	0.374008263	0.582153028
informativeness	0.037629165	0.052033442	0.7231727	0.470663658	-0.065157027	0.140415356	-0.065157027	0.140415356
Customization	0.644395901	0.089002012	7.240239693	1.95671E-11	0.468582472	0.820209331	0.468582472	0.820209331

· Interpretation

1. Regression Statistics:
   ◦ The multiple R value of 0.842 suggests a strong positive correlation between the independent variables (entertainment, informativeness, customization) and the dependent variables (brand awareness, consumer attraction).
   ◦ The R Square value of 0.709 indicates that approximately 70.9% of the variance in brand awareness and consumer attraction can be explained by the independent variables.
   ◦ The Adjusted R Square value of 0.704 adjusts the R Square value for the number of predictors in the model.
   ◦ The Standard Error of 0.390 indicates the average distance that the observed values fall from the regression line.
   ◦ With 159 observations, the model has a decent sample size for analysis.
2. ANOVA:
   ◦ The ANOVA table shows that the regression model is statistically significant, as indicated by the high F-value of 126.054 and a low p-value.
   ◦ The Regression sum of squares (SS) of 57.653 indicates the amount of variance explained by the regression model, while the Residual SS of 23.631 represents the unexplained variance.

- ○ The Total SS of 81.284 is the total sum of squares in the model.
3. Coefficients:
  - ○ The intercept coefficient of 0.142 represents the expected value of the dependent variables when all independent variables are zero.
  - ○ The coefficients for entertainment, informativeness, and customization are 0.478, 0.038, and 0.644, respectively.
  - ○ These coefficients indicate the impact of each independent variable on brand awareness and consumer attraction.
  - ○ The t-statistics and p-values show that entertainment and customization have a significant impact on brand awareness and consumer attraction, while informativeness does not appear to be statistically significant.
4. Overall Interpretation:
  - ○ Entertainment and customization play a crucial role in influencing brand awareness and consumer attraction, with higher values leading to increased brand awareness and consumer attraction.
  - ○ Informativeness, while included in the model, does not seem to have a significant impact based on the coefficients and p-values.
  - ○ Strategies focusing on enhancing entertainment and customization aspects may lead to improved brand awareness and consumer attraction based on the regression analysis results.

This interpretation provides insights into how the independent variables contribute to brand awareness and consumer attraction, guiding potential strategies for enhancing these aspects in a marketing or consumer context.

CONCLUSION

From a theoretical standpoint, first, this study reveals that all the three factors (Entertainment, Customization, Informativeness) in advertising value plays an important role in helping customers with enhancing brand awareness when receiving YouTube & Instagram advertisements and subsequently forming purchase intention. The results indicate the perceived entertainment and the customization of advertisements are the strongest positive drivers of ads value while irritation is the negative drivers, which supports previous studies. Furthermore, in the smart advertising environment, customization plays an important role in advertisement value.

This study provides significant data for organizations who use YouTube and Instagram advertising to reach Gen-Z customers in Delhi-NCR. Marketers targeting this group should focus generating interesting and skip-resistant ad formats, especially on YouTube, where ad-skipping is common. Our findings imply that professional design and relevant information are critical for catching Gen-Z attention in the first few seconds.

Furthermore, customization emerges as a significant driver of ad value. Instagram's existing tailored ad capabilities can serve as a solid example for YouTube's video ad implementation. This would ensure that Gen-Z viewers see advertising relevant to their interests, decreasing aggravation and enhancing ad effectiveness.

For YouTube, the findings emphasize the significance of balancing free and paid offerings. YouTube may create a more favorable advertising climate by providing Gen-Z users both ad-supported free content as well as premium ad-free choices. This can reduce user irritation, resulting in a more sustainable model for both viewers and marketers.

Previous studies have neither paid attention in examining the relationships between our variables in ad value nor the effect on brand awareness and purchase intention. Therefore, the results of this study extend the current literature on social media advertising.

Gen Z in Delhi-NCR is inundated with information. Their attention span is short, and they seek authenticity. Traditional advertising strategies frequently fall short. Our findings highlight the necessity of emphasizing compelling content. Gone are the days of generic advertising. To capture viewers' attention before they click away, YouTube advertising must be appealing within the first few seconds. Consider short, snappy tales, comedy, and influencer partnerships. Instagram thrives off visually attractive content. High-quality pictures, short-form movies (such as Reels), and user-generated content (UGC) have a great appeal. Partnering with local micro-influencers that share your brand values may be very beneficial.

In the Delhi-NCR region, Gen-Z consumers prioritize value. They choose brands that share their social and environmental concerns. Simply posting advertising isn't enough. Marketers must establish trust and promote a feeling of community. YouTube channels and Instagram accounts should serve more than just commercial purposes. Create educational and interesting material that reflects Gen-Z interests. Hold live Q&A sessions with brand ambassadors, promote user-generated content through contests, and aggressively respond to comments and messages. This two-way communication encourages brand loyalty and establishes your organization as a thinking leader.

Personalization is no longer a "nice-to-have" but a "must-have" for Gen-Z marketing. Our research demonstrates the favorable impact of ad customization on ad value. Leveraging the massive amounts of data accessible on these platforms enables tailored messaging. Consider a Gen-Z sneakerhead in Delhi seeing an ad for the latest limited-edition release on their favorite YouTuber's channel, or a young lady who cares about sustainability seeing an Instagram ad for an eco-friendly apparel business. This degree of customization promotes brand connection and raises the possibility of conversion.

Our findings further emphasize the necessity of a healthy advertising ecology on YouTube. While Gen-Z likes free material, an overwhelming ad load can be frustrating. Offering a premium ad-free membership alongside an ad-supported free tier gives viewers options and offers a more sustainable strategy for both advertisers and the platform. Finding this balance is essential for attracting and maintaining Gen-Z customers.

To summarize, our study offers actionable insights not only for established companies, but for any firm looking to interact with Gen-Z consumers in Delhi-NCR via YouTube and Instagram advertising. Marketers can effectively target this crucial demographic by focusing compelling content, customization, and a balanced user experience across all platforms.

LIMITATIONS

First, in this study, sample size could not completely apply to the whole population of YouTube' users as we conducted the research based on small number of populations. University students are the investigated demographic. However, collecting data from only the university student does not cover the all range of YouTube users, which limits the generalizability of the findings

The paper mentions that users might perceive advertising on YouTube as valuable if it aligns with their incentives for using the platform. However, it does not delve into the specific motivations and perceptions of users regarding advertising on YouTube. Further research is needed to evaluate the usage motivations associated with videos on YouTube and provide empirical data on users' perceptions of advertising.

REFERENCES

Albaum, G., Best, R., & Hawkins, D. (1980). Retailing strategy for customer growth and new customer attraction. *Journal of Business Research*, 8(1), 7–19. doi:10.1016/0148-2963(80)90027-2

Ausat, A. M. A.M. A. (2023). The Role of Social Media in Shaping Public Opinion and Its Influence on Economic Decisions. [TACIT]. *Technology and Society Perspectives*, 1(1), 35–44. doi:10.61100/tacit.v1i1.37

Aziza, D. N., & Astuti, R. D. (2019, March). Evaluating the effect of YouTube advertising towards young customers' purchase intention. In *12th International Conference on Business and Management Research (ICBMR 2018)* (pp. 93-98). Atlantis Press. 10.2991/icbmr-18.2019.16

Bendixen, M. T. (1993). Advertising effects and effectiveness. *European Journal of Marketing*, *27*(10), 19–32. doi:10.1108/03090569310045861

Datta, B., & Kaushik, P. (2019). Brand awareness through Instagram advertising. *Asian Journal of Management*, *10*(2), 100–108. doi:10.5958/2321-5763.2019.00017.9

De Mooij, M., & Hofstede, G. (2010). The Hofstede model: applications to global branding and advertising strategy and research. *International Journal of Advertising, 29*(1), 85e110.

Dehghani, M., Niaki, M. K., Ramezani, I., & Sali, R. (2016). Evaluating the influence of YouTube advertising for attraction of young customers. *Computers in Human Behavior*, *59*, 165–172. doi:10.1016/j.chb.2016.01.037

Dehghani, M., Nourani, S., & Choubtarash, H. (2012). *Interdisciplinary journal of contemporary research in business, 4*(8), 774e787.

Dehghani, M., & Tumer, M. (2015). A research on effectiveness of Facebook adver- tising on enhancing purchase intention of consumers. *Computers in Human Behavior, 49*, 597e600.

Djafarova, E., & Kramer, K. (2019). YouTube advertising: Exploring its effectiveness. *The Marketing Review*, *19*(1-2), 127–145. doi:10.1362/146934719X15633618140855

Dong, M., & Saini, R. (2023). Listening to strangers more than friends: How recommendations from close-(vs distant-) others influence consumption. *European Journal of Marketing*, *57*(5), 1327–1351. doi:10.1108/EJM-11-2021-0841

Ducoffe, R. H. (1995a). How consumers assess the value of advertising. *Journal of Current Issues & Research in Advertising, 17*(1), 1e18.

Edell, J. A., & Burke, M. C. (1987). The power of feelings in understanding advertising effects. *The Journal of Consumer Research*, *14*(3), 421–433. doi:10.1086/209124

Edwards, S. M., Li, H., & Lee, J. H. (2002a). *Forced exposure and psychological reactance: antecedents and consequences of the perceived intrusiveness of pop-up ads.*

Ellegaard, C., & Ritter, T. (2006). *Customer attraction and its purchasing potential.* In *22nd IMP Conference*, Milan.

Evans, N. J., Phua, J., Lim, J., & Jun, H. (2017). Disclosing Instagram influencer advertising: The effects of disclosure language on advertising recognition, attitudes, and behavioral intent. *Journal of Interactive Advertising, 17*(2), 138–149. doi:10.1 080/15252019.2017.1366885

Firat, D. (2019). YouTube advertising value and its effects on purchase intention. *Journal of Global Business Insights, 4*(2), 141–155. doi:10.5038/2640-6489.4.2.1097

Gupta, H., Singh, S., & Sinha, P. (2017). Multimedia tool as a predictor for social media advertising-a YouTube way. *Multimedia Tools and Applications, 76*(18), 18557–18568. doi:10.1007/s11042-016-4249-6

Hüttinger, L., Schiele, H., & Veldman, J. (2012). The drivers of customer attractiveness, supplier satisfaction and preferred customer status: A literature review. *Industrial Marketing Management, 41*(8), 1194–1205. doi:10.1016/j.indmarman.2012.10.004

La Rocca, A., Caruana, A., & Snehota, I. (2012). Measuring customer attractiveness. *Industrial Marketing Management, 41*(8), 1241–1248. doi:10.1016/j. indmarman.2012.10.008

Lipsman, A., Mudd, G., Rich, M., & Bruich, S. (2012). The power of"like": How brands reach (and influence) fans through social-media marketing. *Journal of Advertising Research, 52*(1), 40–52. doi:10.2501/JAR-52-1-040-052

Liu, F., Li, J., Mizerski, D., & Soh, H. (2012). Self-congruity, brand attitude, and brand loyalty: a study on luxury brands. *European Journal of Marketing, 46*(7/8),922e937.

McKechnie, S. (1992). Consumer Buying Behaviour in Financial Services: AnOverview. *International Journal of Bank Marketing, 10*(5), 5–39. doi:10.1108/02652329210016803

Mihaela, O. O. E. (2015). The influence of the integrated marketing communication on the consumer buying behaviour. *Procedia Economics and Finance, 23*, 1446–1450. doi:10.1016/S2212-5671(15)00446-3

Patikar, E. T. D. G., & Thangasamy, E. (2014). Factors influencing consumer buying behaviour: a case study. *Global Journal of Management and Business Research: E Marketing, 14*(5).

Pessala, I. (2016). *User experiences and efficiency of Instagram Advertising.*

Ponzoa, J. M., & Erdmann, A. (2021). E-commerce customer attraction: Digital marketing techniques, evolution and dynamics across firms. *Journal of Promotion Management, 27*(5), 697–715. doi:10.1080/10496491.2021.1880521

Pulles, N. J., Schiele, H., Veldman, J., & Hüttinger, L. (2016). The impact of customer attractiveness and supplier satisfaction on becoming a preferred customer. *Industrial Marketing Management, 54*, 129–140. doi:10.1016/j.indmarman.2015.06.004

Ramya, N. A. S. A. M., & Ali, S. M. (2016). Factors affecting consumer buying behavior. *International Journal of Applied Research, 2*(10), 76–80.

Rao, B., & Minakakis, L. (2003). Evolution of mobile location-based services. *Com-munications of the ACM, 46*(12), 61e65.

Rixom, J. M., & Rixom, B. A. (2023). Perceived brand authenticity: Examining the effects of inferred dedication and anticipated quality on consumers' purchase intentions and actual choices. *Journal of Consumer Behaviour, 22*(3), 721–737. doi:10.1002/cb.2156

Rodriguez, P. R. (2017). *Effectiveness of YouTube advertising: A study of audience analysis.* Rochester Institute of Technology.

Sangroya, D., & Nayak, J. K. (2017). Factors influencing buying behaviour of green energy consumer. *Journal of Cleaner Production, 151*, 393–405. doi:10.1016/j.jclepro.2017.03.010

Schiele, H., Calvi, R., & Gibbert, M. (2012). Customer attractiveness, supplier satisfaction and preferred customer status: Introduction, definitions and an overarching framework. *Industrial Marketing Management, 41*(8), 1178–1185. doi:10.1016/j.indmarman.2012.10.002

Tobias-Mamina, R. J., Kempen, E., Chinomona, R., & Sly, M. (2020). The influence of instagram advertising on destination visit intention. *African Journal of Hospitality, Tourism and Leisure, 9*(3), 274–287. doi:10.46222/ajhtl.19770720-18

Tsimonis, G., & Dimitriadis, S. (2014). *Brand strategies in social media.* Marketing. doi:10.1108/MIP-04-2013-0056

Vanwesenbeeck, I., Hudders, L., & Ponnet, K. (2020). Understanding the YouTube generation: How preschoolers process television and YouTube advertising. *Cyberpsychology, Behavior, and Social Networking, 23*(6), 426–432. doi:10.1089/cyber.2019.0488 PMID:32320269

Wardhani, P. K., & Alif, M. G. (2019, October). The effect of advertising exposure on attitude toward the advertising and the brand and purchase intention in Instagram. In *3rd Asia-Pacific Research in Social Sciences and Humanities Universitas Indonesia Conference (APRISH 2018)* (pp. 196-204). Atlantis Press. 10.2991/aprish-18.2019.24

Wu, K. (2016). YouTube marketing: Legality of sponsorship and endorsements in advertising. *JL Bus. & Ethics*, *22*, 59.

Wu, S.-I. (2006). The impact of feeling, judgment and attitude on Purchase intention as online advertising performance measure. *Journal of International Marketing & Marketing Research, 31*(2), 89e108.

Wulandari, L. P. A., & Darma, G. S. (2020). Advertising effectiveness in purchasing decision on Instagram. *Journal of Business on Hospitality and Tourism*, *6*(2), 381–389. doi:10.22334/jbhost.v6i2.220

Zhou, Y., Ahmad, Z., Alsuhabi, H., Yusuf, M., Alkhairy, I., & Sharawy, A. M. (2021). Impact of YouTube Advertising on Sales with Regression Analysis and Statistical Modeling: Usefulness of Online Media in Business. *Computational Intelligence and Neuroscience*, *2021*, 2021. doi:10.1155/2021/9863155 PMID:34539772

Chapter 13
The Metaverse Within the SWOT Framework

Deniz Ünal Adigüzel

https://orcid.org/0000-0002-6275-7434
Pamukkale University, Turkey

ABSTRACT

Metaverse is a huge virtual world in which humans and digital twins (avatars) will interact in real-time, a world created by humans that exists beyond the analog world we live in, where individuals are lonely but also social, with humanoid appearances, traditions, and taboos, but also without rules and boundaries. It is a completely different, relatively free, relatively unregulated virtual world. The interaction of consumers in virtual spaces and the companies investing in this field have not only made some research in this field mandatory but also caused questions to arise in people's minds. The focus of the study is the excitement and anxiety of consumers. In general, the aim is to define the metaverse concept that will affect consumers and the positive and negative effects of the metaverse concept on consumers. On this basis, the concept of the metaverse will be approached from a SWOT perspective and predictions will be made regarding the situations that may be encountered in the metaverse field soon.

INTRODUCTION

Innovations that lead to changes in individuals' lifestyles, starting with the COVID-19 pandemic and continuing until today, are increasing day by day. With the term "untact", a term coined in South Korea, new markets and marketing concepts have begun to emerge in many areas from communication to education, shopping and

DOI: 10.4018/979-8-3693-4167-4.ch013

socialization. (Hwang, Lee, 2022). The most important difference, thanks to metadata, the concept of time and space has begun to disappear and accessibility has increased.

This virtual world, which is surrounded by social networks that individuals can access twenty-four hours a day, seven days a week, without any time constraints, where they have the opportunity to receive education, have the opportunity to shop indefinitely, and also have an entertainment factor, provides endless freedom. This virtual world is becoming an even bigger phenomenon today, as companies that recognize the demand in individuals are included in the Metaverse universe day by day.

However, in an area where there is so much limitlessness and freedom, there will of course be some extremes and some groups who are concerned about the existence of these extremes. For this reason, it is thought that it is useful to look in depth at every aspect when talking about the Metaverse.

CONCEPTUAL FRAMEWORK

The term "Metaverse" comes from Neal Stephenson's science fiction novel Snow Crash, in 1992 Snow Crash focuses on the theme of creating value from the virtual world to the real world through social activities, is a new reality and virtual-physical spaces that emerged with the development of internet technologies and where completely artificial worlds are constructed as well as the reflection of real worlds. Metaverse offers collaboration opportunities that anyone with the necessary means, wherever they are in the world, can participate under certain conditions; providing infrastructure and interaction opportunities for cultural, intellectual and economic production; it is a cyber social plane or new digital world where different advanced technologies are used simultaneously and in an integrated manner. Metaverse is the platform where parties interact in worlds that mirror reality and fictional worlds (Smart, Cascio, Paffendorf, 2007; Kim, 2021; Kuş, 2021; Hollensen et. al., 2022; Park, Kim, 2022; Bozkurt, Gümüş, 2022).

Metaverse is a new word (concept) consisting of the words metaverse transcendence and universality. Metaverse simply refers to a three-dimensional virtual world in which avatars engage in political, economic, social and cultural activities. This world is built on such a structure that it represents a life that is based on daily life but is virtual, where both the real and the unreal coexist (Park, Kim, 2022: 4211). This three-dimensional world is based on a foundation where communication, business and information tools can work together and in a comprehensive manner. In fact, it is a virtual reflection of how it works in the real world. The only difference is that in this digital world, communication can be made through avatars with similar features in real life (Hollensen et. al., 2022).

The Metaverse is based on technologies that enable multi-sensory interaction with virtual environments, digital objects, and people. The metaverse is a created universe beyond reality, a persistent and persistent multi-user environment that combines physical reality with digital virtuality. Virtual environments such as virtual reality (VR) and augmented reality (AR) are technologies that enable multisensory interaction between digital objects, digital universe, digital reality and people. Therefore, the Metaverse is a collection of social and environments interconnected on persistent multi-user platforms. It enables dynamic interaction between digital, i.e. unreal, objects and objects with real time perception (El Beheiry et. al., 2019; Mystakidis, 2022; Barrera, Shah, 2023).

Although Metaverse's entry into the industry was in the field of gaming, it can turn into an all-encompassing structure. It is estimated that it will appear in many sectors in the future, such as healthcare, consumer products, entertainment, and business-to-business technical solutions. As a result, even being in the Metaverse may have an impact on the value measurements of businesses (Hollensen et. al., 2022). Therefore, businesses should adapt to technologies by developing products that will serve in these areas.

This study aims to look at the Metaverse concept, which has a great impact today, from the consumer's perspective. While doing this, it is planned to mention the technological innovations that have been experienced in the world until the Metaverse in chronological order. Afterwards, it is planned to discuss how Metaverse will affect marketing and examples of companies and brands making marketing moves in Metaverse. The study will be concluded by making inferences about the future by conducting a SWOT analysis to evaluate the Metaverse universe from the consumers' perspective. In this way, it is planned to contribute to the literature, especially in a theoretical context.

REFERENCES

Barrera, K. G., & Shah, D. (2023). Marketing in the Metaverse: Conceptual understanding, framework, and research agenda. *Journal of Business Research*, *155*, 113420. doi:10.1016/j.jbusres.2022.113420

Bozkurt, Ö., & Gümüş, İ. H. (2022). Metaverse ve metagirişimcilik: Kavramsal bir çerçeve. *Girişimcilik ve Kalkınma Dergisi*, *17*(1), 75–85.

El Beheiry, M., Doutreligne, S., Caporal, C., Ostertag, C., Dahan, M., & Masson, J.-B. (2019). Virtual reality: Beyond visualization. *Journal of Molecular Biology*, *2019*(431), 1315–1321. doi:10.1016/j.jmb.2019.01.033 PMID:30738026

Hollensen, S., Kotler, P., & Opresnik, M. O. (2022). Metaverse the new marketing universe. *The Journal of Business Strategy*. doi:10.1108/JBS-01-2022-0014

Hwang, R., & Lee, M. (2022). The influence of music content marketing on user satisfaction and intention to use in the Metaverse: A focus on the SPICE Model. *Businesses*, *2*(2), 141–155. doi:10.3390/businesses2020010

Kim, J. (2021). Advertising in the Metaverse: Research agenda. *Journal of Interactive Advertising*, *21*(3), 141–144. doi:10.1080/15252019.2021.2001273

Kuş, O. (2021). "Metaverse: 'Dijital büyük patlamada' fırsatlar ve endişelere yönelik algılar". Intermedia. *International Journal (Toronto, Ont.)*, *8*(15), 245–266. doi:10.21645/intermedia.2021.109

Mystakidis, S. (2022). Entry Metaverse. *Encyclopedia*, *2*(1), 486–497. doi:10.3390/encyclopedia2010031

Park, S. M., & Kim, Y. G. (2022). Metaverse: Taxonomy, components, applications, and open Challenge. *IEEE Access : Practical Innovations, Open Solutions*, *10*, 4209–4425. doi:10.1109/ACCESS.2021.3140175

Smart, J., Cascio, J., & Paffendorf, J. (2007). *Pathways to the 3D Web: A cross-industry public foresight Project*. Metaverse Roadmap. https://www.metaverseroadmap.org/MetaverseRoadmapOverview.pdf

Chapter 14
The Presence of Brands in the Metaverse

Joana Oliveira
ISAG - European Business School, Portugal & Research Center in Business Science and Tourism (CICET-FCVC), Porto, Portugal

Catarina Rocha
ISAG - European Business School, Portugal & Research Center in Business Science and Tourism (CICET-FCVC), Porto, Portugal

Ana Pinto Borges
https://orcid.org/0000-0002-4942-079X
ISAG—European Business School, Porto, Portugal; Research Centre in Business Sciences and Tourism (CICET—FCVC), Porto, Portugal and Research Centre in Organizations, Markets and Industrial Management (COMEGI), Porto, Portugal

Bruno Miguel Vieira
ISAG—European Business School, Porto, Portugal; Research Centre in Business Sciences and Tourism (CICET—FCVC), Porto, Portugal

Elvira Vieira
https://orcid.org/0000-0002-9296-3896
ISAG – European Business School and Research Center in Business Sciences and Tourism (CICET - FCVC), Portugal, Applied Management Research Unit (UNIAG), Instituto Politécnico de Bragança, Bragança, Portugal; IPVC—Polytechnic Institute of Viana do Castelo, Viana do Castelo, Portugal

Victor Tavares
ISAG - European Business School, Portugal & Research Center in Business Science and Tourism (CICET-FCVC), Porto, Portugal

ABSTRACT

This research emerges as a starting point in analyzing the requirements that brand managers should consider leveraging the presence of brands in the metaverse,

DOI: 10.4018/979-8-3693-4167-4.ch014

considering the consumers' degree of knowledge, expectations, and desired experiences, thus contributing with theoretical and practical implications to brand management. Through a qualitative methodology – employing the focus group technique – it was possible to understand the interests of consumers and their metaverse-related associations. The interactivity component is of utmost importance and must be developed, implemented, and complemented with the user's own creativity. This research has also shed light on important dimensions related to virtual content.

INTRODUCTION

According to the study by McKinsey & Company (2022), the value of the metaverse could reach $5 trillion by 2030. Given its business potential, several academic and professional studies have been developed to better understand the nature and challenges of the Metaverse (Lee et al., 2021; Narin, 2021; Park & Kim, 2022), including the development of technological roadmaps of the Metaverse (Mozumder et al., 2023). The concept of the metaverse first appeared in 1992 in the fictional work "Snow Crash" by Neal Stephenson. At the time, this author described the metaverse as a space that simulates physical reality to create "parallel worlds" represented in three-dimensional environments that provide a high level of immersion for users (Duan et al., 2021). That is, it is a kind of virtual world that attempts to replicate reality through a series of digital devices. It is a shared collective and virtual space created through the convergence of physical, virtual and augmented reality (Newzoo, 2021). All its users will create their respective avatars, through a duplication of the real world, similar to their physical "self", in order to experience an alternative life in an unprecedented way (Lee et al., 2021). Currently, the Metaverse is based on the social value of Generation Z, with no differentiation between their online and offline "self" (Park & Kim, 2022). The technological advances in progress and the new consumption needs in the digital market are determining a profound sociocultural transformation, which implies new challenges for the management of brands and the adoption of new behaviors. The development of the Metaverse has been translating this turning point (Lee et al., 2021). Effectively, such a concept is changing people's lives, and brands need to be aware, understanding their consumers' attitudes towards the Metaverse and assessing the impact on their businesses.

As highlighted by Wunderman Thompson (2022), the ongoing digital transformation is redefining the consumer/brand relationship. Consequently, those who are responsible for brands need to design effective strategies aimed at their presence in the Metaverse, considering that virtual worlds and assets can be a business card for their brands, as they presently present profiles on social networks and websites. That is, brands will need to start configuring their management teams to enter the Digital Age (Liffreing, 2021).

Always in constant mutation, the new technological world implies an increase in complexity in the brand management process. Companies will have to develop new strategies, provide new experiences, and better understand their consumers (Agersborg et al., 2020). In fact, aiming at the modernization of the Metaverse reality, several organizations worldwide have already been invested to satisfy the needs, desires and expectations of the new consumers' profiles. For this reason, the Metaverse will become increasingly visible and familiar among people (Duan et al., 2021). Thus, the development of the Metaverse should constitute a crucial research area for brands, requiring special attention from researchers and professionals in the sector, to create perceptible value for their customers (Kim, 2021).

Based on the literature review and a qualitative research strategy, this study aims to identify the factors that brand managers should consider when developing and implementing their strategies for effective presence in the metaverse. To this end, three specific research objectives were defined: (i) to understand consumers' perceptions and knowledge of the Metaverse; (ii) to analyse what factors determine the virtual experience; (iii) to identify consumer behaviour and attitudes. The paper is structured as follows: an extensive literature review was conducted on the main issues related to the Metaverse, followed by the methodology section, the main results and discussion, and conclusion, which ends with future research directions.

LITERATURE REVIEW

The development of virtual worlds is a relatively recent and highly dynamic phenomenon and cannot yet be fully understood and clearly explained (Cagnina and Poian, 2007). For these authors, essentially, the characteristics of digital environments are interactivity, physicality, and persistence. For Castronova (2003), virtual worlds are three-dimensional digital environments in which, through an avatar (a digital representation of oneself), it is possible, for a large number of people, to interact with each other.

Virtual Experience and Virtual Consumption

In the modern world, there is a relationship between consumption and culture. For McCracken (1990), culture refers to ideas and activities that result in interpretations of where we build our world. It is understood that consumption is the process by which consumer goods are created, purchased, and used (Nikolaou, 2009). This author acknowledges that "consumer goods to which consumers dedicate time and attention are loaded with cultural meaning" (p. 7), and that contemporary consumption assumes a playful and imaginative nature, as virtual worlds become attractive to those who inhabit them. These are ideal worlds, created by imagination and simulations that include signs with real-life meaning. Effectively, brands must acknowledge that they can "connect" fantasies to the daily experiences of individuals, as well as organizations must consider the potential customer – the avatar (Nikolaou, 2009).

With the emergence and growing popularity of virtual, animated, and three-dimensional worlds, such as Second Life, new stages for consumption were established. As they are highly immersive, these virtual environments represent interactive consumption spaces (Lee et al., 2021), that overcome limitations of space and time and expand contents as much as possible (Shi et al., 2023). Consequently, brand management has become increasingly complex (Khan & Rahman, 2016; Veloutsou & Guzman, 2017; Yin Wong & Merrilees, 2008), because of the rapid transformation of the world of technology. Structural changes in companies' strategies and business standards are being impacted by breakthroughs in advanced technology (in particular, the metaverse) generating behavioral transformations in consumers (Yin Wong & Merrilees, 2008). For Kerry Murphy, founder and CEO of the digital fashion house "The Fabricant", the resulting transition in the development of augmented and virtual reality has already begun. Murphy believes that this reality will be part of the daily life of many people in the western world.

The great value of brands is related to the daily functional interactive experiences, creating a reality that goes beyond the game environment and is beyond mere entertainment (Wunderman Thompson, 2021). For these authors, it is possible to create avatars on Facebook and other social media platforms, such as IMVU, allowing different people around the world to interact, generating interactions through their 3D avatar. The users are the creators of content - the type of passive consumption for active creation is changing behaviors with creativity being conveyed to the power of the user - digital engagement. Effectively, realizing the need to respond to the digital fashion industry, "The Fabricant" shows a new paradigm to the world - clothes are no longer physical elements. In this sense, brands such as Adidas, Puma and Tommy Hilfiger, were not indifferent to this reality and have already developed garments for the digital fashion house – "The Fabricant". Living as digital assets is becoming a reality resulting in a transition, as digital artist Krista Kim says, for Alpha and Gen Z. This acknowledgment from Keith Stuart – Guardian Games Editor – defines the online experience (Wunderman Thompson, 2022). In this context, creativity will drive the future of digital engagement. According to Park and Kim (2022), content is created with what people create and not content that people consume, and the content produced is personalized and results in the personal experiences of all users. So, it will be important that, within a decade, companies reinvent themselves and understand the importance of generating differentiating contributions to the consumer experience. In fact, the use of immersive technologies in the management of customer experiences in the Metaverse must be a concern integrated into the decision-making processes in the management of organizations (Dieck & Han, 2022). Temporary dissociation, concentration, and heightened pleasure are crucial factors in interaction and control emotions, curiosity, and intrinsic motivations (Park & Kim, 2022).

The Importance of the Metaverse for Consumers

When the metaverse comes to full life as it is being designed, it will be possible to carry out various daily activities in retail, finance, health and wellness, food and drink, work, entertainment and sport, fashion, beauty, society, and government, among others, through a 3D avatar in a digital universe (Wunderman Thompson, 2021). Any changes that users make to the metaverse will be permanently visible to almost all consumers, thus providing a greater identity and continuity of the experience (Narin, 2021). Natural consumer interaction is the essential condition to increase immersion in the metaverse (Park & Kim, 2022), and it is also important to understand what consumers want from the metaverse, so that brands can identify opportunities and make strategic decisions, directing them to their target audiences. According to Trendhunter (2022), analyzing games as a simulation platform will open vast new opportunities. A study conducted by Newzoo (2021) examined consumer behaviors and preferences within the metaverse, focusing on individuals aged 14 to 50. The findings indicated that this demographic is open to engaging in social activities in gaming environments, prioritizing interactions with family and friends. The research identified a range of preferred activities, including watching movies, attending events such as birthdays, Christmas celebrations, concerts, parties, festivals, sporting events, and fashion shows featuring real-life brands. Additionally, participants showed interest in attending conferences, lectures, and flash mobs. Another research by this author revealed that the features consumers want in the metaverse are the ability to choose the physical appearance of their avatar, free sponsor-funded content, the ability to create content for other players, and the ability to jump from game to game, without leaving the game environment, special credits for the ability to buy items from one game and take them to other games, created access to player-created content, buy decorations, pets and clothing for their avatar, watch movies or television shows while in the game world, and buying real-life products while in the game world (Trendhunter, 2022).

New Opportunities for Brands in the Metaverse

Metaverse represents a great opportunity for various sectors, such as industrial, commercial, societal, educational, medical, military, and governmental (Huynh-

The et al., 2023). The major impact of changes in industry and retail is being felt in the digital space – increasingly and rapidly evolving – where the online shopping experience implies that the various business areas are present in e-commerce. Currently, virtual stores offer an organic and natural way for customers to discover products. Brands such as Burberry and Tumi have already created their virtual stores, allowing customers to contact products in full size, generating an experience closer to reality. These digital spaces replicate physical stores, but without borders, generating unlimited creative opportunities (Wunderman Thompson, 2022). The leap from brands to virtual stores is evident. In fact, this author pointed out that, in a field survey with 3011 participants from the United States, United Kingdom and China, carried out between July 9 and July 27, 2021, it was concluded that 81% of global consumers agree that the presence of a brand's digital image is as important as its in-store presence. Another totally new market for consumption, boosted by the growing interest of users in owning and developing their own position in the metaverse, is the virtual real estate market, the reason for this expansion being the Mars House, the first digital home in the world, designed by digital artist Krista Kim. The presence of brands in the metaverse of the fashion industry, real estate and digital automobiles is, therefore, an example of business areas that are clearly being driven by technology, as well as teleportation that allows travelers to have contact with a destination in a virtual format through a sensorial experience. Virtual tourism began as a training tool for new Microsoft Flight Simulator pilots (Wunderman Thompson, 2021). Brands will have to watch as consumers explore the metaverse to connect, explore, create, and seek out entertainment. Thus, they will be able to find their niche from the beginning, if they consider interactivity and immersion, generating new revenue streams, loyalty, and attraction of new consumers (Maher, 2022). The next phase of anti-excess consumption results in virtual goods is seen as the future of sustainability, providing consumers with a new way to prioritize environmental impact. The experience in the metaverse and the increase in the consumption of digital products, in the current business areas, provided new opportunities and opened new paths for brands and for entrepreneurs, forcing organizations to rethink new formats for management and implementation of strategies (Wunderman Thompson, 2022). Metaverse provides retailers and brands with unique opportunities along the customer journey's pre-purchase, purchase, and post-purchase stages, where an important factors are digital economic exchange, complex social relationships, direct environment interaction (Yoo et al., 2023).

METHODOLOGY

This research follows a qualitative research strategy, considering its appropriateness to disclose how individuals perceive new concepts (Veal, 2017), in this case, the Metaverse. It was employed a focus group technique regarding its suitability to extract attitudes and perceptions on a particular subject (Clark et al., 2007), and by exploring in-depth the view of individuals through group discussion (Dwyer et al., 2012) encouraged by the moderator.

The participants were invited through academic and professional networks. The sampling frame included individuals from 18 years old to 45 years old (Generation Z and Y), with some knowledge on the Metaverse, or/and experience with virtual reality and video games. Three focus group sessions were held online, through the Zoom platform, which took place in June and July 2022, and were videotaped and transcribed *verbatim* by the moderator. The thematic analysis was prepared through the software package QSR International NVIVO 12. A focus group interview guide was prepared and divided into two sections. Topics included in the focus group guide were:

- How can you describe the Metaverse?
- Is user interactivity an essential condition in Metaverse?
- What are the activities that should be present in the Metaverse?
- What brands would consumers like to find in the Metaverse?
- Will the user be the creator of their own digital environment?
- Sociodemographic profile of the interviewees.

Data Analysis

An interpretative method for data analysis and an inductive approach to code development (Bustard et al., 2018) was used in this study. The thematic analysis was employed to analyse and report patterns within data (Braun & Clarke, 2006). Table 1 discloses the sociodemographic profile of the focus groups' participants. In total, 17 participants have taken part in the focus groups.

Table 1. Profile of the focus group participants

Focus group	Interviewees codes	Age	Gender	Qualifications
1	P1	25	Male	Bachelor
	P2	29	Male	Bachelor
	P3	24	Male	Bachelor
	P4	45	Male	Bachelor
	P5	29	Male	Bachelor
2	P6	31	Female	Bachelor
	P7	31	Male	Master
	P8	26	Male	Bachelor
	P9	26	Female	Masters
	P10	22	Male	Master
	P11	35	Female	PhD
3	P12	40	Female	Master
	P13	40	Female	Bachelor
	P14	30	Male	Master
	P15	27	Male	Bachelor
	P16	26	Female	Bachelor
	P17	40	Female	Bachelor

Source: Authors' elaboration.

All participants have higher qualifications (Bachelor, Master, and Doctoral studies), with age ranging from 25 years old to 45 years old, and 10 were male while 7 were female.

RESULTS AND DISCUSSION

This section of the paper will present the main results of the research according to the objectives previously established. Focus group participants were requested to describe the Metaverse based on their perceptions.

Characterizing the Metaverse

The participants' perceptions on the Metaverse are described in Table 2.

Table 2. Characterizing the metaverse

How can you describe the Metaverse?		
Themes (Participants)	**Categories**	**Quotations extracted from focus groups**
Reality (P1, P2, P6, P11, P12, P15)	augmented reality physical reality mixed reality parallel reality virtual reality immersive reality	"The Metaverse is […] a mixture of virtual reality, augmented reality and the Internet, people can interact in a virtual way […]".
		"[…] is the creation of a digital life through augmented reality or mixed reality with digital devices […]".
Life (P8, P14, P15, P18)	alternative life digital life real life social life	"The Metaverse is not only a digital platform of alternative life, […] is a digital life through an avatar".
		"[…] a virtual character where he/she can walk around the world and meet other people […] a social life on the computer […].

Source: Authors' elaboration.

The first impressions that focus groups participants disclosed were related to the several types of realities (augmented, virtual, mixed, physical, and parallel) which will allow their users to interact through an avatar, multiplying the opportunities for entertainment but also for businesses purposes (enabling shopping), by replicating real-life scenarios in the digital universe. "The Metaverse is an expansion of the Second Life" (P12). The Metaverse is refereed as augmented reality, mixed reality, parallel reality, virtual reality, immersive reality. "Metaverse ends up being a virtual reality, parallel, which has this social component […] the entertainment part, as well as […], in terms of commerce, being able to shop" (P9). It replicates the real life through digital equipment. "The Metaverse is a term used to indicate the entire virtual world that replicates real-life scenarios through various digital equipment's (P18).

These terms are commonly reported regarding their closeness to the subject of Metaverse, and because they seem to be more familiar concepts to the participants. "People are more familiar with the term virtual reality and not so much with the Metaverse. It is a very recent topic. Not long ago, the Facebook company itself changed the name to meta, referring to the Metaverse" (P9). These results are in line with earlier research, in which virtual reality, augmented reality and mixed reality are concepts commonly used as antecedents of the Metaverse (Han et al., 2022).

Interactivity

The interactivity as a condition of using the Metaverse gathered a common agreement from the participants. "Innovation and new ways of interacting and basically trying to innovate our social interaction to another level I think is the basis of the Metaverse". (P10). Table 3 illustrates the main categories that emerged from the codification process.

Table 3. Do you consider that user interactivity is an essential condition in the metaverse?

Interactivity		
Themes (Participants)	**Categories**	**Quotations extracted from focus groups**
Social interaction (P3, P9, P10, P11, P15, P16)	curiosity innovation new ways of interacting	"[…] interaction can be different and more attractive".
		"[…] the interaction between people is the main point in the Metaverse".
		"Interactivity is one of the great pillars of the Metaverse".

Source: authors' elaboration

It was also highlighted the impact of the Covid-19 pandemic in accelerating the presence of individuals and brands in virtual worlds. "The pandemic [...] I think triggered curiosity for the Metaverse. I believe the pandemic was an enabler for entry (brands) into the Metaverse". Despite the increasing of the virtual worlds and platforms to experience new forms of interaction and access to new realities, some participants also pointed out the negative effects that may be caused by spending time in front of screens, particularly in younger generations. "If you notice, many of the teenagers opted for spent the afternoon with friends on the screen […], […] ant they were already able to walk on the street". (P12). These results follow the research of Park and Kim (2022), reinforcing the relevance of users' interactivity with the Metaverse.

Type of Activities in Metaverse

It was apparent through participant data that businesses' activities were more appealing than entertainment. Table 4 systematizes the main themes that emerged from the thematic analysis.

Table 4. Which typology of activities should be in the metaverse?

Themes (Participants)	Categories	Activities
		Quotations extracted from focus groups
Entertainment (P1, P9)	Music concerts Gaming Events	"[…] an industry that already has a huge brand love from consumers (gaming)".
		"[…] the interaction between people is the main point in the Metaverse".
Education (P18)	Explore museums Visiting a city	"Allowing a student to […], see the inside of an organ, even explore a piece of electronics […] this is a fascinating new world".
Business (P1, P4, P6, P11)	Fashion industry Real estate Conferences Networking	"[…] exclusivity and belonging to the brand […]". "The brand Nike recently created sneakers that are only available in Metaverse".

Source: Authors' elaboration.

Regarding the activities that should be in the Metaverse, these fall mainly on the business dimension. When it comes to the entertainment dimension, only video games (gaming) were identified as appealing to participants. About leisure-related activities, particularly attending concerts, travel, and tourism, these were not identified as essential in the Metaverse, since participants claim the need for personal interaction in these types of experiences. "Social activities like watching a concert, […] traveling, in my opinion it does not make any kind of sense" (P11), "But what is more connected to entertainment there is always the need for personal interaction" (P6). Although the Metaverse has already been recognized as a platform with great potential for gaming, which means, recreational activities, the potential for economic activities has been increasingly identified (Jeong et al., 2022).

Brands in Metaverse

A significant number of participants fundamentally discussed what kind of industries are already promoting their engagement with the Metaverse, disregarding the references to specific brands. Nevertheless, some participants have also emphasized that brands are likely to enter the Metaverse, initially to sell low-involvement products such as the fashion industry, but they believe that very soon all brands selling products and services will have a place in the universe of the Metaverse. In their study, Hollensen et al. (2022) described the opportunities and challenges that companies and consumers will have to deal with a series of interconnected virtual worlds. They also exemplify how some brands already have joined the Metaverse (e.g., Nike has its own branded virtual world called 'Nikeland').

Personalization of the Virtual Environment

Personalization within the Metaverse emerges as a pivotal element, especially for users with prior exposure to virtual worlds like Fortnite. This sentiment is encapsulated by P12, who insightfully notes, "Just as we are creators of communication, we will become architects of our own universes". This notion is further reinforced by P7's assertion that "Personalization is a cornerstone in the Metaverse". The Metaverse stands as a beacon of innovation, where the capacity for customization distinguishes it from other platforms. The concept of personalization, already prevalent in various digital leisure activities—most notably on social media platforms—is highlighted by participant observations. P9 elaborates, "In today's world, personalization is paramount. We craft our own digital spaces on social networks, curating our followings, which in turn shapes a personalized ecosystem we each inhabit."

These perspectives underscore the critical findings of Jeong et al. (2022), who articulated that the Metaverse's unique proposition lies in its ability to enable users to generate bespoke content, transcending the confines of physical space. It offers experiences previously confined to the offline world, now accessible online. This shift not only represents a technological leap but also underscores a significant cultural transformation in how we perceive and interact with digital environments. The Metaverse's personalization capabilities are not merely about aesthetic or superficial customization; they are fundamentally about empowering users to construct personalized narratives and experiences that resonate with their individual identity and preferences.

CONCLUSION

The Metaverse is not only a new digital platform but also a space to foster community and connection, to deepen brand engagement. And in this way, it offers new business models and revenue streams. Brands will need to think beyond physical products and can define what the Metaverse will be.

In this research, through a qualitative methodology - using the focus group technique - it was possible to understand relevant consumers' interests and the associations they make with the Metaverse. Participants associate the Metaverse with digital and/or virtual reality as a process of internet development. The interactivity component is of great importance and therefore needs to be developed, implemented and completed, with the user contributing their own creativity. Users of the Metaverse will demand personalized virtual worlds, so customization of their digital environment will be an absolute must. This study also revealed some important dimensions in terms of content. Participants showed a greater interest in social and leisure activities (entertainment dimension), virtual workspaces and networking (business dimension), and didactic activities (educational dimension). The typology of product and/or service brands must be based on real trends and aligned with the needs of users. Creativity is a crucial factor in the experience and is seen by the respondents as an interesting point that promotes personalization, imagination and interaction.

Theoretically, this article is a contribution to knowledge, especially on the main features that the Metaverse should contain to attract and captivate brand consumers. The practical contributions focus mainly on what kind of brands consumers are more willing to engage with. Through the research findings, it was possible to identify the types of brands by different industries that might have greater potential for immersive consumption with the product and/or service. It should be noted that brands associated with games and technology are more willing to engage in the metaverse, which is also relevant for the automotive industry.

Future Research Directions

Based on the insights derived from the conclusion of this research, future research directions regarding the presence of brands in the Metaverse can be outlined to further explore this emerging field. The following directions can help in understanding the evolving dynamics of brand engagement, consumer behaviour, and technological advancements within the Metaverse: a) evaluating consumer brand engagement strategies in the Metaverse, namely a study focusing on how different brand engagement strategies influence consumer Behaviour within the Metaverse. This could include examining the effectiveness of immersive advertising, virtual events, and branded virtual goods on consumer engagement levels; b) impact of customization and personalization on brand loyalty, including research dedicated to exploring the relationship between the degree of customization and personalization available in branded virtual spaces and its impact on brand loyalty and consumer satisfaction within the Metaverse; c) cross-industry brand presence and performance in the Metaverse, involving an investigation into how brands from various industries (beyond gaming and technology) can establish a presence in the Metaverse and the unique challenges and opportunities each industry faces. This could include in-depth case studies of successful brand integrations and consumer responses; d) consumer privacy and data security concerns, with a critical analysis of consumer privacy and data security concerns within the Metaverse, focusing on how brands can navigate these challenges while maintaining consumer trust and compliance with regulations; e) the role of Artificial Intelligence (AI) and emerging technologies in shaping brand experiences, namely an exploration of how AI, blockchain, and other emerging technologies are being used by brands to create unique, interactive, and personalized experiences in the Metaverse; f) sustainability and ethical considerations of brand activities in the Metaverse, relate with research into the sustainability and ethical implications of brand activities in the Metaverse, including the environmental impact of digital goods and the ethical considerations of virtual consumerism; g) the economic impact of brands in the Metaverse, for an assessment of the economic implications of brand investments in the Metaverse, including the creation of new jobs, the development of new markets, and the potential for economic growth; h) cultural and societal impacts of brand presence in the Metaverse: A study examining the cultural and societal impacts of widespread brand presence in the Metaverse, including issues related to digital identity, community building, and the blurring lines between virtual and physical realities; i) comparative analysis of virtual vs. physical brand experiences, with research comparing consumer experiences with brands in the Metaverse versus traditional physical or online environments, to identify key differences, advantages, and limitations of each, and j) longitudinal studies on brand evolution in the Metaverse, including long-term studies tracking the evolution of brand strategies, consumer engagement, and technological developments in the Metaverse, providing insights into the dynamic nature of this digital space over time. Finally, these research directions could contribute significantly to the academic discourse and practical understanding of brand presence and consumer engagement in the Metaverse, offering valuable insights for marketers, technologists, and policymakers navigating this evolving digital landscape.

ACKNOWLEDGMENT

The authors are deeply grateful to ISAG – European Business School and Research Center in Business Sciences and Tourism (CICET - FCVC) for all support.

REFERENCES

Agersborg, C., Månsson, I., & Roth, E. (2020). *Brand Management and Artificial Intelligence-A World of Man Plus Machine-A qualitative study exploring how Artificial Intelligence can contribute to Brand Management in the B2C sector* [Master's thesis, Univeristy of Gothenburg].

Braun, V., & Clarke, V. (2006). Using thematic analysis in psychology. *Qualitative Research in Psychology*, *3*(2), 77–101. doi:10.1191/1478088706qp063oa

Bustard, J. R. T., Bolan, P., Devine, A., & Hutchinson, K. (2018). The emerging smart event experience: *An interpretative phenomenological analysis. Tourism Review*, *74*(1), 116–128. doi:10.1108/TR-10-2017-0156

Cagnina, M. R., & Poian, M. (2008). *How to compete in the metaverse: the business models in Second Life.* (U of Udine Economics Working Paper).

Castronova, E. (2003). Theory of the Avatar. *SSRN*, *385103*. https://doi.org/http://dx.doi.org/10.2139/ssrn.385103

Clark, M. A., Riley, M. J., Wilkie, E., & Wood, R. C. (2007). *Researching and writing dissertations in hospitality and tourism.* International Thomson Business Press.

Dieck, T. M. C., & Han, D.-D. (2022). The role of immersive technology in Customer Experience Management. *Journal of Marketing Theory and Practice*, *30*(1), 108–119. doi:10.1080/10696679.2021.1891939

Duan, H., Li, J., Fan, S., Lin, Z., Wu, X., & Cai, W. (2021). Metaverse for social good: A university campus prototype. In *Proceedings of the 29th ACM international conference on multimedia* (pp. 153-161). ACM. 10.1145/3474085.3479238

Dwyer, L., Gill, A., & Seetaram, N. (2012). *Handbook of research methods in tourism: Quantitative and qualitative approaches*. Edward Elgar Publishing. doi:10.4337/9781781001295

Han, D.-I. D., Bergs, Y., & Moorhouse, N. (2022). Virtual reality consumer experience escapes: Preparing for the metaverse. *Virtual Reality (Waltham Cross)*, *26*(4), 1443–1458. doi:10.1007/s10055-022-00641-7

Hollensen, S., Kotler, P., & Opresnik, M. O. (2022). Metaverse–the new marketing universe. *The Journal of Business Strategy*, *44*(3), 119–125. doi:10.1108/JBS-01-2022-0014

Huynh-The, T., Gadekallu, T. R., Wang, W., Yenduri, G., Ranaweera, P., Pham, Q.-V., da Costa, D. B., & Liyanage, M. (2023). Blockchain for the metaverse: A Review. *Future Generation Computer Systems*, *143*, 401–419. doi:10.1016/j.future.2023.02.008

Jeong, H., Yi, Y., & Kim, D. (2022). An innovative e-commerce platform incorporating Metaverse to live commerce. *International Journal of Innovative Computing, Information, & Control*, *18*(1), 221–229. doi:10.24507/ijicic.18.01.221

Khan, I., & Rahman, Z. (2016). Retail brand experience: Scale development and validation. *Journal of Product and Brand Management*, *25*(5), 435–451. doi:10.1108/JPBM-07-2015-0943

Kim, J. (2021). Advertising in the metaverse: Research agenda. *Journal of Interactive Advertising*, *21*(3), 141–144. doi:10.1080/15252019.2021.2001273

Lee L.-H. Braud T. Zhou P. Wang L. Xu D. Lin Z. Kumar A. Bermejo C. Hui P. (2021). *All One Needs to Know about Metaverse: A Complete Survey on Technological Singularity, Virtual Ecosystem, and Research Agenda*. doi:10.13140/RG.2.2.11200.05124/8

Liffreing, I. (2021). What brands should know about the metaverse. *Advertising Age*, *92*(1). https://adage.com/article/digital-marketing-ad-tech-news/what-brands-should-know-about-metaverse/2354506

Maher, M. (2022, February 14). Why actions and behaviors — not platforms — are the metaverse's real value for brands, *MarketingDrive*, https://www.marketingdive.com/news/why-actions-and-behaviors-not-platforms-are-the-metaverses-real-value/618529/

McCracken, G. D. (1990). *Culture and consumption: New approaches to the symbolic character of consumer goods and activities* (Vol. 1). Indiana University Press.

McKinsey & Company. (2022). *Value creation in the Metaverse: the real business of the virtual world*. McKinsey. https://www.mckinsey.com/business-functions/growth-marketing-and-sales/our-insights/value-creation-in-the-Metaverse

Mozumder, M. A. I., Athar, A., Armand, T. P. T., Sheeraz, M. M., Uddin, S. M. I., & Kim, H. C. (2023, February). Technological roadmap of the future trend of metaverse based on IoT, blockchain, and AI techniques in metaverse education. In *2023 25th International Conference on Advanced Communication Technology (ICACT)* (pp. 1414-1423). IEEE.

Narin, N. G. (2021). A content analysis of the metaverse articles. *Journal of Metaverse*, *1*(1), 17–24.

Newzoo. (2021). *Introduction to the Metaverse. Trend Report 2021*. Newzoo. https://newzoo.com/insights/trend-reports/newzoo-intro-to-the-metaverse-report-2021-free-version

Nikolaou, I. (2009). Brands and consumption in virtual worlds. *Journal of Virtual Worlds Research*, *2*(5), 3–15.

Park, S.-M., & Kim, Y.-G. (2022). A metaverse: Taxonomy, components, applications, and open challenges. *IEEE Access : Practical Innovations, Open Solutions*, *10*, 4209–4251. doi:10.1109/ACCESS.2021.3140175

Shi, F., Ning, H., Zhang, X., Li, R., Tian, Q., Zhang, S., Zheng, Y., Guo, Y., & Daneshmand, M. (2023). A new technology perspective of the Metaverse: Its essence, framework and challenges. *Digital Communications and Networks*. https://doi.org/https://doi.org/10.1016/j.dcan.2023.02.017

Thompson, W. (2021). *Into the metaverse*. Wunderman Thompson. https://www.wundermanthompson.com/insight/new-trend-report-into-the-metaverse

Thompson, W. (2022). *New realities: Into the metaverse and beyond*. Wunderman Thompson. https://www.wundermanthompson.com/pt/insight/new-realities-into-the-metaverse-and-beyond

Trendhunter. (2022). *Trend Report 2022*. Trendhunter. https://www.trendhunter.com/trends/2022-trend-report

Veal, A. J. (2017). *Research methods for leisure and tourism*.

Veloutsou, C., & Guzman, F. (2017). The evolution of brand management thinking over the last 25 years as recorded in the Journal of Product and Brand Management. *Journal of Product and Brand Management*, *26*(1), 2–12. doi:10.1108/JPBM-01-2017-1398

Yin Wong, H., & Merrilees, B. (2008). The performance benefits of being brand-orientated. *Journal of Product and Brand Management*, *17*(6), 372–383. doi:10.1108/10610420810904112

Yoo, K., Welden, R., Hewett, K., & Haenlein, M. (2023). The merchants of meta: A research agenda to understand the future of retailing in the metaverse. *Journal of Retailing*. https://doi.org/https://doi.org/10.1016/j.jretai.2023.02.002

KEY TERM DEFINITIONS

Consumer Engagement: The connection and interaction between consumers and a brand.

Content Management: Managing digital content creation, modification, and publication.

Digital Consumer Behaviour: How consumers behave and interact in digital environments.

268

Engagement Strategies: Decisions to foster consumer interaction and loyalty.

Experience Design: Designing products and services focusing on user experience.

Focus Groups: Group discussions used to gather insights on consumer opinions.

Metaverse Branding: Developing a brand's identity and experiences in virtual worlds.

Virtual Interactivity: The extent to which users can interact with and influence a virtual environment.

Compilation of References

Abashidze, I. (2023). Permission Marketing Strategy Shaping Consumer Behaviour Through Online Communication Channels. *Baltic Journal of Economic Studies*, *9*(2), 8–18. doi:10.30525/2256-0742/2023-9-2-8-18

Acar, O. A., & Puntoni, S. (2016). Customer empowerment in the digital age. *Journal of Advertising Research*, *56*(1), 4–8. doi:10.2501/JAR-2016-007

Acciarini, C., Cappa, F., Boccardelli, P., & Oriani, R. (2023). How can organizations leverage big data to innovate their business models? A systematic literature review. *Technovation*, *123*, 102713. doi:10.1016/j.technovation.2023.102713

Adenigba, S. A., & Akorede, H. Y. (2023). Implications of Psychological Pricing on Contemporary Muslim Retailers and Consumers in Nigeria. *Journal of Islamic Economic and Business Research*, *3*(1), 1–12. doi:10.18196/jiebr.v3i1.93

Agersborg, C., Månsson, I., & Roth, E. (2020). *Brand Management and Artificial Intelligence-A World of Man Plus Machine-A qualitative study exploring how Artificial Intelligence can contribute to Brand Management in the B2C sector* [Master's thesis, Univeristy of Gothenburg].

Ajzen, I. (1985). From intentions to actions: A theory of planned behavior. In *Action Control* (pp. 11–39). Springer. doi:10.1007/978-3-642-69746-3_2

Aka, C. A. (2022). *LC Waikiki, metaverse mağazasını açtı!* Shiftdelete.net. https://shiftdelete.net/lc-waikiki-metaverse-magazasi-alisveris .

Akbar, M. M., & Parvez, N. (2009). Impact of Service Quality, Trust, and Customer Satisfaction on Customers Loyalty. *ABAC Journal*, *29*(1), 1. http://www.assumptionjournal.au.edu/index.php/abacjournal/article/view/526

Akbas, Y. (2022, April 8). *Vodafone, Decentraland'de metaverse mağaza açıyor.* Doanimhaber. https://www.donanimhaber.com/vodafone-decentraland-de-metaverse-magaza-aciyor--147234 .

Alabau, A., Fabra, L., Martí-Testón, A., Muñoz, A., Solanes, J. E., & Gracia, L. (2024). Enriching User-Visitor Experiences in Digital Museology: Combining Social and Virtual Interaction within a Metaverse Environment. *Applied Sciences (Basel, Switzerland)*, *14*(9), 3769. doi:10.3390/app14093769

Compilation of References

Alaimo, C., Kallinikos, J., & Valderrama, E. (2020). Platforms as service ecosystems: Lessons from social media. *Journal of Information Technology*, *35*(1), 25–48. doi:10.1177/0268396219881462

Albaum, G., Best, R., & Hawkins, D. (1980). Retailing strategy for customer growth and new customer attraction. *Journal of Business Research*, *8*(1), 7–19. doi:10.1016/0148-2963(80)90027-2

Algharabat, R., Rana, N. P., Dwivedi, Y. K., Alalwan, A. A., & Qasem, Z. (2018). The effect of telepresence, social presence and involvement on consumer brand engagement: An empirical study of non-profit organizations. *Journal of Retailing and Consumer Services*, *40*, 139–149. doi:10.1016/j.jretconser.2017.09.011

Alspach, K. (2022) *Why the fate of the metaverse could hang on its security*. Venture Beat. https://venturebeat.com/2022/

An Investigation into the Determinants of Customer Satisfaction—Gilbert A. Churchill, Carol Surprenant, 1982. (n.d.). Sage. https://journals.sagepub.com/doi/10.1177/002224378201900410

Anabila, P., & Awunyo-Vitor, D. (2013). Customer relationship management: A key to organisational survival and customer loyalty in Ghana's banking industry. *International Journal of Marketing Studies*, *5*(1), 107–117. doi:10.5539/ijms.v5n1p107

Anand, A., & Jindal, P. (2024). Brand Building in the Metaverse. In Creator's Economy in Metaverse Platforms: Empowering Stakeholders Through Omnichannel Approach (pp. 58-70). IGI Global. doi:10.4018/979-8-3693-3358-7.ch004

Anderson, J., & Rainie, L. (2022). *The metaverse in 2040*. Pew Research Centre.

Anwar, S. (2023). Understanding the conceptualisation and strategies of service recovery processes in service organisations. *International Journal of Services. Economics and Management*, *14*(2), 175–197.

Arakji, R. Y., & Lang, K. R. (2008). Avatar Business Value Analysis: A Method for the Evaluation of Business Value Creation in Virtual Commerce. *Journal of Electronic Commerce Research*, *9*(3), 207–218.

Ariely, D., Loewenstein, G., & Prelec, D. (2003). Coherent arbitrariness: Stable demand curves without stable preferences. *The Quarterly Journal of Economics*, *118*(1), 73–106. doi:10.1162/00335530360535153

Ariely, D., & Wertenbroch, K. (2002). Procrastination, deadlines, and performance: Self-control by precommitment. *Psychological Science*, *13*(3), 219–224. doi:10.1111/1467-9280.00441 PMID:12009041

Arruda Filho, E. J. M., & Barcelos, A. D. A. (2021). Negative online word-of-mouth: Consumers' retaliation in the digital world. *Journal of Global Marketing*, *34*(1), 19–37. doi:10.1080/08911762.2020.1775919

Arsenyan, J., & Mirowska, A. (2021). Almost human? A comparative case study on the social media presence of virtual influencers. *International Journal of Human-Computer Studies*, *155*, 102694. doi:10.1016/j.ijhcs.2021.102694

Arya, V., Sambyal, R., Sharma, A., & Dwivedi, Y. K. (2024). Brands are calling your AVATAR in Metaverse–A study to explore XR-based gamification marketing activities & consumer-based brand equity in virtual world. *Journal of Consumer Behaviour*, *23*(2), 556–585. doi:10.1002/cb.2214

Au, W. J. (2009a, March 24). *Top Second Life Entrepreneur Cashing Out US$1.7 Million Yearly; Furnishings, Events Management Among Top Earners.* New World Notes. http://nwn.blogs.com/nwn/2009/03/million.html#more

Au, W. J. (2009b, April 23). How's the Second Life Economy Doing? M. and T. Linden (eds.) *Talk Earnings, Land Owning, L$ Transactions, More.* New World Notes. https://nwn.blogs.com/nwn/2009/04/hows-the-second-life-economy-doing.html

Ausat, A. M. A.M. A. (2023). The Role of Social Media in Shaping Public Opinion and Its Influence on Economic Decisions. [TACIT]. *Technology and Society Perspectives*, *1*(1), 35–44. doi:10.61100/tacit.v1i1.37

Aw, E. C.-X., & Agnihotri, R. (2023). Influencer marketing research: Review and future research agenda. *Journal of Marketing Theory and Practice*, 1–14. doi:10.1080/10696679.2023.2235883

Aydın, S., & Nalbant, K. G. (2023). The significance of artificial intelligence in the realms of marketing, advertising, and branding inside the metaverse. *JOEEP: Journal of Emerging Economies and Policy*, *8*(2), 301–316.

Azhari, N. F. B., bin S Senathirajah, A. R., & Haque, R. (2023). The role of customer satisfaction, trust, word of mouth, and service quality in enhancing customers' loyalty toward e-commerce. *Transnational Marketing Journal*, *11*(1), 31–43.

Aziza, D. N., & Astuti, R. D. (2019, March). Evaluating the effect of YouTube advertising towards young customers' purchase intention. In *12th International Conference on Business and Management Research (ICBMR 2018)* (pp. 93-98). Atlantis Press. 10.2991/icbmr-18.2019.16

Bag, S., Srivastava, G., Bashir, M. M. A., Kumari, S., Giannakis, M., & Chowdhury, A. H. (2022). Journey of customers in this digital era: Understanding the role of artificial intelligence technologies in user engagement and conversion. *Benchmarking*, *29*(7), 2074–2098. doi:10.1108/BIJ-07-2021-0415

Bailenson, J. N. (2018). *Experience on demand: What virtual reality is, how it works, and what it can do.* WW Norton & Company.

Baird, C. H., & Parasnis, G. (2011). From social media to social customer relationship management. *Strategy and Leadership*, *39*(5), 30–37. doi:10.1108/10878571111161507

Baker, E. W., Hubona, G. S., & Srite, M. (2019). Does "being there" matter? The impact of web-based and virtual world's shopping experiences on consumer purchase attitudes. *Information & Management*, *56*(7), 103153. doi:10.1016/j.im.2019.02.008

Compilation of References

Bansal, R., & Pruthi, N. (2023). Avatar-Based Influencer Marketing: Demystifying the Benefits and Risks of Marketing Through Virtual Influencers. In R. Bansal, S. A. Qalati, & A. Chakir (Eds.), (pp. 78–86). Advances in Marketing, Customer Relationship Management, and E-Services. IGI Global. doi:10.4018/978-1-6684-8898-0.ch005

Bansal, R., Qalati, S. A., & Chakir, A. (Eds.). (2023). *Influencer marketing applications within the Metaverse.* IGI Global. doi:10.4018/978-1-6684-8898-0

Barnes, S. J., & Mattsson, J. (2011). Exploring the Fit of Real Brands in the Second Life Virtual World. *Journal of Marketing Management, 27*(9-10), 934–958. doi:10.1080/026725 7X.2011.565686

Barrera, K. G., & Shah, D. (2023). Marketing in the Metaverse: Conceptual understanding, framework, and research agenda. *Journal of Business Research, 155,* 113420. doi:10.1016/j. jbusres.2022.113420

Barta, S., Belanche, D., Fernández, A., & Flavián, M. (2023). Influencer marketing on TikTok: The effectiveness of humor and followers' hedonic experience. *Journal of Retailing and Consumer Services, 70,* 103149. doi:10.1016/j.jretconser.2022.103149

Barta, S., Gurrea, R., & Flavián, C. (2023). Telepresence in live-stream shopping: An experimental study comparing Instagram and the Metaverse. *Electronic Markets, 33*(1), 29. doi:10.1007/ s12525-023-00643-6

Baudrillard, J., & Glaser, S. F. (1994). *Simulacra and Simulation.* University of Michigan Press.

Beattie, R. (2023). *Bringing Loyalty to Life: How to earn, build and leverage enduring customer loyalty.* SRA Books.

Belk, R., Humayun, M., & Brouard, M. (**2022**). Money, possessions, and ownership in the Metaverse: NFTs, cryptocurrencies, Web3 and Wild Markets. *Journal of Business Research, 153.*

Bendixen, M. T. (1993). Advertising effects and effectiveness. *European Journal of Marketing, 27*(10), 19–32. doi:10.1108/03090569310045861

Bergman, B., & Klefsjo, B. (2010). *Quality from customer needs to customer Satisfaction,.*

Bhattacharyya, S. S., Goswami, S., Mehta, R., & Nayak, B. (2022). Examining the factors influencing adoption of over the top (OTT) services among Indian consumers. *Journal of Science and Technology Policy Management, 13*(3), 652-682..

Blockchain Türkiye. (2023). *Singapur'un en büyük bankasından sürpriz metaverse konsepti.* Blockchain Türkiye. https://bctr.org/singapurun-en-buyuk-bankasindan-surpriz-metaverse-konsepti-30121/

Blut, M., Kulikovskaja, V., Hubert, M., Brock, C., & Grewal, D. (2023). Effectiveness of engagement initiatives across engagement platforms: A meta-analysis. *Journal of the Academy of Marketing Science, 51*(5), 1–25. doi:10.1007/s11747-023-00925-7 PMID:37359266

Bobier, J., Mérey, T., Robnett, S., Grebe, M., Feng, J., Rehberg, B., Woolsey, K., & Hazan, J. (2022). *The Corporate Hitchhiker's Guide to the Metaverse*. BCG. https://on.bcg.com/3arrxsA

Bolton, R. N., Kannan, P. K., & Bramlett, M. D. (2000). Implications of loyalty program membership and service experiences for customer retention and value. *Journal of the Academy of Marketing Science, 28*(1), 95–108. doi:10.1177/0092070300281009

Bolton, R. N., Warlop, L., & Alba, J. (2003). Consumer Perceptions of Price (Un)fairness. *The Journal of Consumer Research, 29*(4), 474–491. doi:10.1086/346244

Bonifacic, I. (2021). Project Cambria' is a high-end VR headset designed for Facebook's metaverse. TechCrunch. https://techcrunch.com/2021/10/28/project-cambria-is-a-high-end-vrheadset-designed-for-facebooks-metaverse

Borden, N. H. (1964). The concept of the marketing mix. *Journal of Advertising Research, 4*, 2–7.

Boselie, P., Hesselink, M., & van der Wiele, T. (2001). *Empirical Evidence for the Relation between Customer Satisfaction and Business Performance* (SSRN Scholarly Paper 370891). https://papers.ssrn.com/abstract=370891

Bourlakis, M., Papagiannidis, S., & Li, F. (2009). Retail spatial evolution: Paving the way from traditional to metaverse retailing. *Electronic Commerce Research, 9*(1-2), 135–148. doi:10.1007/s10660-009-9030-8

Bousba, Y., & Arya, V. (2022). Let's connect in metaverse. Brand's new destination to increase consumers' affective brand engagement & their satisfaction and advocacy. *Journal of Content Community Communication, 14*(8), 276–293. doi:10.31620/JCCC.06.22/19

Bozkurt, Ö., & Gümüş, İ. H. (2022). Metaverse ve metagirişimcilik: Kavramsal bir çerçeve. *Girişimcilik ve Kalkınma Dergisi, 17*(1), 75–85.

Bratu, S., & Sabău, R. I. (2022). Digital commerce in the immersive metaverse environment: Cognitive analytics management, real-time purchasing data, and seamless connected shopping experiences. *Linguistic and Philosophical Investigations, 21*(0), 170–186. doi:10.22381/lpi21202211

Braun, V., & Clarke, V. (2006). Using thematic analysis in psychology. *Qualitative Research in Psychology, 3*(2), 77–101. doi:10.1191/1478088706qp063oa

Brown, D., & Hayes, N. (2008). *Influencer marketing: Who really influences your customers?* Elsevier/Butterworth-Heinemann. doi:10.4324/9780080557700

Bustard, J. R. T., Bolan, P., Devine, A., & Hutchinson, K. (2018). The emerging smart event experience: *An interpretative phenomenological analysis. Tourism Review, 74*(1), 116–128. doi:10.1108/TR-10-2017-0156

Buyukdumlu, S. (2022, August 22). *Türkiye'nin metaverse odaklı ilk defilesi*. Pazar Lamasyon. https://www.pazarlamasyon.com/turkiye-nin-metaverse-odakli-ilk-defilesi .

Cagnina, M. R., & Poian, M. (2008). *How to compete in the metaverse: the business models in Second Life.* (U of Udine Economics Working Paper).

Cakmak, B. K. (2022). *Lacoste, Metaverse'de Oyunlaştırılmış Mağaza Açıyor.* https://www.bisektor.com/lacoste-metaversede-oyunlastirilmis-magaza/

Campbell, C., & Farrell, J. R. (2020). More than meets the eye: The functional components underlying influencer marketing. *Business Horizons*, *63*(4), 469–479. doi:10.1016/j.bushor.2020.03.003

Canavesi, B. (2022). *What Is the Metaverse: Where We Are and Where We're Headed.* Association for Talent Development. https://www. td. org/atd-blog/whatis-the-metaverse-where-we-are-and-where-were-headed

Casey, P., Baggili, I., & Yarramreddy, A. (2019). Immersive virtual reality attacks and the human joystick. *IEEE Transactions on Dependable and Secure Computing*, *18*(2), 550–562. doi:10.1109/TDSC.2019.2907942

Castronova, E. (2003). Theory of the Avatar. *SSRN*, *385103*. https://doi.org/http://dx.doi.org/10.2139/ssrn.385103

Chakraborty, O. (2024). Introduction to Metaverse: Concept and Evolution. In New Business Frontiers in the Metaverse (pp. 14-33). IGI Global.

Chakraborty, D., Polisetty, A., & Rana, N. P. (2024). Consumers' continuance intention towards metaverse-based virtual stores: A multi-study perspective. *Technological Forecasting and Social Change*, *203*, 123405. doi:10.1016/j.techfore.2024.123405

Chakravorti, S. (2023). Customer Relationship Management: A Global Approach. *Sage (Atlanta, Ga.)*.

Chang, H. H., & Chen, S. W. (2008). The impact of online store environment cues on purchase intention. *Online Information Review*, *32*(6), 818–841. doi:10.1108/14684520810923953

Chang, T. Z., & Wildt, A. R. (1994). Price, product information, and purchase intention: An empirical study. *Journal of the Academy of Marketing Science*, *22*(1), 16–27. doi:10.1177/0092070394221002

Chayka, K. (**2021**). We already live in Facebook's metaverse. *The New Yorker*. https://www.newyorker.com/culture/infinite-scroll/we-alreadylive-in-facebooks-metaverse

Cheah, I., & Shimul, A. S. (2023). Marketing in the metaverse: Moving forward–What's next? *Journal of Global Scholars of Marketing Science*, *33*(1), 1–10. doi:10.1080/21639159.2022.2163908

Chen, J. (2020). *What is influencer marketing: How to develop your strategy.* Sprout Social. https://sproutsocial. com/insights/influencer-marketing/(дата звернення: 25.04. 2020).

Chen, C., Zhang, K. Z., Chu, Z., & Lee, M. (2024). Augmented reality in the metaverse market: The role of multimodal sensory interaction. *Internet Research*, *34*(1), 9–38. doi:10.1108/INTR-08-2022-0670

Chen, H., Li, X., Chiu, T. S., & Chen, F. (2021). The impact of perceived justice on behavioral intentions of Cantonese Yum Cha consumers: The mediation role of psychological contract violation. *Journal of Hospitality and Tourism Management, 49*, 178–188. doi:10.1016/j.jhtm.2021.09.009

Chen, Z., & Xie, J. (2008). Online consumer review: Word-of-mouth as a new element of marketing communication mix. *Management Science, 54*(3), 477–491. doi:10.1287/mnsc.1070.0810

Cheung, C. M., Wong, R. Y. M., & Chan, T. K. H. (2021). Online disinhibition: Conceptualization, measurement, and implications for online deviant behavior. *Industrial Management & Data Systems, 121*(1), 48–64. doi:10.1108/IMDS-08-2020-0509

Chiang, O. (2010, October 27). Creating a $1M Virtual Goods Brand in Second Life. *Forbes*.

Choi, H. Y. (2022). Working in the metaverse: Does telework in a metaverse office have the potential to reduce population pressure in megacities? Evidence from young adults in Seoul, South Korea. *Sustainability (Basel), 14*(6), 3629. doi:10.3390/su14063629

Clark, M. A., Riley, M. J., Wilkie, E., & Wood, R. C. (2007). *Researching and writing dissertations in hospitality and tourism*. International Thomson Business Press.

Clement, J. (2022). *Leading business sectors already investing in the metaverse 2022*. Statista. https://www.statista.com/statistics/1302091/global-business-sectors-investing-in-the-metaverse/

Coelho, P. M., Corona, B., ten Klooster, R., & Worrell, E. (2020). Sustainability of reusable packaging–Current situation and trends. *Resources, Conservation and Recycling. X, 6*, 100037. doi:10.1016/j.rcrx.2020.100037

Corbitt, L. (2022). Influencer marketing in 2022: Strategies + examples. *The BigCommerce Blog*. https://www.bigcommerce.com/blog/influencer-marketing/#what-is-influencer-market-ing.

Costa, T., & Helal, A. E. (2022). *Branding in the Metaverse*. [Master's Thesis, Lund University]. https://lup.lub.lu.se/student-papers/record/9096606

Cowan, K., & Ketron, S. (2019). A dual model of product involvement for effective virtual reality: The roles of imagination, co-creation, telepresence, and interactivity. *Journal of Business Research, 100*, 483–492. doi:10.1016/j.jbusres.2018.10.063

Creamer Media Engineering News. (2022) *Meta safety Meta security*. Metaverse. https://www.engineeringnews

Damar, M. (2021). Metaverse shape of your life for future: A bibliometric snapshot. *Journal of Metaverse, 1*(1), 1–8.

Dasgupta, D., & Grover, D. (2019). Understanding adoption factors of over-the- top video services among millennial consumers. *International Journal of Computer Engineering and Technology, 10*(1).

Datta, B., & Kaushik, P. (2019). Brand awareness through Instagram advertising. *Asian Journal of Management, 10*(2), 100–108. doi:10.5958/2321-5763.2019.00017.9

Compilation of References

De Brito Silva, M. J., De Oliveira Ramos Delfino, L., Alves Cerqueira, K., & De Oliveira Campos, P. (2022). Avatar marketing: A study on the engagement and authenticity of virtual influencers on Instagram. *Social Network Analysis and Mining*, *12*(1), 130. doi:10.1007/s13278-022-00966-w

De Mooij, M., & Hofstede, G. (2010). The Hofstede model: applications to global branding and advertising strategy and research. *International Journal of Adver- tising, 29*(1), 85e110.

De Regt, A., Plangger, K., & Barnes, S. J. (2021). Virtual reality marketing and customer advocacy: Transforming experiences from story-telling to story-doing. *Journal of Business Research, 136*, 513–522. doi:10.1016/j.jbusres.2021.08.004

Dehghani, M., & Tumer, M. (2015). A research on effectiveness of Facebook adver- tising on enhancing purchase intention of consumers. *Computers in Human Behavior, 49*, 597e600.

Dehghani, M., Nourani, S., & Choubtarash, H. (2012). *Interdisciplinary journal of contemporary research in business, 4*(8), 774e787.

Dehghani, M., Niaki, M. K., Ramezani, I., & Sali, R. (2016). Evaluating the influence of YouTube advertising for attraction of young customers. *Computers in Human Behavior*, *59*, 165–172. doi:10.1016/j.chb.2016.01.037

Deighton, J., & Kornfeld, L. (2009). Interactivity's Unanticipated Consequences for Marketers and Marketing. *Journal of Interactive Marketing*, *23*(1), 4–10. doi:10.1016/j.intmar.2008.10.001

DHA. (2022). *Çikolata markası Sagra, Metaverse'de fabrika açacak*. DHA. https://www.dha. com.tr/ekonomi/cikolata-markasi-sagra-metaversede-fabrika-acacak-2028834 .

Dholakia, U. M. (2000). Temptation and resistance: An integrated model of consumption impulse formation and enactment. *Psychology and Marketing*, *17*(11), 955–982. doi:10.1002/1520-6793(200011)17:11<955::AID-MAR3>3.0.CO;2-J

Dieck, T. M. C., & Han, D.-D. (2022). The role of immersive technology in Customer Experience Management. *Journal of Marketing Theory and Practice*, *30*(1), 108–119. doi:10.1080/10696 679.2021.1891939

Djafarova, E., & Kramer, K. (2019). YouTube advertising: Exploring its effectiveness. *The Marketing Review*, *19*(1-2), 127–145. doi:10.1362/146934719X15633618140855

DMD. (2007). *The Virtual Brand Footprint: the Marketing Opportunity in Second Life [Report]*. DMD. http://www.dmdinsight.com/research/

Dong, M., & Saini, R. (2023). Listening to strangers more than friends: How recommendations from close-(vs distant-) others influence consumption. *European Journal of Marketing*, *57*(5), 1327–1351. doi:10.1108/EJM-11-2021-0841

Dos Remedios, L. (2023). The influence of the Metaverse on Brand Management: A study. *Communities*, *2*(2), 5.

Drenten, J., & Brooks, G. (2020). Celebrity 2.0: Lil Miquela and the rise of a virtual star system. *Feminist Media Studies*, *20*(8), 1319–1323. doi:10.1080/14680777.2020.1830927

Du, T. (2022). *Virtual influencers in Metaverse: Discussion and research on the impacts of the purchasing decisions of Generation Z.*

Duan, H., Li, J., Fan, S., Lin, Z., Wu, X., & Cai, W. (2021). Metaverse for social good: A university campus prototype. In *Proceedings of the 29th ACM international conference on multimedia* (pp. 153-161). ACM. 10.1145/3474085.3479238

Ducoffe, R. H. (1995a). How consumers assess the value of advertising. *Journal of Current Issues & Research in Advertising, 17*(1), 1e18.

Duffy, B. E., & Hund, E. (2019). Gendered Visibility on Social Media: Navigating Instagram's Authenticity Bind [social media, visibility, gender, authenticity, Instagram, influencers]. *International Journal of Communication*, *13*, 4983–5002. https://ijoc.org/index.php/ijoc/article/view/11729/2821. doi:10.32376/3f8575cb.3f03db0e

Duhon, S., Ellison, K., & Ragas, M. W. (2016). A whale of a problem: A strategic communication analysis of SeaWorld Entertainment's multi-year Blackfish crisis. *Case Studies in Strategic Communication*, *5*(1), 2–37.

Duncan, R. B. (1972). Characteristics of organizational environments and perceived environmental uncertainty. *Administrative Science Quarterly*, *17*(3), 313–327. doi:10.2307/2392145

Dwivedi, Y. K., Hughes, L., Baabdullah, A. M., Ribeiro-Navarrete, S., Giannakis, M., Al-Debei, M. M., Dennehy, D., Metri, B., Buhalis, D., Cheung, C. M. K., Conboy, K., Doyle, R., Dubey, R., Dutot, V., Felix, R., Goyal, D. P., Gustafsson, A., Hinsch, C., Jebabli, I., & Wamba, S. F. (2022). Metaverse beyond the hype: Multidisciplinary perspectives on emerging challenges, opportunities, and agenda for research, practice and policy. *International Journal of Information Management*, *66*, 102542. doi:10.1016/j.ijinfomgt.2022.102542

Dwivedi, Y. K., Hughes, L., Wang, Y., Alalwan, A. A., Ahn, S. J., Balakrishnan, J., Barta, S., Belk, R., Buhalis, D., Dutot, V., Felix, R., Filieri, R., Flavián, C., Gustafsson, A., Hinsch, C., Hollensen, S., Jain, V., Kim, J., Krishen, A. S., & Wirtz, J. (2023). Metaverse marketing: How the metaverse will shape the future of consumer research andpractice. [AL.]. *Psychology and Marketing*, *40*(4), 750776. doi:10.1002/mar.21767

Dwyer, L., Gill, A., & Seetaram, N. (2012). *Handbook of research methods in tourism: Quantitative and qualitative approaches*. Edward Elgar Publishing. doi:10.4337/9781781001295

Edell, J. A., & Burke, M. C. (1987). The power of feelings in understanding advertising effects. *The Journal of Consumer Research*, *14*(3), 421–433. doi:10.1086/209124

Edwards, S. M., Li, H., & Lee, J. H. (2002a). *Forced exposure and psychological reactance: antecedents and consequences of the perceived intrusiveness of pop-up ads.*

Compilation of References

Eggenschwiler, M., Linzmajer, M., Roggeveen, A. L., & Rudolph, T. (2024). Retailing in the metaverse: A framework of managerial considerations for success. *Journal of Retailing and Consumer Services*, *79*, 103791. doi:10.1016/j.jretconser.2024.103791

El Beheiry, M., Doutreligne, S., Caporal, C., Ostertag, C., Dahan, M., & Masson, J.-B. (2019). Virtual reality: Beyond visualization. *Journal of Molecular Biology*, *2019*(431), 1315–1321. doi:10.1016/j.jmb.2019.01.033 PMID:30738026

El-Deeb, S. (2022, December). Computer-Generated Imagery Influencer Marketing—Which Ends of the Continuum Will Prevail? Humans or Avatars? *In International Conference on Marketing and Technologies* (pp. 3-15). Singapore: Springer Nature Singapore.

Ellegaard, C., & Ritter, T. (2006). *Customer attraction and its purchasing potential*. In *22nd IMP Conference*, Milan.

Elmasry, T., Hazan, E., Hamza, K., Kelly, G., Srivastava, S., Yee, L. & Zemmel, R.W. (2022). *Value creation in the metaverse: The real business of the virtual world*.

Elsharnouby, M. H., Jayawardhena, C., Liu, H., & Elbedweihy, A. M. (2022). Strengthening consumer–brand relationships through avatars. *Journal of Research in Interactive Marketing*.

Epley, N., Waytz, A., & Cacioppo, J. T. (2007). On seeing human: A three-factor theory of anthropomorphism. *Psychological Review*, *114*(4), 864–886. doi:10.1037/0033-295X.114.4.864 PMID:17907867

Erlangga, A. W. (2023). The Effect of Digitalization and Customer Relationship Management on Member Loyalty. *Journal of Digital Business and Data Science*, *1*(1), 1–12.

Eshiett, I. O., Eshiett, O. E., Eshiett, I. O., & Eshiett, O. E. (2024). Artificial intelligence marketing and customer satisfaction: An employee job security threat review. *World Journal of Advanced Research and Reviews*, *21*(1), 1. Advance online publication. doi:10.30574/wjarr.2024.21.1.2655

Evans, L., Frith, J., & Saker, M. (2022). The roots of the metaverse. In *From Microverse to Metaverse: Modelling the Future through Today's Virtual Worlds* (pp. 15–24). Emerald Publishing Limited. doi:10.1108/978-1-80455-021-220221002

Evans, N. J., Phua, J., Lim, J., & Jun, H. (2017). Disclosing Instagram influencer advertising: The effects of disclosure language on advertising recognition, attitudes, and behavioral intent. *Journal of Interactive Advertising*, *17*(2), 138–149. doi:10.1080/15252019.2017.1366885

Eyice Başev, S. (2024). Influencer marketing in the age of Metaverse: Beymenverse and meta-influencer Bella. *International Journal of Eurasian Education and Culture*, *9*(25), 29–41. doi:10.35826/ijoecc.1820

Fernandez, C. B., & Hui, P. (2022). Life, the Metaverse and Everything: An Overview of Privacy. Ethics, and Governance in *Metaverse. arXiv preprint* arXiv.01480 doi:10.1109/ICDCSW56584.2022.00058

Firat, D. (2019). YouTube advertising value and its effects on purchase intention. *Journal of Global Business Insights*, *4*(2), 141–155. doi:10.5038/2640-6489.4.2.1097

Fischer, E., & Reuber, A. R. (2011). Social interaction via new social media: (How) can interactions on Twitter affect effectual thinking and behavior? *Journal of Business Venturing*, *26*(1), 1–18. doi:10.1016/j.jbusvent.2010.09.002

Ford Company. (2024). *Dijital Stüdyo Decentraland Klavuzu*. Ford Company. https://www.ford.com.tr/getmedia/c9a4bc41-fbc8-4d8b-b668-1677dd48f74c/Ford-Metaverse-Klavuz.pdf.aspx .

Fournier, S., & Avery, J. (2011). The Uninvited Brand. *Business Horizons*, *54*(3), 193–207. doi:10.1016/j.bushor.2011.01.001

Foutty, J., & Bechte, M. (2022). *What's all the buzz about the metaverse?* https://bit.ly/3bRH313

Frankish, K. (2010). Dual-process and dual-system theories of reasoning. *Philosophy Compass*, *5*(10), 914–926. doi:10.1111/j.1747-9991.2010.00330.x

Gadalla, E., Keeling, K., & Abosaq, I. (2013). Metaverse-Retail Service Quality: A Future Framework for Retail Service Quality in the 3D Internet. *Journal of Marketing Management*, *29*(13-14), 1493–1517. doi:10.1080/0267257X.2013.835742

Garding, S., & Bruns, A. (2015). *Complaint management and channel choice: An analysis of customer perceptions*. Springer. doi:10.1007/978-3-319-18179-0

Gauttier, S., Simouri, W., & Milliat, A. (2024). When to enter the metaverse: Business leaders offer perspectives. *The Journal of Business Strategy*, *45*(1), 2–9. doi:10.1108/JBS-08-2022-0149

Gemma, W. A. (2023, February 14). *Should Brands Use Virtual Influencers in China?* Business of Fashion. https://www.businessoffashion.com/briefings/china/should-brands-use-virtual-influencers-in-china/

Ghalawat, S., Yadav, E., Kumar, M., Kumari, N., Goyal, M., Girdhar, A., & Agarwal, S. (2021). Factors influencing consumer's choice of streaming over the top (OTT) platforms. *Indian Journal of Extension Education, 57*(3), 99-101.

Ghosh, D. (2018). How GDPR will transform digital marketing. *Harvard Business Review*, 2–4.

Ginzarly, M., & Teller, J. (2021). Online communities and their contribution to local heritage knowledge. *Journal of Cultural Heritage Management and Sustainable Development*, *11*(4), 361–380. doi:10.1108/JCHMSD-02-2020-0023

Glenister, G. (2021). *Influencer Marketing Strategy: How to create successful influencer marketing*. Kogan Page.

Grupac, M., Husakova, K., & Balica, R. Ş. (2022). Virtual navigation and augmented reality shopping tools, immersive and cognitive technologies, and image processing computational and object tracking algorithms in the metaverse commerce. *Analysis and Metaphysics*, *21*(0), 210–226. doi:10.22381/am21202213

Gunarathne, P., Rui, H., & Seidmann, A. (2018). When social media delivers customer service: Differential customer treatment in the airline industry. *Management Information Systems Quarterly*, *42*(2), 489–520. doi:10.25300/MISQ/2018/14290

Gündüz, U., & Demirel, S. (2023). Metaverse-related perceptions and sentiments on Twitter: Evidence from text mining and network analysis. *Electronic Commerce Research*. doi:10.1007/s10660-023-09745-x

Gunyol, A. (2022). *Turkcell çalışanlarına "metaverse" dünyasının kapıları açıldı*. AA. https://www.aa.com.tr/tr/sirkethaberleri/bilisim/turkcell-calisanlarina-metaverse-dunyasinin-kapilari-acildi/675650 .

Gupta, G., Gupta, A., & Joshi, M. C. (2022). A Conceptual and Bibliometric Study to Understand Marketing in Metaverse: A new Paradigm. *2022 5th International Conference on Contemporary Computing and Informatics (IC3I)*, (pp. 1486–1491). IEEE. 10.1109/IC3I56241.2022.10073455

Gupta, H., Singh, S., & Sinha, P. (2017). Multimedia tool as a predictor for social media advertising-a YouTube way. *Multimedia Tools and Applications*, *76*(18), 18557–18568. doi:10.1007/s11042-016-4249-6

Habil, S. G. M., El-Deeb, S., & El-Bassiouny, N. (2024). The metaverse era: Leveraging augmented reality in the creation of novel customer experience. Management & Sustainability. *An Arab Review*, *3*(1), 1–15.

Hackl, C. (2021). *Defining The Metaverse Today*. https://bit.ly/3NVvvHs

Haikel-Elsabeh, M. (2023). Virtual Influencers versus Real Influencers Advertising in the Metaverse, Understanding the Perceptions, and Interactions with Users. *Journal of Current Issues and Research in Advertising*, *44*(3), 252–273. doi:10.1080/10641734.2023.2218420

Haimson, O. L., & Hoffmann, A. L. (2016). Constructing and enforcing" authentic" identity online: Facebook, real names, and non-normative identities. *First Monday*. doi:10.5210/fm.v21i6.6791

Halvorsen, K., Hoffmann, J., Coste-Manière, I., & Stankeviciute, R. (2013). Can fashion blogs function as a marketing tool to influence consumer behavior? Evidence from Norway. *Journal of Global Fashion Marketing*, *4*(3), 211–224. doi:10.1080/20932685.2013.790707

Han, D. I. D., Bergs, Y., & Moorhouse, N. (2022). Virtual reality consumer experience escapes: Preparing for the metaverse. *Virtual Reality (Waltham Cross)*, *26*(4), 1443–1458. doi:10.1007/s10055-022-00641-7

Handley, A., & Chapman, C. (2012). *Content Rules: How to Create Killer Blogs, Podcasts, Videos, Ebooks, Webinars (and More) That Engage Customers and Ignite Your Business*. John Wiley & Sons.

Hanna, R., Rohm, A., & Crittenden, V. L. (2011). We're All Connected: The Power of the Social Media Ecosystem. *Business Horizons*, *54*(3), 265–273. doi:10.1016/j.bushor.2011.01.007

Hassouneh, D., & Brengman, M. (2014). *Shopping for Virtual Products in Social Virtual Worlds: Does Users' Gender Matter?* [Working paper].

Hassouneh, D., & Brengman, M. (2011b). Virtual Worlds: A Gateway for SMEs Toward Internationalization. *Journal of Brand Management*, *19*(1), 72–90. doi:10.1057/bm.2011.24

Hassouneh, D., & Brengman, M. (2015). Metaverse Retailing: Are SVW Users Ready to Buy Real Products from Virtual World Stores? In P. Kommers, P. Isarias, & H. Fernandez Betancort (Eds.), *Proceedings of the 12th International IADIS Conference on e-Commerce and Digital Marketing (EC 2015): Multi Conference on Computer Science and Information Systems (MCCSI2015)* (pp. 104-110). IEEE.

Häubl, G., & Trifts, V. (2000). Consumer decision making in online shopping environments: The effects of interactive decision aids. *Marketing Science*, *19*(1), 4–21. doi:10.1287/mksc.19.1.4.15178

Hazan, E., Kelly, G., Khan, H., Spillecke, D., & Yee, L. (2022). *Marketing in the metaverse: An opportunity for innovation and experimentation.*

Hennig-Thurau, T., & Ognibeni, B. (2022). Metaverse marketing. *NIM Marketing Intelligence Review*, *14*(2), 43–47. doi:10.2478/nimmir-2022-0016

Henry, C. D. (2023). Six strategies to building successful communities in the Metaverse. *Journal of Brand Strategy*, *12*(1), 40–48.

Herman, L. E., Sulhaini, S., & Farida, N. (2021). Electronic customer relationship management and company performance: Exploring the product innovativeness development. *Journal of Relationship Marketing*, *20*(1), 1–19. doi:10.1080/15332667.2019.1688600

Hilken, T., Heller, J., Chylinski, M., Keeling, D. I., Mahr, D., & de Ruyter, K. (2020). Making omnichannel an augmented reality: The current and future state of the art. *Journal of Research in Interactive Marketing*, *14*(1), 55–79.

Hoang, D., Kousi, S., Martinez, L. F., & Kumar, S. (2023). Revisiting a model of customer engagement cycle: A systematic review. *Service Industries Journal*, *43*(9-10), 579–617. doi:10.1080/02642069.2023.2202912

Hofstetter, R., de Bellis, E., Brandes, L., Clegg, M., Lamberton, C., Reibstein, D., Rohlfsen, F., Schmitt, B., & Zhang, J. Z. (2022). Crypto-marketing: How non-fungible tokens (NFTs) challenge traditional marketing. *Marketing Letters*, *33*(4), 705–711. doi:10.1007/s11002-022-09639-2

Hollensen, S., Kotler, P., & Opresnik, M. O. (2023). Metaverse: The new marketing universe. *The Journal of Business Strategy*, *44*(3), 119–125. doi:10.1108/JBS-01-2022-0014

Holzwarth, M., Janiszewski, C., & Neumann, M. M. (2006). The influence of avatars on online consumer shopping behavior. *Journal of Marketing*, *70*(4), 19–36. doi:10.1509/jmkg.70.4.019

Hom, W. (2000). *An Overview of Customer Satisfaction Models*. ERIC. http://www. https://eric.ed.gov/?id=ED463825

Huang, L., Gao, B., & Gao, M. (2023). Comparison of E-Commerce Retail Between China and Japan. In *Value Realization in the Phygital Reality Market: Consumption and Service Under Conflation of the Physical, Digital, and Virtual Worlds* (pp. 151–184). Springer Nature Singapore. doi:10.1007/978-981-99-4129-2_8

Hudders, L., & Lou, C. (2023). The rosy world of influencer marketing? Its bright and dark sides, and future research recommendations. *International Journal of Advertising*, *42*(1), 151–161. do i:10.1080/02650487.2022.2137318

Hughes, C. (2023). *Virtual Influencers and the New Wave of Digital Labour Exploitation* [Thesis for the Degree of Master of Arts, Graduate Program in Communications and Culture, York University]. https://yorkspace.library.yorku.ca/server/api/core/bitstreams/e6cdf2e9-ea96-4e38-964e-92d6cb825d29/content

Hunter, T. (2022). *Surveillance will follow us into 'the metaverse,' and our bodies could be its new data source.*

Hüttinger, L., Schiele, H., & Veldman, J. (2012). The drivers of customer attractiveness, supplier satisfaction and preferred customer status: A literature review. *Industrial Marketing Management*, *41*(8), 1194–1205. doi:10.1016/j.indmarman.2012.10.004

Hu, Y. (2023). Research on Brand Marketing Model of Perfect Diary of Beauty Enterprises based on 4P Theory Framework. *Highlights in Business. Economics and Management*, *6*, 29–35.

Huynh-The, T., Gadekallu, T. R., Wang, W., Yenduri, G., Ranaweera, P., Pham, Q.-V., da Costa, D. B., & Liyanage, M. (2023). Blockchain for the metaverse: A Review. *Future Generation Computer Systems*, *143*, 401–419. doi:10.1016/j.future.2023.02.008

Hwang, R., & Lee, M. (2022). The influence of music content marketing on user satisfaction and intention to use in the Metaverse: A focus on the SPICE Model. *Businesses*, *2*(2), 141–155. doi:10.3390/businesses2020010

Icozu, T. (2022). *The Sandbox Kurucu Ortağı ve COO'su Sebastien Borget: "Türkiye önceki sezonda ilk 5'te yer aldı."* Webrazzi. https://webrazzi.com/2022/11/18/the-sandbox-kurucu-ortagi-ve-coo-su-sebastien-borget-turkiye-onceki-sezonda-ilk-5-te-yer-aldi/ Accessed, May 25, 2023.

Idrees, S., Vignali, G., & Gill, S. (2023). Interactive marketing with virtual commerce tools: Purchasing right size and fitted garment in fashion metaverse. In *The Palgrave Handbook of interactive marketing* (pp. 329–351). Springer International Publishing. doi:10.1007/978-3-031-14961-0_15

Inder, S. (2023). Entrepreneurial opportunities in metaverse. In *Promoting Consumer Engagement Through Emotional Branding and Sensory Marketing* (pp. 52–62). IGI Global.

Insights on the metaverse and the future of gaming . (n.d.). EY. https://www.ey.com/en_us/insights/media-entertainment/what-s-possible-for-the-gaming-industry-in-the-next-dimension/chapter-3-insights-on-the-metaverse-and-the-future-of-gaming

Ioannıdıs, S., & Kontıs, A. P. (2023). The 4 Epochs of the Metaverse. *Journal of Metaverse*, *3*(2), 152–165. doi:10.57019/jmv.1294970

ISACA. (2014). *Generating value from big data analytics* [White paper]. Information Systems Audit and Control Association. https://www.isaca.org/Knowledge-Center/Research/ResearchDeliverables/Pages/Generating-Value-From-Big-Data-Analytics.aspx

Israfilzade, K. (2022). Marketing in the metaverse: A sceptical viewpoint of opportunities and future research directions. [EPESS]. *The Eurasia Proceedings of Educational & Social Sciences*, *24*, 53–60. doi:10.55549/epess.1179349

Istanbul Bar Association. (2023). *Metaverse and Artificial Intelligence*. Istanbul Bar Association. https://www.istanbulbarosu.org.tr/files/komisyonlar/yzcg/metaverse_ve_hukuk.pdf

Istanbulluoglu, D., & Oz, S. (2023). Service Recovery via Twitter: An Exploration of Responses to Consumer Complaints. *Accounting Perspectives*, *22*(4), 1–26. doi:10.1111/1911-3838.12339

Japutra, A., Loureiro, S. M. C., Molinillo, S., & Primanti, H. (2023). Influence of individual and social values on customer engagement in luxury thermal spa hotels: The mediating roles of perceived justice and brand experience. *Tourism and Hospitality Research*, 14673584231188847. doi:10.1177/14673584231188847

Javornik, A. (2016). Augmented reality: Research agenda for studying the impact of its media characteristics on consumer behaviour. *Journal of Retailing and Consumer Services*, *30*, 252–261. doi:10.1016/j.jretconser.2016.02.004

Jeong, H., Yi, Y., & Kim, D. (2022). An innovative e-commerce platform incorporating Metaverse to live commerce. *International Journal of Innovative Computing, Information, & Control*, *18*(1), 221–229. doi:10.24507/ijicic.18.01.221

Jeong, M., Shin, H. H., Lee, M., & Lee, J. (2023). Assessing brand performance consistency from consumer-generated media: The US hotel industry. *International Journal of Contemporary Hospitality Management*, *35*(6), 2056–2083. doi:10.1108/IJCHM-12-2021-1516

Jhunjhunwala, S. (2023). Corporate Social Responsibility: Making a Difference. In *Corporate Governance: Creating Value for Stakeholders* (pp. 145–169). Springer Nature Singapore. doi:10.1007/978-981-99-2707-4_7

Johnston, A. (2016). Creepiness Is in the Eye of the Beholder [Opinion]. *IEEE Technology and Society Magazine*, *35*(1), 27–28. doi:10.1109/MTS.2016.2518254

Jones, W. (2021). *Email Marketing*. Editora Bibliomundi.

Jovanović, A., & Milosavljević, A. (2022). VoRtex Metaverse platform for gamified collaborative learning. *Electronics (Basel)*, *11*(3), 317. doi:10.3390/electronics11030317

Juteau, S. (2023). TheFork by TripAdvisor: A French success story. *Journal of Information Technology Teaching Cases*, 20438869231179989.

Kali, Z. (2023, May 18). *The 2023 Turkish Airlines EuroLeague Final Four Kicks Off This Week with New Metaverse, EuroLeague Land*. Aeroportist. https://www.aeroportist.com/the-2023-turkish-airlines-euroleague-final/

Kalyvaki, M. (2023). Navigating the metaverse business and legal challenges: Intellectual property, privacy, and jurisdiction. *Journal of Metaverse*, *3*(1), 87–92. doi:10.57019/jmv.1238344

Kaplan, A. M., & Haenlein, M. (2010). Users of the World, Unite! The Challenges and Opportunities of Social Media. *Business Horizons*, *53*(1), 59–68. doi:10.1016/j.bushor.2009.09.003

Karaağaoğlu, N., & Çiçek, M. (2019). An evaluation of digital marketing applications in airline sector. *International Journal of Human Sciences*, *16*(2), 606–619. doi:10.14687/jhs.v16i2.5661

Karabacak, Z. İ., & Güngör, İ. (2023). The Metaverse as Influencer Marketing Platform: Influencer-Brand Collaborations of Parıs Hilton with 'Superplastic', 'Bohoo', and 'Levi's'. *Etkileşim*, *6*(11), 176–199. doi:10.32739/etkilesim.2023.6.11.194

Kardes, F. R., Cline, T. W., & Cronley, M. L. (2011). *Consumer Behavior: Science and Practice*. South-Western Cengage Learning.

Karimi, S. (2013). A Purchase Decision-Making Process Model of Online Consumers and Its Influential Factora Cross Sector Analysis (Doctoral dissertation, The University of Manchester, Manchester, UK].

Keegan, B. J., McCarthy, I. P., Kietzmann, J., & Canhoto, A. I. (2024). On your marks, headset, go! Understanding the building blocks of metaverse realms. *Business Horizons*, *67*(1), 107–119. doi:10.1016/j.bushor.2023.09.002

Khan, I., & Rahman, Z. (2016). Retail brand experience: Scale development and validation. *Journal of Product and Brand Management*, *25*(5), 435–451. doi:10.1108/JPBM-07-2015-0943

Khan, S. W., Raza, S. H., & Zaman, U. (2022). Remodeling digital marketplace through Metaverse: A multi-path model of consumer neuroticism, parasocial relationships, social media influencers credibility, and ppenness to Metaverse experience. *Pakistan Journal of Commerce and Social Sciences*, *16*(3), 337–365.

Khatri, M. (2022). Revamping the marketing world with metaverse–The future of marketing. *International Journal of Computer Applications*, *975*(29), 8887. doi:10.5120/ijca2022922361

Kim, D. Y., Lee, H. K., & Chung, K. (2023). Avatar-mediated experience in the metaverse: The impact of avatar realism on user-avatar relationship. *Journal of Retailing and Consumer Services*, *73*, 103382. doi:10.1016/j.jretconser.2023.103382

Kim, D., & Wang, Z. (2023). The ethics of virtuality: Navigating the complexities of human-like virtual influencers in the social media marketing realm. *Frontiers in Communication*, *8*, 1205610. doi:10.3389/fcomm.2023.1205610

Kim, E., Best, A. R., & Choi, K. (2023). Mapping the research trends on social media in the hospitality sector from 2010 to 2020. *Tourism and Hospitality Management*, *29*(2), 167–181. doi:10.20867/thm.29.2.2

Kim, E., Kim, D. E. Z., & Shoenberger, H. (2023). The next hype in social media advertising: Examining virtual influencers' brand endorsement effectiveness. *Frontiers in Psychology*, *14*, 1089051. doi:10.3389/fpsyg.2023.1089051 PMID:36949930

Kim, H. M., & Chakraborty, S. (2023). Exploring the diffusion of digital fashion and influencers' social roles in the Metaverse: An analysis of Twitter hashtag networks. *Internet Research*. Advance online publication. doi:10.1108/INTR-09-2022-0727

Kim, J. (2021). Advertising in the metaverse: Research agenda. *Journal of Interactive Advertising*, *21*(3), 141–144. doi:10.1080/15252019.2021.2001273

Kim, J., & Forsythe, S. (2008). Adoption of Virtual Try-on Technology for Online Apparel Shopping. *Journal of Interactive Marketing*, *22*(2), 45–59. doi:10.1002/dir.20113

Kim, J., Natter, M., & Spann, M. (2009). Pay-what-you-want: A new participative pricing mechanism. *Journal of Marketing*, *73*(1), 44–58. doi:10.1509/jmkg.73.1.044

Kinzinger, A., Steiner, W., Tatzgern, M., & Vallaster, C. (2022). Comparing low sensory enabling (LSE) and high sensory enabling (HSE) virtual product presentation modes in e-commerce. *Information Systems Journal*, *32*(5), 1034–1063. doi:10.1111/isj.12382

Koles, B. (2024). The authentic virtual influencer: Authenticity manifestations in the Metaverse. *Journal of Business Research, 170*, 114325. . Hal-04298734 doi:10.1016/j.jbusres.2023.114325

König, T. M., Hein, N., & Nimsgern, V. (2022). A value perspective on online review platforms: Profiling preference structures of online shops and traditional companies. *Journal of Business Research*, *145*, 387–401. doi:10.1016/j.jbusres.2022.02.080

Koohang, A., Nord, J. H., Ooi, K. B., Tan, G. W. H., Al-Emran, M., Aw, E. C. X., Baabdullah, A. M., Buhalis, D., Cham, T.-H., Dennis, C., Dutot, V., Dwivedi, Y. K., Hughes, L., Mogaji, E., Pandey, N., Phau, I., Raman, R., Sharma, A., Sigala, M., & Wong, L. W. (2023). Shaping the Metaverse into Reality: A Holistic Multidisciplinary Understanding of Opportunities, Challenges, and Avenues for Future Investigation. *Journal of Computer Information Systems*, *63*(3), 735–765. doi:10.1080/08874417.2023.2165197

Ko, S. Y., Chung, H. K., Kim, J. I., & Shin, Y. (2021). A study on the typology and advancement of cultural leisure-based metaverse. *KIPS Transactions on Software and Data Engineering*, *10*(8), 331–338.

Kotler, P. (2017). Customer value management. *Journal of Creating Value*, *3*(2), 170–172. doi:10.1177/2394964317706879

Kotler, P., & Armstrong, G. (2018). *Principles of Marketing*. Pearson.

Compilation of References

Kotler, P., Kartajaya, H., & Setiawan, I. (2023). *Marketing 6.0: The Future Is Immersive*. John Wiley & Sons.

Kotler, P., & Keller, K. L. (2009). *Marketing Management*. Pearson Prentice Hall.

Kotler, P., Pfoertsch, W., & Sponholz, U. (2021). *H2H marketing: The genesis of human-to-human marketing* (M. Haas, Ed.). Springer. doi:10.1007/978-3-030-59531-9

Kotler, P., Pfoertsch, W., Sponholz, U., & Haas, M. (Eds.). (2024). *H2H Marketing: Case Studies on Human-to-Human Marketing*. Springer Nature.

Kour, M., & Rani, K. (2023). Challenges and Opportunities to the Media and Entertainment Industry in Metaverse. *Applications of Neuromarketing in the Metaverse*, 88-102.

Kowalczuk, P., & Siepmann, C. (2021). Cognitive, affective, and behavioral consumer responses to augmented reality in e-commerce: A comparative study. *Journal of Business Research*, *124*, 357–373. doi:10.1016/j.jbusres.2020.10.050

Krafft, M., Arden, C. M., & Verhoef, P. C. (2017). Permission marketing and privacy concerns— Why do customers (not) grant permissions? *Journal of Interactive Marketing*, *39*(1), 39–54. doi:10.1016/j.intmar.2017.03.001

Krasonikolakis, I. G., Vrechopoulos, A., & Pouloudi, A. (2011). Defining, Applying and Customizing Store Atmosphere in Virtual Reality Commerce: Back to Basics? *International Journal of E-Services and Mobile Applications*, *3*(2), 14. doi:10.4018/jesma.2011040104

Kshetri, N. (2014). Big data's impact on privacy, security and consumer welfare. *Telecommunications Policy*, *38*(11), 1134–1145. doi:10.1016/j.telpol.2014.10.002

Kshetri, N. (2022). Web 3.0 and the metaverse shaping organizations' brand and product strategies. *IT Professional*, *24*(02), 11–15. doi:10.1109/MITP.2022.3157206

Kumar, V., & Reinartz, W. (2018). *Customer relationship management*. Springer-Verlag GmbH Germany.

Kumari, N., Zhang, B., Zhang, R., Shechtman, E., & Zhu, J. Y. (2023). Multi-concept customization of text-to-image diffusion. In *Proceedings of the IEEE/CVF Conference on Computer Vision and Pattern Recognition* (pp. 1931-1941). IEEE.

Kumar, P., & Pandey, M. (2017). A review on the impact of psychological pricing on consumer perception. *International Journal of Management, IT, and Engineering*, *7*(3), 331–343.

Kumar, V., & Reinartz, W. J. (2006). *Customer relationship management: A databased approach*. Wiley.

Kunathikornkit, S., Piriyakul, I., & Piriyakul, R. (2023). One-to-one marketing management via customer complaint. *Social Network Analysis and Mining*, *13*(1), 83. doi:10.1007/s13278-023-01082-z

Kuntze, R., Crudele, T. R., Reynolds, D., & Matulich, E. (2013). The Rise and Fall of Virtual Reality Retailing in Second Life: An Avatar's Perspective. *Journal of Management and Marketing Research*, 13.

Kuş, O. (2021). "Metaverse: 'Dijital büyük patlamada' fırsatlar ve endişelere yönelik algılar". Intermedia. *International Journal (Toronto, Ont.)*, *8*(15), 245–266. doi:10.21645/intermedia.2021.109

La Rocca, A., Caruana, A., & Snehota, I. (2012). Measuring customer attractiveness. *Industrial Marketing Management*, *41*(8), 1241–1248. doi:10.1016/j.indmarman.2012.10.008

Labrecque, L. I., Markos, E., & Milne, G. R. (2011). Online Personal Branding: Processes, Challenges, and Implications. *Journal of Interactive Marketing*, *25*(1), 37–50. doi:10.1016/j.intmar.2010.09.002

Lahtinen, N., Pulkka, K., Karjaluoto, H., & Mero, J. (2023). *Digital Marketing Strategy: Create Strategy, Put It Into Practice, Sell More*. Edward Elgar Publishing. doi:10.4337/9781035311316

Lamberton, C., & Stephen, A. T. (2016). A thematic exploration of digital, social media, and mobile marketing: Research evolution from 2000 to 2015 and an agenda for future inquiry. *Journal of Marketing*, *80*(6), 146–172. doi:10.1509/jm.15.0415

Lambillotte, L., & Poncin, I. (2023). Customers facing companies' content personalisation attempts: Paradoxical tensions, strategies and managerial insights. *Journal of Marketing Management*, *39*(3-4), 213–243. doi:10.1080/0267257X.2022.2105384

Lane, M. (2023). Social Media Marketing: Learn how to build a great brand. *Master the secrets of influencing*.

Lau, P. L. (2022). The metaverse: three legal issues we need to address. *The conversation, 1*.

Laudon, K. C., & Traver, C. G. (2016). *E-Commerce: Business, Technology, Society*. Pearson.

Lee, L. H., Braud, T., Zhou, P., Wang, L., Xu, D., Lin, Z., & Hui, P. (2021). All one needs to know about metaverse: A complete survey on technological singularity, virtual ecosystem, and research agenda. *arXiv preprint arXiv*:2110.05352.

Lee, C. T., Ho, T.-Y., & Xie, H.-H. (2023). Building brand engagement in metaverse commerce: The role of branded non-fungible tokens (BNFTs). *Electronic Commerce Research and Applications*, *58*, 101248. doi:10.1016/j.elerap.2023.101248

Lee, H. W., Chang, K., Uhm, J. P., & Owiro, E. (2023). How avatar identification affects enjoyment in the metaverse: The roles of avatar customization and social engagement. *Cyberpsychology, Behavior, and Social Networking*, *26*(4), 255–262. doi:10.1089/cyber.2022.0257 PMID:37001178

Lee, H., & Han, J. Y. (2021). A study on classification and charact eristics of metaverse platforms according to experience type s. *Journal of the Korea Institute of the Spatial Design*, *16*(8), 427–436.

Lee, K. C., & Chung, N. (2008). Empirical Analysis of Consumer Reaction to the Virtual Reality Shopping Mall. *Computers in Human Behavior*, *24*(1), 88–104. doi:10.1016/j.chb.2007.01.018

LeeL.-H.BraudT.ZhouP.WangL.XuD.LinZ.KumarA.BermejoC.HuiP. (2021). *All One Needs to Know about Metaverse: A Complete Survey on Technological Singularity, Virtual Ecosystem, and Research Agenda.* doi:10.13140/RG.2.2.11200.05124/8

Lepkowska-White, E., & Kortright, E. (2018). The business of blogging: Effective approaches of women food bloggers. *Journal of Foodservice Business Research*, *21*(3), 257–279. doi:10.1 080/15378020.2017.1399046

Liang, T. P., & Lai, T. P. (2000). Electronic Store Design and Consumer Choice: an Empirical Study. *Proceedings the 33rd Hawaii International Conference on System Sciences, (vol. 6,* pp. 60-42). IEEE.

Liang, T. P., & Lai, T. P. (2002). Effect of Store Design on Consumer Purchases: Van Empirical Study of Online Bookstores. *Information & Management*, *39*(6), 431–444. doi:10.1016/S0378-7206(01)00129-X

Lichtenstein, S., Burton, S., & Karson, M. J. (1993). The effect of semantic cues on consumer perceptions of reference price ads. *The Journal of Consumer Research*, *20*(4), 566–575.

Lifestyle, F. E. (2023, 06 28). Prajakta Koli to Bhuvan Bam: Here are the highest-paid Indian Influencers. *Financial Express.* https://www.financialexpress.com/lifestyle/prajakta-koli-to-bhuvan-bam-here-are-the-highest-paid-indian-influencers-know-about-their-net-worth-and-more/3145723/

Liffreing, I. (2021). What brands should know about the metaverse. *Advertising Age*, *92*(1). https://adage.com/article/digital-marketing-ad-tech-news/what-brands-should-know-about-metaverse/2354506

Li, M., Zhao, L., & Srinivas, S. (2023). It is about inclusion! Mining online reviews to understand the needs of adaptive clothing customers. *International Journal of Consumer Studies*, *47*(3), 1157–1172. doi:10.1111/ijcs.12895

Linden Lab. (2013, June 20). *Infographic: 10 Years of Second Life*. Linden Lab. https://www.lindenlab.com/releases/infographic-10-years-of-second-life

Lipsman, A., Mudd, G., Rich, M., & Bruich, S. (2012). The power of "like": How brands reach (and influence) fans through social-media marketing. *Journal of Advertising Research*, *52*(1), 40–52. doi:10.2501/JAR-52-1-040-052

Liu, F., Li, J., Mizerski, D., & Soh, H. (2012). Self-congruity, brand attitude, and brand loyalty: a study on luxury brands. *European Journal of Marketing, 46*(7/8),922e937.

Liu, H., Chu, H., Huang, Q., & Chen, X. (2016). Enhancing the flow experience of consumers in China through interpersonal interaction in social commerce. *Computers in Human Behavior*, *58*, 306–314. doi:10.1016/j.chb.2016.01.012

Liyanaarachchi, G., Mifsud, M., & Viglia, G. (2024). Virtual influencers and data privacy: Introducing the multi-privacy paradox. *Journal of Business Research*, *176*, 114584. doi:10.1016/j.jbusres.2024.114584

Lou, C. (2022). Social media influencers and followers: Theorization of a trans-parasocial relation and explication of its implications for influencer advertising. *Journal of Advertising*, *51*(1), 4–21. doi:10.1080/00913367.2021.1880345

Lu, S., & Mintz, O. (2023). Marketing on the metaverse: Research opportunities and challenges. *AMS Review*, *13*(1), 151–166. doi:10.1007/s13162-023-00255-5

Luthra, S. (2021). The Impact of Covid-19 on Consumer Perception towards Subscription Based OTT Platforms. *International Journal of Management (IJM)*, *12*(3), 537-549.

Lu, X., Liu, Z., & Yang, C. (2022, June). Research on Touchpoint Management in the Catering Industry——Taking Haidilao as an Example. In *International Conference on Human-Computer Interaction* (pp. 443-454). Cham: Springer International Publishing. 10.1007/978-3-031-05900-1_31

MacKenzie, K., Buckby, S., & Irvine, H. J. (2013). Business Research in Virtual Worlds: Possibilities and Practicalities. *Accounting, Auditing & Accountability Journal*, *26*(3), 352–373. doi:10.1108/09513571311311856

Maher, M. (2022, February 14). Why actions and behaviors — not platforms — are the metaverse's real value for brands, *MarketingDrive*, https://www.marketingdive.com/news/why-actions-and-behaviors-not-platforms-are-the-metaverses-real-value/618529/

Mandal, P. C. (2022). Generation of customer insights–roles of marketing information and marketing intelligence. *International Journal of Business and Data Analytics*, *2*(2), 111–124. doi:10.1504/IJBDA.2022.126794

Mandal, P. C. (2023). Engaging Customers and Managing Customer Relationships: Strategies and Initiatives. [JBE]. *Journal of Business Ecosystems*, *4*(1), 1–14. doi:10.4018/JBE.322405

Mandel, G. N. (2003). Gaps, inexperience, inconsistencies, and overlaps: Crisis in the regulation of genetically modified plants and animals. *SSRN*, *45*, 2167. doi:10.2139/ssrn.418221

Mangold, W. G., & Faulds, D. J. (2009). Social Media: The New Hybrid Element of the Promotion Mix. *Business Horizons*, *52*(4), 357–365. doi:10.1016/j.bushor.2009.03.002

Martínez-Navarro, J., Bigné, E., Guixeres, J., Alcañiz, M., & Torrecilla, C. (2019). The influence of virtual reality in e-commerce. *Journal of Business Research*, *100*, 475–482. doi:10.1016/j.jbusres.2018.10.054

Marwick, A. E. (2018). The algorithmic celebrity. In C. Abidin & M. L. Brown (Eds.), *Microcelebrity Around the Globe* (pp. 161–169). Emerald Publishing Limited. doi:10.1108/978-1-78756-749-820181015

Compilation of References

McCracken, G. D. (1990). *Culture and consumption: New approaches to the symbolic character of consumer goods and activities* (Vol. 1). Indiana University Press.

McKechnie, S. (1992). Consumer Buying Behaviour in Financial Services: AnOverview. *International Journal of Bank Marketing*, *10*(5), 5–39. doi:10.1108/02652329210016803

McKinsey & Company. (2022). *Value creation in the Metaverse: the real business of the virtual world*. McKinsey. https://www.mckinsey.com/business-functions/growth-marketing-and-sales/our-insights/value-creation-in-the-Metaverse

McKinsey & Company. (2022, June 1). *road to change Value creation in the Metaverse*. McKinsey & Company. https://www.mckinsey.com/capabilities/growth-marketing-and-sales/our-insights/value-creation-in-the-metaverse

McKinsey & Company. (2022a). *Value creation in the metaverse*. McKinsey & Company. https://www.mckinsey.com/business-functions/growth-marketing-and-sales/our-insights/value-creation-in-the-metaverse .

McKinsey & Company. (2022b). *Marketing in the metaverse: An opportunity for innovation and experimentation*. McKinsey & Company. https://www.mckinsey.com/business-functions/growth-marketing-and-sales/our-insights/marketing-in-the-metaverse-an-opportunity-for-innovation-and-experimentation .

Measuring customer satisfaction: Why, what and how ? (n.d.). UQ eSpace. https://espace.library.uq.edu.au/view/UQ:127560

Mediacat (n.d.). *Metaverse'ün Türkiye'deki ilk dijital otomotiv stüdyosu Ford Türkiye'den*. Mediacat. https://mediacat.com/metaverseun-turkiyedeki-ilk-dijital-otomotiv-studyosu-ford-turkiyeden/

Mengalli, N. M., & Carvalho, A. A. (2023). The Intrinsic Property of a Representation in the Phygital Transformation: A (Meta) Influence as a Force With Magnitude and Direction in the Metaverse. In S. Teixeira, S. Teixeira, Z. Oliveira, & E. Souza (Eds.), (pp. 147–162). Advances in Marketing, Customer Relationship Management, and E-Services. IGI Global. doi:10.4018/979-8-3693-0551-5.ch007

Mero, J., Vanninen, H., & Keränen, J. (2023). B2B influencer marketing: Conceptualization and four managerial strategies. *Industrial Marketing Management*, *108*, 79–93. doi:10.1016/j.indmarman.2022.10.017

Merre, R. (2022). *Security Will Make Or Break The Metaverse*. NASDAQ. https://www.nasdaq.com/articles/security-will-make-or-break-themetaverse

Metaverse – Prepare to Win . (n.d.). NASSCOM. https://www.nasscom.in/knowledge-center/publications/metaverse-prepare-win

Metaverse: The Hype Possibilities and Beyond. (2022, December). Deloitte. https://www2.deloitte.com/content/dam/Deloitte/in/Documents/technology/in-metaverse-2022-report-noexp.pdf

Metin, U. (2022, September 30). *Kiğılı Türkiye'nin ilk canlı meta defilesini gerçekleştirdi*. Pazar Lamasyon. https://www.pazarlamasyon.com/kigili-turkiye-nin-ilk-canli-meta-defilesini-gerceklestirdi

Miao, F., Kozlenkova, I. V., Wang, H., Xie, T., & Palmatier, R. W. (2022). An emerging theory of avatar marketing. *Journal of Marketing*, *86*(1), 67–90. doi:10.1177/0022242921996646

Mihaela, O. O. E. (2015). The influence of the integrated marketing communication on the consumer buying behaviour. *Procedia Economics and Finance*, *23*, 1446–1450. doi:10.1016/S2212-5671(15)00446-3

Ming, F. (2023). Total Quality Management (TQM) Influence on the Service Quality of Services Companies in China. *Journal of Digitainability* [DREAM]. *Realism & Mastery*, *2*(01), 28–33.

Mirabi, V., Akbariyeh, H., & Tahmasebifard, H. (2015). A study of factors affecting on customers purchase intention. [JMEST]. *Journal of Multidisciplinary Engineering Science and Technology*, *2*, 267–273.

Mishra, M. K., & Singh, L. (2023). Customer Empowerment, Customer Retention, and Performance of Firms: Role of Innovation and Customer Delight as Mediators Through Satisfaction. In Handbook of Research on the Interplay Between Service Quality and Customer Delight (pp. 112-132). IGI Global.

Mishra, P., & Singh, A. (2019). Impact of Transparency on Consumer Trust and Purchase Intention: The Moderating Role of Brand Commitment. *Journal of Promotion Management*, *25*(3), 336–354.

Mittal, G., & Bansal, R. (2023). Driving force behind consumer brand engagement: the metaverse. In *Cultural Marketing and Metaverse for Consumer Engagement* (pp. 164–181). IGI Global. doi:10.4018/978-1-6684-8312-1.ch012

Mollen, A., & Wilson, H. (2010). Engagement, telepresence and interactivity in online consumer experience: Reconciling scholastic and managerial perspectives. *Journal of Business Research*, *63*(9-10), 919–925. doi:10.1016/j.jbusres.2009.05.014

Moochhala, Q. (2018). The future of online OTT entertainment services in India. *Actionesque Consulting, Pune–India, 4*, 2581-5792.

Morino, N. (2022). *Metaverse: 5 questions shaping the next frontier of human experience*. EY. https://www.ey.com/en_tw/digital/metaverse-5-questions-shaping-the-next-frontier-of-human-experience

Morrison, D. G. (1979). Purchase intentions and purchase behavior. *Journal of Marketing*, *43*(2), 65–74. doi:10.1177/002224297904300207

Morrongiello, C., N'Goala, G., & Kreziak, D. (2017). Customer psychological empowerment as a critical source of customer engagement. *International Studies of Management & Organization*, *47*(1), 61–87. doi:10.1080/00208825.2017.1241089

Compilation of References

Moustakas, E., Lamba, N., Mahmoud, D., & Ranganathan, C. (2020, June). Blurring lines between fiction and reality: Perspectives of experts on marketing effectiveness of virtual influencers. In *2020 International Conference on Cyber Security and Protection of Digital Services (Cyber Security)* (pp. 1-6). IEEE. DOI: 10.1109/CyberSecurity49315.2020.9138861

Mozumder, M. A. I., Athar, A., Armand, T. P. T., Sheeraz, M. M., Uddin, S. M. I., & Kim, H. C. (2023, February). Technological roadmap of the future trend of metaverse based on IoT, blockchain, and AI techniques in metaverse education. In *2023 25th International Conference on Advanced Communication Technology (ICACT)* (pp. 1414-1423). IEEE.

Mukherjee, A., & Nath, P. (2003). A model of trust in online relationship banking. *International Journal of Bank Marketing*, *21*(1), 5–15. doi:10.1108/02652320310457767

Mukherjee, D., Debnath, R., Chakraborty, S., Jena, L. K., & Hasan, K. K. (2023). Performance Improvement in Budget Hotels Through Consumer Sentiment Analysis Using Text Mining. In *Smart Analytics, Artificial Intelligence and Sustainable Performance Management in a Global Digitalised Economy* (pp. 67–85). Emerald Publishing Limited. doi:10.1108/S1569-37592023000110A004

Mull, I., Wyss, J., Moon, E., & Lee, S. E. (2015). An exploratory study of using 3D avatars as online salespeople: The effect of avatar type on credibility, homophily, attractiveness and intention to interact. *Journal of Fashion Marketing and Management*, *19*(2), 154–168. doi:10.1108/JFMM-05-2014-0033

Mystakidis, S. (2022). Entry Metaverse. *Encyclopedia*, *2*(1), 486–497. doi:10.3390/encyclopedia2010031

Nagle, T. T., & Holden, R. K. (1994). *The strategy and tactics of pricing: A guide to growing more profitably*. Prentice Hall.

Na, H. J., Choi, S., & Kwon, O. (2019). The association of institutional information on websites with present and future financial performance. *Journal of Society for E-business Studies*, *23*(4), 63–85.

Narin, N. G. (2021). A content analysis of the metaverse articles. *Journal of Metaverse*, *1*(1), 17–24.

Neupane, R. (2014). Relationship between Customer Satisfaction and Business Performance: A Case Study of Lloyds Bank UK. *International Journal of Social Sciences and Management*, *1*(2), 74–85. doi:10.3126/ijssm.v1i2.10019

Neves, J., Bacalhau, L. M., & Santos, V. (2022, December). A Systematic Review on the Customer Journey Between Two Worlds: Reality and Immersive World. In *International Conference on Marketing and Technologies* (pp. 401-416). Singapore: Springer Nature Singapore.

Newzoo. (2021). *Introduction to the Metaverse. Trend Report 2021*. Newzoo. https://newzoo.com/insights/trend-reports/newzoo-intro-to-the-metaverse-report-2021-free-version

Ngah, A. H., Thurasamy, R., & Han, H. (2023). If you don't care, I will switch: Online retailers' behaviour on third-party logistics services. *International Journal of Physical Distribution & Logistics Management*, *53*(7/8), 813–837. doi:10.1108/IJPDLM-04-2022-0124

Ngo, M. V., & Nguyen, H. H.Tomas Bata University in Zlín. (2016). The Relationship between Service Quality, Customer Satisfaction and Customer Loyalty: An Investigation in Vietnamese Retail Banking Sector. *Journal of Competitiveness*, 8(2), 103–116. doi:10.7441/joc.2016.02.08

Nguyen. D., Pham, V., Tran, M., & Pham, D. (2020). Impact of Service Quality, Customer Satisfaction and Switching Costs on Customer Loyalty. *The Journal of Asian Finance, Economics and Business, 7*, 395–405. 10.13106/jafeb.2020.vol7.no8.395

Nigam, A., Behl, A., Pereira, V., & Sangal, S. (2023). Impulse purchases during emergency situations: Exploring permission marketing and the role of blockchain. *Industrial Management & Data Systems*, 123(1), 155–187. doi:10.1108/IMDS-12-2021-0799

Nikhashemi, S. R., Knight, H. H., Nusair, K., & Liat, C. B. (2021). Augmented reality in smart retailing: A (n)(A) Symmetric Approach to continuous intention to use retail brands' mobile AR apps. *Journal of Retailing and Consumer Services*, 60, 102464. doi:10.1016/j.jretconser.2021.102464

Nikolaou, I. (2009). Brands and consumption in virtual worlds. *Journal of Virtual Worlds Research*, 2(5), 3–15.

Nisbett, R. E., & Wilson, T. D. (1977). Telling More Than We Can Know: Verbal Reports on Mental Processes. *Psychological Review*, 84(3), 231–259. doi:10.1037/0033-295X.84.3.231

Nisbett, R. E., & Wilson, T. D. (1977). The halo effect: Evidence for unconscious alteration of judgments. *Journal of Personality and Social Psychology*, 35(4), 250–256. doi:10.1037/0022-3514.35.4.250

Nuseir, M. T., El Refae, G. A., Aljumah, A., Alshurideh, M., Urabi, S., & Kurdi, B. A. (2023). Digital Marketing Strategies and the Impact on Customer Experience: A Systematic Review. *The Effect of Information Technology on Business and Marketing Intelligence Systems*, 21-44.

Nyrhinen, J., Kemppainen, T., Grénman, M., Frank, L., Makkonen, M., & Wilska, T. A. (2021, December). Positive Online Customer Experience as an Antecedent of the Willingness to Share Information with an E-Commerce Retailer. In *European, Mediterranean, and Middle Eastern Conference on Information Systems* (pp. 376-383). Cham: Springer International Publishing.

Oetarjo, M., Rohim, D. A. G., Firdaus, V., & Togayev, S. S. (2023, May). Online Reviews and Ratings Shape Purchasing Decisions in Indonesian E-Commerce. In *International Conference on Intellectuals' Global Responsibility (ICIGR 2022)* (pp. 557-566). Atlantis Press. 10.2991/978-2-38476-052-7_61

Oey, E., Puspitasari, P. P. M., Fransiska, F., & Polla, J. R. (2023). Identifying and improving customer preferences of frozen tuna for the export market. *International Journal of Productivity and Quality Management*, 39(4), 512–535. doi:10.1504/IJPQM.2023.132831

Oh, H. (1999). Service quality, customer satisfaction, and customer value: A holistic perspective. *International Journal of Hospitality Management*, 18(1), 67–82. doi:10.1016/S0278-4319(98)00047-4

Özkan, A., & Özkan, H. (2024). Meta: XR-AR-MR and Mirror World Technologies Business Impact of Metaverse. *Journal of Metaverse*, *4*(1), 21–32.

Pandey, N., Nayal, P., & Rathore, A. S. (2020). Digital marketing for B2B organizations: Structured literature review and future research directions. *Journal of Business and Industrial Marketing*, *35*(7), 1191–1204. doi:10.1108/JBIM-06-2019-0283

Papadopoulou, P. (2007). Applying Virtual Reality for Trust-building E-commerce Environments. *Virtual Reality (Waltham Cross)*, *11*(2), 107–127. doi:10.1007/s10055-006-0059-x

Papagiannidis, S., & Bourlakis, M. (2010). Staging the New Retail Drama: At a Metaverse Near You! *Journal of Virtual Worlds Research*, *2*(5). doi:10.4101/jvwr.v2i5.808

Papagiannidis, S., Pantano, E., See-To, E. W. K., & Bourlakis, M. (2013). Modelling the Determinants of a Simulated Experience in a Virtual Retail Store and Users' Product Purchasing Intentions. *Journal of Marketing Management*, *29*(13-14), 1462–1492. doi:10.1080/026725 7X.2013.821150

Park, S., & Kwon, Y. (2019). *Research on the Relationship between the Growth of OTT Service Market and the Change in the Structure of the Pay-TV Market*.

Park, J., Stoel, L., & Lennon, S. J. (2008). Cognitive, Affective and Cognitive Responses to Visual Simulation: The Effects of Rotation in Online Product Presentation. *Journal of Consumer Behaviour*, *7*(1), 72–87. doi:10.1002/cb.237

Park, S. M., & Kim, Y. G. (2022). Metaverse: Taxonomy, components, applications, and open Challenge. *IEEE Access : Practical Innovations, Open Solutions*, *10*, 4209–4425. doi:10.1109/ACCESS.2021.3140175

Park, S. R., Nah, F. F., & Dewester, D., & Eschenbrenner. (2008). Virtual World Affordances: Enhancing Brand Value. *Journal of Virtual Worlds Research*, *1*(2), 1–18.

Patikar, E. T. D. G., & Thangasamy, E. (2014). Factors influencing consumer buying behaviour: a case study. *Global Journal of Management and Business Research: E Marketing, 14*(5).

Payal, R., Sharma, N., & Dwivedi, Y. K. (2024). Unlocking the impact of brand engagement in the metaverse on Real-World purchase intentions: Analyzing Pre-Adoption behavior in a futuristic technology platform. *Electronic Commerce Research and Applications*, *65*, 101381. doi:10.1016/j.elerap.2024.101381

Pessala, I. (2016). *User experiences and efficiency of Instagram Advertising*.

Piller, F. T., & Walcher, D. (2006). Toolkits for idea competitions: A novel method to integrate users in new product development. *R & D Management*, *36*(3), 307–318. doi:10.1111/j.1467-9310.2006.00432.x

Platforms/Players in Anand City. (2020). Gujarat, India. Asian Journal of Agricultural Extension. *Economia e Sociologia*, *40*(12), 254–264.

Plotkina, D., & Saurel, H. (2019). Me or just like me? The role of virtual try-on and physical appearance in apparel M-retailing. *Journal of Retailing and Consumer Services*, *51*, 362–377. doi:10.1016/j.jretconser.2019.07.002

Ponathil, A., Bhanu, A., Piratla, K., Sharma, V., & Chalil Madathil, K. (2022). Investigation of the factors influencing the online consumer's choice of a service provider for home improvement. *Electronic Commerce Research*, 1–28. doi:10.1007/s10660-022-09621-0

Ponzoa, J. M., & Erdmann, A. (2021). E-commerce customer attraction: Digital marketing techniques, evolution and dynamics across firms. *Journal of Promotion Management*, *27*(5), 697–715. doi:10.1080/10496491.2021.1880521

Pradhan, D., Kuanr, A., Anupurba Pahi, S., & Akram, M. S. (2023). Influencer marketing: When and why gen Z consumers avoid influencers and endorsed brands. *Psychology and Marketing*, *40*(1), 27–47. doi:10.1002/mar.21749

Prahalad, C. K., & Ramaswamy, V. (2004). Co-creation experiences: The next practice in value creation. *Journal of Interactive Marketing*, *18*(3), 5–14. doi:10.1002/dir.20015

Pulizzi, J., & Barrett, N. (2008). *Get Content Get Customers: Turn Prospects into Buyers with Content Marketing*. McGraw-Hill.

Pulles, N. J., Schiele, H., Veldman, J., & Hüttinger, L. (2016). The impact of customer attractiveness and supplier satisfaction on becoming a preferred customer. *Industrial Marketing Management*, *54*, 129–140. doi:10.1016/j.indmarman.2015.06.004

Puthiyakath, H. H., & Goswami, M. P. (2021). Is over the top video platform the game changer over traditional TV channels in India? A niche analysis. *Asia Pacific Media Educator, 31*(1), 133-150.

PwC 2022 US Metaverse Survey. (n.d.). PwC. https://www.pwc.com/us/en/tech-effect/emerging-tech/metaverse-survey.html

Ramadan, Z. (2023). Marketing in the metaverse era: Toward an integrative channel approach. *Virtual Reality (Waltham Cross)*, *27*(3), 1905–1918. doi:10.1007/s10055-023-00783-2 PMID:37360809

Ramadan, Z. B., & Farah, M. F. (2020). Influencing the influencers: The case of retailers' social shopping platforms. *International Journal of Web Based Communities*, *16*(3), 279–295. doi:10.1504/IJWBC.2020.108626

Ramya, N. A. S. A. M., & Ali, S. M. (2016). Factors affecting consumer buying behavior. *International Journal of Applied Research*, *2*(10), 76–80.

Rao, B., & Minakakis, L. (2003). Evolution of mobile location-based services. *Com-munications of the ACM, 46*(12), 61e65.

Rathore, B. (2018). Metaverse marketing: Novel challenges, opportunities, and strategic approaches. *Eduzone: International Peer Reviewed/Refereed Multidisciplinary Journal, 7*(2), 72-82.

Rauschnabel, P. A., Babin, B. J., tom Dieck, M. C., Krey, N., & Jung, T. (2022). What is augmented reality marketing? Its definition, complexity, and future. *Journal of Business Research*, *142*, 1140–1150. doi:10.1016/j.jbusres.2021.12.084

Rauschnabel, P. A., Felix, R., & Hinsch, C. (2019). Augmented reality marketing: How mobile AR-apps can improve brands through inspiration. *Journal of Retailing and Consumer Services*, *49*, 43–53. doi:10.1016/j.jretconser.2019.03.004

Reimer, T. (2023). Environmental factors to maximize social media engagement: A comprehensive framework. *Journal of Retailing and Consumer Services*, *75*, 103458. doi:10.1016/j.jretconser.2023.103458

Rese, A., Baier, D., Geyer-Schulz, A., & Schreiber, S. (2017). How augmented reality apps are accepted by consumers: A comparative analysis using scales and opinions. *Technological Forecasting and Social Change*, *124*, 306–319. doi:10.1016/j.techfore.2016.10.010

Riva, G., Wiederhold, B. K., & Mantovani, F. (2024). Searching for the metaverse: Neuroscience of physical and digital communities. *Cyberpsychology, Behavior, and Social Networking*, *27*(1), 9–18. doi:10.1089/cyber.2023.0040 PMID:37057986

Rixom, J. M., & Rixom, B. A. (2023). Perceived brand authenticity: Examining the effects of inferred dedication and anticipated quality on consumers' purchase intentions and actual choices. *Journal of Consumer Behaviour*, *22*(3), 721–737. doi:10.1002/cb.2156

Robinson, B. (2020). Towards an Ontology and Ethics of Virtual Influencers. *AJIS. Australasian Journal of Information Systems*, *23*, 333–345. doi:10.3127/ajis.v24i0.2807

Rodriguez, P. R. (2017). *Effectiveness of YouTube advertising: A study of audience analysis.* Rochester Institute of Technology.

Rogers, E. (2023). Impossible Foods: Growing the Plant-Based Meat Sector at Home and Abroad. *Journal for Global Business and Community*, *14*(1). doi:10.56020/001c.71493

Roh, M. H., Oh, W. Y., & Shin, D. (2003). The Discount Heuristic: Simple Arithmetic vs. Complex Information in Making Numerical Estimates. *JMR, Journal of Marketing Research*, *40*(4), 399–414.

Saffari, F., Kakaria, S., Bigné, E., Bruni, L. E., Zarei, S., & Ramsøy, T. Z. (2023). Motivation in the metaverse: A dual-process approach to consumer choices in a virtual reality supermarket. *Frontiers in Neuroscience*, *17*, 1062980. doi:10.3389/fnins.2023.1062980 PMID:36875641

Samriti, D., & Sharma, P. (2020). OTT-existing censorship laws and recommendations. Available at SSRN 3735027. http://dspace.christcollegeijk.edu.in:8080/jspui/bitstream/123456789/1043/24/CC AS BCM023.pdf

Sandhusen, R. (2008). *Marketing.* Barrons.

Sands, S., Campbell, C., Plangger, K., & Ferraro, C. (2022). Unreal influence: Leveraging AI in influencer marketing. *European Journal of Marketing*, *56*(6), 1721–1747. doi:10.1108/EJM-12-2019-0949

Sands, S., Ferraro, C., Demsar, V., & Chandler, G. (2022). False idols: Unpacking the opportunities and challenges of falsity in the context of virtual influencers. *Business Horizons*, *65*(6), 777–788. doi:10.1016/j.bushor.2022.08.002

Sangroya, D., & Nayak, J. K. (2017). Factors influencing buying behaviour of green energy consumer. *Journal of Cleaner Production*, *151*, 393–405. doi:10.1016/j.jclepro.2017.03.010

Sangroya, D., Yadav, R., & Joshi, Y. (2021). Does gamified interaction build a strong consumer-brand connection? A study of mobile applications. *AJIS. Australasian Journal of Information Systems*, *25*, 25. doi:10.3127/ajis.v25i0.3105

SanMiguel, P., Sádaba, T., & Sayeed, N. (2024). Fashion brands in the metaverse: Achievements from a marketing perspective. *Journal of Global Fashion Marketing*, 1-21.

Sann, R., & Lai, P. C. (2023). Topic modeling of the quality of guest's experience using latent Dirichlet allocation: Western versus eastern perspectives. *Consumer Behavior in Tourism and Hospitality*, *18*(1), 17–34. doi:10.1108/CBTH-04-2022-0084

Schall, J. D. (2001). Neural basis of deciding, choosing and acting. *Nature Reviews. Neuroscience*, *2*(1), 33–42. doi:10.1038/35049054 PMID:11253357

Schiele, H., Calvi, R., & Gibbert, M. (2012). Customer attractiveness, supplier satisfaction and preferred customer status: Introduction, definitions and an overarching framework. *Industrial Marketing Management*, *41*(8), 1178–1185. doi:10.1016/j.indmarman.2012.10.002

Schindler, R. M. (1989). The excitement of getting a bargain: Some hypotheses concerning the origins and effects of smart-shopper feelings. *Advances in Consumer Research. Association for Consumer Research (U. S.)*, *16*(1), 447–453.

Schindler, R. M. (1989). The psychology of pricing. *Psychology and Marketing*, *6*(4), 307–324.

Seaborn, K., & Fels, D. I. (2015). Gamification in theory and action: A survey. *International Journal of Human-Computer Studies*, *74*, 14–31. doi:10.1016/j.ijhcs.2014.09.006

Seok, W. H. (2021). Analysis of metaverse business model and ecosystem. *Electronics and Telecommunications Trends*, *36*(4), 81–91.

Shah, D., & Murthi, B. P. S. (2021). Marketing in a data-driven digital world: Implications for the role and scope of marketing. *Journal of Business Research*, *125*(March), 772–779. doi:10.1016/j.jbusres.2020.06.062

Sharma, W., Lim, W. M., Kumar, S., Verma, A., & Kumra, R. (2024). Game on! A state-of-the-art overview of doing business with gamification. *Technological Forecasting and Social Change*, *198*, 122988. doi:10.1016/j.techfore.2023.122988

Shavkatovna, R. D. (2023). A new tendency of Virtual Economics and its influence on the social life. *Scientific Impulse, 15*(100). http://nauchniyimpuls.ru/index.php/ni/article/download/12940/8928

Shen, B., Tan, W., Guo, J., Cai, H., Wang, B., & Zhuo, S. (2020). A Study on Design Requirement Development and Satisfaction for Future Virtual World Systems. *Future Internet, 12*(7), 112. doi:10.3390/fi12070112

Shen, B., Tan, W., Guo, J., Zhao, L., & Qin, P. (2021). How to promote user purchase in metaverse? A systematic literature review on consumer behavior research and virtual commerce application design. *Applied Sciences (Basel, Switzerland), 11*(23), 11087. doi:10.3390/app112311087

Shen, P., Wan, D., & Li, J. (2023). How human–computer interaction perception affects consumer well-being in the context of online retail: From the perspective of autonomy. *Nankai Business Review International, 14*(1), 102–127. doi:10.1108/NBRI-03-2022-0034

Sheper, A., & Speros, W. (2022). *The hotel industry enters the Metaverse*. Hospitality Design. https://hospitalitydesign.com/news/development-destinations/hotel-industry-nfts-metaverse/

Shevlin, R. (2022). JP Morgan opens a bank branch in the metaverse. *Forbes*. https://www.forbes.com/sites/ronshevlin/2022/02/16/jpmorgan-opens-a-bank-branch-in-the-metaverse-but-its-not-for-what-you-think-its-for/?sh=9e1cf2c158d3

Shi, F., Ning, H., Zhang, X., Li, R., Tian, Q., Zhang, S., Zheng, Y., Guo, Y., & Daneshmand, M. (2023). A new technology perspective of the Metaverse: Its essence, framework and challenges. *Digital Communications and Networks*. https://doi.org/https://doi.org/10.1016/j.dcan.2023.02.017

Shi, H., Liu, G., Zhang, K., Zhou, Z., & Wang, J. (2022). Marl sim2real transfer: Merging physical reality with digital virtuality in metaverse. *IEEE Transactions on Systems, Man, and Cybernetics. Systems, 53*(4), 2107–2117. doi:10.1109/TSMC.2022.3229213

Shi, X., & Chen, Z. (2021). Listening to your employees: Analyzing opinions from online reviews of hotel companies. *International Journal of Contemporary Hospitality Management, 33*(6), 2091–2116. doi:10.1108/IJCHM-06-2020-0576

Siby, A., & George, J. P. (2022). Influence of customer relationship management for the success of E-business. In Information and Communication Technology for Competitive Strategies (ICTCS 2020) ICT: Applications and Social Interfaces (pp. 473-481). Springer Singapore. doi:10.1007/978-981-16-0739-4_45

Singh, A., Sharma, S., Singh, A., Unanoglu, M., & Taneja, S. (Eds.). (2023). *Cultural marketing and metaverse for consumer engagement*. IGI Global. doi:10.4018/978-1-6684-8312-1

Singla, B., Shalender, K., & Singh, N. (Eds.). (2024). *Omnichannel Approach to Co-Creating Customer Experiences Through Metaverse Platforms*. IGI Global. doi:10.4018/979-8-3693-1866-9

Sivadas, E., & Baker-Prewitt, J. L. (2000). An examination of the relationship between service quality, customer satisfaction, and store loyalty. *International Journal of Retail & Distribution Management, 28*(2), 73–82. doi:10.1108/09590550010315223

Smart, J., Cascio, J., & Paffendorf, J. (2007). *Pathways to the 3D Web: A cross-industry public foresight Project*. Metaverse Roadmap. https://www.metaverseroadmap.org/MetaverseRoadmapOverview.pdf

Smink, A. R., Frowijn, S., van Reijmersdal, E. A., van Noort, G., & Neijens, P. C. (2019). Try online before you buy: How does shopping with augmented reality affect brand responses and personal data disclosure. Electronic Commerce Research and Applications, 35, 100854.

Smith, A. N., & Chaffey, D. (2005). *E-Marketing Excellence: Planning and Optimizing your Digital Marketing*. Butterworth-Heinemann.

Smith, R. (2012). Psychological Pricing: A Strategy for Maximizing Revenue. *Entrepreneurship & Organization Management, 1*(2), 1–2.

Smith, T. A. (2022). A Qualitative Inquiry into Marketing Effectiveness of SMEs. In *Marketing Effectiveness and Accountability in SMEs: A Multimethodological Approach* (pp. 81–106). Springer International Publishing. doi:10.1007/978-3-031-09861-1_4

Smith, W. K., & Zook, M. A. (2011). *The Wealth of Networks: How Social Production Transforms Markets and Freedom*. Yale University Press.

Statista. (2023). *Value of influencer marketing industry in India from 2021 to 2022, with projections until 2026*. Statista. https://www.statista.com: https://www.statista.com/statistics/1294803/india-influencer-marketing-industry-value/

Stefanic, D. (2022). *Gamification for Metaverse events: The ultimate guide + 8 examples*. Mootup. https://mootup.com/gamification-for-metaverse-eventsthe-ultimate-guide-8-examples/

Stephenson, N. (1992). *Snow Crash*. Bantam Books.

Suchánek, P., & Králová, M. (2015). Effect of Customer Satisfaction on Company Performance. *Acta Universitatis Agriculturae et Silviculturae Mendelianae Brunensis, 63*(3), 1013–1021. doi:10.11118/actaun201563031013

Suh, K. S., & Lee, Y. E. (2005). The effects of virtual reality on consumer learning: An empirical investigation. *Management Information Systems Quarterly, 29*(4), 673–697. doi:10.2307/25148705

Sullivan, M. (2021). *What the metaverse will (and won't) be, according to 28 experts*. FastCompany. https://www.fastcompany.com/90678442/what-is-the-metaverse

Sunny, E. E., & Anael, O. (2016). Mobile marketing in a digital age: Application, challenges & opportunities. *British Journal of Economics. Management & Trade, 11*(1), 1–13.

Sveder, M., & Lundbäck, E. (2023). *Gamification within the Metaverse: A quantitative study to understand how consumer engagement is influenced by gamification strategies in the Metaverse.*

Tan, E., Cherapanukorn, V., Kim, H. H., & Chon, K. (2014). The art of service in Asia: A conceptual framework through a case study of hospitality industry in Thailand. In *Proceedings of the Global Tourism and Hospitality Conference and 11th Asia Tourism Forum* (pp. 1217-1244). Research Gate.

Taneja, S., & Shukla, R. P. (2024). Omnichannel Retailing: A Comprehensive Exploration of Integration, Customer Engagement, and Market Share in Today's Retail. In Omnichannel Approach to Co-Creating Customer Experiences Through Metaverse Platforms (pp. 60-76). IGI Global.

Taneja, N. K. (2016). *The Passenger Has Gone Digital and Mobile: Accessing and Connecting Through Information and Technology*. Routledge. doi:10.4324/9781315554792

Tang, Y., & Chan, E. Y. (2023). Name reminders and customization preferences: The role of perceived control. *International Journal of Hospitality Management*, *109*, 103425. doi:10.1016/j.ijhm.2022.103425

Tariq, M. U. (2024). Metaverse in Business and Commerce. In *Exploring the Use of Metaverse in Business and Education* (pp. 47–72). IGI Global. doi:10.4018/979-8-3693-5868-9.ch004

Tarnanidis, T. K. (Ed.). (2024). *Consumer Experience and Decision-Making in the Metaverse*. IGI Global.

Tarnanidis, T. K., & Sklavounos, N. (Eds.). (2024). *New Trends in Marketing and Consumer Science*. IGI Global. doi:10.4018/979-8-3693-2754-8

Tarnanidis, T., & Manaf, A. H. (2024). Research Notes on the Future of Marketing and Consumer Insights. In T. Tarnanidis & N. Sklavounos (Eds.), *New Trends in Marketing and Consumer Science* (pp. 324–336). IGI Global. doi:10.4018/979-8-3693-2754-8.ch017

Tarnanidis, T., Papathanasiou, J., Mareschal, B., & Vlachopoulou, M. (2025). MCDM Review in marketing and managerial decisions: Practical implications and Future research. *Management Science Letters*, *15*(1), 45–54. doi:10.5267/j.msl.2024.3.004

Tarnanidis, T., Papathanasiou, J., Vlachopoulou, M., & Mareschal, B. (2023). Review and the Use of PROMETHEE Methods in Marketing (Problems). In T. Tarnanidis, M. Vlachopoulou, & J. Papathanasiou (Eds.), *Influences of Social Media on Consumer Decision-Making Processes in the Food and Grocery Industry* (pp. 196–212). IGI Global. doi:10.4018/978-1-6684-8868-3.ch009

Tayal, S., Rajagopal, K., & Mahajan, V. (2022, March). Virtual reality based metaverse of gamification. In *2022 6th International Conference on Computing Methodologies and Communication (ICCMC)* (pp. 1597-1604). IEEE. https://egitimkatalogu.tbb.org.tr/Seminer/Detay/2372/9436/metaverse-hukuku.

Teoh, K. K., & Cyril, E. U. (2008). The role of presence and para social presence on trust in online virtual electronic commerce. *Journal of Applied Sciences (Faisalabad)*, *8*(16), 2834–2842. doi:10.3923/jas.2008.2834.2842

Thaichon, P., Surachartkumtonkun, J., Quach, S., Weaven, S., & Palmatier, R. W. (2018). Hybrid sales structures in the age of e-commerce. *Journal of Personal Selling & Sales Management*, *38*(3), 277–302. doi:10.1080/08853134.2018.1441718

Thakur, A. (2022). Technological Innovations in the Hospitality and Tourism Industry. In *Mobile Computing and Technology Applications in Tourism and Hospitality* (pp. 72–97). IGI Global. doi:10.4018/978-1-7998-6904-7.ch004

The Verge. (2021). Mark in the Metaverse. *The Verge.* https://www.theverge.com/22588022/mark-zuckerberg-facebook-ceo-metaverse-interview

Thomas, M., & Morwitz, V. G. (2005). Penny Wise and Pound Foolish: The Left-Digit Effect in Price Cognition. *The Journal of Consumer Research*, *32*(1), 54–64. doi:10.1086/429600

Thompson, W. (2021). *Into the metaverse.* Wunderman Thompson. https://www.wundermanthompson.com/insight/new-trend-report-into-the-metaverse

Thompson, W. (2022). *New realities: Into the metaverse and beyond.* Wunderman Thompson. https://www.wundermanthompson.com/pt/insight/new-realities-into-the-metaverse-and-beyond

Tiffany, L. (2007, January 9). *Starting a Second Life Business.* Entrepreneur.

Tobias-Mamina, R. J., Kempen, E., Chinomona, R., & Sly, M. (2020). The influence of instagram advertising on destination visit intention. *African Journal of Hospitality, Tourism and Leisure*, *9*(3), 274–287. doi:10.46222/ajhtl.19770720-18

Trendhunter. (2022). *Trend Report 2022.* Trendhunter. https://www.trendhunter.com/trends/2022-trend-report

Tsimonis, G., & Dimitriadis, S. (2014). *Brand strategies in social media.* Marketing. doi:10.1108/MIP-04-2013-0056

Turkyilmaz, F. (2023, January 6). *Yüzü aşkın eserin sergileneceği "NFT Biennial" Zorlu PSM'de başladı.* AA. https://www.aa.com.tr/tr/kultur/yuzu-askin-eserin-sergilenecegi-nft-biennial-zorlu-psmde-basladi/2781618

Tversky, A., & Kahneman, D. (1974). Judgment under uncertainty: Heuristics and biases. *Science*, *185*(4157), 1124–1131. doi:10.1126/science.185.4157.1124 PMID:17835457

Uusitalo, K., Hakala, H., & Kautonen, T. (2011). Customer complaints as a source of customer-focused process improvement: A constructive case study. *Operations Management: A Modern Approach, 29*(2), 107-133.

Vahoniya, D. R., Darji, D. R., Baruri, S., & Halpati, J. R. (2022). Awareness, Preferences, Perception, and Satisfaction about the Over-The-Top (OTT) Platforms/Players in Anand City, Gujarat, India. *Asian Journal of Agricultural Extension, Economics & Sociology, 40*(12), 254-264.

Value creation in the metaverse . (2022, June). McKinsey. https://www.mckinsey.com/~/media/mckinsey/business%20functions/marketing%20and%20sales/our%20insights/value%20creation%20in%20the%20metaverse/Value-creation-in-the-metaverse.pdf

Van Kerrebroeck, H., Brengman, M., & Willems, K. (2017). When brands come to life: Experimental research on the vividness effect of Virtual Reality in transformational marketing communications. *Virtual Reality (Waltham Cross)*, *21*(4), 177–191. doi:10.1007/s10055-017-0306-3

Vanwesenbeeck, I., Hudders, L., & Ponnet, K. (2020). Understanding the YouTube generation: How preschoolers process television and YouTube advertising. *Cyberpsychology, Behavior, and Social Networking*, *23*(6), 426–432. doi:10.1089/cyber.2019.0488 PMID:32320269

Vargo, L. (2022). *Council post: How the metaverse is shaping consumer behavior*. Forbes Business Development Council. com/sites/forbesbusinessdevelopmentcouncil/2022/07/05/how-the- metaverse-is-shaping-consumer-behavior/?sh=572c5c493079 Accessed 4 July 2023.

Veal, A. J. (2017). *Research methods for leisure and tourism*.

Veloutsou, C., & Guzman, F. (2017). The evolution of brand management thinking over the last 25 years as recorded in the Journal of Product and Brand Management. *Journal of Product and Brand Management*, *26*(1), 2–12. doi:10.1108/JPBM-01-2017-1398

Venetis, K., & Ghauri, P. (2004). *Service Quality and Customer Retention: Building Long-Term Relationships* (SSRN Scholarly Paper 2844589). https://papers.ssrn.com/abstract=2844589 doi:10.1108/03090560410560254

Venkatesh, V., Morris, M. G., Davis, G. B., & Davis, F. D. (2003). User acceptance of information technology: Toward a unified view. *Management Information Systems Quarterly*, *27*(3), 425–478. doi:10.2307/30036540

Verhoef, P. C., & Lemon, K. N. (2013). Successful customer value management: Key lessons and emerging trends. *European Management Journal*, *31*(1), 1–15. doi:10.1016/j.emj.2012.08.001

Vigneron, F., & Johnson, L. W. (2004). Measuring perceptions of brand luxury. *Journal of Brand Management*, *11*(6), 484–506. doi:10.1057/palgrave.bm.2540194

Von Hippel, E. (1986). Lead users: A source of novel product concepts. *Management Science*, *32*(7), 791–805. doi:10.1287/mnsc.32.7.791

Vrontis, D., Makrides, A., Christofi, M., & Thrassou, A. (2021). Social media influencer marketing: A systematic review, integrative framework and future research agenda. *International Journal of Consumer Studies*, *45*(4), 617–644. doi:10.1111/ijcs.12647

Vukmir, R. B. (2006). Customer satisfaction. *International Journal of Health Care Quality Assurance Incorporating Leadership in Health Services*, *19*(1), 8–31. doi:10.1108/09526860610642573 PMID:16548396

Wang, X., & Karmina, N. (2023, February). *Theoretical Approaches to the Concept of Marketing Strategies.* In 4th International Conference on Economic Management and Model Engineering, ICEMME 2022, November 18-20, 2022, Nanjing, China. 10.4108/eai.18-11-2022.2327135

Wang, J. (2021). Genre change in the online context: Responding to negative online reviews and redefining an effective genre construct on Amazon. Com. *Journal of Business and Technical Communication, 35*(3), 297–332. doi:10.1177/10506519211001113

Wang, J., Lai, J. Y., & Lin, Y. H. (2023). Social media analytics for mining customer complaints to explore product opportunities. *Computers & Industrial Engineering, 178,* 109104. doi:10.1016/j. cie.2023.109104

Wang, K. L., & Groth, M. (2014). Buffering the negative effects of employee surface acting: The moderating role of employee–customer relationship strength and personalized services. *The Journal of Applied Psychology, 99*(2), 341–350. doi:10.1037/a0034428 PMID:24079672

Wanick, V., & Stallwood, J. (2023). Brand storytelling, gamification and social media marketing in the "metaverse": A case study of the Ralph Lauren winter escape. In *Reinventing fashion retailing: Digitalising, gamifying, entrepreneuring* (pp. 35–54). Springer International Publishing. doi:10.1007/978-3-031-11185-3_3

Warden, C. A., Chen, J. F., & Yen, W. H. (2024). Metaverse Servicescape: Emotional Response to Virtual Retail Design. *International Journal of Human-Computer Interaction,* 1–14. doi:10. 1080/10447318.2024.2322200

Wardhani, P. K., & Alif, M. G. (2019, October). The effect of advertising exposure on attitude toward the advertising and the brand and purchase intention in Instagram. In *3rd Asia-Pacific Research in Social Sciences and Humanities Universitas Indonesia Conference (APRISH 2018)* (pp. 196-204). Atlantis Press. 10.2991/aprish-18.2019.24

What is the metaverse ? (2024). Accenture. https://www.accenture.com/in-en/insights/metaverse

Wicaksono, Y. M., & Utami, C. W. (n.d.). *THE EFFECT OF SERVICE QUALITY AND FOOD QUALITY ON CUSTOMER SATISFACTION AND CUSTOMER RETENTION AT PRIDE COFFEE AND KITCHEN.* Semantic Scholar.

Williams, P., & Naumann, E. (2011). Customer satisfaction and business performance: A firm-level analysis. *Journal of Services Marketing, 25*(1), 1. doi:10.1108/08876041111107032

Wirtz, B. W., Schilke, O., & Ullrich, S. (2010). Strategic development of business models: Implications of the Web 2.0 for creating value on the internet. *Long Range Planning, 43*(2–3), 272–290. doi:10.1016/j.lrp.2010.01.005

Wong, Q. (**2022**). Shopping in the Metaverse could be more fun than you think. Cnet. https://www. cnet.com/tech/computing/features/shopping-in-the-metaversecould-be-more-fun-than-you-think/

Wongkitrungrueng, A., & Suprawan, L. (2023). Metaverse meets branding: Examining consumer responses to immersive brand experiences. *International Journal of Human-Computer Interaction,* 1–20. doi:10.1080/10447318.2023.2175162

World Economic Forum. (2024) *Navigating the Industrial Metaverse: A Blueprint for Future Innovations*. WEF. https://www3.weforum.org/docs/WEF_Navigating_the_Industrial_Metaverse_A_Blueprint_2024.pdf

Wu, S.-I. (2006). The impact of feeling, judgment and attitude on Purchase intention as online advertising performance measure. *Journal of International Marketing & Marketing Research, 31*(2), 89e108.

Wu, K. (2016). YouTube marketing: Legality of sponsorship and endorsements in advertising. *JL Bus. & Ethics*, *22*, 59.

Wulandari, L. P. A., & Darma, G. S. (2020). Advertising effectiveness in purchasing decision on Instagram. *Journal of Business on Hospitality and Tourism*, *6*(2), 381–389. doi:10.22334/jbhost.v6i2.220

Wunderman Thompson Intelligence. (2021). *Into the Metaverse*. WTI. https://www.wundermanthompson.com/insight/new-trend-report-into-the-metaverse

Yadav, M., Joshi, Y., & Rahman, Z. (2015). Mobile social media: The new hybrid element of digital marketing communications. *Procedia: Social and Behavioral Sciences*, *189*, 335–343. doi:10.1016/j.sbspro.2015.03.229

Yang, S., Li, T., Chen, S., & Li, B. (2020). When and why do negative reviews have positive effects? An empirical study on the movie industry. *Nankai Business Review International*, *11*(1), 87–101. doi:10.1108/NBRI-11-2018-0063

Yang, T., Wu, J., & Zhang, J. (2023). Knowing how satisfied/dissatisfied is far from enough: A comprehensive customer satisfaction analysis framework based on hybrid text mining techniques. *International Journal of Contemporary Hospitality Management*, *36*(3), 873–892. doi:10.1108/IJCHM-10-2022-1319

Yang, Y., Wang, Y., & Zhao, J. (2023). Effect of user-generated image on review helpfulness: Perspectives from object detection. *Electronic Commerce Research and Applications*, *57*, 101232. doi:10.1016/j.elerap.2022.101232

Yao, Q. (2023). When in Rome, Do as the Romans Do: Differences of Interactive Behaviors Across Social Media Networks. In *The Palgrave Handbook of Interactive Marketing* (pp. 451–473). Springer International Publishing. doi:10.1007/978-3-031-14961-0_20

Yildiz, G. (2022, January 27). *İş Bankası'nın reklamları Metaverse'te*. MarketingTürkiye. https://www.marketingturkiye.com.tr/kampanyalar/is-bankasi-roblox/

Yim, M. Y. C., Chu, S. C., & Sauer, P. L. (2017). Is augmented reality technology an effective tool for e-commerce? An interactivity and vividness perspective. *Journal of Interactive Marketing*, *39*, 89–103. doi:10.1016/j.intmar.2017.04.001

Yin Wong, H., & Merrilees, B. (2008). The performance benefits of being brand-orientated. *Journal of Product and Brand Management*, *17*(6), 372–383. doi:10.1108/10610420810904112

Yoo, K., Welden, R., Hewett, K., & Haenlein, M. (2023). The merchants of meta: A research agenda to understand the future of retailing in the metaverse. *Journal of Retailing*. https://doi.org/https://doi.org/10.1016/j.jretai.2023.02.002

Yoo, K., Welden, R., Hewett, K., & Haenlein, M. (2023). The merchants of meta: A research agenda to understand the future of retailing in the metaverse. *Journal of Retailing*, *99*(2), 173–192. doi:10.1016/j.jretai.2023.02.002

Yousaf, A., Mishra, A., Taheri, B., & Kesgin, M. (2021). A cross-country analysis of the determinants of customer recommendation intentions for over-the-top (OTT) platforms. *Information & Management, 58*(8), 103543.

You, Y., He, Y., Chen, Q., & Hu, M. (2021). The interplay between brand relationship norms and ease of sharing on electronic word-of-mouth and willingness to pay. *Information & Management*, *58*(2), 103410. doi:10.1016/j.im.2020.103410

Yurduneri, D. (2022, November 8). Halkbank, yerli metaverse GoArt'ta şube açtı. *Coin Telegraph*. https://tr.cointelegraph.com/news/halkbank-partners-with-turkish-metaverse-goart

Zarantonello, L., & Schmitt, B. H. (2023). Experiential AR/VR: A consumer and service framework and research agenda. *Journal of Service Management*, *34*(1), 34–55. doi:10.1108/JOSM-12-2021-0479

Zhang, J., & Krishna, A. (2009). The comprehensive assortment-as-variety hypothesis: How the interplay of per-option and per-category assortment influences perceived variety and choice. *The Journal of Consumer Research*, *36*(6), 1006–1020.

Zhang, K. Z., & Benyoucef, M. (2016). Consumer behavior in social commerce: A literature review. *Decision Support Systems*, *86*, 95–108. doi:10.1016/j.dss.2016.04.001

Zhang, S., & Krishna, A. (2009). The Effect of Decoy Pricing on Consumer Choice: Understanding When a "Low-Price" Option Serves as a "Dominated Alternative.". *JMR, Journal of Marketing Research*, *46*(6), 767–779.

Zhang, Y., Lu, X., & Prombutr, W. (2022). The asymmetric online talk effect. *Review of Behavioral Finance*, *14*(2), 157–182. doi:10.1108/RBF-05-2020-0117

Zhou, Y., Ahmad, Z., Alsuhabi, H., Yusuf, M., Alkhairy, I., & Sharawy, A. M. (2021). Impact of YouTube Advertising on Sales with Regression Analysis and Statistical Modeling: Usefulness of Online Media in Business. *Computational Intelligence and Neuroscience*, *2021*, 2021. doi:10.1155/2021/9863155 PMID:34539772

About the Contributors

Theodore Tarnanidis is a marketing scholar, adjunct professor at the International Hellenic University and researcher in Applications of D.Sc. and MCDA. Theodore has six years experience as a marketing and decision making practitioner. He made his post-doc research in the area of sustainable entrepreneurship from the University of Macedonia. He obtained a Ph.D. from the University of London Met., UK. He received his M.B.A from Liverpool University, UK and is a graduate from the University of Macedonia (Business Administration) and Alexander Technological Educational Institute (Marketing). His research focuses on International Marketing, Multi-cultural Marketing, Marketing Management, Consumer Science by Means of Rank-Coded Data, Preference Measurement Techniques, Quantitative Methods & Structural Equation Modelling. His work has been published in various internationally renowned scientific conferences (Academy of Marketing, European Marketing Academy, PROMETHEE Days, Hellenic Operational Research) and in journals (Journal of Business Ethics, World Review of Entrepreneurship, Management and Sustainable Development, Journal of Retailing and Consumer Services, Current Issues in Tourism, Marketing Science & Inspirations, Management Science Letters).

***

Karan Anand, a student at Christ University's School of Business and Management, brings a unique blend of creativity and analytical prowess to the study of OTT platform consumption. His fascination with the entertainment industry is interwoven with a keen interest in business trends. This research project allowed him to explore this intersection, leveraging his analytical skills honed through his business studies to dissect user behavior and content preferences within the OTT ecosystem.

Babita is a faculty member in Finance and Accounts at CHRIST (Deemed to be University). She is NET/JRF qualified and completed her Ph.D. at Guru Jambeshwar University of Science and Technology, Hisar. She holds a Master's degree in Finance and HR, and a Bachelor's in Business Administration from MDU Rohtak.

Currently, she is an Assistant Professor at CHRIST (Deemed to be University). Previously, she was associated with JC Bose University of Science and Technology, YMCA (Faridabad). She also has two years of corporate experience. Her research interests include economic growth, corporate finance, and international trade. Dr. Babita has published in SAGE, Inderscience, and Bloomsbury. She has presented at various national and international conferences and has attended over 20 FDPs.

Divya Bansal is working as an Assistant Professor, Management at Amity University. Have published various articles, books and book chapters at reputed journals.

Jitta Mallikharjuna Rao is a Ph.D Research Scholar in Marketing stream in GITAM School of Business, GITAM University located at Visakhapatnam, India. His educational background includes a Bachelor of Technology (B.Tech) degree in Mechanical Engineering from Jawaharlal Nehru Technological University which he obtained in 1994. He started his professional career as a Management Trainee in Steel Authority of India Limited (SAIL) in 1995 and worked till 1998 as Jr Manager. He later joined at Vizag Steel Plant, Rashtriya Ispat Nigam Limited (RINL) in Visakhapatnam. He has pursued his Master of Business of Administration (MBA) while working at Vizag Steel Plant from Indira Gandhi National Open University (IGNOU). Spanning from 1998 to 2006 he held various roles in Steel Melting Shop of Vizag Steel Plant. In 2007 Jitta assumed the role of Technical Advisor to Chairman cum Managing Director of RINL marking a transition to the corporate office. Presently he is working as Deputy General Manager & TA to CMD at RINL. Concurrently, he has embarked on a part-time Ph.D. journey at GITAM University, focusing his research endeavors within the realm of marketing.

Manjit Kour is working as a Professor at University Business School at Chandigarh University. She is a PhD in Business Management. She has a good research record with several research papers published in reputed journals. She has presented numerous papers at international/national conferences and seminars. She has two books to her credit as well. She is an editorial board member and reviewer of many reputed journals including ABDC-indexed journals. She has acted as a resource person in many seminars and workshops. She has also received International Researcher Award 2021 from the International Institute of Organized Research (I2OR). Her areas of interest include sustainability, green practices, Fintech, online marketing trends and business ethics.

Vijaya Kittu Manda is a multi-dimensional personality. He has nearly 13+ years of experience in capital markets, financial planning, and investing. He is a Researcher at PBMEIT, India. He is an Advocate, a technocrat, an academician, a book writer, and a stock market enthusiast. He has 11 University Postgraduate Degrees and is a Ph.D. in Management / Finance with focus on Mutual Funds and their Market Competition. His thesis won the prestigious NSE-IEA Best Thesis Award in 2023. He is currently pursuing his second Ph.D. in Computer Science with focus on Blockchain. He contributed over 750 articles to various magazines. He is the Chief Editor for a Management Book Series, is a Peer Review, is a Certified Peer Review Supervisor, is a Session Chair and an Advisor for various academic and industrial conferences, Writers Research Papers and Case Studies, sits on Editorial Boards of various publishers, and is a guest speaker for colleges and universities.

Pratap Chandra Mandal is an Assistant Professor (Marketing) at Indian Institute of Management, Shillong, India. He has completed graduate degree from the reputed Indian Institute of Technology, Kharagpur (IIT Kharagpur), India (Bachelor of Technology in Mechanical Engineering), post-graduate degree from Vinod Gupta School of Management, IIT Kharagpur (Masters in Business Adminstration), PhD (Marketing) from Vinod Gupta School of Management, IIT Kharagpur. His research concerns customer relationship management, customer satisfaction, services marketing, marketing intelligence, and qualitative methods in management. He is the editor-in-chief of two international journals and is on the editorial board of journals like Journal of Global Marketing. Pratap has won several prestigious scholarships and awards throughout his academic career.

Ana Pinto Borges holds a PhD in Economics, Faculty of Economics, University of Porto, in 2009. Since 2010 is Coordinating Professor at ISAG - European Business School specializing on the areas of Economics, Management, and Finance, and since 2015 Coordinator of the Master's Degree in Business Management and President of the Pedagogical Council of ISAG. She is Scientific Coordinator of Research Centre in Business Sciences and Tourism (CICET – FCVC) since 2021 and coordinated the ISAG Research Centre (NIDISAG) between 2015 and 2021. Since 2018, she is researcher of the Centre for Research in Organizations, Markets and Industrial Management (COMEGI). She supervised 2 PhD theses and is now supervising other 2, in addition to having supervised more than 40 master's theses. She published more than 180 publications (around 120 indexed in Scopus/WoS databases) in journals/book chapters/proceedings and 5 books (3 indexed in Scopus). She is associate editor at the Eurasian Business Review (indexed by Scopus/WoS – Q1) and editor and one of the founding members of the European Journal of Applied Business and Management (EJABM). She founded, integrated the organizer and scientific committees, and did the co-editor of the proceedings of International Conference in Applied Business and Management (ICABM – 5 eds since 2016), International Workshop in Tourism and Hospitality Management (IWTHM – 3 eds since 2017), and in Accounting and Taxation (IWAT – 3 eds since 2021). All these academic events have been indexed or are in evaluation by WoS and by EBSCO, among others. Furthermore, she is the coordinator and co-author of several applied projects financed by external entities (companies, municipalities, among others). She is Economist at the Portuguese Health Regulatory Authority since 2010 with the main function of carrying out sectoral studies and issuing opinions in the scope of access, quality and competition. Member of the Associação Portuguesa de Economia da Saúde (since 2005).

Praneet Poddar is a student at the School of Business and Management, Christ University, Bangalore, India. He is an emerging scholar with a strong interest in consumer behavior and digital media trends. Praneet has been involved in various research projects, showcasing his analytical skills. His recent research on consumer ethnocentrism and buying behavior on OTT platforms highlights his dedication to understanding contemporary management issues. Praneet aims to further his research in digital media and consumer behavior, focusing on enhancing consumer experiences through technological advancements.

Victor Tavares, Business Sciences, PhD, Master's in Business Management and Degree in Economics. Coordinating Professor in Business Strategy and Brand Management, at ISAG - EBS. He was a professor at the Faculty of Economics of Porto and Researcher, at CICET – FCVC. President of the Technical-Scientific Council of ISAG – EBS. Coordinator of the Master in Commercial Management and Marketing. Business consultant in the areas of Brand Management, Strategy and Marketing

Tyagi is working as an assistant professor of marketing at KIET Group of Institutions Ghaziabad, India. Her area of expertise is online marketing.

Mani is an educationist and researcher; who has completed her doctorate in Management. She is a double post-graduate in MBA and PGDMM from Narsee Monjee University. She is a White Belt holder of Six Sigma from MSI, USA. She has 10 years of experience in industry and teaching. She has 12 copyrights registered under the Government of India.

Bruno Miguel Vieira attends the PhD Program in Informatics MAP-i of the Universities of Minho, Aveiro and Porto, with international partnerships, namely, with Carnegie Mellon University, under the CMU-Portugal program, conferring a double degree in informatics and the partnership with the University of Texas in Austin. He completed the Master's Degree in Teaching of Informatics from the

University of Minho in 2012, completed the University Master in Experimental, Mathematical and Technology Sciences from the University of Vigo in 2011. He is a Lecturer in the category of assistant at the ISAG – European Business School. He works in the areas of exact sciences, with an emphasis on computer and information sciences, mathematics and technologies and social sciences, with an emphasis on economics and management.

Elvira Vieira holds a PhD in Applied Economics at the University of Santiago de Compostela, in 2007. Since 2012, is Dean of ISAG ¿ European Business School, where she is also Principal Coordinating Professor and Member of the Technical-Scientific Council. Invited Adjunct Professor at the Polytechnic Institute of Viana do Castelo - School of Business Sciences. Integrated Member at the Applied Management Research Unit (UNIAG) since 2010, and Collaborator Member at the Research Centre in Business Sciences and Tourism (CICET - FCVC), since 2021. Coordinated the ISAG Research Centre (NIDISAG) between 2009 and 2021. Author of more than 160 publications in scientific journals with peer reviewd, some indexed in the various international databases (WoS - Clarivate Analytics and Scopus). Published 12 book chapters and 3 books. Supervised 4 doctoral theses and 25 master's dissertations. Received 2 awards and/or honours. Has participated as a researcher in 30 projects and has been the lead researcher on 15. Works in the areas of Social Sciences with an emphasis on Economics, Management, Tourism, Regional and Cross-border Development, Innovation and Entrepreneurship, -Information and Communication Technologies and Corporate Governance.

Anuradha Yadav is an Assistant Professor at the Department of MBA at Dayananda Sagar College of Engineering (DSCE), a premium institution at Bengaluru, India. She is an MBA, MA, PGDJM and a Ph.D. in Marketing. Her teaching and research focus is on Product and Brand Management, Strategic Management, and Marketing Management. She is a prolific author of several research papers, book chapters and case studies. She is a resource person to various research conferences and passionately guides researchers and students in management domain.

Index

S

Second Life 127, 209, 219-222, 224, 255, 260, 266
services 2-3, 5-8, 16, 19, 22, 24, 33, 37-39, 41, 44, 52, 55-56, 58-64, 67, 69-70, 79, 89, 100, 113, 115-120, 122, 125, 130-131, 133, 135-136, 145, 151, 155-156, 158-159, 167-168, 171, 173-175, 179-181, 184, 186, 190-191, 193-194, 203, 205, 213, 219, 221, 223, 225, 245-246, 262, 269
Social Media 12, 17, 19, 32, 35, 58-62, 65-69, 71, 73-77, 120, 130-133, 135, 137-138, 143, 147, 150, 152, 154, 156, 160, 170-171, 178-180, 182, 186-187, 189, 191, 193, 211, 213, 220, 226-231, 233-234, 242-243, 245-246, 255, 263
Social Media Influencer 133, 156

U

User Experience 25, 39, 66, 73, 156, 225, 243, 269
User Generated Content 136
User preferences 39, 69
User-Generated Content 58, 60-62, 74, 120, 130, 137, 144, 146-147, 157, 203, 211-212, 217, 227, 242

V

Video Advertising 57-59, 67-68, 229
Virtual Community 19

Virtual Events 20, 24, 64, 122, 140, 145-146, 156, 159, 164, 166, 264
Virtual Influencer (VI) 157
Virtual Influencers 136-138, 141-142, 147-148, 150-155, 169
Virtual Interactivity 269
Virtual Reality 30, 33-34, 57-59, 63, 72, 74, 99-103, 105, 108-109, 113-116, 119-121, 123-124, 132-133, 139, 143, 156-157, 159, 162, 166, 171, 196-197, 200, 202, 207, 210-211, 215, 219-225, 250, 255, 258, 260, 263, 266
Virtual Reality (VR) 59, 63, 72, 74, 101, 103, 105, 108, 143, 157, 159, 171, 196-197, 200, 202, 210, 215, 225, 250
Virtual universe 197
Virtual World 19, 29, 104, 106, 115, 120, 124, 127-128, 132-134, 137, 147, 156, 166, 199, 201, 203, 209-210, 223-224, 248-249, 253, 260, 263, 267

W

Web 3.0 32, 130-133, 138, 157
Word of Mouth 76, 172-173, 178-179, 181, 184-186, 194

Y

Youtube 59, 68, 112, 116, 133, 182, 226-233, 235, 241-247

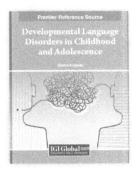

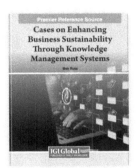

Ensure Quality Research is Introduced to the Academic Community

Become a Reviewer for IGI Global Authored Book Projects

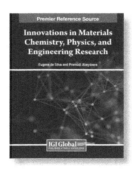
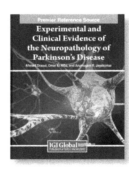

The overall success of an authored book project is dependent on quality and timely manuscript evaluations.

Applications and Inquiries may be sent to:
development@igi-global.com

Applicants must have a doctorate (or equivalent degree) as well as publishing, research, and reviewing experience. Authored Book Evaluators are appointed for one-year terms and are expected to complete at least three evaluations per term. Upon successful completion of this term, evaluators can be considered for an additional term.

If you have a colleague that may be interested in this opportunity, we encourage you to share this information with them.